DUNGEONS & DRAGONS

DUNGEON MASTER'S GUIDE 2

ROLEPLAYING GAME SUPPLEMENT

James Wyatt · Bill Slavicsek · Robin D. Laws

CREDITS

Design
James Wyatt (lead),
Bill Slavicsek, Mike Mearls, Robin D. Laws

Additional Design
Andy Collins, Rob Donoghue, Johnn Four, Greg Gorden,
Yacine "Yax" Merzouk, Stephen Radney-MacFarland,
Stephen Schubert, Matthew Sernett

Development
Stephen Schubert (lead),
Andy Collins, Stephen Radney-MacFarland

Editing
Michele Carter (lead),
Kara Hamilton, Miranda Horner, Cal Moore

Additional Editing
Greg Bilsland, Torah Cottrill

Managing Editing
Kim Mohan

Text Review
George Strayton

Director of D&D R&D and Book Publishing
Bill Slavicsek

D&D Creative Manager
Christopher Perkins

D&D Design Manager
James Wyatt

D&D Development and Editing Manager
Andy Collins

D&D Senior Art Director
Jon Schindehette

Art Director
Mari Kolkowsky

Graphic Designer
Soe Hemmi

Cover Illustration
Wayne Reynolds

Interior Illustrations
Steve Argyle, Ryan Barger, Kerem Beyit, Zoltan Boros
& Gabor Szikszai, Nicole Ashley Cardiff, Chippy, Julie
Dillon, Vincent Dutrait, Jason A. Engle, Randy Gallegos,
Tomás Giorello, Ralph Horsley, Howard Lyon, Raven
Mimura, Lucio Parrillo, Georgi Simeonov "Calader,"
Amelia Stoner, Eva Widermann

Cartographer
Jason A. Engle

D&D Brand Team
Liz Schuh, Scott Rouse, Kierin Chase, Sara Girard,
Martin Durham

Publishing Production Specialist
Erin Dorries

Prepress Manager
Jefferson Dunlap

Imaging Technician
Carmen Cheung

Production Manager
Cynda Callaway

Game rules based on the original DUNGEONS & DRAGONS® rules created by **E. Gary Gygax** and **Dave Arneson**, and the later editions by **David "Zeb" Cook** (2nd Edition); **Jonathan Tweet, Monte Cook, Skip Williams, Richard Baker,** and **Peter Adkison** (3rd Edition); and **Rob Heinsoo, Andy Collins,** and **James Wyatt** (4th Edition).

Dedicated to the memory of Dave Arneson

620-24206000-001 EN
9 8 7 6 5 4 3 2 1
First Printing:
September 2009
ISBN: 978-0-7869-5244-1

U.S., CANADA, ASIA, PACIFIC,
& LATIN AMERICA
Wizards of the Coast LLC
P.O. Box 707
Renton WA 98057-0707
+1-800-324-6496

EUROPEAN HEADQUARTERS
Hasbro UK Ltd
Caswell Way
Newport, Gwent NP9 0YH
GREAT BRITAIN
Please keep this address for your records

WIZARDS OF THE COAST, BELGIUM
Industrialaan 1
1702 Groot-Bijgaarden
Belgium
+32.070.233.277

VISIT OUR WEBSITE AT WWW.WIZARDS.COM/DND

CONTENTS

Introduction

PLAYER'S HANDBOOK 2 introduced eight new classes and five new races to the D&D® game. It presented racial paragon paths, character backgrounds, and new feats and rituals for every character.

Monster Manual® 2 presented over 300 new monsters to the game, covering every level and role. From the humble ankheg broodling to the mighty Prince of Demons, Demogorgon, it's full of monsters to challenge your players and add new life to your dungeons.

So what's in *Dungeon Master's Guide*® 2 that will make your game better?

JUICY RULES BITS

Let's start with the juicy rules bits you can drop in your game right away–like the eight pages of new traps in Chapter 2. You also get solid guidelines for creating your own traps, covering everything from getting the numbers right to making sure your trap threatens the characters–not the fun of your game.

Chapter 2 also includes new types of fantastic terrain you can add to your encounters, as well as introducing the concept of "terrain powers"–attack powers built in to an encounter's environment.

Chapter 4 is about tweaking and adjusting monsters. It rounds out the rules presented in the first 4th Edition *Dungeon Master's Guide* with additional rules for making minions and refined guidelines for elite and solo monsters. It presents new templates, including class templates for the classes in *Player's Handbook*® 2, and introduces monster themes–a great way to tweak the flavor and powers of a monster to make it fit whatever kind of adventure you want to run.

You'll find new artifacts in Chapter 5, including old favorites such as the *Rod of Seven Parts* and the *Cup and Talisman of Al'Akbar* (both of which appeared in the original *Dungeon Master's Guide* back in 1979) as well as all-new artifacts designed to appeal to pairs or whole groups of characters.

Chapter 5 also sets out a new system of rewards you can use instead of (or as a supplement to) magic items. Divine boons represent gifts from the gods or their agents, legendary boons express the accomplishment of great deeds of power, and grandmaster training reflects what happens when a player character learns from a legendary master.

Near the end of Chapter 1, you'll find rules for companion characters–a great way to round out a small party or bring an important NPC along for the ride with your player characters. That chapter also includes handy rules for altering a character on the fly so he or she can fit in with a party of characters of much higher or lower level.

EXPERT ADVICE

A *Dungeon Master's Guide* isn't just about rules, it's about helping you be a better Dungeon Master. Whether you're a veteran DM or a first-timer, this book has ample expert advice to improve your game.

Chapter 1, "Group Storytelling," focuses on the cooperative experience of creating a dramatic narrative. Whether you're looking to inject a little more drama into your game or you want a group-created story to drive your campaign, you'll find advice that will help you bring the characters at your table to life.

Chapter 2, "Advanced Encounters," extends that advice to the level of the individual encounters that make up your adventures, offering advice to help make each encounter an important part of the plot. This chapter also includes advice on how to tailor encounters for different player motivations, how to deal with large and small groups, how to encourage movement in combat, and how to pace encounters to build dramatic tension. If you've wondered how to encourage characters to press on without taking an extended rest, or how to handle a long fight with wave after wave of onrushing enemies and no time for a short rest, this chapter has the advice you need.

Chapter 2 ends with a sample encounter that pulls many of the elements discussed in the chapter together into a single, dynamic fight.

Chapter 3, "Skill Challenges," focuses on using skill challenges in your game, combining extensive, detailed advice with lots of examples. It sums up the basic rules of skill challenges (as already expanded and clarified in rules updates found on www.wizards.com), moves on to discuss five key elements of skill challenges, and wraps up with a series of examples.

In among the rewards and artifacts in Chapter 5, "Adventures," you'll also find plenty of advice to help you build your campaign. Sample campaign arcs, including a hands-on example of how to build a campaign arc, help you form the skeleton of your campaign, and information about using artifacts and organizations can help you flesh out the details.

If the characters in your campaign have advanced to paragon level, be sure to take a look at Chapter 6, "Paragon Campaigns." This chapter offers tips and suggestions for campaigns set in the paragon tier, presents the city of Sigil as a home base for characters' adventures through the paragon tier, and includes a short adventure for 11th-level characters.

D&D INSIDER

Throughout this book, you'll find excerpts of material from the pages of *Dungeon*™ magazine, particularly Stephen Radney-MacFarland's "Save My Game" column and James Wyatt's "Dungeoncraft" column. Some other material in this book originally appeared in the "Ruling Skill Challenges" column by Mike Mearls or in feature articles in *Dragon*™ magazine.

These columns and features are part of *D&D Insider*™, an online subscription-based service designed to bring new life and new ideas to your D&D game. *D&D Insider* is a suite of content and tools for better gaming, including:

✦ *Dragon* magazine, which features new material and expanded content to help make your characters and campaigns more fun and more compelling: character options, powers, feats, magic items, paragon paths, epic destinies, monsters, campaign setting source material, and more. *Dragon* magazine also regularly features material slated for inclusion in future print products, giving you the opportunity to share your feedback with the Wizards of the Coast design and development teams.

✦ *Dungeon* magazine, which provides three to five new adventures every month–something for each tier of play (heroic, paragon, and epic)–so you'll always have a game that's ready to run. Whether you run those adventures, or play your own home-brewed adventures and campaigns, *Dungeon* offers a continuous source of articles, features, hints, and tips, to help make the job of DMing even easier.

✦ The D&D Character Builder, a stand-alone application that puts information from every printed book and online article at your fingertips as you build and level your character. In addition to providing an updatable and easy-to-read character sheet, the Character Builder generates power cards for you to quickly reference and track your character's powers.

✦ The *D&D Compendium*, a searchable online database of the complete rules text for every race, class, paragon path, epic destiny, skill, feat, power, item, and ritual–from every D&D rulebook and online magazine article.

Wizards of the Coast is working constantly to expand and improve the tools and content available on *D&D Insider*, so be sure to check www.dndinsider.com for the latest updates. And if you like the excerpts from *D&D Insider* you find within these pages, become a subscriber and check out what you've been missing!

PUTTING IT ALL TO USE

Since the release of the *Dungeon Master's Guide* in 2008, the D&D game has grown. Besides *Player's Handbook 2* and *Monster Manual 2*, you and your players might own *Martial Power*™, *Draconomicon*™: *Chromatic Dragons*, *Open Grave*™, *Adventurer's Vault*™, the FORGOTTEN REALMS® or EBERRON® Campaign Guide and *Player's Guide*, and any number of other supplements and adventures. How do you put it all to work for your game?

Start by knowing when to say no. If a player brings a new option to your table that doesn't fit in your game, it's okay to tell the player to hold on to that idea until this campaign wraps up and you (or someone else in your group) starts something new. Balance this, of course, with the advice to say yes as much as possible (see page 28 of the *Dungeon Master's Guide*), but know the limits you want in your game and don't be afraid to enforce them.

If your players are eager to try a new class or build they found in *Player's Handbook 2* or a power source book such as *Arcane Power*™, check out the sidebar on page 35, which discusses how to let players take on multiple characters. You should also feel free to let your players tweak aspects of their characters when new options become available. If the guardian druid in your party wants to become a swarm druid once *Primal Power*™ comes out, and the player can make that change without doing violence to the story of your game, let it happen.

The *D&D Compendium*, part of the *D&D Insider* suite of tools, is a great way to keep track of information that appears in multiple books. If you're trying to find the caller in darkness, the *Compendium* can tell you quickly that it appears in *Open Grave: Secrets of the Undead* (and that it's a level 19 elite soldier). Using the *Compendium* to build encounters keeps all the information from your books at your fingertips.

Loot freely. For instance, you don't have to be running a game set in the world of Eberron to find something worth using in the EBERRON Campaign Guide. Maybe the idea of characters with dragonmarks tied to a mysterious prophecy fits in with the ideas you have for your own campaign. Letting your characters take dragonmark feats—and then pitting them against agents of the Chamber and the Lords of Dust—makes everyone at the table happy.

Delves (short, three-encounter adventures), lairs, and even single encounters are easy to work in to whatever adventure you're running, whether it's a published adventure or one of your own creation. If you craft your own adventures but find yourself underprepared for a session, picking up a delve from *Dungeon Delve*™, a dragon lair from *Draconomicon*, or even a couple of encounters from one of the dozens of adventures found in *Dungeon* magazine is a great way to keep your game on track.

– James Wyatt

GROUP STORYTELLING

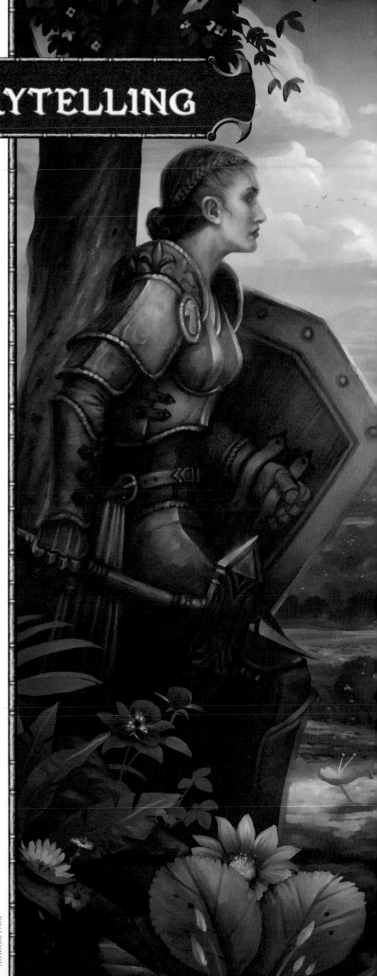

T HE D&D game offers a Dungeon Master and the other players the ability to craft a story out of each session and each adventure. Sometimes a gaming group creates a straightforward story, with sword-and-sorcery action and little character development or few plot twists. Other times, a group weaves a magical tale with dramatic layers of complex storytelling.

This chapter focuses on the narrative side of the game from the DM's point of view, offering techniques to encourage your group of players to help you shape the story of the game.

This chapter includes the following topics.

✦ **Story Structure:** The basic building blocks of narrative storytelling.

✦ **Branching:** Consider the narrative as a series of choices leading to multiple possible destinations.

✦ **Cooperative Arcs:** Consult with your players to build a campaign from the ground up.

✦ **Your Cast of Characters:** Help players work with you and each other to create dynamic characters.

✦ **Cooperative World Building:** The cooperative storytelling approach builds a story through joint improvisation. Players feel they have a stake in the story when they participate in building the plot.

✦ **Roleplaying Hooks:** Strong personality and plot hooks established at the start keep the characters involved throughout the life of the campaign.

✦ **Vignettes:** Short, directed scenes allow players to see events from a different point of view.

✦ **Drama Rewards:** Significant, dedicated role-playing deserves XP rewards.

✦ **What Your Players Want:** Create surveys so you can adapt the game to your players'–and their characters'–requests.

✦ **Companion Characters:** Your story might call for an ally to join the PCs for a time, or maybe they need help in overcoming a challenge you want to use. These rules work independent of the storytelling style you adopt for your game.

✦ **Making Things Level:** Guidance for handling the situation when a character of higher or lower level joins the party.

HOWARD LYON

To create any story—whether prepared in advance or improvised, whether for your D&D game or for a creative writing project—begin with the basic building blocks that construct all narratives.

CLASSIC STORY STRUCTURE

Fantasy stories draw on the great myths of various world cultures and make heavy use of traditional structures. You can create strong effects by deviating from an expected structure, but doing so requires a thorough knowledge of the subject.

The following elements comprise a traditional story.

Introduction: An opening sequence that identifies the viewpoint characters, or protagonists, and the basic situation. The introduction also establishes the antagonists, the forces that impede the progress of the protagonists.

Rising Action: A series of events that makes the characters' situation more complex and urgent. As these events progress, the consequences become more significant. You can map the rising action as an upward-trending line with peaks and valleys. Through a series of turning points, you create tension, release it periodically, and then build it up again to a higher pitch.

The Climax: A pivotal moment of maximum tension, in which the opposed forces driving the central conflict of the story conclusively clash, resolving the situation established in the introduction.

STORY ISN'T EVERYTHING

You can run a thrilling D&D campaign that keeps your players coming back for more even if you don't give a single thought to story structure, character motivations, cooperative world building, or any of the other concepts described in this chapter. Using these ideas makes you a better DM only if doing so enhances the collective fun of a receptive group. Before introducing the cooperative techniques discussed in this chapter, poll your players and confirm that they are interested.

Consider the types of players in your group (as discussed on pages 8–10 of the *Dungeon Master's Guide*). Explorers, instigators, and storytellers thrive in a cooperative game. Power gamers and slayers might approve, as long as the focus on characterization doesn't cut into their fighting time. Watchers remain content if they are allowed to shy from the creative spotlight. Thinkers might feel frustrated by a cooperative game's focus on drama and tension. Some actors might love the cooperative style of dramatic creation, but others could find it distracting.

Denouement: A brief wrap-up sequence in which the players glimpse the lasting consequences of the story's climactic events.

TURNING POINTS

Every peak or valley in the rising action pivots around a turning point. At the end of a turning point, players feel the tension either increase or decrease. Turning points fall into two main categories: problem solving and dramatic turns.

PROBLEM SOLVING

Problem-solving turning points make up the majority of an adventure story. A protagonist faces an external obstacle, attempts to overcome it, and either passes or fails the test. For this reason, the structure of adventure stories is sometimes referred to as "the pass/fail cycle." External obstacles that stand in the way of pragmatic or tactical goals include:

✦ a hidden item the characters must find.

✦ a wall the characters must climb.

✦ a witness the characters must convince to talk.

DRAMATIC TURNS

Tension also rises or falls when a protagonist pursues emotional goals through interaction with other characters. These turning points make up a large part of conventional dramas, from soap operas to classic plays. In adventure stories, dramatic turns most often appear as interludes of emotional reaction interwoven with active pass/fail obstacles.

Dramatic scenes occur when outside characters such as the PCs' friends, family members, loved ones, rivals, and enemies hold emotional power over the player characters. These scenes offer a shift in power from one character to another. Tension decreases if the protagonist retains or increases his or her emotional power. If she loses it, tension increases.

TENSION AND RELEASE

Maintain the tension and release of the pass/fail cycle by adjusting DCs or encounter levels to reflect the party's recent record of loss and gain. When a string of failures discourages players, adjust the numbers downward to make their subsequent success more likely. If the PCs are cocky in the wake of successive wins, tighten the screws.

Satisfying D&D stories differ from other narrative forms in one major way: D&D stories don't follow a single predetermined storyline through a series of turning points. Instead, each turning point presents the opportunity for the story to branch in an unexpected direction. By anticipating branches, you can ensure that the story keeps moving in an exciting—and unexpected—direction.

A strong branch point engages players and can move the story in two or more directions.

PASS/FAIL BRANCHING

Every time you call on a D&D mechanic to resolve an action and the result affects the story, you create a pass/fail branch point.

When players successfully complete encounters or skill challenges or make successful skill checks, the PCs pass a test and gain a benefit. Tension is released. Success carries them to the next turning point.

When they flee an encounter or fail a skill challenge or skill check, they suffer a negative consequence.

Tension increases as they move toward a new turning point—possibly one not of their choosing.

A null result—one that is not a success and does not move the story forward—could frustrate players and create a negative play experience. If the PCs fail to overcome the current obstacle, they must find another way to surmount it—and there should always be another way.

To create a strong pass/fail branch point, build tension by showing players the negative consequences of failure. Even if the players see the negative consequences already, increase the thrill level with vivid description. Describe the yawning chasm the paladin will fall into if he fails to clamber up onto the ledge. Alternatively, tantalize your group with a tempting reward they will gain if they succeed.

AVOIDING DEAD BRANCHES

When you look at the two possible outcomes of any branch point, don't let either choice lead you into a narrative dead end. This situation could occur when the PCs can't devise a solution to a problem, or if a sequence of dull, repetitive, or petty obstacles hinders their progress.

Eventually, a dead branch will stump you. You just can't imagine a consequence of failure that takes the story anywhere fun or interesting. In this case, allow the players an automatic success. Either secretly set the DC of the check to 1, or drop the pretense and tell the players that they overcome the obstacle without resorting to a die roll. If this easy success feels like a lapse in story logic, describe a fortuitous event that makes the obstacle suddenly surmountable. The PCs locate a crack in a supposedly impregnable wall, find the guards asleep at their post, or stumble upon the dragon after a wagonload of ale has left him in a magnanimous mood. Turn a dead branch into an opportunity to create a scene to move the story forward.

Repeated null results are a particularly difficult form of dead branches. The story stalls, and the players' frustration

This diagram maps out a D&D session's major events in a pass/fail cycle. The PCs first learn that an astral pirate fleet threatens the friendly dominions. The characters successfully recruit Dezarran, an expert on the pirates, passing that obstacle (represented by an upward arrow). During the PCs' return from this journey, an astral kraken attacks them, and they fail to defeat it before it shatters their ship. A downward arrow represents their failure. They wash ashore on Kalandurren. This event leads to a successful skill challenge to escape a demon chief (pass) and the capture of an astral skiff from slaad guards (pass again). They fall short on a skill challenge to repair the skiff (fail), leading them to search for a blue diamond to power its engines, which they successfully locate (pass).

builds with each failed attempt at the same task. Before this type of dead branch spoils everyone's enjoyment of the game, drop the DCs in order to allow the characters to move on. Plan ahead to avoid the frustration of repeated null results by devising obstacles that create a new situation after a failure.

Sometimes story logic dictates a difficult challenge even though one of its possible branches leads to a dead end. In this case, focus the challenge on what the PCs' necessary victory costs them, rather than on winning or losing. On either a success or a failure, the characters will move on to the same obstacle. However, on a failure, they move on at a significant disadvantage.

ENCOUNTERS AS BRANCH POINTS

The aftermath of a typical encounter has two or more branches. Lucky, smart PCs walk away from a fight having spent relatively few daily powers, action points, and healing surges. Bad luck or poor tactics in the same encounter leaves the PCs in worse shape and force them to rest to replenish their resources. Occasionally, a party member will die, exacting an even higher cost in lost time and payment for a ritual to bring back the dead character.

You can turn encounters into genuine pass/fail turning points, with possible branches for both outcomes. One way to accomplish this is by staging a nonlethal fight against superior opponents. Pit the group against more creatures than the standard encounter rules call for, or increase the encounter level by one or two notches. Success gives the group a benefit and sends them to obstacle A, whereas failure has a negative consequence and takes them to less desirable obstacle B.

Another technique is to give the PCs a secondary goal to fulfill during the encounter, in addition to overcoming the traps and defeating the creatures. If the PCs achieve the goal in a set number of rounds, the plot takes a positive turn. If the PCs take longer or fail, their next obstacle reflects a narrative setback. A secondary goal might include a simple task, such as reaching a specified square and then succeeding on a skill check. Chapter 2 discusses encounter goals in more depth, but simple objectives could include the following accomplishments:

✦ Capturing an enemy noncombatant.
✦ Defeating a particular creature before dealing with the rest of its comrades.
✦ Destroying a magic device before it harms a distant person, place, or object.
✦ Grabbing an artifact before it is somehow lost.
✦ Hitting a button to keep a dimensional gate open.
✦ Rescuing a hostage.
✦ Stopping a sinister ritual.

Make sure to tailor the encounter for the additional goal the PCs must accomplish. Ease back on encounter difficulty if necessary by reducing creature numbers or the overall encounter level. Consider introducing a creature or two in the middle of a fight if the PCs meet the secondary goal with anticlimactic ease. You could also stage an encounter of higher level than the level of the PCs. Build in a goal that, if it is reached, removes some of the creatures from the fray, putting the encounter back into the group's comfort zone.

DECISION BRANCHING

Strongly plotted adventures provide players with multiple opportunities to make decisions that insert branch points into the story. These branches might lead to obstacles that don't involve the PCs defeating monsters or traps, such as:

✦ Opening the door on the left instead of the one on the right.
✦ Choosing which witness to talk to next.
✦ Deciding to go to the tavern in the dangerous part of town instead of the one that seems more safe.
✦ Going home to challenge your evil stepbrother for superior status in the family.
✦ Demanding that your father, the king, recognize you as a worthy heir.

CHAPTER 1 | *Group Storytelling*

Sometimes, players make unexpected choices, forcing you to improvise a suitable response. A DM who prefers to prepare every encounter before starting an adventure might try to nullify the players' choice, encouraging their return to the preplanned set of obstacles. DMs who like to improvise might use these unanticipated decision branches as opportunities to allow the players to take the story in a new direction.

Strong decision points give the players a sense of freedom and influence over the course of events. Describe the situation so they can make a clear decision between contrasting outcomes, not a random choice between unknowns. Simply choosing between a dungeon corridor to the right and one to the left is not as satisfying a decision for the players as the choice between a corridor that reeks of necromantic magic and a hallway that echoes with a strange siren song.

When a decision point lies between action and inaction, heighten the stakes by making both options seem risky in different ways. If a player tries to decide whether he should return home to confront his character's stepbrother, raise the stakes: Suggest to him the consequences of putting off the showdown, as well as what might happen if he goes through with it.

DM'S WORKSHOP: ROYAL SUMMONS

Previously in the campaign, the paragon-level PCs had begun exploring the Underdark. They know of a dwarven stronghold that they hope to make their base of operations for their delving, but encounters with dwarf patrols have warned them that the dwarf king is unstable.

In this example of branching, the king of the stronghold summons the PCs. The stronghold's sergeant, Thangur, arrives with a heavily armed escort to take the PCs to the royal audience chamber. As a consequence of success in a previous pass/fail scene when the PCs met a patrol led by Thangur, they have earned the sergeant's grudging approval.

You have built a decision branch into the opening of the encounter: Do the PCs try to flee the escort, or do they obediently accompany Thangur? Plan ahead to ensure that both choices pose risks to the party and offer up interesting branches.

Fleeing poses risks; if the PCs fail the resulting skill challenge to get away, they face capture and King Fyolf's wrath. If they succeed, they must fend for themselves in the depths of the Underdark without the dwarves' aid. So, one course of action offers two branches that move the story toward new obstacles.

Following Thangur has its risks, too. He reluctantly explains that a brush with a mind flayer has made King Fyolf increasingly capricious. Depending on how deftly they deal with Fyolf, he might throw them in his dungeon or send them on a mission. Again, this outcome branches toward two interesting obstacles: escaping from a dungeon or going on a mission the PCs might not have chosen for themselves.

Having planned ahead in two directions, you have preparations in place for the players to make either available decision, and you can plan strong pass/fail results for both outcomes.

The players discuss their options and decide to accompany Thangur. As you might expect, they pump him for further information about Fyolf. Use this opportunity to heighten the tension with a description of the king's unpredictability. Obsequious words sometimes anger him, but he also erupts if petitioners fail to bow and scrape before him.

After some discussion, the PCs decide to present themselves as proud and unapologetic, befitting their paragon status.

After checking your notes, you see that the PCs easily succeeded on their last skill challenge, so you might decide to use high DCs this time.

With both possible branches from this challenge planned, the scenario plays out. The PCs fail the skill challenge, and a furious Fyolf imprisons them. The players react with dismay when the king threatens to jail their characters, and they consider fighting their way out of his court.

Because you have described in great detail the formidable retinue attending the king, it seemed unlikely that the PCs would present you with this decision point. You might think about shutting off this option by simply declaring the opposition to be overwhelming. But before you do that, remind yourself that cooperative DMs take cues from their players; rethink the situation, and look for a way to resolve this scenario with a fight that makes sense. You decide that Fyolf, bored and seeking entertainment, dispatches just enough guards to make for a tough but fair fight against the party. If the PCs defeat the guards without being foolish enough to kill any of them, he'll merely exile them from his kingdom. If they lose the fight, or if they kill any guards, they wind up in chains. Armed with two interesting yet believable branches, you can now create a dwarf encounter and haul out the battle grid.

Then, as you begin to assemble the encounter materials, the players perform an about-face. Cooler heads maintain that attempting to escape from Fyolf's prison presents less difficulty than fighting an entire court of dwarf warriors—so the characters surrender and allow themselves to be taken into custody.

While you describe the group's trip to jail, at the same time, anticipate the possible branches that could arise from an escape sequence. Being unable to escape from confinement exemplifies a classic dead branch—possibly the deadest of all because it leads to frustration. So you assume the characters manage to escape, perhaps without attracting any attention from their guards or perhaps after fighting their way out. In both cases, the PCs wind up without civilized shelter in the Underdark and must take and hold a hideout of their own.

A sense of shared authorship between you and the players can begin before you start playing, when you create a campaign. Convene with your group and ask them to help you create a campaign arc from the ground up. Have each player bring a pitch, a basic idea for the campaign, to this meeting. The pitch is a simple sentence that describes how the player characters fit into their world. Here are a few examples.

✦ The resurrected heroes of a long-dead empire fight to prevent the disaster that claimed their civilization from destroying another.

✦ Outcasts and scavengers vow to gather a barbarian army and conquer the world.

✦ Bickering half-siblings set out to gather unique items for their father's magic item shop.

✦ In a Roman-style empire, high-status slaves capture live monsters for combat in the coliseum run by their master, a senator.

You serve as editor and mediator, guiding the process until you assemble a blueprint for the campaign. After each player makes a pitch, let the group discuss and rank the possible choices. They might take elements of several pitches and combine them into a favorite pick. Cross-fertilization promotes engaging storylines. Aim for a concept open enough to allow variety while still revolving around a distinct, central idea.

Having hammered out the basic premise, expand and refine it by establishing the basic arcs of the three tiers. (You can skip this step if you plan to run a shorter campaign.) Use the examples beginning on page 168 in Chapter 5 for inspiration and guidance as you build the basic structure of your storyline.

Earthbound and practical, the heroic tier focuses on the steady emergence of the characters from obscurity to fame. The paragon tier thrusts them into strange environments and raises the stakes to national or global levels. In the epic tier, the stakes go up yet again, with the cosmos possibly hanging in the balance.

Don't worry if an obvious take on the later tiers fails to present itself. You can schedule a new pitch meeting later, as the new tier draws closer.

DM'S WORKSHOP: CONCEIVING THE REVIVED

Now that another DM's campaign is about to wrap up, you take the reins for your group's next campaign. You decide to create a cooperative campaign arc, pitch-meeting style. Your group consists of the players Amy, Ben, Carlos, and Deena. When you solicit pitches from the group, one suggestion immediately captures everybody's attention:

"How about a game where we bring our favorite characters back for an all-star team-up?" Amy says.

The other players immediately reel off exploits of favorite PCs from past campaigns. You recall some details, others you don't.

You can tell that the players like the idea because the other players begin riffing on it:

"How do they all know each other?"

"They don't have to be from the same world, I hope. My paladin is from the FORGOTTEN REALMS campaign—"

"—but I want to play my first character, from my big brother's homebrewed world."

"And they were all different levels, and different editions," muses Carlos. "You want to start out at 1st level, right?"

The group suggests ideas until the wrinkles are ironed out, and here's where things stand: The PCs have the same names and appearances as their favorite past PCs and live as peasants in the same village. As they advance through the heroic tier and they manifest their various powers, they slowly recall their past lives. Initially, they remember only flashes of their old lives. At the end of the heroic tier, they have recovered their memories entirely.

Ben suggests that during the paragon tier, they discover why fate reincarnated them together. "We won't know what it is; maybe something cosmic in scope requires the universe's greatest heroes to gather."

Deena nods, seeing his direction. "And then the epic tier focuses on fighting a world-threatening force."

As you furiously jot down ideas, Carlos pipes up with a request of his own: "You know, my monk never defeated his archenemy, the Flower King. If I convince Keith, who DMed that campaign, to write him up for you, can you make him a major villain?"

"Yes!" Amy exclaims. "Every hero team-up needs its rogue's gallery."

Now that the players have an excuse to tell you about their characters, they spend the evening giving you the details you need to reveal their old histories, and to introduce their villains. Meanwhile, you might ponder various possible cosmic menaces to propel the plot forward.

You don't have to confine the storytelling process to a dialogue between you and the players. Encourage players to cooperate with each other, to build relationships and connections between their characters. This approach lends a greater sense of cohesion to the developing story. Your campaign's memorable and entertaining moments of interaction likely happen between player characters. Similar to the leading characters of an ensemble TV show, the PCs should contrast with one another to make dramatic sparks fly.

CORE MOTIVATIONS

Strong characters build strong ensembles. Compelling, dramatic characters actively propel themselves into the story by pursuing powerful core motivations. Ask each player to spell out his or her reason for adventuring. Motivations can suggest what the characters have encountered before they meet each other, as well as what kind of actions they might take during the game. Here are a few examples to get your players thinking.

✦ "An obsessive curiosity about arcane secrets propels me."

✦ "The destruction of my village drives me to vengeance against bandits and anyone else who reminds me of them."

✦ "In tribute to the brother who died saving my life, I have sworn to spread the worship of Pelor."

✦ "If I don't use my brilliant mind to solve mysteries, I'll go mad."

✦ "An oracle told me I'd learn the secret of my true parentage somewhere deep in the Underdark."

Work with a player if he or she creates a passive, vague, or impersonal motivation; help the player sharpen it and give it emotional weight.

Motivations contain specifics. If the campaign frame specifies the PCs' courses of action, help players tie their motivations into the arc's main activity.

Players' conceptions of their characters might change over time, especially after the first few sessions of a campaign. Allow them to modify their core motivations–provided that the new motivation also provides compelling story hooks.

MAKING USE OF MOTIVATIONS

When designing adventures, use motivations to draw the characters into encounters, skill challenges, and decision points. Make sure characters can act on their motivations in more than one way, so they don't feel trapped.

Devise adventure plot lines around character motivations. Wherever possible, develop story ideas so that they advance the agendas of multiple PCs. This method divides attention between players more evenly. It also covers you when a player whose motivation you planned as a story springboard can't play during a critical session or leaves the campaign.

Over time, balance your use of motivations to shine the spotlight on everyone. Make an exception for watchers, players who prefer having a secondary role in others' stories to taking center stage in their own. Some motivations can easily generate stories, whereas others might require effort to incorporate. If you consistently find it difficult to connect a PC's motivation with the action in your game, revisit the motivation. Work with the player to adjust the motivation so that it inspires specific action.

INTERRELATIONSHIPS

To create reasons for the PCs to spend all their time together and entrust each other with their lives, ask each player to specify a preexisting tie between his character and at least one other PC. The tie should involve strong positive feelings toward the chosen PC. Both of the players must agree to the relationship; negotiate the original suggestion until it makes sense for both. When a player's turn comes up, he or she should specify a new tie, rather than repeating one already established. However, the player might also

DISTRACTED

After having gone to the trouble to create them, players probably stick to their motivations. When a PC ignores his motivation to gain a short-term advantage, or for other reasons that seem out of character, declare him distracted. The stress of acting against his instincts costs him precious mental concentration. Until he reverts to his established motivation, he labors under some or all of the following consequences.

✦ Grants combat advantage.
✦ Takes a -2 penalty to saving throws.
✦ Loses one healing surge after each rest.
✦ Can't regain action points.

A player who wants to alter his character's motivation to fit an evolving conception of the character can do so without penalty. A character who constantly shirks his motivation to suit momentary circumstances is a shifty opportunist, and his motives should reflect that. Work with the player to recast his character's motivation to match his behavior.

confirm that he or she reciprocates the loyalty given by another PC.

Such a relationship might pair two characters as members of the same family, romantic partners, a mentor and a protégé, comrades-in-arms, coworkers, dedicated worshipers of the same deity, or political allies.

CONTRASTS

Next, have each player outline a source of conflict between his or her character and another PC. Unlike the strong feelings represented by motivations and interrelationships, you can make these points of

DM'S WORKSHOP: CASTING THE REVIVED

Amy, Ben, Carlos, and Deena gather for the preamble session of "The Revived."

Amy introduces her PC as Arisana, a budding wizard, and provides her motivation: "Since childhood, the villagers have feared me, saying I had 'witch eyes.' I had to sneak away and learn magic from books I found beneath a deserted hut. I need to prove to them—and myself—that they were wrong to fear me, and I am not a creature of evil."

Ben says, "My character is Bob the Ranger. He didn't have a motivation when I played him in my big brother's campaign, so I'll say he feels he has a great destiny, and he wants to find out what that feeling means."

(The others in the group object to his character's name, and Ben agrees to the more formal-sounding "Brom.")

"I'm Caliban, and I have developed unarmed fighting powers at odds with the surrounding culture," says Carlos, explaining that he chose to play a monk. "He has recurring nightmares about this dread figure who wears a crown and a wreath of toxic blossoms. Caliban seeks combat experience, so he can defeat this menace when it arrives."

Deena says, "My character is Diani, a fierce devotee of Bahamut. I intend to perform great deeds in the name of my deity to erase the memory of my treacherous father. He betrayed a cohort of his allies to Tiamat before she devoured him."

Now each player establishes a tie to another PC. "Arisana feels grateful to Diani," says Amy. "She saw virtue in me despite the villagers' fears."

Ben takes his turn: "Brom thinks Caliban's weird powers are cool. They show that Caliban has a great destiny, just like me, so I stick close by his side."

Carlos says, "Caliban adores Arisana, though he worries that if he shows it, he'll make her a target for the evil being in his dreams. So instead, he keeps a protective, brotherly watch over her."

"Hmm," says Deena, "that leaves Brom. I know—he's my husband! We were betrothed as children, and I went through with the marriage out of loyalty to my long-suffering mother. I feel no great passion for him, but I honor him out of duty."

"Wow, weird," says Ben, taking in this suggestion. Since the idea impinges on his character, he could ask for a modification. Instead he thinks for a moment and decides to roll with it. "I never thought of Brom as being married. This process has made him more interesting than when I played him as a kid. Well, Brom's kind of clueless, so he figures Diani loves him the way he loves her."

In the second-to-last round of collaborative party building, players pick their contrasts.

Amy says, "I don't fully trust Caliban. I don't understand why he watches an outcast like me so closely, and I sense that he hides his true intentions toward me. No one could ever love me, so it can't be that."

Carlos clutches his chest. "Oh, no! Poor Caliban!"

Ben's up next: "I choose Diani—I keep bugging her to settle down and have my kids."

"I try to restrain myself," adds Deena, "but Brom doesn't make it easy."

"Brom can be an insensitive numbskull," says Carlos. "Caliban finds it hard to maintain his sense of mystical detachment around the guy."

"Who hasn't been contrasted with yet?" asks Deena. Amy holds up her hand.

"Interesting. I'm your tie, right?" Deena continues. "Um, well, let's say I fear your outsider ways, how you skulk around and separate yourself from society. Diani believes in duty and conformity and obedience to legitimate authority."

Finally, each player specifies a recurring character who might play a role in the campaign.

"I'm an outcast," muses Amy. "So I only speak to these three individuals in the village. How about the shade of the old hermit who owned the books of magic I found? It appears by moonlight, sometimes, and it listens more than it talks."

"I had a henchman in the old campaign called Bodo," says Ben. "I'll have a servant named Bodo who follows me around, listens to my stories, and picks up after me."

"We must be well off, hubby," says Deena.

"I guess. Can I say I'm the son of a landowner?" Ben asks you.

"Sure, but you don't score any extra starting equipment."

In fact, Ben has just created two recurring characters—Bodo and Brom's father—giving you more grist for your story-making mill.

"I already named my contrasting character," says Carlos. "The Flower King."

"Me too," says Deena. "My father's treachery broke the heart of Diani's mother, Eloan."

"And your treacherous father?" Ben points out.

Deena shakes her head. "No, he's dead."

I'm sure you believe he's dead, you think to yourself, already hatching a plan for his eventual appearance.

contrast relatively mild, even humorous. You want to achieve amusing banter, not genuine rancor.

For example, differences over minor theological points provide fodder for fun in-character debates. On the other hand, a character's vow to take fatal vengeance on another PC poses an obvious threat to group harmony. Contrasts that tie into another PC's motivations highlight both characters. Help the players work together to modify suggestions to bring any differences in line with their intended character portrayals.

Recurring Characters

You might also ask players to invent one or two NPCs to whom they have important ties. These can be ties of loyalty, similar to what a character might share with another group member. Alternatively, these NPCs might despise the character, and you can use the NPCs as obstacles to the character's goals.

This option works best if you expect the PCs to spend frequent periods of downtime in a single home base. You might have trouble incorporating casts of recurring NPCs into a campaign that features a band of constantly roving PCs.

Predestined

This approach comes into play when players want to decide ahead of time what, in general, happens to their characters at a campaign's end. A story that ends with one or more characters suffering a tragic fate (perhaps dying in a final heroic gesture) or an ironic reversal is especially appropriate for this sort of approach. In the latter case, a player might ask for story hooks that help his or her character evolve over time. Each step is part of a gradual progression, but the contrast between the beginning character and the end result is extreme. A foolhardy character might grow wise. An avatar of virtue could slowly become corrupted until the player hands his or her character over to you as an NPC adversary. A rambling explorer might end up finding true happiness in his hometown.

A character's core motivation culminates in predestined fates. They finish a PC's story. The character achieves his or her ultimate goal, rises above it to discover and complete a more profound objective, or is destroyed. In a tragic ending, either the goal inherently leads to doom, or the character's inner flaws prevent his or her success.

The process of shared creation doesn't need to stop during your campaign's prep phase. You can continue it by allowing players a role in inventing your D&D world.

The default D&D setting provides an ideal basis for definition on the fly. It establishes a few cornerstone elements, such as the planes of existence and the way magic works, and then you can fill in the rest. Traditionally, DMs flesh out these details on their own, as part of their prep work. Engage your players—and ease your workload—by inviting them to join in the process and help you create the world.

If you like the idea of player input but feel more comfortable working from detailed notes, assign your players homework. Ask them to describe which elements of the world their characters closely engage with. These background elements might include their cultures, religions, and organizations. This method preserves suspension of disbelief by creating relevant world details. If your group enjoys this approach, consider opening up the world as a joint setting, one in which all of you run games. You might establish separate campaigns based in different parts of the same world, or rotate DMing duties in a single, long-running game.

LIMITS OF COLLABORATION

Even though the first rule of improvisation is never to negate someone else's idea, sometimes rules are meant to be broken.

When you and your players brainstorm to design a world, you can feel free to alter pure flavor elements of published D&D works. On the other hand, avoid suggestions that require you to alter game mechanics. "This world contains no necrotic energy" might sound like the seed for an interesting variant setting. However, many creatures, powers, and magic items in the game rules have necrotic attacks, resistances, and vulnerabilities hardwired into them. Removing such elements changes the game balance, making some game properties more powerful than intended and other abilities useless.

Also, player suggestions must remain consistent with the world's previously established continuity. If players declared the Raven Queen to be the city's patron deity last week, a new idea should usually not be allowed to override that fact. (You might make an exception for a truly compelling suggestion, provided that the player can convincingly justify the inconsistency.) This stipulation applies only to facts about the world that have come up in play. You can contradict a detail about your setting that, so far, appears only in your notes. If your players don't know about it, changing it won't impair their suspension of disbelief.

NEVER NEGATE

A DM serves as an arbiter, deciding which player suggestions to incorporate into the world directly and which suggestions need to be modified to fit into your broader plans.

When you are presented with player input into your world, start by repeating to yourself the first rule of improvisation: Never negate.

With few exceptions (see the "Limits of Collaboration" sidebar), following this rule means incorporating at least part of every suggestion into your world. If an idea contradicts something you plan to introduce, don't reject the conflicting idea out of hand. Put a new spin on it instead. Even when you hear no objections to a suggestion, consider adding an additional element to it. This approach surprises the players, and it encourages a sense of creative back-and-forth. Approving the players' suggestions pleases them, and it encourages all participants to build on each other's ideas.

Add a new detail or caveat to a proposed idea instead of altering it beyond recognition. What you lose in control, you gain in player engagement.

Players might unintentionally add details to your world by confusing elements of the default D&D

DM'S WORKSHOP: CHAMPIONS OF HONOR

In this example of an incidental reference, a player named Ed responds haughtily on behalf of his character, Erekam, when challenged by sentinels at a city gate:

"I bang vigorously on my shield, showing them the emblem of my warrior order."

Ed has never before referenced an emblem on his shield, but since it's his character, he can introduce it without any adjustment by you.

"Do you not recognize this symbol?" Ed exclaims, in his deep Erekam voice. "It identifies me as a member of the Champions of Honor! Do you not know us?"

You've never heard of the Champions of Honor. You reach for your notepad, ready to scrawl the necessary notation.

In character as the indifferent guard, you scratch your head and say, "We don't receive visitors hereabouts, stranger."

"Why, for a hundred years the Champions of Honor have protected the good folk of this region, driving off orcs and bandits alike!"

Through this exchange, Ed establishes that this organization exists as he has described and that Erekam belongs to it. After brainstorming for a moment, you prepare a bandit encounter—now someone can spot Erekam's shield, tell him about a brigand problem, and motivate the group's trip to the wilderness to engage them.

setting with past or alternate versions. Stave off other players' natural impulses to correct these mix-ups. Take advantage of fortuitous errors, and incorporate them the same as you would a purposeful suggestion. For instance, if a player misremembers the life expectancy of elves and cites a vastly longer figure, you can decide that the elves in your world enjoy greater longevity than the norm. These accidental improvisations help you to foster the idea of a mutually developed world. Their example helps to overcome any initial reluctance either to step on your toes or to adjust official source material.

INTRODUCING PLAYER SUGGESTIONS

Three main techniques allow you to bring player suggestions to the fore: incidental reference, solicited input, and the turnaround. Proactive players might employ a fourth method, the direct assertion.

DM'S WORKSHOP: FORKS IN THE ROAD

In this example of solicited input, the players are traveling along an ancient road through a dense forest.

"After turning to avoid a rocky outcrop," you narrate, "the road forks to the east and northwest."

This fork offers a decision point to the PCs, as well as a chance to tailor its branches to their interests. Ben and Deena dominated an earlier interaction scene, so you solicit input from Amy and Carlos.

"Amy, you've heard that something dangerous lies to the east. What is it?"

Amy thinks for a moment. "Um, it's bird people. I hate bird people."

For a moment, you panic. You don't have stat blocks for any bird people. But you realize that, with minimal effort, the creatures in your bugbear and goblin encounter can be reskinned into hostile, flightless birds. You affirm Amy's choice by adding a new detail.

"Oh, yes," you reply. "They have a new leader, Rakak, who has sworn vengeance on all mammals."

"Okay, Carlos, what trouble lies to the northwest?"

Carlos takes the opportunity to bring his character's core motivation back into the storyline.

"The Pagoda of the Poison Blossom, a haunted place where explorers vanish. Rumor has it that the Flower King once lodged there and might have hidden secret texts on its grounds."

You decide on a twist: If the PCs go to the grounds, they find monks of the Flower King searching for lost scrolls. But you can reveal this surprise later.

Now that the players have established their options, they debate the merits of the two choices: Do they head toward the hostile bird people, or do they explore the haunted pagoda?

INCIDENTAL REFERENCE

This situation arises when a player makes an offhand remark, possibly as in-character dialogue, concerning a fact about the world. You then treat it as true.

If you need to adjust the idea, do not interrupt an unfolding scene to footnote the setting detail. Wait until a suitable break in the action, and then go back and clarify.

SOLICITED INPUT

In the solicited input technique, you ask each player to supply a detail of your world. You could ask a particular player—perhaps one who hasn't had enough spotlight time—or throw it open to the group and take the first suggestion offered.

THE TURNAROUND

Players are accustomed to asking the DM for details of the world. In the turnaround technique, you take a player's question and turn it around on the group, asking the players what they think the answer might be.

Use the stock phrases of the turnaround: "You tell me" and "What do you think?"

DIRECT ASSERTION

Players who are accustomed to the DM's traditional control over setting elements will wait for you to

---

DM'S WORKSHOP: DEEP GNOME RULE

In this example of a turnaround, the players are traveling through the Underdark, debating whether to seek hospitality at a deep gnome enclave far underground.

"Do I know anything about the deep gnome culture?" Amy inquires.

You consider requiring her to make a History check but instead give her an automatic success, because having information seems more interesting here than not having it. (In other words, failure would be a dead branch; see page 9.)

"You've read tomes on the subject," you answer.

"So, this enclave—how do the gnomes rule it?

"You tell me."

"Uh, well . . . I consider surface gnomes to be sneaky Feywild skulkers, and I think Underdark gnomes act especially paranoid. So its defenders rule its society, maybe? Sort of a combination of a police state and a ninja clan?"

That idea sounds pretty cool, and it's complicated enough that it doesn't require additional details.

"Exactly right," you say.

Amy realizes that she might have just invented the group out of a suitable hideaway. She quickly adds, "But paranoid ninja police state in a good way."

"Yep, that's what the deep gnomes say," you answer, keeping open a hint of uncertainty and danger.

prompt them before supplying world details. In a cooperative campaign, more assertive players might catch on to the technique and start giving you input unbidden. Give these ideas extra scrutiny to ensure that the players don't wreck the suspension of disbelief by proposing details that give their characters an advantage. If the players make slanted suggestions, spin the proposals to counterbalance the idea's intended benefits.

When given in good faith, direct assertions make good gifts for a harried DM. Proposals show what interests the players and what they want to do next.

AREAS OF INPUT

You can seek player input for any aspect of your setting, from the fine details to the world-spanning back story. Common areas of input include the following elements.

BACKGROUND INFORMATION

Draw on players for details of your world's history, cultures, economy, or religious practices. By inviting them to add to your world maps, you recruit them as geographers. See the DM's Workshop sidebars "Champions of Honor," "Deep Gnome Rule," and "Dragons Love Elves" for examples of player input into world background.

DESCRIPTIVE CONTROL

When you grant partial descriptive control to your players, you allow them to specify what they see and hear in a scene.

DMs might prefer to make encounters off limits for descriptive control. Allowing players to add obstacles and features might unbalance carefully planned combats. A daring DM might let the PCs play in this sandbox if he or she feels confident enough to countermand advantages that players try to sneak into the situation.

The DM's Workshop sidebars "Tentacle Temple" and "Forks in the Road" provide examples of descriptive control.

SUPPORTING CHARACTERS

If you used the collaborative cast-building techniques when preparing your campaign, the players might have already invented NPCs that tie into their characters' backgrounds. Extend this approach by allowing them to describe other minor characters.

Initially, you might blanch at the thought of allowing players to invent NPCs who make the PCs' lives easier. In practice, those NPCs can make your job easier. First, characters whom your players can interact with (and are interested in interacting with) make the story more dramatically interesting. Second, when you give your players the means to overcome minor inconveniences, you speed up play. In roleplaying, as in any story, you want to edit out the boring bits. If allowing a player to immediately flag down a messenger or find a blacksmith advances the story, all the better.

As with any PC advantage gained through improvised player input, you can change a situation and introduce it as a bit of complication. The bad guys might kidnap the messenger and grill him for information, prompting a rescue attempt. That seemingly helpful blacksmith could be a spy for the illithid conspiracy.

To help players invent minor characters on the fly, supply a list of names appropriate to the location. Players pick one that suits the new character and cross it off the list. When the players specify a name, you add that nonplayer character to your notes.

Once the players create an NPC, you control his or her words and actions, as you normally would.

DM'S WORKSHOP: TENTACLE TEMPLE

In this example of a direct assertion, the party has entered a demon-occupied city.

"Do I see a watchtower?" Carlos asks you.

Before you can reply, Ben, feeling a creative surge, supplies an answer of his own: "Look! Over there! That horrible tower, rising from the central plateau! Oh, my goodness, its tiles writhe! And tentacles dangle from the spire!"

You might instinctively want to slap down this seizure of your narrative prerogative. Then you remember that you encouraged the players to collaborate in building the world. You affirm Ben's idea by building on it.

"Yep, those are tentacles, all right. A strange bird that looks like a black-feathered albatross circles slowly near the spire. Suddenly, a tentacle zaps out, like the tongue of a frog, and grabs the bird, pulling it into the tower. You hear a chewing noise."

"You mean the tower is alive?" Deena exclaims. She knows your DMing style includes vivid details to encourage the PCs to move in closer to explore. "Thanks a lot, Ben!" she jokes.

DM'S WORKSHOP: DRAGONS LOVE ELVES

In this example, you turn around an abusive suggestion intended only to grant an advantage to a player.

The party finds itself in the treasure chamber of an ancient dragon. The characters have no hope of defeating the dragon in combat and must resort to persuasion to avoid becoming its midday snack.

"Luckily, dragons in this world famously love and respect the elven people," says Paul. Not coincidentally, he plays an elf.

In character as the dragon, you growl menacingly in Paul's direction. "The others I might forgive," you boom, "but to have my lair invaded by an elf, a member of a people who allied with the dragons at the dawn of time . . . why, it is enough to rouse me to homicidal fury!"

"Whoops," says Paul.

You could take the idea of player-created NPCs one step further. Let players momentarily play these NPCs as secondary characters. Choose when they gain or relinquish control. Different players might take on recurring characters over the course of a campaign.

Player-controlled recurring NPCs come in handy in open-ended adventures in which PCs split up and fan out to pursue separate agendas in parallel. The NPCs allow you to engage your players in the action when their characters are otherwise occupied.

Make a player-controlled NPC a noncombatant who, like any sensible, ordinary citizen, avoids the dangers of an adventuring life. You can play NPCs without set statistics, and without treating them as minions or designing creature stat blocks for them. Sometimes, they might morph into full-fledged companion characters (page 27) as the campaign develops.

TIMING AND FREQUENCY

Using the techniques of cooperative world building at the right times, and not too often or too seldom, gives them maximum impact. If you continually ask players to describe your world for you, they lose belief in it and come to think of it as malleable. Call on them too infrequently, and your requests for input seem jarring when they do occur.

To achieve balance, seek input no more than three or four times per session. Invite collaboration when you experience one of the following situations:

✦ You can't think of an answer.

✦ You don't see why the question matters.

✦ The party is stumped and seeking a new plot thread.

✦ You cannot envision the party's next obstacle.

✦ Your players haven't made a significant story choice recently.

✦ Players are focusing on the mechanics of the game and you want to engage their creative energy.

DM'S WORKSHOP: TANIS

During the party's first trip to the city of Sigil, Brom decides to find a local to show them the ropes. "I look for a street urchin. Are any around?"

"You see a bunch of them," you reply. "Describe the one you want to talk to."

"Uh, okay. I see a young girl, dressed in rags with a mop of dark hair, and something about her makes the others treat her as a pariah."

"I know," suggests Amy. "She has a clawed hand, as if she has a demon or monster in her ancestry."

"Yeah, a clawed hand, that's awesome. She looks hungry; she doesn't receive the handouts that the others do." Ben takes the sheet of Sigil character names. "Her name's Tanis."

You note this detail, and take on the role of Tanis. For the first few sessions of play, you retain control of the character in order to convey information about the city.

Later, Brom and Diani conduct a dangerous negotiation with the githyanki leader Yultang. Caliban descends into a mazelike pocket dimension, attempting to track down a doppelganger who has been posing as him. You

cut between the two sequences. Amy thought it out of character for Arisana to go on either errand. Rather than cook up a third plot line just for her, you offer her the chance to tag along in the githyanki sequence, temporarily playing Tanis. Amy decides that it would be a fun contrast to portray Tanis as an enthusiastic fan of the githyanki. Although others shun Tanis's ugliness, Amy explains, the pirates of the Astral Sea have engaged her services on numerous occasions. The others dislike her affinity for the githyanki, but they end up letting her lead the negotiation with Yultang.

Two sessions later, Brom dies. His comrades, low on funds but unwilling to sell their equipment, scour Sigil for someone willing to perform a Raise Dead ritual in return for future favors. You ask Ben if he wants to play Tanis, and he agrees. Picking up on the previously established githyanki connection, he has her suggest Yultang as a possible financier of the revivifying ritual. Although Brom would shudder at the thought of owing the githyanki, Ben enjoys having his temporary character skillfully back his permanent one into a corner filled with juicy plot hooks.

JULIE DILLON

—by Stephen Radney-MacFarland,
from "Save My Game!" in *Dungeon #155*

The narrative part of roleplaying has a more free-form nature than the game rules. This aspect of playing the game makes people nervous and self-conscious, especially if they prefer not to act. Sometimes you have to ease players into roleplaying by making it work like other game aspects. The following ideas show you how.

CREATE HOOKS

A lot of D&D games involve the bare-bones, smash-and-grab model of roleplaying, filled with stats, action, monster killing, and treasure. Players in these games need less story to guide them. They don't care about the implausible. They have fun because they buy into the game. Why? Because the game and its design have built-in hooks.

What do I mean by hooks? The parts that grab your audience, pull them in, and never let them go. D&D has them in spades. Classes and races both function as hooks; their concepts, art, and application reach out and grab people. The "simple rules with exceptions" principle of D&D offers another hook. You have a firm idea of the general rules, and you can reference the specific. A hook pokes its head up and says, "Hey, I'm here, and I think you'll like me." The people who do like it, grab it and run. As a fantasy game, D&D has its own hook, too.

DMs sometimes forget the general principle of hooks when they make their campaigns. DMs might create a place they believe could be real, not realizing that few players care for the models of trade and agriculture in the game world—since the game functions as a power fantasy. Others fixate on their campaign's overarching story and overlook that this form of storytelling already has an audience (and cast) of real people in the form of players and their characters. In the end, these DMs might find themselves trapped when they create hooks interesting only to them. And as the DM, if you interest only yourself, you don't have an audience.

Use a sandbox approach to story and roleplaying. Throw out loose threads, see who bites, figure out why they bite, and react to the story rather than driving it autocratically from the start. You might guide your players in class and race choices, but don't make those decisions for them. Don't try to make roleplaying decisions for them, either. You can use an open approach in your details of your world and story vision without losing it completely. Pick up on good ideas and suggestions from your players. As your players feel more attached to the story, their immersion levels rise, especially when they

figure out they can drive the story rather than have it unfold around them. When players have more investment in the storytelling and roleplaying parts of the game, they focus on these parts rather than ignoring or avoiding them.

I'll give you an example by briefly outlining what I'm doing in my current campaign—my first, full-fledged levels 1–30 D&D 4E campaign—the *Days of Long Shadows*. When my players made their characters, I gave them a list of seven backgrounds they could choose from. I told them from the start that choosing a background would ensure that their characters had a stronger connection to the overall plot of the campaign, but that they didn't need to take one. I made these backgrounds simple, with few restrictions. Two examples follow.

The Hexed (Half-Elf, Human, or Tiefling): A mysterious master cursed you; you don't know his identity. All you know is that his raspy voice occasionally compels you to do as he bids. His commands sometimes demand terrible deeds, but far worse consequences ensue when you refuse to obey.

The Orphan (Human): You're an orphan of the disappeared village of Fadail. A wandering oracle of Ioun prophesized that only Fadail's last scion could find the village. Presumably, that person is you.

These raw hooks have a purpose. I combined the interesting themes I wanted to explore in the campaign into a form that might interest my players, and made the themes available to my players.

Allowing my players to pick their backgrounds achieved a couple of objectives. First, it gives them a focused hook into one or more of the stories and themes of the campaign. Having a choice strengthens their story investment, and it gives me a tool that simultaneously focuses their plot-seeking activity and helps me create stories that speak to their characters personally—even before the campaign begins.

For instance, I had a specific player in mind when I wrote the hexed, and I was not surprised when the player took that background. He enjoys playing these mysterious, tormented characters that have a secret. I knew he would gravitate toward this background.

As for the backgrounds not chosen (such as the orphan above), I have a page of rough ideas I won't use in this particular campaign. I can learn a lot from what my players didn't pick, such as what kind of game interests them.

More important, these backgrounds bridge the gap between game and story. Since I made backgrounds a character choice, the players feel a sense of ownership. I created roleplaying and story hooks the same way the rest of the game hooks worked—I let my players choose what they wanted.

KEEP THOSE LINES TAUT

So you have the hooks. Next step: Don't let them go. And keep a lookout for new and interesting hooks. Every time you identify what players find interesting in your game, pull them in with it. As the first order of business in my campaign, I make sure the background choice of each player remains important and relevant. Don't make a background a wasted choice by never incorporating its themes and ideas in the game; that approach makes the hook irrelevant and pointless. After all, my PCs can't retrain their backgrounds! At the same time, a D&D game has an ensemble cast. Game sessions rarely tug every line—save some lines for when they have the best effect.

For instance, if the hexed character never heard the voice, that situation would be silly and counterproductive. But the opposite holds true as well. You don't want every game session to start with the voice telling him what to do. Save these reveals for the right moments, and until then, leave them hanging over the character's head. After a few sessions, and when something interesting occurs, I bring in the mysterious agenda to create drama and conflict, and to give the player interesting choices to make.

As my second order of business, I observe how my players interpret those hooks, and how they use the hooks to flesh out their characters and inform their actions. My backgrounds lack detail for a reason—I want to see how each player interprets and weaves them into the story. As the hexed player comes up with past stories on how the voice guided him, I can ensure that future instances of the voice act in a similar manner.

DON'T BE A SINKER

Finally, don't sink honest effort even if it's awkward. It takes practice to do anything well. Some individuals might have a native ability to succeed, but most goals require trial and error until we hit our groove.

The same holds true for roleplaying. Although the drama major in your group might excel, your group introvert might have a hard time with it at first. And although pointing out someone's awkward attempt at roleplaying might give you a brief moment of amusement, a friendly guiding hand works better than sarcasm if you want to promote roleplaying and deeper story interaction. Don't worry; no one is up for an Oscar. No talent agent will knock on your door in the morning. People continue to roleplay as long as they have fun. You might enjoy being critical, but others rarely find it fun.

MY SON, THE FIRE ARCHON

D&D builds monsters and characters differently. Characters have more complexity than monsters because PCs live longer. A single player normally controls a single character, whereas the DM runs multiple monsters at a time.

So what happens when your 11-year-old son wants to play a fire archon as a character?

My son enjoys the tactile elements of the game. He loves it when I bring new miniatures home, he builds sprawling dungeons out of my *Dungeon Tiles*, and he designs his characters with specific minis in mind.

So his favorite mini from the *Desert of Desolation* set is the fire archon, and he wants to play that creature as his character. What do I do? Fire archons don't appear in the *Monster Manual* appendix of playable monster races.

I'm still amazed at how easily I constructed a fire archon character. I built him a 7th-level rogue, and I picked powers that I could rework to add a fiery touch:

✦ 7th-level encounter attack: *cloud of steel*, which I turned into *cloud of flame* (a close blast 5 of fire damage).
✦ 5th-level daily attack: *deep cut* became *blazing strike* (dealing ongoing fire damage).
✦ 3rd-level encounter attack: *bait and switch* turned into *flame's dance* but remained a power concerned with mobility.

✦ 1st-level daily attack: *blinding barrage* turned into *blinding flames* (a blast of blinding fire).
✦ 1st-level encounter attack: *dazing strike* transformed into *dazing flame* (a simple dazing attack).
✦ 1st-level at-wills: *piercing strike* became *fiery blast* (it already targets Reflex instead of AC), and *deft strike* for mobility again.

I made his sneak attack damage fire damage, just for flavor. Then, for racial powers, I copied the tiefling's fire resistance and added poison resistance in the same amount. I gave him immunity to disease and made his speed 8. That was enough—he didn't need an additional racial power.

Did I create a character identical to the fire archons in the *Monster Manual*? No, and I didn't make it a standard human rogue, either. I made it resemble the fire archon in all the ways that matter.

A player's character is an important aspect of the game for that player. So a DM should help every player create a fun character who won't unbalance the game (which would hinder the fun of the other players). Sometimes it proves easy within the limits of the rules. Other times, you have to be more creative.

–James Wyatt, originally posted on Wizards.com staff blogs

Add moments of character interaction to your game with vignettes—specially shaped scenes in which players respond to dramatic situations you create for them.

VIGNETTE TYPES

Vignettes can fill a number of roles in your story.

✦ Interactions dramatize current conflicts between PCs or other characters.

✦ Flashbacks illuminate past events in the characters' lives.

✦ Dream sequences bring a character's inner conflicts to life in a surreal mental environment.

✦ Transitions leap the campaign forward in time.

✦ Third-person teasers use NPCs, portrayed by the players, to foreshadow events that enmesh the PCs.

INTERACTIONS

Interactions resolve conflicts that arise during standard play between PCs. Push for resolution cautiously; preserve player autonomy by allowing some interactions to end in standstills. Interactions make useful session starters. They can kick-start a campaign after a long break. Use them as reminders when your planned adventure riffs on a previous PC conflict that might have receded into the background.

FLASHBACKS

Flashback sequences move the character's background story into the spotlight for the entire group to imagine. These vignettes can sharpen the portrayal of unfocused PCs by playing out the pivotal moments that shaped their core motivations.

You can also use flashback sequences to introduce elements of the character's past that later resurface in the main action. For example, if a previously unmentioned old mentor of a PC shows up to send the party on a mission, a flashback can add weight to the idea of their preexisting relationship.

In campaigns featuring elements of destiny or prophecy, flash forward to possible futures that provide a fun variation on the flashback. You might specify that these predictions offer glimpses into an immutable future. You might find it easier, though, to portray these sequences as possible futures (or

DM'S WORKSHOP: BANISHED

After several sessions of play, you realize that one of the PCs seizes the lead role in encounters and takes a back seat in interaction scenes. The player, Greg, enjoys the story side of D&D. His shifter character, Grath, has yet to display a personality. You start the next session with a flashback sequence featuring Grath. Greg established that Grath chose the life of a wandering adventurer after his people banished him. You ask him to explain why his people banished him.

"My brother stole cattle belonging to the clan chief and traded them for silk for his trading company," Greg says. "The clan soothsayer performed a divining ritual and saw that I knew the culprit. Although I despised my brother, family loyalty prevented me from turning him in. So the townsfolk banished me, though my brother remains with them to this day."

"All right, we're flashing back to the moment before your final audience with the clan chief. You stand in the family tent. What's your brother's name?"

"I hadn't decided."

"Okay, how about Yaroth." You point to another player, Haru. "You play Yaroth. You must convince him not to turn you in."

Turning back to Greg, you ask, "Who was Grath's best friend and confidante?"

"A comrade-in-arms."

You select a third player, Inez, to play Grath's best friend, Uchig. "Your goal is to convince Grath not to throw away his position for the sake of his thieving, no-good brother."

Haru, as Yaroth, kicks off with a wheedling plea to protect his life. "They'll just banish you, but if you turn me in, they'll execute me!"

"And so you deserve!" cries Inez, as Uchig. "Why, I have a mind to tell the clan chief myself."

"Remember," says Greg, "you have sworn on your honor to keep this secret."

"What good is my honor, if he takes yours unfairly from you?"

Greg's addition to the scene gives him a goal, too—to persuade his friend not to besmirch his own honor over Yaroth's misdeeds.

The scene continues. When it becomes repetitive, you address Greg: "Okay, let's identify one more unknown detail about Grath's banishment. Steer the scene toward that revelation."

Greg nods and waits until Inez makes a strong point in favor of informing on Yaroth. He jumps in, now switching to narrative mode: "At that point my elderly father enters the tent, clutching his chest. I realize that if the elders execute Yaroth, it will also kill my father. Now I see my destiny laid out before me—as a wandering, masterless noble."

Move back into standard action when the scene reaches a natural climax. As you steer the group toward a choice of encounters, you can plan how to introduce a scene that recalls Grath's pivotal moment.

hallucinations) that the PCs can avert or move toward, according to their actions in the present.

DREAM SEQUENCES

Dream sequences allow you to portray a PC's inner turmoil with surreal imagery. The PC stands at one point of the triangle while other players try to pull him in opposite directions. They might play dream versions of themselves, figures from the PC's past, or surreal personifications of abstract forces. For that matter, the other PCs can shift identities according to the whims of dream logic.

TRANSITIONS

Transitions acknowledge the progression of time in the campaign since the last session. They create the sense that the character's life continues between adventures. In campaigns that use them, transitions can cover long jumps in time, taking the characters through months or years of unseen action.

Transitions require open-ended framing led by player input. Ask the players to describe a conflict that occupied them during the elapsed time period. Together, choose a dramatic moment, and frame a vignette around it. You might construct one vignette per character, or cast vignettes together into a scene of combined struggle.

THIRD-PERSON TEASERS

Scenes featuring a cast of player-controlled NPCs foreshadow events for their PCs. Third-person teasers provide snappy openers to sessions that might otherwise begin with a gathering of PCs in a tavern.

Dialogue might drive third-person teasers, but they might depart from other vignettes by featuring descriptions of physical action.

For inspiration, look at the opening credit sequences of TV shows, especially openers that feature only members of that week's guest cast. Horror

---

DM'S WORKSHOP: CALLED TO ACCOUNT

Brom, who believes himself destined for greatness, ended last session with a craven surrender to the bandit queen, Isolta. To explore the gap between his self-image and his actions, you create a dream sequence in which Brom's hero, the legendary warrior Ambek, calls him to account. You assign Amy to play Ambek, who wishes to convince Brom to follow in his footsteps. Deena also appears in his dream, as Isolta, who argues that Brom, as an ordinary man, took the only reasonable action when he bowed and scraped before her.

You want this scene to pose a question, not to answer one, so interrupt it as it reaches a crescendo. Brom, you narrate, jolts awake in his bedroll, drenched in icy sweat.

procedurals, such as *Supernatural* or *The X-Files*, start with teasers that introduce an unknown threat to the main characters.

This device allows you to introduce your players to the bad guys before their characters kill them. They learn to dread and loathe the villains long before the climactic encounter, increasing its emotional impact.

Preserve future surprises by withholding information from the players. A monster attack scene might allow their temporary characters to see shadowy figures materialize from nothing and attack. In a scene of political negotiation or criminal plotting, you might not tell the PCs what characters they're playing.

Third-person vignettes require players who can separate their knowledge of the events portrayed from what their characters know.

DM'S WORKSHOP: REPORT TO THE EMPEROR

In a saga-length campaign in which each of the PCs rules a province of the Arcathian Empire, the characters level up, triggering one of the campaign's periodic one-year breaks. You ask each player to come to the next session, which starts with a meeting of provincial governors before the emperor, with an accomplishment to brag about. A dry recap of interim events becomes a fun competitive scene, in which each player jockeys for recognition.

DM'S WORKSHOP: ILLITHID ATTACK

As the kickoff to an adventure in which the heroes fight mind flayers, assign each player a new character to play in a third-person teaser. Each character plays a soldier guarding a frontier outpost. Assign each soldier a name. Half of the six characters work toward a goal that forces them to interact with one another. After playing dice all night, Conrad, Aldfrid, and Ellis have lost their wages to Imric, Oswyn, and Hengist, and the former group wishes the latter group to forgive their debts.

After the players roleplay their temporary characters long enough to make them feel real and engaging, you describe the horrible results of a mind flayer attack on the outpost. Although you allow the players to describe their temporary characters' responses to the attack, don't use dice or rules to resolve the results. These poor soldiers have no hope. The two players who can convincingly describe countermeasures survive the longest. The illithid leader, Khardaghk, as played with sinister relish by you, interrogates and toys with the last two survivors. By the time he slays the last of the soldiers, the players despise Khardaghk and want to see him laid low—even though their characters have yet to hear of him.

VIGNETTE STAGES

Vignettes break down into three stages:

+ Framing, when you establish the parameters of the interaction.
+ Development, in which the scene plays out.
+ Conclusion, the wrap-up.

FRAMING

When framing a vignette, you establish a current situation, as well as the conflict the vignette resolves. Start by designating which players you want to participate in the vignette. Tell them whom they will portray—their own characters or other NPCs important to the scene. You might have a mix—part of your group plays characters, and the other part plays NPCs.

Second, briefly describe the physical environment and the participants' starting situations.

Then lay out the conflict that drives the scene, preferably between two characters or sets of characters. Establish the goal each side pursues.

DEVELOPMENT

Sit back as the players, through dialogue and action description, play out the scene. Depending on the conflict you design, the players might employ a mixture of debate, emotional pleas, and offered inducements. As they do, the scene heads in one of two directions. Either the players resolve the conflict, or each side digs in. You can tell that players have dug in their heels when proponents of each side begin to restate their positions. If this stalemate happens, nudge the proceedings along by suggesting a new argument or negotiating position that one or the other side might adopt. If the players remain dug in, move to the next stage.

CONCLUSION

If the conflict resolves itself naturally, the players either compromise, allowing both sides to achieve their goals, or one side capitulates to the other. The players have done your job for you: Declare the scene over and cut back to the main action.

If both sides refuse to budge, ask yourself if it seems unsatisfying to end the scene at a standstill.

An impasse can be a strong outcome because it leaves unanswered questions the players can deal with in subsequent scenes.

If an impasse disappoints the players, decide who gives in. When PCs face off against NPCs, the PCs should have more influence over the conflict. In a conflict between two PCs, or one between NPCs, judge which side offers the most persuasive argument. Instruct the players on the losing side to convincingly relent. If players seem unhappy to relent for their PCs, default to an impasse.

DRAMA REWARDS

When asked to recall their favorite D&D experiences, players might recall a session made up only of roleplaying interaction. You might hear the capper phrase, "And we didn't roll dice once!"

If you aspire to this style of play, you can give player characters experience rewards for time spent in dramatic scenes of interaction, as well as for their triumph over more traditional encounters. Award the characters experience as if they had defeated one monster of their level for every 15 minutes they spend in significant, focused roleplaying that advances the story of your campaign. Don't count time the players use to digress, idly chatter, repeat themselves, wander off topic, argue to a standstill, or engage pointlessly with minor characters.

Because vignettes are short, and because you steer them to maintain focus, you should grant drama rewards for vignettes only if you rely on them in any given session. Don't bother to calculate experience for one or two typical vignettes.

If you think a player is clearly drawing out an interaction to score a drama reward, subtract an amount of time that you estimate is equal to the entire time that player spent in the interaction.

This technique compensates players for the time they devote to interaction without judging any participant's skill at portraying his character. Instead, it rewards the entire group's focus and efficiency of communication.

MAINTAINING PLAYER AUTHORITY

Be prepared to accept input from players when placing their characters in vignettes. If your framing places the PCs in a situation they don't think they would have put themselves in, or assigns them a goal they don't agree with, revise the framing to meet their objections. Tell the players what the scene is intended to accomplish and solicit their input to adjust the situation and goal to better reflect their characters' intentions.

ACTION RESOLUTION

Vignettes can unfold through dialogue alone, without resorting to skill checks. When participants physically clash or otherwise engage in activities that game mechanics ordinarily resolve, you can break out the dice, allow a directly concerned player to decide the outcome, or put it up to a group vote, with yourself as the tiebreaker.

Players whose PCs appear in flashback sequences decide how past conflicts panned out. Use mechanics only if different players' ideas conflict, and they can't agree on what should have happened.

You'll find it easier to create adventures and encounters your players enjoy once you know what your players like about gaming. If you serve up game sessions that cover exactly what the group enjoys, then the players will have fun. Plus, you can prepare with more confidence and fewer contingencies because you know what material the players gravitate toward and what hooks and encounters they avoid, meaning faster and easier session preparation.

To find out what the members of your group like and dislike, ask them. Player and character surveys allow you to discover this information. What would you like to know about your players' gaming preferences? Write down a wish list. If you knew whether your group preferred city, wilderness, or urban settings, would that affect your campaign plans? What about favorite gaming moments, combats, and encounter setups? That information might give you great ideas for future sessions that your players find exciting.

Once you compile a list of details you want to know about your group, turn each item into a question, and then compile your questions into surveys. Use anything related to characters' wants, dreams, and goals in a character survey. Ask each player to answer this survey from his or her character's point of view. You could roleplay to make responses more interesting, since players could consider questionnaires a chore. Place questions related to player preferences and experiences in a separate player survey.

Dividing your queries and the players' answers into character and player categories helps you plan better adventures. Take character answers and weave those elements directly into encounters by way of monster, terrain, and treasure selection. Factor PC preferences into your plots, as well. Characters might want to visit certain places, take certain actions, and earn specific achievements. Modify your short- and long-term plans, the setting, and the villains to include character desires. You best serve a player through his or her character. Fulfilling the PCs' survey requests makes a group eager to play and happy with your games.

The second part of the equation serves player-specific preferences. You can serve these inclinations in the same way you serve character preferences—with in-game content and design. However, you might serve your friends better through new house rules, changes to the gaming environment or schedule, session management, and other metagame issues.

When you read player survey responses, consider how you can improve the game and campaign based on player feedback. Discuss major items such as session length or location, new house rules, or game world changes with your group. Implement changes one or two at a time, in trial periods. If someone expresses unhappiness with a change, roll it back. Set proper expectations and follow a process that respects individuals while trying to please the group.

To avoid overwhelming busy players, consider spacing out your questions. Perhaps supply one or two questions during sessions that players can think about while their characters are idle. Post a question of the week on your gaming group website, or follow up every session with a short feedback form.

Revisit your surveys. Sometimes player and character tastes change, and you want to keep your information fresh. Administer the entire survey again, or just pick key questions. A healthy frequency for surveys might be every five character levels, ten sessions, or four months.

Example character survey questions:

✦ Describe yourself in ten words or fewer.
✦ What do you think is your greatest strength?
✦ What do you think is your biggest weakness?
✦ What is your most distinguishing feature?
✦ Why did you choose an adventuring life?
✦ Which family members or friends do you hold most dear?
✦ What people, groups, or objects hold your greatest loyalty?
✦ What career do you want to have one year from now? Five years?
✦ What place do you wish to visit?
✦ Consider your skills. How did you acquire them?
✦ What do you like to do when not adventuring or training?
✦ What magic items do you crave?
✦ Where do you enjoy hanging out?
✦ How do you want people to remember you after your death?

Example player survey questions:

✦ What monsters do you like most?
✦ Rate your enjoyment of each of the following environments from 1-10, 10 being best: a) wilderness encounters, b) city encounters, c) dungeons, and d) unusual locations such as cloud homes or underwater.
✦ Rate your enjoyment of each of the following types of adventures from 1-10, 10 being best: a) long

adventures, b) short adventures, c) linear adventures, and d) open play with no prepared plot.

✦ Rate your enjoyment of each of the following types of play from 1–10, 10 being best: a) combat, b) interaction with NPCs, c) puzzles, d) investigation, and e) mystery.

✦ Do you have any session location requests or preferences?

✦ What times can you play each week?

✦ How do you prefer I contact you about game details? Please provide your contact information.

✦ How do you prefer we handle characters of absent players?

✦ What three gaming moments would you like to recreate in this campaign?

Keep replies and craft profiles for each player in one place, so you can read up on a player when desired. Profiles might contain survey answers, player knowledge, trivia, a spreadsheet, or paper forms you maintain.

At reasonable intervals, review your player and character profiles so you can adjust your DMing style. Approach each encounter with character and player preferences in mind. Even if you want to retain the original content of the encounters you've designed, realize that subtle tweaks during play can make games more enjoyable. For example, make a foe's magic weapon one a PC desires, change an NPC's surname and make him a distant cousin of a character, or use extra description for magical effects because one of your players loves spells and wizardry.

You can also make checklists of requests and ideas for each player and character. Then, try to add items from these checklists into the game. Check off an equal number of items for each player by session's end to maintain balance and fairness. Keep the checklists on hand behind your DM screen to make adding items easier during the game.

If you have a top-down DMing style, you do not need to throw out all your plans and designs in order to craft game sessions based on player and character preferences. Just change a few details, because the group will notice a little customization and campaign personalization, and this approach makes everyone excited to play.

COMPANION CHARACTERS

A paladin rescues an imprisoned knight who swears to follow her as a faithful companion for a year and a day. A shaman tends to the wounds of a young black bear, and the friendly animal follows the shaman on his quest. A wizard takes on an apprentice, a youthful elf eager to learn the ways of magic and use them to battle evil.

The young sidekick, the eager beast follower, and the faithful henchman feature regularly in fantasy novels, comics, and movies. Although adding an extra character to the adventuring group might make perfect sense from a story point of view, instantly recognizable pitfalls can make this decision a bad one:

✦ Players might consider running a single character to be a full-time job; running two adds a lot of work and slows down the game.

✦ Allowing one player to run two characters diminishes the participation of the other players in the game, which can lead to frustration and disappointment from those players.

✦ Adding characters can dilute the individual strengths of other party members by doubling (or even tripling) particular roles, which can lead to player feeling as though his or her character isn't important anymore.

If you can cope with these issues, adding an extra character can yield significant benefits. No matter how compelling the story angle, however, remember one rule: Add an extra character only when it helps fill out a small party or an underserved role.

If fewer than five players participate in a game, your group probably struggles with standard encounters designed for groups of five PCs. In addition, your group probably lacks one or more character roles. Adding the right companion character can solve both problems.

Even in full-size groups, having a few companion characters available for use helps you cope with unexpected player absences. When the party's leader misses a gaming session, that friendly local priest of Kord willing to adventure with you can keep the game on track.

COMPANION CHARACTERS VS. NPCS

The rules for building companion characters are similar to the "Creating NPCs" rules presented on page 186 of the *Dungeon Master's Guide*. However, these new rules are better at crafting an adventuring ally for the PCs, whereas the NPC rules are better at helping you build enemies for your characters.

These new rules are more abstract than the NPC rules: They focus entirely on the companion character's role in the party, rather than building the character through the filter of its class. That makes it simpler to create and use the companion character.

COMPANION CHARACTERS IN THE GAME

Companion characters fill a role similar to that of NPCs because you don't design and detail companion characters like player characters, nor do companion characters have key roles in the story as PCs do.

Companion characters exist first and foremost to ensure a fun and exciting game. A companion character should never disrupt anyone's enjoyment. You control a companion character's presence and role in the game and must allow him or her to come and go as appropriate to the story. Remove a companion character from the game (or modify the character's statistics) if she creates an inappropriate impact on the game, or if her presence overshadows the PCs.

The rules for companion characters relate to monsters more than to PCs, though companion characters share some aspects with PCs. Overall, a companion character's abilities offer function over flavor: a small array of powers and skills, a few personality elements, and the other basic mechanical elements of a character such as defenses, hit points, and healing surges. These rules aim to make the companion character easy to run, so a single player can handle both a PC and a companion character with little extra effort.

Of course, statistics represent only a portion of what makes companion characters fun. As the DM, you have to bring a companion character to life. A character who has an engaging personality and good story adds a layer of fun to the game. A companion character who doesn't exhibit such details behaves like a game piece, nothing more than a convenient tool for fighting monsters.

Allowing players to run a companion character can ease your burden (you have enough to do handling monsters, traps, and refereeing the game), but you still have control over the character's personality, motivations, and important choices. The players might dictate the companion character's tactics, but you can overrule them if the players push the companion character into a suicidal position ("I'll hold off this dragon while you guys flee!") or attempt to exploit him.

CREATING A COMPANION CHARACTER

You can craft a companion character by adapting a monster from the *Monster Manual* or another source, or by building one from scratch, the same way you create an NPC opponent.

When you create a companion character, consider involving the players in the process, particularly any player whose character has strong ties to the companion character. For example, if the paladin PC decides to take on a squire, the paladin's player might want to determine the characteristics of that companion character. You can allow that player to sketch out or design the squire, but you have ultimate veto authority. If you want to change something in the player's design, explain your reason to avoid appearing arbitrary or unfair. Maybe the companion character's race doesn't fit into your world, or maybe you think the powers the player chose for the character are inappropriate.

USING AN EXISTING MONSTER

As an easy solution, use an existing creature from the *Monster Manual* or some other resource to create a companion character. You can use an "out of the box" monster as a hired mercenary, a tamed beast, or a formerly evil creature that turned its back on its heritage. Just find a monster of the appropriate level and role, and apply a few adjustments to its statistics.

Simple monsters make good companion characters because they don't burden a player the way a more fleshed-out character would. The "Suggested Companion Characters" sidebar gives a list of appropriate monsters; use the following criteria to find a good fit.

Keep it Simple: As a rule of thumb, allow a companion character no more than three different attack powers. Otherwise, he or she approaches the complexity of a PC. You made the companion character to fill a party role or pad out the group's numbers. A complex monster defeats that purpose and might overshadow the characters.

Standard Monsters Only: Avoid elite and solo monsters because they make overpowered companion characters. Conversely, minions are too weak to help out the party.

Medium Is Best: Although Small companion characters pose no problems, Large creatures crowd the characters in a dungeon. Don't use Huge or Gargantuan companion characters except for brief guest appearances on enormous fields of battle.

DM BUILT, PLAYER RUN

The rules for companion characters rest on a simple assumption: The DM builds the character, and the players use the companion character for as long as his or her presence remains appropriate.

Don't allow players to exploit and abuse the *Monster Manual* to build a powerful ally. Instead, use a companion character when the party needs the help of an ally, or to fill out an empty role at a short-handed table.

At the table, assign the companion character to a player, preferably one whose character's background somehow links to the companion character. In combat situations, the player can run the companion character.

If a particular adventure does not require the companion character, tell your group he has an important errand that prevents him from assisting the PCs (just as you might do for an absent player's PC).

TURNING A MONSTER INTO A COMPANION CHARACTER

When you use an existing monster as a companion character, keep these rules in mind.

1. Level. Make a companion character of the same level as the party. You can adjust an existing monster's level up or down to bring it in line with the party's level. If you increase a monster's level to make it a companion character, advance it according to the rules in "Companion Characters in Play" on page 33. Reduce the companion character's level by reversing the same process. For example, if you reduce a human mage's level from 4 to 3, reduce her hit points by 4, lower her attack bonus and defense scores by 1, and apply a –1 penalty to her damage rolls.

2. Role. A monster's normal role helps determine its appropriate role in the party. Use the following guidelines to determine a monster's appropriateness for a particular role in the PC party.

Controller: Controller monsters obviously work well for this role. Look particularly for controllers with area attacks. Artillery monsters that use area attacks also count as controllers.

Defender: Soldiers make good defenders. If a creature can mark its enemies as an at-will attack, consider it a defender regardless of its monster role. Controller monsters, particularly ones that prefer to engage in melee and control a limited swath of the battlefield immediately around their own space, can act as defenders in a PC party.

Leader: Few monsters fit this role because only a small number have the ability to bolster their allies. A monster that has the leader subtype can function as a backup leader in the party, but many of these monsters have more complicated arrays of powers that make them otherwise inappropriate. Instead, choose a monster that fits the controller or defender role, and add the default power for leader companion characters detailed in step 8 for creating companion characters, "Assign Feature," on page 31.

Striker: Brutes, lurkers, and skirmishers function well as strikers. Artillery monsters that use single-target ranged attacks also fit the striker role.

3. Hit Points and Healing Surges. Do not use the monster's normal hit points. The role you assign to a companion character determines its hit points as shown on the Companion Character Statistics table on page 30. It also gains healing surges, according to the same table.

4. Defenses. If you want to tweak the monster's defenses, increase one or two defenses while reducing other defenses. Don't adjust any defense by more than 2 from the baseline given in the Companion Character Statistics table.

✦ +1 AC: Reduce two other defenses by 1.

✦ +2 Fortitude, Reflex, or Will: Reduce AC by 1 or reduce one other non-AC defense by 2.

5. Powers. You might have to adjust a monster's powers to make them fit a companion character.

Recharge: If the creature has a power that recharges during the encounter, treat it as a normal, nonrechargeable encounter power.

Swapping Powers: If a monster's power causes trouble in the game because it's overly complicated or powerful, trade one of the creature's encounter attack powers for an encounter attack power from a class that shares the companion character's party role.

SUGGESTED COMPANION CHARACTERS

Here are a few monsters from the *Monster Manual* and other sources that make good companion characters. They have attacks and abilities on par with PC at-will or encounter abilities.

Level	Monster	Role
1	Fire beetle	Striker
1	Halfling slinger	Striker
2	Elf scout	Striker
2	Gray wolf	Striker
2	Human bandit	Striker
2	Kobold dragonshield	Defender
3	Gnome arcanist	Controller
3	Human guard	Defender
3	Iron defender	Defender
3	Spitting drake	Striker
4	Dwarf bolter	Striker
4	Human berserker	Striker
4	Human mage	Controller
4	Warforged soldier	Defender
5	Dragonborn soldier	Defender
5	Dwarf hammerer	Defender
5	Human noble^M	Leader
5	Rage drake	Striker
6	Ambush drake^D	Striker
6	Dire boar	Striker
6	Dragonkin defender^D	Defender
7	Eladrin fey knight	Soldier
7	Hell hound	Striker
7	Human cavalier^M	Defender
7	Macetail behemoth	Defender
8	Eladrin twilight incanter	Controller
8	Warforged forgepriest^M	Leader
9	Gnome wolverine^M	Striker
9	Human pirate^M	Striker
10	Minotaur warrior	Defender
13	Hill giant	Striker
14	Angel of protection	Defender
14	Azer foot soldier	Defender
15	Thunderfury boar	Striker
17	Firebred hell hound	Striker

D: Appears in *Draconomicon: Chromatic Dragons*
M: Appears in *Monster Manual 2*

Choose a power of a level equal to or lower than the companion character's level. For instance, you can trade a human mage's *thunder burst* attack for *shock sphere* (a 3rd-level wizard encounter power).

Avoid Record-Keeping Effects: Powers that have effects that a saving throw can end, or that a monster can sustain, burden the player (and frequently prove too powerful in the hands of a companion character). Either avoid these monsters or remove the aspect of the power that requires record-keeping. For example, change a "save ends" duration to make the effect last until the end of the companion character's next turn.

Avoid Immediate Actions: Players should have to worry about immediate actions for only one character at a time. If a player's PC has no immediate actions, allow his companion character to have one.

Beware of Gamebreakers: Don't allow a companion character to have abilities that allow that character (and potentially the party) to avoid common obstacles or ignore normal resource management, particularly in the heroic tier. Your own experience at the table can tell you what powers or abilities would offer too much of an advantage to the party. For example:

+ A companion character who has darkvision, blindsight, or tremorsense gives the party a warning system beyond their normal abilities.

+ A companion character who can fly, particularly one capable of carrying another character, eliminates too many challenges and potential risks to the PCs. The same holds true for companion characters who have teleportation or phasing.

+ A companion character who can daze, stun, or immobilize foes with an at-will power has too much clout. If you want to use such a creature, change the at-will power to an encounter power.

+ A power that restores hit points without costing a healing surge makes a companion character too potent. Make such a power a daily power.

6. Magic Items. As a general rule, companion characters don't use magic items. A PC might give a magic item to a companion character, but if one does so, do not add the magic item's enhancement bonus to the companion character's statistics. The companion character's attack and defense values are already set at appropriate values for the character's level, so adding these bonuses could lead to an overpowered character.

A companion character can use only one daily magic item power per day. The character doesn't

gain additional uses at higher tiers or when the party reaches a milestone.

CRAFTING A UNIQUE COMPANION CHARACTER

If no monster matches your vision for a follower, or if you want a particular kind of character for your campaign world and your current story arc, you can create a unique companion character from scratch.

Crafting a unique companion character resembles creating a PC or making a unique monster. To do so, follow the steps outlined below.

1. Choose Level: Set a companion character's level within one level of the PCs. This practice keeps the companion character relevant and prevents him or her from outshining the player characters.

2. Choose Role: A companion character doesn't have a character class, but each one does need a party role to generate numerical statistics and to clarify the character's place in the adventuring group. Page 16 of the *Player's Handbook* describes the party roles of controller, defender, leader, and striker.

3. Choose Race: If the companion character is a member of a PC race, he or she gains all the racial traits of that race, including the racial power. If you don't choose a PC race for the companion character, ignore this step.

4. Generate Ability Scores: Generate a unique companion character's ability scores just as you would for a 1st-level player character (as described on page 17 of the *Player's Handbook*). Unlike with a PC or an NPC, a companion character's ability scores don't improve at higher levels.

Ability modifiers don't influence a companion character's attack or defense numbers. Ability modifiers still apply when determining hit points and healing surges, damage values, skill check modifiers, ability check modifiers, and initiative check modifier.

5. Determine Hit Points and Healing Surges: The role you assign to a companion character dictates his or her hit points and healing surges, as shown on the Companion Character Statistics table.

6. Calculate Defenses: A companion character's defenses depend on the role and level you choose, as shown on the Companion Character Statistics table. Do not apply modifiers for ability scores or equipment.

At your option, increase any non-AC defense by 2. If you do, reduce a different non-AC defense by 2 to compensate.

COMPANION CHARACTER STATISTICS

Statistic	Controller	Defender	Leader	Striker
Hit points	(level × 4) + 6 + Con score	(level × 6) + 9 + Con score	(level × 5) + 7 + Con score	(level × 5) + 7 + Con score
Healing surges	6 + Con modifier	9 + Con modifier	7 + Con modifier	6 + Con modifier
Armor Class	13 + level	17 + level	15 + level	15 + level
Other defenses	13 + level	13 + level	13 + level	13 + level

7. Select Powers: Choose a character class that has the same role as the companion character. Note that class's appropriate melee and ranged basic attacks. Then select one other at-will attack power, one encounter attack power, and one utility power from that class. Each of these powers must be no higher in level than the companion character's level. As the companion character gains levels, replace these powers with new powers of the companion character's level or lower.

If the companion character is 11th level or higher, it gains an encounter attack power or utility power of 10th level or lower. If the companion character is 21st level or higher, it also gains an encounter attack power or utility power of 17th level or lower.

8. Assign Feature: Each companion character also gains one of the following four features, as appropriate to his or her role.

Controller: Once per encounter as a free action, a controller can extend an effect on an enemy to end at the end of his next turn, rather than his current turn.

Defender: When a defender hits an enemy with a melee basic attack, the defender marks that target until the end of her next turn.

Leader: Twice per encounter as a minor action, a leader can allow an ally within 5 squares of the leader to spend a healing surge. A leader of 16th level or higher can use this feature three times per encounter.

Striker: Once per round, a striker deals 1d6 extra damage when he hits an enemy he has combat advantage against. This extra damage increases to 2d6 at 11th level and 3d6 at 21st level.

9. Calculate Attack Bonus: A companion character's attack bonus equals 4 + level. For attacks with weapons, add the weapon's proficiency bonus. Do not apply modifiers for ability scores or magic items.

10. Calculate Damage Bonus: A companion character adds the appropriate ability modifier to damage rolls as normal. In addition, the character adds one-half his or her level to all damage rolls. This value replaces the damage bonuses that PCs derive from feats and other special benefits.

11. Choose Skills: Choose two trained skills for the companion character. Make at least one of these skills one in which a PC has training, so the companion character doesn't steal the limelight.

If necessary, you can give the companion character one or two additional trained skills to fill out key gaps in the party's array of trained skills.

Calculate skill check modifiers the same as for a PC (one-half level + ability modifier + training, if any). Skill check modifiers include racial bonuses, if applicable.

At 11th level, and again at 21st level, companion characters gain a +3 bonus to each of their trained skills.

12. Choose Equipment: Assign gear to the companion character as appropriate his or her their role, powers, and appearance.

Armor and Shield: Even though the companion character's armor and shield do not modify his or her AC, assign such gear as desired for the appropriate appearance. Defenders and leaders, for example, might wear heavy armor. Apply any armor check and speed penalties.

Weapons and Implements: Give the companion character weapons or implements appropriate for his or her powers. Remember to apply the weapon's proficiency bonus to attack rolls.

Mundane Equipment: You can provide various mundane gear—rope, trail rations, torches—to a companion character.

Magic Items: Don't equip companion characters with magic items. A companion character doesn't need magic items to be a viable party member. A companion character's presence doesn't result in extra magic items placed as treasure (see "Companion Characters in Play" on page 33), so they shouldn't have any when they join the party.

13. Roleplaying Details: Flesh out the companion character with details about his or her alignment, personality, appearance, and beliefs as appropriate.

What a Companion Character Doesn't Receive: A companion character doesn't receive class features or any benefits related to class features that appear in his or her powers.

A companion character gains only limited benefits from equipment. In particular, a companion character gains no enhancement bonuses from magic items.

A companion character has no feats.

A companion character should know rituals only if such knowledge is important to your story. You decide if a companion character learns additional rituals as the campaign continues.

A companion character doesn't select a paragon path at 11th level or an epic destiny at 21st level.

COMPANION CHARACTER TRAITS

No matter how you create companion characters, assign them key personality traits. Make companion characters more than a collection of numbers.

Don't go overboard; a few key aspects go a long way toward defining a companion character. You can summarize a companion character's essential elements in five sentences, covering the following topics.

Occupation: Outside of life with the PCs, what does the companion character do for a living?

Physical Description: Provide a brief summary of the companion character's appearance. In addition to covering the basics (height; build; color of skin, hair, and eyes), consider a distinctive quirk to help set the character apart in the players' minds. You can choose a quirk from the NPC Quirks table on page 186 of the *Dungeon Master's Guide*, roll on the table to generate a quirk randomly, or come up with one of your own.

one-handed halfling mage who has been so helpful to the party struck a bargain with a demon that holds her missing hand captive and uses it as a ritual focus to temporarily seize control of her. Use the secret to inject surprise into a mundane encounter or session. Make the secret lead to another storyline or resolve a key element in the story. Roll or choose a secret from the Secrets table below.

AGENDAS

d10	Agenda
1	Wants revenge
2	Needs the PCs' help on a quest
3	Needs money
4	Bored, seeks excitement
5	Seeks magic
6	Seeks lost relative or friend
7	Seeks fame
8	Looks up to PCs (hero worship)
9	Owes PCs a favor
10	Wants to chronicle PCs' adventures

BEHAVIORAL TRAITS

d20	Trait
1	Sunny optimist, unflappable
2	Gloomy pessimist, sees doom everywhere
3	Religious fanatic, tries to convert others
4	Superstitious, sees ill omens in everything
5	Hedonistic, gambler and drinker
6	Violent, eager to attack
7	Greedy, takes risks for treasure
8	Barbaric, knows little of civilization
9	Patriotic, fights for a noble or a country
10	Careless, sloppy, makes casual mistakes
11	Bookish, studious, takes copious notes
12	Loyal, fights to the death for friends
13	Suspicious, trusts no one
14	Altruistic, easy target for a person in need
15	Honorable, follows rigid code
16	Grim, suicidally brave
17	Vengeful, seeks payback for a wrong
18	Abrasive, insults others
19	Finicky, overly polite and formal
20	Rude, ill-mannered

Agenda: Why is the character with the party? Although a strong personality makes a companion character memorable, a clear (and perhaps secret) agenda gives you a direction for the character. You can roll on the Agendas table below, choose one from the table, or come up with one of your own.

You could make the companion character want something that conflicts with the PCs' goals. A larcenous dwarf could sneak back to an abandoned temple in the dungeon and steal the sacred ingots that the party decided to leave behind. A knight might promise the mayor to defend the town against an attacking kobold horde, forcing the PCs into a tough decision: remain behind and help their friend, or push onward to chase down a fleeing villain.

Behavior: How does the companion character interact with other characters? Does he or she have a pessimist attitude, seeing doom around every corner? You might create a religious fanatic who preaches religious doctrine and finds a deity's hand in every event. One key behavioral trait provides enough distinction to make a companion character stand out. Come up with a behavioral trait that works for the character, or roll or choose one from the Behavioral Traits table below.

Secret: Finally, give each companion character a secret. If that secret surfaces in play, it could provide an interesting plot twist or an unexpected complication. The PCs discover that their trusted guide is a reformed criminal with a price on his head. Or, the

SECRETS

d10	Secret
1	In debt to crime lord
2	Spy for a villain
3	Spy for a rival organization
4	Works for villain but wants to change sides
5	Worships an evil god
6	Once belonged to evil cult
7	Fleeing from powerful enemy
8	Has a deep phobia
9	Once famous in particular city or region
10	Noble in hiding

COMPANION CHARACTERS IN PLAY

Regardless of how you create companion characters, the following rules apply to them in play.

Encounters: When you build encounters, treat the companion character like a full member of the party.

If the companion character's level is one level higher or lower than the party's level, first determine your experience budget for the party as if the companion character didn't exist. Then add the experience value of a standard monster of the companion character's level to the encounter.

Treasure: When you determine treasure, don't count the companion character as a party member. The party should receive treasure, and magic items, appropriate for the number of player characters.

If the characters negotiate payment to the companion character, increase the treasure payout to support this payment. Make sure players understand that companion characters have no need for magic items.

Gaining Levels: A companion character begins with experience points equal to the minimum amount that the character needed to attain his or her current level. Companion characters gain a full share of the experience points earned by the party.

When a companion character gains a level, he or she receives the following benefits:

Hit Points: Controller companion characters gain 4 hit points, leaders or strikers gain 5 hit points, and defenders gain 6 hit points.

Attack Bonus: A companion character's attack bonus increases by 1.

Defenses: Each of the character's defenses increases by 1.

Damage: When a companion character achieves an even-numbered level, increase his or her damage rolls by 1.

Powers: You can replace one of the companion character's encounter powers with a new encounter power from a class that has a matching role. The level of the new power must be equal to or lower than the companion character's new level.

SAMPLE COMPANION CHARACTER

Orryn Glittercave is a gnome warrior, a knight, and champion for his people.

Orryn is big and tough for a gnome, and he walks with a limp (the result of an old injury).

Maybe he wants to join the party to help protect gnomes and other friendly fey creatures. Or the PCs could have rescued him from captivity at the hands of foul monsters, in which case Orryn swears to help the PCs complete their current quest. In either case, he aids the characters in a couple adventures before returning home.

Orryn displays fierce loyalty to his friends and risks his life to protect people he cares about. And he expects the same loyalty in return.

Unknown to the PCs, Orryn was briefly a member of an evil cult in his youth. When he discovered the truth about the cult, he quit the group, but its members still hold a grudge against Orryn.

Mechanically, you built Orryn as a 4th-level defender with fighter powers. His Fortitude is 2 points higher than normal, resulting in a corresponding drop in his Will. This adjustment reflects his tough but sometimes rash nature.

Orryn Glittercave	Level 4 Defender
Small fey humanoid, gnome	XP–

Initiative +2   **Senses** Perception +2; low-light vision
HP 46; **Bloodied** 23; **Healing Surges** 10
AC 21; **Fortitude** 19, **Reflex** 17, **Will** 15
Saving Throws +5 against illusions
Speed 4

⊕ **Battleaxe** (standard; at-will) ✦ **Weapon**
  +10 vs. AC; 1d10+5 damage, and the target is marked until the end of Orryn's next turn.

↗ **Shortbow** (standard; at-will) ✦ **Weapon**
  Ranged 15/30; +10 vs. AC; 1d8+2 damage.

↓ **Sure Strike** (standard; at-will) ✦ **Weapon**
  +12 vs. AC; 1d10 damage.

↓ **Steel Serpent Strike** (standard; encounter) ✦ **Weapon**
  +10 vs. AC; 1d10+5 damage, and until the end of Orryn's next turn, the target is slowed and cannot shift.

Master Trickster (minor; encounter)
  Orryn can use the *ghost sound* cantrip (*Player's Handbook*, page 158).

Unstoppable (minor; daily)
  Orryn gains 2d6+1 temporary hit points.

Fade Away (immediate reaction, when Orryn takes damage; encounter) ✦ **Illusion**
  Orryn is invisible until he attacks or until the end of his next turn.

Reactive Stealth
  If Orryn has any cover or concealment when he makes an initiative check, he can make a Stealth check.

Alignment Good   **Languages** Common, Elven
Skills Arcana +6, Diplomacy +10, Heal +7, Stealth +3
| **Str** 16 (+5) | **Dex** 11 (+2) | **Wis** 10 (+2) |
| **Con** 13 (+3) | **Int** 14 (+4) | **Cha** 16 (+5) |

Equipment chainmail, battleaxe, dagger, shortbow with 20 arrows

Even though the *Dungeon Master's Guide* recommends that all characters gain levels at the same rate, you might have characters of different levels who want to adventure together. Perhaps an old gaming buddy drops in for a guest appearance and wants to play a character six months out of date, or a new player arrives with a character who doesn't measure up to the rest of the PCs. In such a circumstance, you might intentionally set up a situation in which one PC acts as a sidekick to a group of higher-level characters.

You can adjust a character to fit in with a group of characters of significantly higher or lower level. Use the adjustments described in this section as a temporary fix—if a character wants to join the group permanently, adjust the character's level according to the parameters in the *Player's Handbook*.

Use this approach for no more than one or two characters in a party and only as a short-term solution. Although a sidekick of this nature can keep up with higher-level comrades for a few encounters, he or she doesn't have a full range of powers and might quickly run out of options. Similarly, a character scaled down to adventure in a lower-level group still has advantages over his or her allies; such a character outshines the other characters if he or she hangs around for too long.

Don't use this system unless at least two levels separate the characters. A difference of just one level between characters is not enough to worry about.

Up from a Lower Level

If you need to temporarily boost a character's abilities and don't want to use the normal process, this section offers a simple system that keeps the lower-level character on par with the challenges in your adventure.

These adjustments might represent a short-cut abstraction of the abilities possessed by higher-level characters: "Garik is 12th level. His character sheet lists him as 6th level because I haven't had time to advance him yet." Alternatively, you might make the boosts temporary: The character draws on the talents and insights of his higher-level allies to survive battles in which the challenges are over his head.

To adjust a character's statistics, use the following guidelines. In each case, "level difference" is the difference between the level of the character you want to adjust and the level of the rest of the party.

Attacks: Increase the character's attack bonus by the level difference.

Defenses: Increase all the character's defenses by the level difference.

Skill Checks: Increase all the character's skill check modifiers by one-half the level difference (round down).

Ability Checks: Increase all the character's ability check modifiers by one-half the level difference (round down).

Hit Points: Increase the character's hit points by an amount equal to the level difference × the number of hit points the character normally gains per level.

Damage Rolls: The character gains a bonus to damage rolls with encounter and daily attack powers equal to one-half the level difference (round down).

If the party is 21st level or higher and the character is not, treat the character's at-will attack powers as if the character were 21st level.

What the Character Doesn't Receive: New powers, new feats, ability score increases, improved class features, paragon path benefits, epic destiny benefits, additional magic items, extra uses of daily magic item powers, or any other benefits normally gained by a character of the new level.

Experience Points: The character gains the same amount of experience from encounters as everyone else. This adjustment allows the character to rapidly close the level gap with the rest of the party.

Example: A visiting player brings a 5th-level fighter to your table, whereas the rest of the group has 10th-level characters (a level difference of 5). You give the character a +5 bonus to attack rolls and defenses, a +2 bonus (one-half the level difference, rounded down) to skill checks and ability checks, and 30 additional hit points (a level difference of 5 × 6 hit points per level). The character receives a +2 bonus to damage rolls with encounter and daily attack powers.

When the party overcomes a 10th-level encounter, this 5th-level character gains 500 XP. The 10th-level characters need eleven of those encounters to reach 11th level, whereas five encounters bring the 5th-level fighter to 6th level. After those five encounters, start with the base character again, advance the character to 6th level normally, and repeat this process (this time with a level difference of 4).

Down from a Higher Level

Although low-level characters more commonly tag along with high-level characters, the converse can also occur. If you need to add one character to a party whose level is significantly lower—perhaps a grandmaster joining the group for an adventure with his students—use the following guidelines to adjust statistics accordingly.

Attacks: Reduce the character's attack bonus by the level difference.

Defenses: Reduce all the character's defenses by the level difference.

Skill Checks: Reduce all the character's skill check modifiers by one-half the level difference (round down).

Ability Checks: Reduce all the character's ability check modifiers by one-half the level difference (round down).

Hit Points: Reduce the character's hit points by an amount equal to the level difference × the number of hit points the character normally gains per level.

Powers: The character loses all utility powers of higher level than the party level. The character also loses all powers gained from a paragon path or epic destiny if those powers are higher in level than the party level.

Damage Rolls: The character takes a penalty to damage rolls with encounter and daily attack powers equal to one-half the level difference (round down).

If the character is 21st level or higher and the party is lower in level, treat the character's at-will attack powers as if the character was 20th level.

Don't Change: Don't reduce the character's ability scores. Don't adjust any class features. Keep the character's paragon path features and epic destiny features (if any). Don't remove any feats. Don't change any magic items, and don't change the number of uses of daily magic item powers the character gains.

Experience Points: The character gains the same amount of experience from encounters as everyone else. This practice prevents the character from outpacing the rest of the party (and encourages the character to return to adventures more appropriate to his or her level).

Example: A 20th-level wizard tags along with a group of 10th-level characters (a level difference of 10). Impose a –10 penalty to the character's attack rolls and defenses and a –5 penalty to skill checks and ability checks. Reduce the character's hit points by 40 (a level difference of 10 × 4 hit points per level). Impose a –5 penalty to the character's damage rolls with encounter and daily attack powers. He loses his 12th-level utility power and all his paragon path powers (his 11th-level encounter attack power, his 16th-level utility power, and his 20th-level daily attack power).

The 500 XP award this character receives from completing a 10th-level encounter does little to help him reach the next level—he needs 64 such encounters to reach 21st level. Of course, during that time, the rest of the party gains several levels, decreasing the level difference. And as the rest of the party advances, the character looks forward to facing more challenging encounters that earn him more experience.

MULTIPLE CHARACTERS PER PLAYER

With each release of new player options, the expanding D&D game offers ever more possibilities—more than players can explore in the course of a normal campaign. What do you do if your players, excited by the classes and races in *Player's Handbook 2*, want to start new characters? Do you deny their requests? Do you throw your campaign continuity out the window and let a whole new party pick up where the old one left off? Or do you jettison your whole campaign and start again?

Using a solution less drastic than all of these can keep your players happy and your campaign stable.

If your campaign uses a "dungeon of the week" approach (see page 134 of the *Dungeon Master's Guide*), your players could bring different characters on different adventures. Perhaps the player characters (including multiple characters per player) belong to an exploration society. For any particular mission, they assemble a group of adventurers that changes from mission to mission. In this situation, a player could play a tiefling paladin in one session and a goliath warden in the next. Just make sure that the party remains balanced and that each of its different configurations includes a proper mix of roles. Whenever a character gains a level, all other characters of that player should also gain a level, so the player can swap his or her characters in and out of the group.

You might use a similar solution if you plan a campaign that's particularly lethal to adventurers. If you intend to formulate encounters and story lines that result in character death on a regular basis (and your players agree that this approach sounds fun), tell your players to keep a backup character on hand, of the same level as the rest of the party.

If your campaign involves world-shaking events unfolding in multiple places across the globe, you might invite your players to create two different parties of characters, and then switch the action between groups for different adventures. One group of characters searches for the hilt of the legendary sword Durindana while another group of heroes looks for pieces of the shattered blade. The goal of both groups is to reforge the sword and wield it against Vecna. You might run one group's adventure for a few sessions, and then switch to the other group for the next few. All the characters in each group should be the same level, though the two groups might differ in levels. For example, one band of epic-level characters deals with a terrible threat against the entire fabric of the universe, while their heroic-level counterparts contend with the local repercussions of that threat.

If you have a small number of players and you want each player to play multiple characters at once to have a group of four or five characters, you should use the rules in this chapter for companion characters rather than making any player take on more than one full-fledged player character.

—James Wyatt

ADVANCED ENCOUNTERS

THIS CHAPTER expands on the information presented in Chapter 4 of the *Dungeon Master's Guide* to give you tips, techniques, and a few tricks to make dynamic, exciting combat encounters for your game. The chapter covers a wide range of topics.

✦ **Encounter as Story:** Building on the story foundations laid out in Chapter 1, this section discusses encounters as turning points in the story of your adventure and focuses on encounter objectives that add purpose to a combat encounter.

✦ **Player Motivations:** This section focuses on the player motivations described in the *Dungeon Master's Guide* and describes how to tailor combat encounters to the players at your table.

✦ **Large and Small Groups:** This information can help you design encounters for unusually large or small groups of player characters.

✦ **Encounters and Attrition:** This section includes a discussion of encounter pacing and suggestions for how to push characters onward when they want to stop for an extended rest.

✦ **Creating Movement:** Learn how to avoid static encounters.

✦ **Terrain:** Using additional terrain in your encounters, including terrain with inherent attack powers, can make each encounter unique.

✦ **Designing Traps:** Use this guide to create traps for your adventures; you'll find plenty of examples.

✦ **Pulling It All Together:** An example encounter combines the elements of this chapter into a dynamic fight.

JASON A. ENGLE

A well-crafted encounter is a key scene in the story of your adventure and in the overarching story of the characters in your campaign. If you build your adventure like a structured fantasy story, sharing a similar dramatic structure with novels, movies, and plays, then an encounter equals a scene in that story. The encounter acts as a discrete element in which tension builds in steady increments toward the climax of the adventure. (See Chapter 1 for more discussion of story structure.)

Viewed as part of a larger story, a great encounter has three key ingredients.

History: It builds on what the characters have learned in past encounters and previous game sessions.

Clear Objective: The characters must try to accomplish a specific task.

Significant Outcome: The characters might easily accomplish the objective, barely succeed, or fail entirely. However the encounter resolves, the outcome matters and relates to later encounters.

BUILDING ON THE PAST

A strong encounter builds on information the characters have acquired in the course of previous encounters. You can create stronger encounters by foreshadowing what lies ahead.

Introducing information about an encounter ahead of time builds anticipation or apprehension. For example, if you know the climactic battle in an orc-filled adventure features the brutal orc chieftain and his ogre bodyguard, orcs in earlier encounters could name the chieftain and speak fearfully of the ogre. When one orc suggests running from the PCs' onslaught, another says, "No! Angarr will feed us to the ogre if we flee!"

Laying the groundwork for future encounters can also help the players succeed. For example, the party seeks an audience with a grand duke who has no tolerance for rudeness or insolence. When the duke is introduced to the characters, tell the players that the duke frowns at them and acts condescending. This information might keep the PCs on their toes particularly if you also tell them the grand duke recently imprisoned someone who was rude to him during an audience. This setup builds the players' anticipation as they prepare for the audience and helps them avoid imprisonment.

You can use the same technique to prepare the characters for random wilderness encounters. Let players know what to expect if they wander off the beaten path or stray into the nearby forest: Perhaps woods folk warn the PCs of deadly spiders or fey-haunted clearings. Foreshadowing what lies ahead fills your players with anticipation and tension as your adventure progresses toward its climax.

SETTING ENCOUNTER OBJECTIVES

Players can quickly grasp the objective of an encounter in which their characters face a horde of savage orcs. The characters understand that they must fight for their lives, and they either try to kill all the orcs or escape from them. Other encounters have less obvious goals, such as finding an important clue, securing an alliance with a group of NPCs, or defeating a monster before it kills innocent bystanders or assassinates the baron. Every encounter should have a specific objective, even if it's straightforward. Ambiguous goals could leave your players frustrated or bored.

An encounter's objective also links the encounter into the adventure story. If the overall story of your campaign involves a quest that the characters embark on to deliver a precious relic to a remote monastery, then each encounter in your campaign should have an objective that moves that quest forward. For example, during encounters along the way, the characters might have to protect the relic from enemies who want to steal or destroy it. These encounters build toward a climactic showdown with the leader of those evil forces.

The use of a secondary objective can make straightforward combat encounters more interesting. The secondary objective might force characters to approach the encounter differently, using their powers or strategizing in ways they normally wouldn't. A time limit is a simple example of a secondary objective: Not only do the characters have to overcome a gang of bandits, they have to do so in a small number of rounds. If they don't beat the clock, the hostage awaiting rescue in the next room will succumb to his wounds.

THE OUTCOME MATTERS

A clear objective can make it easy to determine the consequences of success or failure in an encounter. If the characters' objective is to protect a relic from shadar-kai that plan to steal it, then failure might mean the PCs must reclaim the item from the victorious thieves. Success, on the other hand, could mean that the players come across fewer shadar-kai in a later encounter, or it could mean that the characters must face the shadow dragon that commands the shadar-kai. (See the discussion of branching in Chapter 1 for more ideas about how to use the result of an encounter as a way of determining the characters' next encounters.)

STEVE ARGYLE

Failure is a possibility in any encounter; the more pertinent question is how successfully the characters deal with a challenge during an encounter. Following are some examples of possible outcomes.

✦ The characters take advantage of their opportunities and deal with the threat successfully. The PCs use few of their resources and enjoy the rewards of the encounter with few setbacks.

✦ The characters overcome the obstacles facing them—at a cost. The PCs might head into the next encounter with fewer healing surges or daily powers at their disposal. Worse, an enemy that fled the fight could raise an alarm (leading to tougher encounters ahead) or escape with important information.

✦ The characters fail to overcome the challenge. They might flee from a combat encounter, or their enemies could capture them. They don't receive a reward for the encounter, they suffer a serious setback, and they might have to work hard to overcome the consequences of their failure.

The outcome of one encounter should play into the next encounter. Success in an encounter carries the characters toward completing the overall goal of the adventure. Failure leads the characters to a new turning point.

FINISHING STRONG

Players find the end of a great encounter meaningful and memorable. No matter what the scene is about, spice it up and leave them wanting more. If the characters just vanquished the main villain of the adventure, they might stumble upon a mysterious fact or witness a strange event that leaves them wondering if they have wrapped up the adventure as neatly as they thought.

A sense of resolution can also provide a strong finish to an encounter. When the characters achieve one of the main goals of the campaign, give them an appropriately lavish reward. Make it a truly memorable scene, full of pomp and gravity. Allow the characters to bask in their own glory.

Then set up your next adventure with a surprising twist in the middle of the celebration! End your session with a cliffhanger, and your players will be hungry for more.

—Yax and James Wyatt

SAMPLE ENCOUNTER OBJECTIVES

Use the following story-rich objectives as foundations for complex and compelling encounters. Although these objectives focus on a single encounter during an adventure, you can use them in multiple encounters that combine to form one obstacle or problem the PCs must overcome.

MAKE PEACE

Through a misunderstanding, the characters must fight monsters or nonplayer characters who should be allies. Perhaps the characters' enemies have deceived the leader of the NPCs into attacking the PCs, or maybe the NPCs are xenophobic or territorial.

Objective: The characters must convince the members or the leader of the opposing group that the two groups should work together.

Possible Outcomes: The characters need allies, so skill at negotiation is more important than martial prowess. If the party's diplomatic attempts falter, the PCs face a fight. This encounter could produce these outcomes:

✦ The characters avert a fight, prevent injury or loss of life on both sides, and convince the NPCs to become their allies.

✦ Fighting breaks out, but the characters convince the other side of their good intentions and stop the conflict. One or both sides are bloodied or suffer casualties.

✦ The characters break off the fight without securing the aid of the NPCs, opting to flee rather than harm potential allies.

✦ The characters fail to secure the NPCs' aid and defeat them in combat, perhaps knocking them unconscious or taking them prisoner. At worst, the PCs kill the opposing group and lose these potential allies.

PROTECT A PERSON OR AN ITEM

The characters act as bodyguards, or they have an ancient or fragile item they must transport to a specific location. In every challenge they face the risk of breaking the item or endangering the character they're protecting.

The nature of the nonplayer character the PCs must protect can affect the difficulty of the encounter. In an easy encounter, the NPC could be a smart warrior, capable of aiding the characters in combat if necessary. For a tougher encounter, make the NPC incompetent, prone to panicking in combat, or apt to risk the lives of PCs through dubious decisions. Alternatively, you could create NPCs who are grievously injured, too young or too old to fend for themselves, or wracked by debilitating diseases. If the characters

are escorting an NPC to a destination where he or she can be cured of a crippling condition, they might create an ally if they succeed.

If the characters protect an item, it might be an artifact they need to complete an important ritual, a gift meant to seal an alliance with another group, or a religious icon that could end a struggle that has torn apart a religious order. The villains could send thugs after the characters with the sole intention of destroying the item.

Objective: Keep the NPC alive or the item intact for the duration of the encounter.

Possible Outcomes: Although this sort of encounter looks like an all-or-nothing proposition, a middle ground exists. For example, the characters could avert failure by using a Raise Dead ritual to revive a dead NPC. The characters might also achieve different degrees of success based on whether the NPC or the item takes damage during the fight, whether the party's enemies recognize the NPC or the item, or whether the NPC completes a specific task before dying.

✦ The characters protect their charge by avoiding combat, either hiding from their enemies or fleeing before their foes engage them.

✦ The characters fight off the attackers and protect the NPC or item.

✦ The characters protect the NPC or the item, but their enemies see and identify the NPC or the item and use this information against the PCs later.

✦ The NPC survives but is wounded. This injury could hinder the character's ability to perform the required task or could otherwise diminish his or her usefulness to the player characters.

✦ The item breaks but is not rendered useless. The characters can recover enough of the item to undertake a quest to repair it, or they can use the item for its intended purpose at a less effective level.

✦ Enemies capture or kill the NPC, or the PCs lose or destroy the item. The characters must rescue or resurrect the NPC or repair the item, or else they must find a new way to accomplish their goal.

✦ The characters keep the NPC alive long enough for him or her to complete a necessary task but not long enough for him or her to give the PCs a reward or important information needed for a later encounter. For instance, the elderly sage completes the ritual to seal the demongate but dies under a demon's claws before he can warn the characters of a threat he discovered in the course of the ritual.

RETRIEVE AN OBJECT

In this objective, the characters must gain possession of a specific object in the room or area, preferably before combat finishes. This type of encounter has two basic scenarios. First, the enemies the PCs face are overwhelmingly powerful, creating a situation where the characters must retrieve the object and then either flee or use its powers for protection. Second, the enemies desire the item as much as the characters do, and both parties race to obtain it.

Objective: Reach and secure an object in the encounter area. Securing the object could mean pocketing a small item, activating a large object in the room, or opening a locked chest containing the object. During an encounter, the characters might have to search the area to find a hidden item.

Possible Outcomes: If the characters acquire the object, they succeed. If they don't, more possibilities open up.

✦ The characters retrieve the object and either escape with it or use it to defeat their enemies in the encounter.

✦ The characters obtain the object, use it once, and then lose it to their enemies. The object helps them, but not as much as they had hoped it would.

✦ The characters fail to retrieve the item and must either pursue the enemies who took it or find a way to achieve their goal without it.

SNEAK IN

The characters need to move through the encounter area without raising an alarm. Succeeding could mean killing the guards and thereby ensuring that none of them reach the enormous gong on one side of the chamber, or it could mean sneaking through a maze of rooms undetected.

Objective: Reach a destination or kill all the defenders without raising an alarm.

Possible Outcomes: The outcome of an infiltration encounter can have a dramatic effect on future encounters, or on the rest of the adventure. If the characters succeed, they can bypass significant obstacles. If they fail, they face stiffer resistance in the encounters ahead.

✦ The characters succeed—no alarm is raised, and anyone who became aware of their presence is dead or disabled.

✦ The characters fail to sneak through the area, and guards attack them. This outcome can lead to a second encounter with the same objective, since the characters must defeat these guards before the guards raise an alarm.

✦ One guard manages to alert more guards in the next room, making for a tougher encounter.

✦ The guards sound an alarm. Reinforcements could arrive immediately, or the characters might find future encounters more difficult because the enemies are prepared for the characters' arrival.

STOP A RITUAL

An evil cult leader, a malevolent sorcerer, or a demon performs a ritual that has dire consequences if the PCs fail to stop it. A gateway to the Ninth Hell could open, a terror from beyond the stars could make its way into the world, or a horde of slavering demons could erupt from the Abyss at the completion of the ritual. Only the characters can prevent these events from happening.

Objective: The characters must interrupt the ritual before their enemy completes it. They might have to kill the ritual caster quickly, fighting their way past bodyguards to reach their target. Or they might have to destroy special focus items used in the ritual (smash statues, extinguish candles or burning braziers, or splash holy water on the infernal altar).

The ritual caster's participation adds an interesting element to this type of combat encounter. You might determine in advance that the caster must spend five standard actions to perform the ritual and also use a minor action to sustain the ritual each round. Stunning the caster disrupts the ritual, and the caster could participate in combat at the cost of not making progress with the ritual. Alternatively, the ritual caster could remain absorbed in performing the ritual until the characters successfully disrupt it, at which point the caster joins the combat in an effort to destroy them. As a third possibility, the ritual caster takes an active role in the combat until the characters disrupt the ritual, which causes the caster to flee or to be destroyed by the failed ritual.

Possible Outcomes: To prevent this sort of encounter from dead-ending the adventure or your entire campaign, set it up so that either the characters have excellent odds of disrupting the ritual, or the ritual's completion doesn't have world-shattering consequences.

✦ The characters stop the ritual in time and avert catastrophe.

✦ Each round the characters spend in combat without stopping the ritual, more combatants join the fray—cultists hurry into the room from elsewhere in the temple complex, or demons spill up from the yawning chasm in the floor. The characters succeed in stopping the ritual but suffer significant losses during combat.

✦ The characters fail to prevent the ritual and must find a way to undo what the ritual accomplished.

Different players have different motivations. Pages 8-10 of the *Dungeon Master's Guide* outline eight archetypal player motivations you might find at your game table. If you understand these motivations and know how to encourage your players, you can tailor the encounters in your adventures to better suit your players' tastes. The following pages suggest specific ways to make encounters appeal to your players, helping each player have more fun at every session.

These suggestions include seating arrangements, based on the idea that adjacent players influence one another. You might not want to assign seats to your group and might instead allow your players to choose their own seating arrangement. However, if you have trouble engaging the players in your group, review the seating suggestions and see if steering players to different seats helps.

THE ACTOR

One actor at your table can inspire the rest of your group to roleplay, bringing all the player characters to life. At their best, actors make the game feel like more than a game—something more akin to a fantasy novel or movie.

Seating: The best seat for an actor is directly opposite you, perhaps at the far end of a table. With all the other players between you and the actor, the actor's dramatics won't close you off from the other players. A clear view of the actor's body language might make you feel more engaged in roleplaying, and the two of you can encourage the rest of the group to be more involved.

An actor seated beside a shy player can help to draw that player out over several game sessions.

Encounter Types: Actors thrive in skill challenges of all sorts, and they especially flourish in challenges that involve interaction with NPCs. Combat doesn't necessarily leave the actor cold—vivid descriptions of powers and other actions in combat can engage the actor the same way dramatic interaction draws in other characters.

Provide Vivid NPCs: Quirks and mannerisms that bring NPCs to life (see page 186 of the *Dungeon Master's Guide*) give the actor ideas for interacting with the NPCs. With actors in your group, you can spend more time in the characters' home base with NPCs who offer the players adventure hooks or important clues, turning what might otherwise be a bland information dump into a lively interaction. In a straightforward dungeon crawl, detailed descriptions of key monster opponents can immerse the actor in the action.

Add Roleplaying Elements to Combat: From lowly kobolds to mighty dragons, the monsters the characters face in combat can come alive if you imbue them with personality. Challenges, taunts, and insults can be fun and particularly appropriate when a character marks a monster or vice versa. Monsters might gloat or curse during the ebb and flow of battle. Describe the monsters' attacks the way actors would describe their own actions, even when the monsters miss. Keep a list of taunts, curses, and dramatic descriptions on hand in case inspiration fails.

You might let characters use Bluff, Diplomacy, or Intimidate checks to influence monster actions during combat. This tactic allows players to trick enemies into taking actions that benefit the characters. Characters might goad their foes into entering hazards, draw enemies into positions that give characters combat advantage, lure enemies away from a bloodied character, or convince a monster to attack the character who has the best defenses. Actor players might want to try these tactics; you must determine an appropriate skill check and assign a DC for the check.

Leverage Character Details: Make an effort to include characters, locations, and events from the actor player's character background in encounters, particularly in climactic fights against major villains. For example, if the actor PC's father died in a duel with a tiefling, you could choose that same murderous tiefling darkblade as the adventure's villain. When the characters confront this villain, the tiefling recognizes the daughter of the human he killed years ago and taunts her: "So you're Andrunn's brat? No better at swordplay than your father, I see." The actor might find that villain more satisfying to defeat than just another tiefling darkblade, and you didn't need to make a single change to the monster's statistics.

ACTORS IN KOBOLD HALL

As written, Kobold Hall (in Chapter 11 of the *Dungeon Master's Guide*) offers few opportunities for interaction encounters in which actors thrive. However, you could roleplay the kobolds before and during the combat encounters—the kobolds in area 3, for example, could taunt the player characters and berate them for interrupting a skull-skull game. You might also have the dragon talk before attacking, giving the characters a chance to plead for their lives and the actor players a chance to shine.

—James Wyatt, from
Dungeon Master 4th Edition for Dummies

The Explorer

Having an explorer at your table can keep the players interested when the action stalls, because explorers enjoy seeking information. They help the group find clues and secret doors and help keep the adventure on track—except when the explorer derails it by looking for secrets that don't exist. You can satisfy explorers by giving them plenty of clues to find.

Seating: If the explorer likes to draw maps of the adventure area, then have that player sit next to you, so you don't have to talk across other players to resolve the map details. Explorers can inspire new players with their curiosity and enthusiasm, so seat new players next to explorers when possible.

Encounter Types: Similar to actors, explorers thrive in skill challenges, particularly ones that involve research, puzzles, or digging up hidden information. Explorers also enjoy the time between encounters, so be sure not to gloss over the ancient dungeon corridors and grand entry halls devoid of monsters. To engage your explorer, plan combat encounters that include puzzle elements, such as complex traps, to make the encounter area livelier, or insert surprising hazards to navigate around.

Monsters with Secrets: Explorers enjoy combat scenarios that offer a secret about the monsters they face. For example, when ghosts and the wights attack, the explorer might want to know who these undead creatures were in life, why they were cursed with undeath, and how that information might pertain to the current adventure. Make a straightforward combat encounter with undead more appealing to an explorer by explaining that the tiefling ghosts think the PCs are the dragonborn soldiers of Arkhosia who killed them the first time around.

You can achieve the same effect with mundane monsters if the combat encounter reveals interesting details, such as those of a hobgoblin culture in this region. The newly acquired knowledge that hobgoblins take pride in being the first to score a hit during combat enriches the explorer's satisfaction of emerging victorious from a tough combat encounter.

Monsters with Weaknesses: Throw the party into a challenging encounter, but give them a way to even the odds, possibly hidden in the terrain or on a monster. For example, the characters encounter a dragon in a large room with a shrine in one corner. When the fight starts, the players might notice that the dragon avoids the shrine, focusing its attacks on the characters farthest away from it. If the characters force the dragon closer to the shrine, they discover that the dragon's defenses drop, and if they stand adjacent to the shrine, it boosts their defenses. The characters eventually learn that the individuals who built the shrine dedicated it to Bahamut, and the dragon's attempts to defile it have failed to sever the shrine's connection to the deity of justice and honor.

The combination of history and tactics pleases the explorer's sense of world logic.

Puzzle Encounters: Create encounters—combat or otherwise—that have elements the players need to figure out. Perhaps the characters encounter a group of hobgoblins in a room that features alternating black and white squares on the floor. Through trial and error, the PCs learn that they have to move like chess pieces or take damage: On the "board," the first square a character enters determines how that character must move for the duration of the encounter. Or maybe four pillars pop up from the ground, creating dangerous arcs of lightning across the

EXPLORERS IN KOBOLD HALL

Kobold Hall used to be a walled keep for a minor human lord whose name and history are long forgotten. You can engage explorer players by inventing a history for the place and providing clues to the background you invent. Explorers might be intrigued to learn that the altar now dedicated to Tiamat (in area 2) used to be a shrine to Ioun and that the stone coffins hold the remains of a long-lost noble line. What if the players find an heirloom of the family that spurs them to find any surviving heirs to the line?

—James Wyatt, from
Dungeon Master 4th Edition for Dummies

JULIE DILLON

room in a regular pattern. The characters can avoid and then exploit the hazard by maneuvering their enemies into the path of the lightning. These types of puzzle elements engage explorers—and make combat encounters more memorable for all your players.

THE INSTIGATOR

Like an explorer, an instigator at the table can be an ally to the DM by preventing the group from getting bogged down in indecision or caution. Instigators need little help to enjoy the game because they amuse themselves. Engage instigators in the game by allowing them to affect their surroundings. Nothing frustrates instigators more than trying to cause trouble and failing, with the result that their actions don't necessarily benefit the party. Be prepared to downgrade the consequences of an instigator's actions if necessary to prevent him or her from getting the party killed.

Seating: Assign an instigator to a seat next to you, where he or she can easily attract your attention when he or she wants to try something. An instigator seated next to indecisive players can help spur them to action.

Encounter Types: Combat encounters offer the most action choices to instigators, and a wide-open skill challenge that brings numerous skills into play can be an instigator's playground.

Battle Grid Surprises: Allow instigators to explore everything on the battle grid. If you use *Dungeon Tiles* or preprinted maps, prepare notes about the minute details and mundane features of the map to determine what happens when the instigator pokes, prods, opens, or breaks these features. If the map shows crates and barrels stacked in the room, the adventure text might give a generic description of what players can find inside. Your instigator might also knock over braziers, spill casks onto the floor, lift carpets, and tear down tapestries. Use the guidelines for terrain powers (pages 62–63) in these situations. Although toppling a brazier onto an enemy should cause less damage than being hit by the characters' powers, instigators might find it more entertaining.

You can also allow instigators to find unexpected ways to move around the encounter area. Secret passages that circle around, perhaps bypassing blocking terrain, can reward the instigator with an opportunity to sneak up on the monsters.

The two most disheartening words for an instigator player might be "Nothing happens." Instigators enjoy interacting with their surroundings, so prepare consequences ahead of time for the instigator's actions—consequences that make the game more fun for everyone. Create a group of possible results to keep your game moving when an instigator's character tries something unexpected. Your results might include the following events.

✦ If a character tinkers with an item, it explodes in a burst 2 or a blast 3, making an attack against Reflex with a modifier equal to the party's level +3 and dealing damage on a hit equal to the appropriate medium limited damage expression on page 42 of the *Dungeon Master's Guide*. As a positive side effect, the explosion could harm enemies as well as the instigator; place the item in an area where the instigator's foes are likely to take more damage than his or her allies.

✦ Liquid or sludge spills over the floor, creating an area of difficult terrain.

✦ A cloud of dust erupts into the air, obscuring an area for 1 or 2 rounds.

✦ The character disturbs a sleeping monster—typically a dungeon denizen such as a dire rat, a kruthik, or a carrion crawler.

✦ A dimensional rift tears open and teleports the character 1d10 squares in a random direction.

✦ The character finds an injured creature caught in a trap. Freeing the creature secures its help for 1 or 2 rounds.

✦ The character finds a secret compartment containing a treasure parcel, perhaps including an item that can help the party in the current encounter.

Busy Work: Instigators pose the risk of setting the pace for the game and interfering with other players' enjoyment. If your instigator has no patience for interactions that your actors and storytellers thrive on, he or she might disrupt those scenes and spoil the other players' fun. As a solution, occupy the instigator with tasks unrelated to the game's action. This tactic occupies an instigator while the other players engage in activities they enjoy.

When you sense a restless instigator, ask him or her to do one of the following quick favors.

✦ Clear away the map or tiles from the last combat encounter to make room for the next.

✦ Set up *Dungeon Tiles* or gather miniatures for the next encounter.

✦ Tally up and divide experience points from the last encounter or the session so far.

✦ Refresh everyone's drinks or open a new bag of chips.

THE POWER GAMER

Your group can overcome challenges more efficiently and have fun in the process if the group includes a power gamer. Power gamers have extensive rules knowledge, since they must know the rules to take advantage of them. This type of player can serve as a valuable resource, saving you from having to look up rules you don't remember.

Seating: Seat the power gamer near you if you plan to use him or her as a ready rules reference. Similarly, a power gamer can bring a new player up to speed if you seat them together. Be sure the power gamer doesn't dictate the new player's actions; the power gamer should only help a new player understand what's going on.

Power gamers sometimes downplay the importance of story and roleplaying, so you might want to place them near actors and storytellers. This proximity can lead to productive synergy, but sometimes it leads to conflict, depending on the personalities of the players involved.

Encounter Types: Power gamers optimize their characters for combat, and if you establish that your campaign will feature skill challenges and other types of encounters, die-hard power gamers will optimize their characters for those challenges as well. For instance, in ordinary circumstances power gamers might not be inclined to take the Linguist feat, but if your campaign rewards characters who have a mastery of multiple languages, power gamers in your group will probably take it.

Play to Strengths: Let the power gamer shine by showing how his or her character excels. If the character has a high AC, allow that character to hold the front line from time to time, standing firm against monsters while the rest of the party snipes from safety. If you feature the same kinds of monsters in more than one of your encounters, the power gamer can determine the best tactics to use against them. For example, after a fight with trolls, inform the players that more trolls lie ahead. The power gamer can then work out the best way to overcome their regeneration.

Exploit Weaknesses: Identify the weaknesses of a power gamer's character and design encounters to target those vulnerable spots. Use monsters that attack the character's weakest defense. Create situations that require checks with the character's poorest skills or abilities. You don't want to punish the player or try to defeat the character; rather, you want to offer a broad range of challenges. Testing a character's weaknesses encourages the player to improve his her play style. This technique motivates the player to acquire items or find other ways to shore up those weaknesses—and to learn to rely on the other characters in the group.

Make Villains Learn: If you can manage to keep a recurring villain alive over the course of a long adventure, make sure that the villain learns from each encounter with the characters and adapts his or her tactics to counter the characters' strengths. By the third time a villain meets the characters, that villain has a good idea of what they're capable of and has come up with ways to frustrate them. The power gamer will be challenged to explore new tactics rather than to simply replay the same old fights.

Reward Engagement: Power gamers respond to rewards. In the same way that a power gamer will take the Linguist feat if your campaign clearly rewards that knowledge, a power gamer will remember details of your campaign world and story if that knowledge pays off. Likewise, power gamers care about the story of an adventure when it translates into experience points and treasure rewards for completing minor and major objectives. Use magic items the player wants (perhaps drawn from a wish list of items) to draw the power gamer into adventures.

THE SLAYER

The slayer at your table plays the game to experience the visceral thrill that D&D offers: A slayer wants to fight monsters and villains every week—and save the world in the process. To keep the slayer happy, include villains and monsters in your adventure that have to be eradicated. If slayers have plenty of targets to kill, you can expect a lively dose of energy that can inspire the rest of your group in return.

KEEPING ANTAGONISTS ALIVE

Exciting adventure stories slowly build up their villains and then introduce them in dramatic fashion. Then the bad guy acts in a way that makes the audience hunger for his comeuppance. The first clash between hero and antagonist usually results in awful defeat for the hero. Finally, after delayed gratification and numerous trials, the hero triumphs against the villain, and all is well again in the universe.

In a D&D game, you might find it tough to keep a villain alive past his first appearance in a storyline. But if you kill your villains as soon as you introduce them, they can't acquire the iconic quality of classic villains.

The following points summarize my favorite methods of preserving villains for another day.

- ✦ Use introductory interaction scenes in which the antagonist's villainy is not apparent.
- ✦ Cheat the stats by making the villain impossibly tough during his or her first encounter and weaker later on when you mean to allow the PCs to defeat him or her. Give the villain a good reason to keep the defeated PCs alive during the initial encounter.
- ✦ Use interaction scenes in which the PCs can't fight the villain, possibly for legal or political reasons, or in order to ensure the safety of innocents.
- ✦ Give the PCs reasons to keep the villain alive if they defeat him.
- ✦ Create situations when the heroes and the villain temporarily have to work together.

—Robin Laws

Seating: Place the battle grid within reach of the slayer to ensure that the player gets to manipulate his or her character's miniature (and perhaps also those of players who are seated too far from the grid to reach their own miniatures). Seated beside a new player, a slayer makes a great mentor because his or her enthusiasm and energy can rub off.

Encounter Types: Slayers enjoy combat in all its glorious variety: wading through hordes of minions, facing off against a villainous mastermind and his squad of bodyguards, or going toe to toe with a solo dragon. Whatever the scenario, slayers want to use their attack powers to destroy their enemies.

Bring on the Villains: Give at least one villain a significant role in your campaign, and make sure your slayer (in particular) knows and despises the villain early on. At least once each session, have the villain's servitors disrupt the PCs' plans to irritate them and load the encounter with emotional power. Defeating an annoying villain gives the slayer a supremely satisfying moment of victory.

Bring on the Minions: Make liberal use of minions. They might fall quickly under the slayer's assault, but he or she will enjoy being the architect of the onslaught. Also, by unleashing a horde of minions, you can start the combat with a shock to the

players. Have one group of minions quickly engage the characters, and maneuver the remaining minions to gain a tactical advantage. This tactic satisfies the slayer and ensures that a single area attack doesn't wipe out all the minions at once.

Combat Interruptions: If the slayer becomes restless during a skill challenge, have enemies kick in the door and start a fight to add an adrenaline jolt. This interruption works best if a necessary skill challenge preoccupies the players. Maybe the PCs must disable a magic ward, which requires the uninterrupted work of a few of the characters, or the characters might need to extract information from an NPC before his ship sails away on the next tide. If you throw an easy fight in the middle of such a challenge, perhaps triggered by a failed skill check, the slayer and one or two other characters can fight off the monsters while the rest of the party continues working on the challenge.

ACHIEVEMENTS

Many computer and video games track player achievements, giving players a sense of accomplishment and sometimes unlocking additional content in the game. Players—particularly slayers—might enjoy tracking similar achievements in the context of a D&D campaign. If your group likes this idea, consider recruiting a slayer at your table to be the official record-keeper for group and individual achievements, such as the following:

+ Highest damage dealt with a single attack (you might have one entry for single-target attacks and one for multiple-target attacks, in which you add up the damage dealt to each creature).
+ Most damage taken in a single encounter.
+ Killing blows scored.
+ Critical hit tally (by character, per encounter, and ongoing).
+ Natural 1 tally (by character, per encounter, and ongoing).
+ Most failed saving throws (consecutive or not).
+ Highest attack roll that missed.
+ Creatures killed (by origin, type, or specific attribute).
+ Unusual or dramatic events, such as a prone character scoring a critical hit.

THE STORYTELLER

A storyteller in your group can help you tie together all the rules, numbers, and encounters into an entertaining narrative. DMs sometimes lose themselves in the details and forget to step back and look at the story unfolding on the other side of the DM screen. Engage storytellers by frequently including narrative elements: Tie together quests and plots, and mine character backgrounds for story possibilities.

Seating: Seat the storyteller near the middle of the table. From this location, the storyteller can immerse the other players in the unfolding story of the adventure and the campaign.

Encounter Types: Any kind of encounter engages the storyteller, as long as it makes sense in the adventure's story. If the party has a good reason to be in the dungeon fighting orcs, and each combat encounter moves the characters measurably closer to their goal, the storyteller can be just as invested in the fights as the slayer is.

Storytellers lose interest when encounters fill up the session and nothing ties together—no large goals drive the characters, no common cause motivates their efforts, no connections link events in the campaign, and no consequences arise from the characters' actions. When the characters emerge from the dungeon, the storyteller wants what happened in the adventure to matter, to have an effect on the game world, and to drive the characters on to the next adventure. Storytellers don't find gaining levels and acquiring treasure to be sufficient motivation.

Tie Encounters to Larger Goals: To storytellers, the orc leader the party just killed could represent a terrible force of violence and suffering. Or the PCs

might have made the region safer by eliminating one of the villain's lieutenants. Make sure to give storytellers a way to connect the events in each encounter to the adventure's larger goals.

Explicitly link one encounter in every session to the party's overall goal in the campaign, and move the characters closer to achieving that goal—or farther away if they fail to overcome that encounter's challenge. When the characters finish that encounter, recount what just happened through descriptive narrative; highlight important character contributions without using numbers. Connect encounter events to the characters' personalities, backgrounds, details, and goals. You might ask a storyteller in your group to perform this function.

Create Cause and Effect: Make sure the actions of both player characters and nonplayer characters in the game have consequences. Use these repercussions to tie together encounters and campaign elements, so that the storyteller understands the overall narrative. Keep a log of the events in your campaign, and build encounters that are the clear result of the PCs' actions. For example, the characters delve into the dungeons of Greenbrier Chasm and fight goblins. When the characters return to town, goblins begin raiding the farms around the village of Greenbrier in retribution for the PCs' actions. What's more, because of a specific action the characters took in the dungeon, such as opening a sealed door, the goblins have a new ally or an artifact that empowers them. Storytellers thrive on connecting such details and figuring out the underlying plot.

Monster Stories: Give the characters' enemies their own stories, and make sure the players can learn those stories. If your villain has a legion of human soldiers at his disposal, ensure that the players eventually realize that the human soldiers they repeatedly fight belong to the villain's army and aren't random monsters. The monster themes presented in Chapter 4 add a layer of story to a variety of monsters the characters could face in an adventure. The players might suspect a connection if they repeatedly encounter enemies that have a similar origin or similar powers.

THE THINKER

Thinkers reward your clever planning by scrutinizing villainous machinations, taking the time to solve your puzzles, and using calculated actions and good tactics to keep fellow characters safe.

Seating: Thinkers ask questions, making a seat near you ideal for easy access. Give the thinker a seat with a clear view of the battle grid. Be aware that if you place a thinker adjacent to a power gamer, they might form a decision-making team that excludes other player types.

STORYTELLERS IN KOBOLD HALL

It's important to help storyteller players understand that any adventure is both an individual story and part of a larger story of the campaign and its heroes. Don't gloss over the adventure hooks and quests, which provide the context for the characters' excursion into Kobold Hall. Storytellers will be eager to learn why these kobolds seem so organized and aggressive, and you should make it clear that the dragon's influence is to blame. Pay attention to the suggestions for further adventures on page 219 of the *Dungeon Master's Guide*, and consider how you can tie this adventure in with the next one you plan to run. Finally, look for ways to make the adventure personal for the storytellers in your group, such as hooking them with individual quests that relate to their character backgrounds. For example, in a raid on the King's Road, kobolds might have captured or injured a friend or relative of one of the characters.

—James Wyatt, from
Dungeon Master 4th Edition for Dummies

Encounter Types: Thinkers, like explorers, enjoy any encounter that includes puzzle elements, such as tactical challenges to overcome and riddles to solve outside combat. Thinkers might appreciate the puzzle material on pages 81–84 of the *Dungeon Master's Guide*. They also thrive on complex combat encounters that incorporate different kinds of challenges, including monsters, traps or hazards, interesting terrain features, and perhaps a skill challenge.

Avoid the Linear Path: Rigidly linear adventures frustrate thinkers, who prefer to weigh their options. Offer numerous choices, from branching dungeon passages to forking plot lines. Branching passages make dungeon exploration more interesting, and they can enrich tactical combat encounters by offering multiple lines of engagement, which creates a more dynamic confrontation.

Be Generous with Clues: Give your thinker player plenty to contemplate by providing information about foes, dangers, and challenges in advance. These clues work best if you can use them to maintain a sense of surprise. Dispense partial facts by combining them with treasure, dropping them into interactions with NPCs, and working them into the background scenery of other encounters. Reward successful skill checks with new information combined with vivid descriptions to entertain everyone at the table.

Use the following clues as examples.

✦ **Enemy Powers and Abilities:** A scrawled message in a treasure cache reads "Beware the serpent guardian's word of pain that roots you to the ground, and fear the resounding force of its thunderstrike!"

✦ **Weak Defenses:** A captured bandit tells the PCs about the inn his cohorts use as a headquarters: "Numerous guards watch the front door, but only two guards protect the kitchen entrance around back."

✦ **NPC Personality Weaknesses:** During their first meeting with the duke, a character who makes a successful Insight check notices that the duke can't keep his eyes off the warlock's ruby ring.

✦ **Terrain Hazards:** A tapestry in a temple antechamber depicts the altar in the main sanctuary erupting with bolts of lightning.

✦ **Maps and Location Layouts:** The characters find a map in a dragon's treasure hoard depicting an ancient stronghold, and their next adventure takes them to the stronghold's ruins.

✦ **Villain's Plans:** A soldier in the villain's elite guard says, "Fools! Before the next dawn my master's armies will march through the streets of Winterhaven, and nothing will stop them!"

Start Battles with a Clear Overview: You risk frustrating thinkers when you forget to reveal options and hazards the characters would have noticed. When you start a combat round, provide a fast overview of observable and important details before you call for initiative checks. This quick overview informs the players and helps the thinker understand what he or she has to work with in the encounter. Make sure to cover these points.

✦ Visible foes and their placement, including anything characters can detect with a high enough passive Perception check.

✦ Terrain features and known attributes.

✦ Furnishings and tactically important objects.

✦ Enemy equipment.

✦ Visible rewards and treasure.

Reward Sound Tactics: When the thinker concocts a sound plan from the information you provide, let the plan pay off. Without altering a combat encounter significantly, you can give the characters an edge in the fight in a variety of ways.

✦ Award a surprise round to the characters if they catch their foes off guard.

✦ Show the characters a map of the encounter area and let them choose where they want to enter for the best tactical advantage.

✦ Give the characters combat advantage against their enemies for the first full round of combat.

ALLOW CHAT TIME

Off-topic digressions are the scourge of roleplaying. They're also an irresistible common currency in all conversations between members of our glorious geek tribe. Even while you're serving as DM, you might fall prey to the opportunity to throw in a clever reference to the Internet meme of the day or a classic pop culture property.

During sessions, I try limit my group's off-topic conversations. But people play D&D to hang out with friends. Even when personal schedules press my session length down to the bare minimum, I make sure to include a healthy period of chat time before we start recapping the events of the previous session. By granting time up front for the inevitable socializing, I keep digressions to a minimum for the first couple of hours of gaming. Then, personal discussions return as the night progresses and attention spans wane.

—Robin Laws

TAKE A MOMENT . . .

To run better encounters, make sure you take 30 seconds before rolling initiative to study your monster and NPC tactics, as well as the creatures' Intelligence scores. Then you can decide how well they will carry out their tactics.

—Yax

CHAPTER 2 | *Advanced Encounters*

THE WATCHER

Although watchers might seem disinterested, they are a valuable part of the group. Watchers can help to round out the roles in a party, because they are not as committed to playing a specific type of character as some other kinds of players are. Watchers can also help defuse the tension created when players' motivations clash by reminding everyone that D&D is a game, and the players are supposed to have fun. Bear that fact in mind if you start to feel frustrated that watchers don't involve themselves more or take the game more seriously.

Seating: Place verbose and enthusiastic watchers next to shy or quiet players. A power gamer might express frustration with the watcher's choice of character skills and actions, so separating these two types of players might benefit the group. Placing the watcher at the far end of the table can prevent his or her socializing from interrupting you.

Encounter Types: You might find that a watcher participates more in a combat encounter than in a skill challenge or some other form of interaction that doesn't involve combat. This is often true because a combat encounter offers a relatively limited set of options (the character's powers) that define the actions the watcher can take, and the encounter has a clear goal.

Ham It Up: The more you bring an encounter to life, the more likely the watcher will pay attention. Vivid descriptions of monster actions and environments, or the player's own actions, can draw a watcher in. For example, if the watcher says, "I use *eldritch blast* on the orc, and I rolled a 22," you might expound with: "A dark bolt of energy flies from your fingertip and erupts around the orc, making it howl in pain. What's your damage?" This technique keeps the rest of the group immersed in the action and encourages the watcher to use the flavor text for the powers in the *Player's Handbook*. In turn, the watcher might want to roleplay and participate more.

Have Fun! The watcher wants to have a good time with the group, so have fun. Don't take the game too seriously, and don't let it start arguments among the players.

DON'T TAKE IT PERSONALLY

By definition, watchers are difficult to engage, so remember that it's okay—watchers have fun because of the company around the table, not because they're hooked by the game. Don't take it personally. Also, make sure that whenever any player comes up with an unexpected strategy or an innovative idea, you reward it and run with it. This example shows the watcher that involved, engaged players make the game fun for everyone at the table.

—James Wyatt, from
Dungeon Master 4th Edition for Dummies

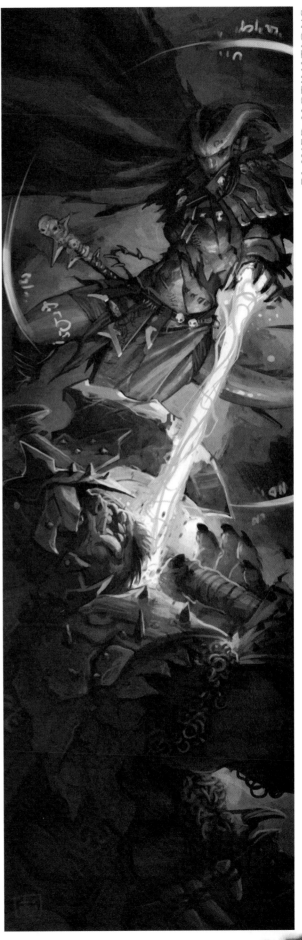

GEORGI SIMEONOV "CALADER"

Large groups can be fun to DM. Imagine a big bunch of your friends gathered together around a table determined to defeat monsters you conjure up, overcome mighty challenges you set before them, and roleplay through grand adventures. A game table with numerous players will test your skills differently than a smaller group. To succeed, be organized and prepared, and don't be afraid to delegate.

More Monsters, not Tougher Ones

According to the math of encounter building outlined in the *Dungeon Master's Guide,* four 10th-level monsters are an appropriate encounter for ten 5th-level characters. However, think twice before you throw such an encounter at your players. An encounter with two minotaur warriors (level 10 soldiers), a gibbering mouther (level 10 controller), and a wyvern (level 10 skirmisher) adds up to the right experience point total. But because the minotaurs have AC 26, and the player characters attack at about +11, the PCs would hit only 30% of the time. At best, the characters take so long to kill the monsters that the fight drags on for hours of playing time. At worst, the minotaurs

(hitting about 70% of the time) kill all the characters before taking serious damage.

A better encounter for ten 5th-level characters is a collection of monsters that are all around 5th level. Ten monsters could be challenging for you to manage, so choose elite and solo monsters to reduce your burden. Four dragonborn soldiers (level 5 soldier), a goblin underboss (level 4 elite controller leader), and a young green dragon (level 5 solo skirmisher) have nearly the same experience point total as the monsters in the first example (2,150 XP rather than 2,000 XP). Because this encounter features monsters that have attacks and defenses comparable to the characters' capabilities, it's more balanced. And because the encounter includes elite and solo monsters, the number of monsters should be manageable.

Larger Encounter Areas

Design encounter areas that can accommodate a large group of player characters as well as numerous monsters. Rather than using a single open space, create several rooms with multiple connections to enable the monsters to attack the characters from different directions. This technique encourages characters to engage the monsters on multiple front lines.

RECRUIT LIEUTENANTS

Players can be a great help when you become overwhelmed or when the game slows down because large groups take longer to cycle through encounters. Pick two experienced players who know the rules, and ask them to take the seats on your left and right as your lieutenants. Having them nearby makes it easy to assign tasks and duties to them.

Minions: Have minions' stats and basic tactical advice ready to hand out, so your lieutenants can manage these foes during combats.

Battle Grid Setup: Sometimes just clearing the table to make way for maps and tiles takes time. Ask your lieutenants to lay out your maps and arrange unconcealed enemies according to the encounter diagram. Before everyone rolls initiative, briefly inspect the setup and tweak as desired.

Initiative: Have a lieutenant handle initiative setup and order, with you reporting to them on enemy results. If possible, post the order in a visible place, such as on a whiteboard. Have your aide keep the combat pace going by prompting players for actions and nudging you when a foe's turn is next.

Battlefield Description: While one lieutenant gathers initiative rolls, give your other lieutenant an overview of all the unconcealed features on the battlefield, so he can be the group's go-to person for questions about terrain

effects, hazards, and combat props. This technique will save you from having to deal with repeated questions every combat.

Monster Managers: Have your lieutenants be your hands and eyes on the battlefield. On each monster's turn, have a lieutenant hold a finger on the monster's mini on the battle grid. This system shows you which enemy is currently active, and it focuses the group's attention on the game. Ask your aide to report ongoing damage at a turn's start and saving throws at turn's end. For movement, tell your aide the foe's intended action, ask your aide to choose optimal routes, and have him announce any opportunity attacks.

Foe Wounds and Status Markers: Ask the lieutenants to track ongoing damage and effects on foes during combat. Have your helpers report total damage to you as it is dealt, so you can quickly check for bloodied status.

Opportunity Attacks: As the PCs and their enemies move around the battle grid, ask one of your lieutenants to handle opportunity attacks for you. If a PC provokes an opportunity attack, the lieutenant grabs the player's attention and informs you of attack and damage results. If a foe receives an opportunity attack, the lieutenant attracts your attention so you can resolve the attack.

—Johnn Four

Sometimes you have only a small group to play with, or you want a small-scale D&D experience. You might be teaching the game to your children or leading a small group that has limited membership. Building encounters for small groups can be tricky, but it can lead to rewarding game time.

MORE MONSTERS AGAIN

The rule of thumb for creating encounters suggests that a group of two 5th-level characters should face two 5th-level monsters. That encounter works, but compared to a five-on-five encounter, such a small encounter might feel lackluster. As discussed previously, you can create dynamic encounters by using larger numbers of lower-level monsters. A more exciting encounter might be two 5th-level characters facing three 2nd- or 3rd-level monsters.

Weaker monsters also offer the player characters a better chance of surviving despite the group's lack of key party roles. Weaker monsters don't hit as often or deal as much damage, so if a party lacks a leader, it can still hold its own. At the same time, the monsters have fewer hit points, so a party without a striker can still take them down in a reasonable amount of time.

MORE MINIONS

Use minions to keep encounters dynamic and interesting without overwhelming a small party of characters. Be careful, though, if your characters don't have attacks that affect multiple targets. To a party that lacks a controller or at least some blast and burst attacks, minions can be troublesome.

DIFFERENT CHALLENGES

You can turn an apparent weakness into a great strength by using more encounters that don't involve combat. Encounters that feature lots of interaction, stealthy infiltration, puzzle solving, or skill use are

well suited for small groups. As a guideline, make skill challenge complexity no higher than 1 above the number of characters in the party.

ALLIED NPCS

You can supplement a small group with allied NPCs that help the player characters in combat and non-combat situations. Companion characters, detailed in Chapter 1, can increase the number of effective characters in the party without overwhelming the players with multiple full-fledged PCs to run.

MINIONS IN ENCOUNTERS

If you're using minions in an encounter, a couple of tips can help make them more effective.

+ Don't clump them together at the start of the encounter. Spread them out.
+ Reveal minions in stages—maybe two are visible at the start of the encounter, another one runs in during the second round, and the rest come up behind the characters in the next round.
+ Use more minions at higher levels. Use four minions at minimum in heroic tier encounters, at least five in paragon tier encounters, and six or more in epic tier encounters.

FINDING PLAYERS

If you have a small group because you don't know more people who play D&D, it might be time to find or recruit more players. Where do you find more people for your game? Try these suggestions.

Friends and Relatives: Start with people you know who might be interested in the game, such as fans of fantasy movies, books, or TV shows.

School: High schools and colleges sometimes have organized gaming clubs. If you're a student, check to see if your school has an active gaming club, and if it doesn't, you might try starting one to recruit more players.

Work: If school is behind you, your workplace might contain folks with an interest in D&D who could join your regular game group.

The D&D Website: The D&D website at www.wizards. com/dnd is home to a huge community of D&D players, probably including people who live near you. In the Community section of the website, you can find game stores, events and conventions, and gamers in your area.

Game Store: Your local game or hobby store might have a space where people play D&D, or at least a bulletin board where you can advertise to find more players for your game.

Conventions: From large conventions such as GenCon (www.gencon.com) and Origins (www.originsgames.com) to smaller local and regional gatherings, gaming cons provide a weekend full of activity and abundant opportunities to meet other gamers from your area. In addition, comic book and fantasy conventions sometimes include programming related to gaming and draw a sizable population of gamers.

RPGA: Wizards of the Coast's Organized Play department runs the Roleplaying Gamers Association (or RPGA)—a program devoted to making it easier to find face-to-face gaming experiences. Joining is easy and free, and membership provides you with free DM material and access to hundreds of events at conventions and in your community. Check it out at www.wizards.com/rpga.

—James Wyatt, Bill Slavicsek, and Richard Baker, adapted from *Dungeon Master 4th Edition for Dummies*

When characters run out of daily powers or spend all their healing surges, after perhaps four or five encounters, they probably stop for an extended rest. You can manipulate the pacing of encounters in your game to change the pattern of the PCs' rests and alter the buildup and release of tension in the game.

PACING

Pacing is the rhythm of action and story progression that unfolds in encounters over the course of a game session.

You can keep the tension building in your game sessions by pacing your encounters. Consider three different models of encounter pacing: a standard, balanced model; one with a single, intense spike in the action; and one that features a slow escalation of danger. This section discusses how to use these models to plan encounters for a single game session or an in-game day of adventuring.

When you offer choices to your players during an adventure, they might tackle encounters in a sequence different from what you had planned. Be flexible, and be prepared to modify encounters to fit with the pacing model you have in mind. For example, you can take enemies from one encounter and add them to a later or earlier one if your sense of dramatic pacing demands it. If you want to aim for a balanced pace, and the characters just finished two easy encounters, you might add monsters to the next fight if the PCs choose a path that leads to another easy encounter.

When setting a pace, consider these two time scales: what happens in a single game session and what happens in an adventuring day between extended rests. You'll find pacing easier to manage if you design those periods equivalently, meaning that the characters start a new day at the beginning of every session. You might not be able to utilize that method, particularly if your sessions last only one or two hours. Conversely, long game sessions might cover two in-game days, with characters taking an extended rest in the middle of the session.

BALANCED PACING

In a balanced pacing model, aim for a balance of action, roleplaying, and storytelling—fast and furious segments that alternate with slower, calmer periods. You don't need to strictly alternate between difficult and easy encounters or scenes of high drama and slower exposition. Instead, watch the trends and aim for a balance over the course of a session.

A straightforward dungeon-based adventure follows this model, with slow, relatively calm periods of exploration broken occasionally by scenes of intense and life-threatening combat. If you use a mix of encounter difficulties as suggested on page 104 of the *Dungeon Master's Guide*, you can easily fall into a rhythm of harder and easier encounters to complement the alternation of exploration and encounter.

This model works effectively when you start and end each session (and each adventuring day) with an exciting high note, such as a difficult encounter or a dramatic turning point. Grab your players' attention at the outset, and then finish with a cliffhanger, leaving them eager for your next session.

A smart party spends its resources slowly over a series of encounters that feature balanced pacing. If the characters use up their daily powers and spend all their healing surges early in the session, they might stop for an extended rest and disrupt your pacing. Use easier encounters and slower periods to ease up on the tension and encourage them to continue adventuring.

Balanced pacing is a versatile model that allows a variety of different encounter types, including combat and noncombat encounters, as well as exploration, interaction with NPCs, investigation, puzzles, and administration. Give your players a variety of encounter types to hold their attention.

THE SPIKE

A spike is a single encounter so difficult that the characters need to use every power, spend every action point, and utilize smart tactics to overcome the challenge. The characters will likely face only one encounter of this type in a day of adventuring; if you play short sessions, it could be the only encounter. However, you can use minor build-up and aftermath encounters to serve as rising action and ending for the story of the session (see "Classic Story Structure," page 8). Players enjoy the adrenaline rush and excitement of a single battle in which their characters fight for their lives, unleashing every resource at their disposal.

A spike works most effectively when paired with a dedicated build-up, especially if you foreshadow this dramatic conflict over the course of days or weeks of game time. Increase the players' fear, uncertainty, and tension with clues about the opponents they face.

You want the characters to reach a spike fresh. They should have most of their daily powers, an action point apiece to spend, and perhaps consumable magic items to use in the fight. For this reason, the spike model works well as the centerpiece of a short adventure, or in an adventure when the characters are in no particular rush, such as a long trek through the wilderness during which the characters

can take an extended rest before reaching the monster's lair at the end of the journey.

You can present the characters with a few easy encounters after the spike as they deal with scattered enemy forces or minor remaining threats, or let them spend the conclusion dealing with the consequences of the outcome, in interaction with NPCs, or in exploration.

Escalation Pacing

In a model of escalation pacing, you put the characters (and players) on a steady upward ramp of increasingly difficult challenges until they reach the top—a huge dramatic climax featuring a major villain, world-shattering revelations, or both. The key to this model is to deplete the characters' resources, so that when the PCs reach the climax, they're exhausted and face serious trouble.

Because the escalation model relies on depleting the characters' resources, consider depriving the characters of extended rests to ensure that they're nearly tapped out when they reach the final encounter. The characters could be on a tight deadline, they might be racing across the countryside in pursuit of fleeing bandits, or they could be suffering from a curse that prevents them from gaining any benefit from an extended rest. You want to motivate characters to proceed from one encounter to the next without stopping for an extended rest (see the next section, "Drawing Characters Onward").

The escalation model works particularly well in a game that has strong elements of horror or drama. Ideally, the characters don't realize what serious trouble they face until it's too late. Then they have to do battle with no daily powers at their disposal and precious few healing surges remaining.

The goal of escalation pacing is to build to a terrible climax in which the players fear for their characters' lives. It's not to wipe out the party or force them to flee in defeat. The climactic encounter should be big and scary, but it shouldn't be more than a level or two above their level. With their resources drained, the characters will have trouble enough with an encounter of around their level without trying to handle something far more powerful than they are.

Drawing Characters Onward

When DMs discuss, analyze, and create games, they often try to find a way to evoke one particular reaction: "Just one more turn," or sometimes "Just one more quest." This phrase refers to the game's ability to engross and invest a player in the game's progress, making him or her want to continue playing, just as reading a novel might make you say, "Just one more chapter" until you finish the book at three in the morning.

How can you involve your players in your adventure so deeply that they say, "Just one more encounter" until they find themselves in a tough fight with no remaining daily powers or healing surges? In an escalation model, you want to overcome their natural caution and force them to extend themselves beyond their comfort zone in their eagerness to reach the next encounter. Four basic techniques can help you draw your players into one encounter after another: momentum, rewards, deadlines, and prohibitions.

Momentum

Let the momentum of the adventure story carry the characters from one encounter to the next. Short, relatively easy combat encounters draw the players forward—if no single encounter feels too difficult, characters might underestimate the value of the resources they have spent. Make sure combat encounters don't increase while character resources diminish, and cut encounters short if characters seem fatigued from a long fight.

Use compelling hooks to make the characters eagerly anticipate the next encounter. A pair of doors in a dungeon room can be a compelling hook for players. Each choice the characters make draws them onward, particularly if the players know that their decisions affect the outcome of the adventure.

Respect the Dynamic

Whenever I start a new campaign, I frame it in a distinctive way. And the plan I have in mind for a new campaign slowly mutates during play. What might seem like a failure to adhere to an original concept becomes one of the great strengths of the roleplaying experience. Each campaign develops a dynamic beyond the control of the DM, or any other single participant. I might try to implement a sweeping plot line of epic proportions, only to find my players drifting into a trading-and-fighting game. Improvised events might veer a lighthearted campaign into angst, darkness, and bloodshed.

When a campaign takes on an unintended shape, I take a deep breath and remember to respect the dynamic. What we create together at the table trumps my initial plans.

–Robin Laws

When the characters open a dungeon door and see monsters they defeated easily before, they're more likely to charge ahead than if they see unknown, dangerous-looking foes. You can use rumors of familiar monsters to draw the characters deeper and deeper into the dungeon, bolstered by the confidence that they can handle these weak opponents.

Rewards

You can use rewards to encourage players to continue adventuring without resting. Milestones and the benefits associated with them (action points and magic item daily power uses) are rewards built in to the game to counteract the effect of depleted resources. Magic rings also have powers that function better or function only if the wearer reaches at least one milestone in a day, which can be an incentive to seek out additional encounters before starting a climactic battle.

You can also use the promise of treasure as a hook to draw characters on to the next encounter. A dungeon door inscribed with the words "Royal Treasury" practically begs characters to open it to acquire the treasure inside—after fighting its guardians. Beyond the simple promise of a tangible reward, certain kinds of treasure can encourage characters to press onward as well. Consumable magic items, such as potions and whetstones (see page 189 of *Adventurer's Vault*), can bolster player confidence, especially if the players believe that the items they find will help in the next encounter. For example, the characters find a cache of alchemist's fire (*Adventurer's Vault*, page 24), and they know trolls lie in wait in the next room. An exciting magic item—an item that has an interesting power or a useful property—gives the player who acquires it an incentive to press on for one more encounter and test the item out.

You can also use the alternative rewards detailed in Chapter 5 to encourage characters to push on through additional encounters. A divine boon might come with a specific duration that drives the characters to use that reward as much as possible before it expires. Or, a grandmaster might promise training if the characters complete a task within a specific time.

Deadlines

A deadline amounts to a strong disincentive to take an extended rest. If the characters have to accomplish a specific goal within a limited time, a 6-hour rest could ruin their ability to meet the deadline. An adventure deadline might fall into one of these categories.

Specific Date or Time: The characters must meet certain requirements before a specific date or time. For example, the dead will rise on an upcoming holiday, or cultists plan to perform a sinister ritual on the night of the full moon, or the bandits demand delivery of the ransom before sunset.

Race Against Time: The characters know a deadline looms but have no specifics. For example, rumblings in the earth indicate the volcano above the village will erupt soon, but the PCs don't know how soon. This type of deadline enables you to adapt the deadline to the characters' actions, although it's not as effective in motivating the characters to hurry.

Limited-Time Resource: The characters have a boon or an alchemical concoction that loses its effectiveness after a certain time. This category works the same as a specific-time deadline or a race against time, but it gives the characters a personal investment in the passage of time.

Race or Chase: The characters need to reach their goal before a rival or enemy does, or maybe they have to catch up with a group on the move. They have no reason to believe that their rivals will stop for an extended rest, so stopping to rest will set the PCs behind. For example, the characters must retrieve a treasure before a band of evil NPCs does, or the PCs must catch up to a group of bandits racing across the wilderness.

You can allow the characters to gain the benefit of a short rest while they hurry through empty dungeon corridors or across the wilderness between encounters. Then, your story maintains a sense of urgency without limiting characters to relying on at-will attacks and healing potions.

PROHIBITIONS

Another way to prevent players from stopping too frequently for extended rests that disrupt your planned pacing is to create situations when characters can't benefit from an extended rest until they have met certain conditions. Here are a few ideas for the kinds of situations that can motivate your players to keep going.

✦ A curse afflicts the characters, preventing them from sleeping until they complete a quest to remove the curse. Or maybe a magical obligation placed on the PCs prevents them from resting until they fulfill their duty.

✦ The characters must perform an extended skill challenge that lasts several days, with combat encounters interspersed throughout. Tell the players up front that an extended rest in the course of the skill challenge will interrupt it and cancel their progress, forcing them to start over.

✦ As a house rule, change the requirements of an extended rest to prevent the characters from benefiting from it until they reach two milestones in a day. Make sure your players know and understand this rule at the start of the campaign.

Use these techniques sparingly, because overusing them can lead to player resentment. These tactics can be effective in horror-themed campaigns that use the escalation pacing model.

LONG FIGHTS

Closely related to these methods for pacing encounters between extended rests is the question of how to handle rapid-fire encounters that don't allow characters to take short rests. How do you model the fights you see in movies, where waves of enemies rush the characters without a moment's pause? How do you make your characters hurry from one encounter to the next to stop an assassin from killing the high priest?

To create these long encounters, you can allow characters to refresh themselves in the middle of the fight. Devise specific objectives and turning points in the battle, and give each one an associated refresh. These objectives could include any of the following examples.

✦ Defeat a designated champion monster. One champion emerges from each wave of enemies, or one appears early in the running fight.

✦ Reinforcements arrive to help the PCs and bolster their courage. These reinforcements might be companion characters (see Chapter 1) who help the PCs in the fight, or they could be part of a larger force if the PCs are fighting an enemy army.

✦ The characters battle their way to an ancient altar and complete a simple skill challenge during the encounter to claim a blessing from a deity.

✦ The PCs defeat one-half, one-third, or another designated fraction of the enemy forces.

✦ The characters secure a solid defensive position on the battlefield, allowing them to catch their breath.

When the characters fulfill your predetermined requirements, you might give them one or more of the following benefits.

✦ Each character can choose one expended encounter power and regain its use.

✦ Every character regains the use of his or her second wind or can spend a healing surge (even if unconscious).

✦ Each character gains an action point and can spend it later in the encounter, even if he or she has already spent an action point in the encounter.

✦ Each character gains another use of a magic item daily power as if he or she had reached a milestone.

✦ Each character can regain the use of an expended daily power. Save this benefit for a significant accomplishment in the middle of a battle.

Terrain features, such as energy nodes (see page 59), which allow characters to recharge spent powers, also prove useful in long fights.

—James Wyatt

Every class has attack powers and utility powers related to movement, such as powers that let characters push and slide enemies, and powers that let them shift or teleport themselves or their allies. Racial features such as the eladrin's *fey step* and the elf's *wild step* make movement a significant tool for the player characters. Monsters also have numerous movement powers, particularly skirmisher monsters. Racial abilities, such as those possessed by goblins and kobolds, give them the potential to shift during combat.

Sometimes, no number of movement powers can convince characters to change position, especially ranged attackers such as wizards, invokers, warlocks, archer rangers, and some clerics and bards. Even a rogue—one of the most mobile melee characters in the game—might stand still for round after round if he or she has an enemy pinned in a flanked position.

You'll find encounters more dynamic and exciting when everyone changes position on their turn. The following section offers techniques you can use to keep characters and monsters moving.

Circular Paths: The basic shape of your encounter area is important.

Attractive Terrain: Use terrain that gives characters an advantage or offers other reasons for them to reach specific locations.

Terrain to Avoid: Terrain, traps, and hazards that the characters want to avoid can also encourage movement, if you use them with care.

Starting the Encounter: The first round of combat can determine how much movement takes place in the encounter.

Enemy Tactics: Monsters on the move can force characters to move as well, so keeping monsters mobile—even moving them into positions of disadvantage—can be worthwhile.

Encounter Objectives: Encounter objectives that discourage the characters from remaining stationary can make movement a more significant part of the encounter.

CIRCULAR PATHS

Your room layout can encourage movement in an encounter. Create an area that suggests a continuous path of movement: a pair of rooms connected by two different hallways, a room split by a chasm spanned by two bridges, or a twisting maze of interconnecting goblin warrens. That type of circular path allows combat to unfold on multiple fronts. Once fighting starts in one area, either side can gain an advantage by circling around to approach from a different side.

Create a more dynamic encounter area by using a more complex shape—three areas connected to the others by multiple pathways. Start the encounter with the characters in the middle, the room connected to both of the other rooms. The map on page 77 shows an example of an encounter area designed with circular paths: The characters enter the area in the largest room, where three passages lead to smaller rooms that form part of the same encounter area.

Don't stop at designing an encounter area around a circular path; take advantage of the looping corridors to encourage movement. If every monster in the encounter area confronts the characters in the doorway on the first round of combat and never leaves the entry area, the PCs might as well be fighting in a small room with one entrance.

ATTRACTIVE TERRAIN

Force PCs to move around by creating attractive locations within an encounter, such as advantageous terrain, a place behind cover, or some other sort of defensive position. Desirable locations might also involve an objective of the encounter, such as an object in the room that the characters need to reach (see "Encounter Objectives," below).

An example of advantageous terrain is a bottleneck location where outnumbered characters can limit the number of monsters that can attack them at one time. Five characters facing a horde of angry minions create an advantage by retreating into a 10-foot-wide corridor. This approach allows only two minions at a time to attack the party defenders while the rest of the party makes ranged attacks or assists the front-line defenders. Maneuvering into that position can produce an interesting, dynamic couple of rounds. Once the characters settle into place, don't allow them dig in until all the minions are dead; put the PCs on the move again by changing the enemies' tactics (see "Enemy Tactics," below).

Some terrain features that give advantages to characters can be found on pages 67-68 of the *Dungeon Master's Guide*. These include blood rock, cloudspores, a font of power, mirror crystal, a pillar of life, and a sacred circle. The following section of this chapter describes more terrain features that can be used to add interest to encounters. Those that could be used as attractive terrain include an eldritch influx, an energy node, and healing ground.

TERRAIN TO AVOID

Difficult or dangerous terrain, along with traps and hazards, can hinder, discourage, or punish characters when they change position, so use these features carefully. You can also combine them with other methods of encouraging motion, or use them in conjunction with powers that push, pull, or slide. Both monsters and characters have access to forced movement powers, so the fight could involve maneuvering for the best position to push enemies into the hazardous terrain.

Another way to use hazardous terrain and traps is to have the danger travel around the encounter area, encouraging players to keep away from it as it moves. The *vexing cloud* power of the goblin hexer (*Monster Manual*, page 137) is an example of this sort of terrain—the goblin can move the cloud to pursue characters who try to escape or avoid it. Terrain examples might include a lava flow, a drifting cloud of noxious gas, a slowly spreading fire, or motes of raw chaotic energy that dart around the area and teleport each creature they touch, dealing damage in the process.

You can also move dangerous terrain in a regular pattern (such as the rolling boulder trap in Kobold Hall on page 217 of the *Dungeon Master's Guide*). Use dangerous terrain to propel the characters out of combat inertia and away from their current locations. You can use moving terrain to give an advantage to either side of the combat or to make the outcome of the battle feel more uncertain.

Finally, dangerous terrain can draw characters to it if it offers a potential reward. For example, bolt stone (page 58) damages a character who enters its space, and the discharge has a chance to create more bolt stone around it, hurting any enemies that move adjacent to the character. Players might find that the potential payoff is worth taking minor damage. However, for this kind of terrain to attract characters, they must understand how it works. Plant clues in the environment or let characters make Dungeoneering checks to identify terrain features—and be sure to tell them the benefits as well as the perils.

STARTING THE ENCOUNTER

One common DM mistake that can ruin an encounter can happen in the first round of combat. When the characters break down the door, they see a room full of monsters, interesting terrain features, and awe-inspiring wall carvings. The DM calls for initiative checks, and the players roll low. The monsters go first, and the problem begins. Each monster moves up to the PCs on its turn and attacks. None of that interesting terrain comes into play, and little movement occurs because the monsters and characters are stuck fighting in the doorway.

When the monsters have higher initiative counts than the characters, it's not a given that every one of them will rush forward to attack in melee. You can delay some of the monsters' turns or ready their attacks for when the characters move closer. Hold the monsters in their defensive positions and allow the characters to move into the room before the fight breaks out in earnest.

If the encounter includes artillery monsters that can attack from a distance, then the remaining monsters could charge the characters in the entryway. The monsters' ranged attacks might encourage one or more player characters to break through the front line of monsters to deal with the snipers. Or you could include attractive terrain or an encounter objective that draws the characters into the room before they change their focus to killing the monsters on the front line.

ENEMY TACTICS

All other particulars being equal, if the monsters don't move, the characters have little reason to move. Move your monsters, even if it means that they provoke opportunity attacks or attacks from the fighter's Combat Challenge class feature. Don't keep a monster stationary just because it might miss a chance to attack if it moves. Monsters should make the following choices:

✦ Move out of positions where characters flank them.
✦ Take cover from ranged attacks when possible.
✦ Avoid hazardous terrain they know about.

Reasonably intelligent monsters should also use these tactics:

✦ Move into flanking positions.
✦ Take advantage of circular paths to outflank the party.
✦ Make use of attractive terrain they know about.

ENCOUNTER OBJECTIVES

Clear encounter objectives can encourage movement. Several of the sample objectives described on pages 40-41 can spur characters to change positions during encounters.

For example, when characters have to protect an NPC, that person's actions can propel the characters around the battlefield—especially if the NPC panics or otherwise doesn't cooperate with the player characters. The characters could spend move actions chasing after an NPC who flees every time a monster moves into proximity. Alternatively, a battle-tested NPC could encourage the player characters to move by taking up a position that offers the PCs flanking opportunities.

If the characters have to retrieve an item or stop a ritual by manipulating objects in the room, the position of the significant items becomes attractive terrain, a place the characters want to reach.

The *Dungeon Master's Guide* presents a variety of terrain features to use when fleshing out your dungeons and encounter areas. This section presents more examples of fantastic terrain, and also introduces the concept of terrain powers.

Terrain is more interesting if the player characters know that something will happen when they try to interact with it. Some terrain types have obvious cues that should tip the players off, such as a cloud of magical energy or an ice-covered floor. For such terrain types, the players should at least be aware that those spaces aren't normal, and they should have the opportunity to identify the terrain if they interact with it or if they observe its effects on another creature.

If a monster uses terrain to its advantage, be sure to describe to the players how the terrain affected the monster's action. For instance, if a mind flayer uses a blast cloud to increase the size of its *mind blast*, be sure to describe the amplifying effect of the blast cloud so the characters know they can use the terrain in the same way.

In the absence of any clue the characters might get from how a monster acts, the effects of fantastic terrain are seldom obvious. However, you can allow characters to attempt Dungeoneering, Nature, or Arcana checks against a hard difficulty for their level. (See the Difficulty Class and Damage by Level table on page 65.) Choose a skill based on the environment where the encounter takes place or the nature of the terrain. A successful check means the character has a general idea of the terrain's effects and how to avoid them.

MORE FANTASTIC TERRAIN

The fantastic terrain types described on the following pages supplement the terrain types detailed on pages 64–69 of the *Dungeon Master's Guide*. These entries expand on what's presented there by giving advice on how best to use the terrain in constructing your own encounters.

Tier and Skill Checks and Ability Checks: Throughout these examples, the term "per tier" is used to show how an effect should scale. Multiply the per tier value by one for heroic tier, two for paragon, and three for epic. If a terrain feature grants a +1 bonus to attack rolls per tier, the bonus is +1 at heroic tier, +2 at paragon tier, and +3 at epic tier.

BLAST CLOUD

Rust-hued dust hangs in the air. The dust particles conduct and amplify certain types of energy and elemental forces.

Effect: The squares containing the cloud are lightly obscured. When a burst or a blast created by a fire, force, lightning, psychic, or thunder power touches a square of blast cloud, the size of the burst or blast is increased by 1.

Usage: A blast cloud encourages the characters (and their opponents) to remain farther apart than normal to avoid the enlarged areas of effect. Use this terrain in encounters featuring monsters that can take advantage of it, or when it can allow player characters who have attacks that might benefit from the blast cloud to take up an attractive combat position that utilizes the terrain's effect.

BLOOD MIDGE CLOUD

A swarm of biting insects fills the area.

Effect: The squares occupied by the cloud are lightly obscured, and the cloud is difficult terrain. If no creature is in the cloud when a creature starts its turn within 3 squares of a blood midge cloud, the cloud moves 5 squares and attempts to cover as many living creatures as possible. If an area or close attack includes squares occupied by the cloud, the cloud is destroyed in those squares. If a cloud is broken into smaller pieces by an attack, each piece acts as a separate terrain feature.

Usage: A blood midge cloud is interesting because it is mobile obscured terrain that can move to engulf the greatest number of creatures. The concealment granted by the cloud helps anyone in the cloud, and it's particularly beneficial to ranged attackers, who can fire out of it easily.

BOLT STONE

In some areas, lightning energy fuses with rock to form a highly unstable, dangerous mixture. In various regions of the Elemental Chaos, and in dungeons located near the conflux of different types of elemental energy, blue-tinged areas of bolt stone appear.

Effect: When a creature enters a square of bolt stone, it takes 5 lightning damage per tier. Roll a d20; on a 10 or higher, the bolt stone's energy is discharged, and the stone becomes inert. Otherwise, the lightning energy is transferred to all unoccupied squares adjacent to the origin square, and those squares become bolt stone.

Usage: Bolt stone works best when you scatter it across an encounter area. It offers some risk and reward. A player character might enter a square and take the damage in the hope of creating a barrier to hold back monsters or eliminate minions.

CREEPING ICE

In some areas infused with cold energy, particularly where icy parts of the Elemental Chaos erupt into the world, a strange form of ice crawls toward any kind of heat. Living creatures that stand on the ice are slowly drained of life.

Effect: Any creature that starts and ends its turn in any square of creeping ice takes 5 cold damage per tier.

Usage: Creeping ice is a great tool to persuade the characters to move around an encounter area, particularly if you place it in spots where characters who have ranged attacks are likely to position themselves.

DEFILED GROUND

The dead do not always rest in peace. Some cemeteries are darker than others, and ancient events leave unseen traces of their former presence. Defiled ground sometimes attracts undead.

Effect: Undead gain a +1 bonus to rolls to recharge their powers while on defiled ground. In addition, if an undead creature is reduced to 0 hit points while on defiled ground, roll a d20; on a 10 or higher, the undead creature rises with 1 hit point on its next turn. If radiant damage reduces an undead creature to 0 hit points, it can't rise again in this manner.

Usage: Defiled ground makes undead encounters somewhat more dangerous. Use it for encounters that are meant to have a feel of horror, or to evoke the atmosphere of a site sacred to undead, such as a temple to Orcus.

DIMENSIONAL TURBULENCE

Instability in the fabric of a plane makes teleportation difficult and inaccurate. Dimensional turbulence is visible as a faint rippling of space with an occasional twinkling of purple light.

Effect: A creature that teleports into a square of dimensional turbulence slides 1d4 squares in a random direction after teleporting.

Usage: Most useful at the paragon and epic tiers, dimensional turbulence turns normally dependable teleportation powers into a risky proposition.

DOOMLIGHT CRYSTAL

These rare, glowing rock formations exist in the Underdark and deep caverns. The glow comes from the gas inside the crystals, which explodes if it comes in contact with air.

Effect: A fist-sized doomlight crystal emits dim yellow light in a 3-square radius. If a character in a square with a doomlight crystal is hit by a close or an area attack, the crystal is destroyed as well—and the gas inside it explodes, dealing 5 damage per tier to the character in its square.

Usage: Obviously, this terrain feature makes area and close attacks more powerful. It can also add an interesting lighting element to a battle if the doomlights are the only source of illumination. As they are destroyed, the battlefield grows darker and darker.

ELDRITCH INFLUX

One or more squares reflect light, as if a metallic object hung suspended in the air. Characters entering these squares feel energy surrounding them and hear a faint hum in the air. Magical energy pools in this area, flowing into the void left behind by the expenditure of magic item powers.

Effect: As a standard action, a character in a square of eldritch influx can channel its energy to recharge an expended magic item power. Recharging a power in this way does not grant the item's wielder the ability to make use of more daily magic item powers between milestones. Using an eldritch influx for this purpose depletes its energy, and it can't be used again until 24 hours have passed.

Usage: Since monsters rarely use magic items, this terrain feature is a great magnet for player characters. Place it so they have to work to reach it during a fight, encouraging movement and rewarding risk. Use it for paragon characters or in the first encounter after a milestone, when you know the characters have magic item activations available to them.

ELEMENTAL WINDCHURN

The powerful, swirling wind in this area makes flying difficult. The elemental turbulence crackles with energy, bringing with it a strong ozone odor.

Effect: An area of elemental windchurn is difficult terrain for creatures that are flying, and a creature that ends its turn aloft in the area slides 1d6 squares in a random direction.

Usage: Elemental windchurn adds a touch of chaos to a battle while discouraging flight. Use it as an excuse to ground flying monsters at the heroic tier, while at higher tiers it makes an aerial duel far less predictable.

ENERGY NODE

An energy node is a particularly strong confluence of arcane, divine, and other forms of power. The air above it shimmers with energy, and anyone standing upon it feels fresh and reinvigorated.

Effect: A creature that starts its turn in an energy node's square can spend a minor action while in the square to regain a single encounter or recharge power. Using a node for this purpose depletes its energy, and it can't be used again until 24 hours have passed.

Usage: Energy nodes work well in long, running battles and in encounters with solo monsters. Not only do they allow the characters (and monsters) to use encounter powers multiple times, but they also create a situation in which the player characters might be racing against their opponents. Only one creature can benefit from each energy node, forcing the characters to fight for access to any nodes in an area. In a fight against a solo monster, consider placing more than one node around the perimeter of the encounter area, or in hard-to-reach places, which can force PCs to disengage in order to draw upon the power of a node.

FEY CIRCLE

Often distinguished by the presence of tangled vines or large toadstools, this location is empowered with the extraordinary energy of the Feywild.

Effect: A creature can spend a minor action while in a fey circle's square to teleport 5 squares.

Usage: A fey circle can add unpredictability to a combat area, and it can level the playing field somewhat when the player characters are fighting monsters that teleport–or when monsters familiar with the circle face player characters who teleport all the time. A fey circle is also a great addition to an encounter area that features a treacherous chasm or similarly dangerous terrain, giving the player characters a way to bypass the danger if they can figure out the purpose of the fey circle.

GRASPING BOG

A grasping bog is an area of deep, viscous mud that not only hampers movement but also clings to characters who tumble into it.

Effect: A grasping bog is difficult terrain. In addition, a creature that falls prone in a square of grasping bog is restrained (save ends).

Usage: Combine grasping bog terrain with monsters that can knock their enemies prone.

HEALING GROUND

This area is infused with primal energy that allows life of all sorts to flourish. Undergrowth or fungus that thrives on the primal energy in the place grows wildly and chokes the area with its profusion.

Effect: If a creature in this terrain spends a healing surge, it regains an additional 2 hit points per tier. Healing ground is also difficult terrain due to the abundant plant life.

Usage: Healing ground, assuming that the characters can recognize it, is a good example of attractive terrain that gives characters an incentive to move into a room and take up advantageous positions.

INFERNAL FUMES

Most common in regions of the Nine Hells and certain volcanic regions of the world, infernal fumes are great clouds of gray smoke that glow red with inner heat. Infernal fumes drift as if alive, apparently seeking concentrations of multiple creatures.

Effect: Squares filled with infernal fumes are lightly obscured. The fumes can move up to 4 squares each round. A creature that ends its turn in a square of infernal fumes takes 5 fire and poison damage per tier and is dazed until the end of its next turn.

Usage: Infernal fumes are an effective way to chase player characters around an encounter area. This terrain is similar to a blood midge cloud, but has a significant harmful effect to characters and monsters inside it. Few monsters, even devils, are immune to the effect of infernal fumes, so they challenge both sides of a fight equally. Creatures that remain outside the cloud are hindered in their attempts to attack creatures inside the cloud as a result of the concealment it grants.

JADE FLAME

This strange, vibrant green fire burns everything that comes near it, yet the nature of its magic is such that a creature it burns cannot be harmed by other sources of heat for a limited time.

Effect: A creature that enters a square of jade flame or that starts its turn adjacent to such a square takes ongoing 5 radiant damage per tier (save ends). However, until the creature saves against the ongoing damage, it has resist fire equal to 10 per tier.

Usage: Jade flame offers the characters a choice. They can accept some constant radiant damage in return for protection against a potentially more dangerous threat. The characters might need to use jade flame to protect themselves before they race across a lava chamber or face another sort of fire hazard.

MARTYR'S MONUMENT

This area contains the life energy of an ancient and powerful champion of the gods, embodied in a statue or some other holy icon.

Effect: The monument grants a +2 bonus to saving throws to all creatures within 5 squares of it.

In addition, a creature adjacent to the monument can touch it as a minor action to make a saving throw. Each time a creature touches the monument to make a saving throw, roll a d20; on a 5 or lower, the monument loses all its magical properties for 24 hours.

Usage: A martyr's monument gives characters a new option for their minor actions. Such terrain is also great for monsters that have nothing else to do with their minor actions. Characters and monsters can use forced movement powers to drive their enemies away from the monument so they can't gain the saving throw bonus it grants. Use this feature in combination with monsters whose attacks impose effects that a save can end, or if the characters have been making particularly effective use of such attacks against previous foes.

NECROTIC GROUND

This area is infused with necrotic energy. All light sources appear slightly dimmer, and the air is cold and still. Creatures that enter this area feel tired and drained.

Effect: A creature that spends a healing surge in an area of necrotic ground recovers only half the normal number of hit points. (All other effects, such as additional hit points regained or the bonus to defense from using second wind, are unaffected.)

Usage: Unless an encounter area consists entirely of necrotic ground, characters will wisely do anything they can to avoid being in the area when they spend healing surges. If you combine necrotic ground with a strong defensive position or another advantageous location, you might force characters into the difficult choice of staying in their good position but gaining less benefit from healing effects, or abandoning their position so that they can regain as many hit points as possible.

NEEDLE HEDGE

Areas of sharp-needled bushes grow in the dark forests of the Shadowfell and in areas of the world where shadow's influence is strong. The plants are covered in long, sharp spines and thorns, forcing creatures to slow down as they move through the bushes or suffer a multitude of small cuts.

Effect: A needle hedge is difficult terrain, and it grants cover to a creature within it or behind it. If a creature moves through more than 1 square of needle hedge during a single move action or incident of forced movement, that creature takes 5 damage per tier.

Usage: Characters are likely to consider a needle hedge an effectively solid barrier until they're pushed through it. Use it with monsters that can force movement, or with elves or other skirmishers that can shift

KEREM BEYIT

freely in difficult terrain (including creatures that have the forest walk ability).

PHASE MIST

Phase mist is an extremely rare phenomenon. It appears as a hazy cloud of swirling colors similar to those found in the Astral Sea. When a creature steps into phase mist, its body phases into the strange spaces that exist between the planes.

Effect: A square of phase mist is lightly obscured. A creature that starts its turn in a square of phase mist gains phasing until the end of its turn.

Usage: Use phase mist to create encounters that force the characters to split up. For example, the characters might use the mist to enter a chamber that lacks a door. Within the chamber is another patch of phase mist and an object that the characters need. In addition, monsters that have phasing, or undying guardians that lurk in the inaccessible chambers, wait to ambush lone characters.

QUICK SEAR

This mixture of acid and quicksilver is a viscous, silvery green liquid. It appears as a small puddle in a single square.

Effect: A creature that starts its turn in a square of quick sear or adjacent to such a square takes 5 acid damage per tier. If a square of quick sear is within the area of effect of a close or an area attack, it moves 1d6 squares in a random direction.

Usage: Quick sear adds a random element to an encounter that could otherwise prove dull or static. Use it in encounters where a sense of randomness and an unexpected twist seems appropriate.

RAGE STONE

This expanse of black-veined crimson stone is infused with the psychic residue of pitched battles and brutal atrocities. A creature standing on a square of rage stone feels itself consumed with negative and violent emotions that it must unleash.

Effect: A creature that starts its turn in a square of rage stone must make a melee attack on that turn or takes 5 psychic damage per tier.

Usage: Creatures that are comfortable making melee attacks suffer few ill effects from rage stone, aside from lingering emotional turmoil that has no game effect. Creatures that prefer to stay away from melee combat (including most PC controllers, for example) are the most likely to take damage from rage stone. Putting rage stone at the periphery of an encounter area can play havoc with PC controllers and ranged strikers, as well as with artillery monsters.

THUNDER SHARDS

These crystalline shards of solidified thunder energy are both unstable and dangerous. They rumble and shudder as they course with the energy within them. Most creatures avoid them, but occasionally orcs, ogres, and other battle hungry creatures dwell near them. Although thunder shards are dangerous, they also make useful defensive fortifications if used properly.

Effect: Squares of thunder shards are difficult terrain. If a creature makes a melee attack against a target in a thunder shard square, roll a d20; on a 10 or higher, both the attacker and the target take 5 thunder damage and are pushed 1d4 squares from each other.

Usage: Thunder shards are useful barriers to encourage movement and add a random element to the fight. The random push is especially useful if the area has pits or other dangerous terrain.

TERRAIN POWERS

The barbarian pushes against a broken stone wall, causing it to topple over and crush the orcs on the other side. An ogre slams its club into the ship's wooden floor, causing the floor to shudder and knocking the wizard prone.

Sometimes, characters and their enemies can use the terrain around them as weapons. Adding this terrain to an encounter provides for an added layer of excitement, inventiveness, and danger. When the players see that terrain can function as a weapon against their characters' enemies, they seek out creative tactics and novel ways to deal with encounters.

A terrain power is a description of what happens when a creature uses a feature of the terrain to attack its enemies. It can be a prepared part of an encounter, perhaps even key to the characters' success in the encounter, or it can be an improvised action invented on the spur of the moment.

Terrain powers are interesting in an encounter when the characters can use them. You might prepare terrain powers for a climactic encounter and lay them out on the table (perhaps literally, on index cards, or else verbally as you describe the area) when the encounter starts, or let characters discover them on their own. On the other hand, exciting uses of terrain powers can include the unusual tactics that players think up when their characters are caught in desperate situations. Be flexible!

Terrain powers function like character or monster powers, with just a few important differences. Any creature in or adjacent to the terrain can use the power without any special training.

READING TERRAIN POWERS

Like character powers, terrain powers are described in a specific format.

Name and Usage: The header line gives the name of the power and how often it can be used.

Single-Use Terrain: Sometimes using a terrain power destroys the terrain. Once the ogre collapses the hut's roof on the PCs, the roof can't attack the characters anymore. The first time a creature succeeds on a check to use a single-use terrain power, or attacks with it if the power requires no check, that terrain power is no longer available for use. The terrain is destroyed or otherwise ineffective if used to attack again.

At-Will Terrain: Terrain powers of this sort can be used over and over. The terrain's attack can be repeated. Attacking with it might cause the terrain some damage, but the object or area remains intact.

Flavor Text: Beneath the header line is a brief description of how the terrain looks and what its power might do.

Action: The kind of action needed to use the power is called out here.

Requirement: Some terrain powers can be used only if a certain precondition is met.

Check: A terrain power requires an attack roll, a skill check, or an ability check to prepare it for use. A tiefling archer takes careful aim, firing an arrow and trying to sever the rope holding up a chandelier. The archer must first hit the rope. Or, an ogre pushes against a wall, attempting to topple it over onto nearby enemies. First the ogre has to make a successful skill check to push the wall over.

A terrain power's "Check" entry specifies the kind of roll or check required to use the power. Usually, the entry describes the DC of a skill check or ability check as easy, moderate, or hard. Use Difficulty Class and Damage by Level table (page 65) to determine the exact DC based on the level of the encounter.

Success: This entry describes what happens if a character succeeds on the check. That character can then use the terrain power.

Failure: As a default, if a character fails the check, he or she cannot use the terrain power. If the terrain power is single-use, the power is not expended on a failed check. This entry appears only if a failure requires some further explanation about the terrain or the outcome of the usage attempt.

Attack and **Hit:** The attack of a terrain power is part of the same action needed to make the check. These and other entries in a terrain power description sometimes refer to "level," which is the level of the encounter. For example, the attack of a falling chandelier is level + 3 vs. Reflex, and a hit deals 2d8 + one-half level damage. In a 10th-level encounter, its attack would be +13 vs. Reflex, and its damage would be 2d8 + 5.

Miss: This entry appears only if an attack deals half damage or imposes some other damage or condition on a miss.

Effect: A terrain power can have an effect that occurs regardless of whether the attack hit or missed.

Sample Terrain Powers

You can adapt these example terrain powers to a variety of situations, using the same rules but providing different descriptions. For example, when a player character (or an ogre) wants to push a wagon down a slope, use the boulder terrain power. Any heavy object suspended above the encounter area can fill in for a chandelier, including the tiefling archer's drawbridge.

Boulder — Single-Use Terrain

This large boulder is perched atop a long slope. One strong shove could send it hurtling into an oncoming mob of enemies.

Standard Action

Requirement: You must be adjacent to the boulder.
Check: Athletics check (hard DC) to shove the rock.
Success: The boulder rolls forward and down the slope, stopping after moving 1d6 squares away from the slope's base. The boulder can move through a creature's space. When it does so, make the following attack.
Target: Each creature whose space the boulder enters
Attack: Level + 3 vs. Fortitude
Hit: 2d10 + one-half level damage, and the target is knocked prone.
Miss: Slide the target 1 square out of the boulder's path.

Chandelier — Single-Use Terrain

A large, ornate chandelier of iron and crystal hangs over the battlefield. It would be a pity if it fell to the ground.

Standard Action

Check: From a distance, to sever or loosen the rope or chain holding the chandelier aloft, make a ranged attack (the chandelier's defenses are level + 5).
   Alternatively, you can spend a standard action to cut the rope while adjacent to either the chandelier or the rope or chain keeping it aloft.
Success: The chandelier falls to the ground and smashes to pieces.
Target: Each creature in an area burst 1 beneath the chandelier
Attack: Level + 3 vs. Reflex
Hit: 2d8 + one-half level damage.
Miss: Half damage.
Effect: The area where the chandelier fell becomes difficult terrain.

Rope Bridge — At-Will Terrain

This rickety bridge spans a deep gap. One sudden move, and it sways perilously, threatening to put anyone on it over the side.

Standard Action

Requirement: You must be on or adjacent to the bridge.
Check: Athletics check (moderate DC) to sway the bridge.
Success: The bridge sways.
Target: Each creature standing on the bridge (including you, if applicable)
Attack: Level + 3 vs. Reflex
Hit: The target is knocked prone. If the target is already prone, it falls off the bridge.

Ruined Wall — Single-Use Terrain

This sagging wall is ready to fall over with just the right application of force.

Standard Action

Requirement: You must be adjacent to the wall.
Check: Athletics check (hard DC) to topple the wall.
Success: The wall collapses.
Target: Each creature in a close blast 3 in the direction the wall fell
Attack: Level + 3 vs. Reflex
Hit: 1d10 + one-half level damage, and the target is knocked prone.
Miss: Half damage.
Effect: The space the wall covered and the area of the blast become difficult terrain.

Swinging Rope or Vine — At-Will Terrain

A vine hangs down from the treetops over a deep chasm.

DM Note: When placing a swinging vine or rope in an encounter, you must determine the rope's starting square, its path of travel, and its ending square. Keep in mind that some vines or ropes can travel in both directions.
Move Action

Requirement: You must be in the vine or rope's starting square to use this terrain power.
Check: Athletics check (moderate DC) to swing from the vine's starting square to its ending square.
Success: You move from the vine's starting square to its ending square along the vine's path. This movement provokes opportunity attacks, and you can let go from the vine at any point during this movement. If you reach the ending square, you can make an Athletics check to jump at the end of the swing, treating it as a jump with a running start, but you must jump in the same direction as the movement of the swinging vine.
Failure: You do not move, and your move action ends.

Table of Combustibles — Single-Use Terrain

A table holds beakers and vials containing volatile combustibles that have a violent reaction when mixed together or thrown to the ground.

Standard Action

Requirement: You must be adjacent to the table.
Check: Athletics check (hard DC) to overturn the table. You can drop prone as part of the standard action to avoid the attack.
Success: The table is overturned.
Target: Each creature in a close burst 2 centered on the table
Attack: Level + 3 vs. Reflex
Hit: Ongoing 5 fire and poison damage per tier (save ends).

Tapestry — Single-Use Terrain

A quick tug, and the tapestry hanging on the wall flutters to the ground, trapping anyone next to it.

Standard Action

Requirement: You must be adjacent to the tapestry.
Check: Athletics check (moderate DC) to pull the tapestry down.
Success: The tapestry falls.
Target: Each creature in a close blast 3 out from the tapestry
Attack: Level + 3 vs. Reflex
Hit: The target is blinded and slowed until it is no longer underneath the tapestry.

DESIGNING TRAPS

No dungeon is complete without a few devious devices. Sometimes, though, traps have a nasty habit of reducing a dungeon run to a crawl. Take care to put traps in the right setting to make their inclusion fun and to keep them from dragging your game down.

When setting out to design a trap for your game, consider basing it on the traps you already have available to you. If you're thinking about a gauntlet of shuriken-spitting statues for an 8th-level party, you can probably use either the spear gauntlet or poisoned dart wall from the *Dungeon Master's Guide*. Replace the numbers for DCs, attack bonus, and damage using the tables in this section. This method is a lot easier and faster than designing from scratch.

You can also use the tables to increase or decrease the level of a trap that you already have available. Maybe you like one of the traps in this chapter, but its level is too high. Just consult the tables and adjust it. If the existing trap doesn't match the numbers for its level in the tables, compare the trap's numbers to the table's numbers and then eyeball a proportional difference based on the numbers for the level you want.

You can even take a trap and "reskin" it to your needs without changing any numbers. Perhaps you want to fill an area with deadly but random arcs of lightning. Take the pendulum scythes trap from the *Dungeon Master's Guide* and have it deal lightning damage instead of normal damage. Instead of slots, hidden lightning generators create the effect. Your players have what feels like a new trap experience, and you didn't have to do a lot of work.

If no existing trap serves your needs, you can design one using the tables here with other traps as your guide. When setting out to design a trap for an encounter, don't get hung up on whether it's a trap or a hazard, or if it qualifies as a blaster, a lurker, an obstacle, or a warder. These terms exist to provide mental cues that suggest the uses of traps. You already know how you want to use your trap.

1. Choose the Trap's Level: This is probably either the level of the player characters or the level of the encounter in which the trap appears. The level determines the trap's numbers as described in the tables below. You can deviate from these numbers, but you should have good reason to do so. Your players aren't likely to realize small changes in difficulty (a point or two up or down), but noticeable changes in the numbers can cause the trap to become either too easy or too hard for the XP it provides, which likely translates to less fun at the table. If you look at the numbers and want your trap to be more dangerous, consider making a higher-level trap.

Trap DCs: Use the Difficulty Class and Damage by Level table to generate appropriate DCs for

interacting with traps of a given level. Perception is typically used to detect a trap, though other skills might also come into play if thematically appropriate. Such DCs typically start as moderate or hard, and in many cases progressively more difficult DCs might provide more information. If detecting a trap, or some fact about a trap, needs to be more challenging than hard difficulty, use a value no more than 5 greater than the hard DC.

When setting the DCs for disabling or delaying a trap using the Thievery skill, consider rudimentary traps, such as concealed pits or tripwire triggers, to be of moderate difficulty, while a more complex trap should use DCs appropriate for a hard challenge. Traps might have alternative ways of delaying or disabling them, with varying DCs. For instance, a trap could have a moderate DC check that involves some risk (such as requiring the PC to be attacked or to place himself in a precarious situation), while also allowing a hard DC check with reduced or no risk. In some cases, you might even allow a character who accomplishes a difficult success to find an even easier way to disable the trap. For example, a PC might succeed on a hard DC Perception check to notice the panel that hides a trap's control mechanism, after which an easy DC Thievery check allows her to use those controls to stop the trap.

2. Determine How the Trap Threatens the Characters: A trap that attacks once and is done should have different numbers from a trap of the same level that attacks multiple times. Similarly, a trap that attacks a large area or many characters functions differently from a trap that endangers just one character.

Single-Shot Traps: Single-shot traps attack once and are done. A trap that resets might still be a single-shot trap if a character must choose to do something active to set it off again. Being attacked every round as long as you stand in a square is not a single-shot trap, because the character could be paralyzed in that location or forced to fight in that square, but getting shot every time you open a particular door qualifies as a single-shot trap. The trap resets whenever the door is closed, but the character could leave the door open or not use it again.

A single-shot trap uses the Limited Damage Expressions part of the table. For a single-shot trap that affects a single target, use the Medium damage column. For one that affects an area, use the Low damage column. For an elite trap, use the damage column one step up (Low becomes Medium, Medium becomes High).

Ongoing Attack Traps: These traps continually attack the targets while they are in the area.

DIFFICULTY CLASS AND DAMAGE BY LEVEL

	Difficulty Class (DC) Values			Normal Damage Expressions			Limited Damage Expressions		
Level	Easy	Moderate	Hard	Low	Medium	High	Low	Medium	High
1st–3rd	5	10	15	1d6 + 3	1d10 + 3	2d6 + 3	3d6 + 3	2d10 + 3	3d8 + 3
4th–6th	7	12	17	1d6 + 4	1d10 + 4	2d8 + 4	3d6 + 4	3d8 + 4	3d10 + 4
7th–9th	8	14	19	1d8 + 5	2d6 + 5	2d8 + 5	3d8 + 5	3d10 + 5	4d8 + 5
10th–12th	10	16	21	1d8 + 5	2d6 + 5	3d6 + 5	3d8 + 5	4d8 + 5	4d10 + 5
13th–15th	11	18	23	1d10 + 6	2d8 + 6	3d6 + 6	3d10 + 6	4d8 + 6	4d10 + 6
16th–18th	13	20	25	1d10 + 7	2d8 + 7	3d8 + 7	3d10 + 6	4d10 + 7	4d12 + 7
19th–21st	14	22	27	2d6 + 7	3d6 + 8	3d8 + 7	4d8 + 7	4d10 + 7	4d12 + 7
22nd–24th	16	24	29	2d6 + 8	3d6 + 8	4d6 + 8	4d8 + 8	4d12 + 8	5d10 + 8
25th–27th	17	26	31	2d8 + 9	3d8 + 9	4d6 + 9	4d10 + 9	5d10 + 9	5d12 + 9
28th–30th	19	28	33	2d8 + 10	3d8 + 10	4d8 + 10	4d10 + 9	5d10 + 9	5d12 + 9

An ongoing attack trap uses the Normal Damage Expressions part of the table. For an ongoing-attack trap that affects a single target, use the Medium damage column. For one that affects an area, use the Low damage column. For an elite trap, use the damage column one step up (Low becomes Medium, Medium becomes High).

No-Damage Traps: Traps that deal no damage might still otherwise harm the characters (blocking their movement, making them weakened or slowed, and so on). In a noncombat situation, a no-damage trap probably isn't much of a threat, but in a combat encounter, this sort of trap can be just as tough to deal with as a monster. You're firmly in the realm of art when designing a no-damage trap, so don't be afraid to change the XP you give for it based on the difficulty of the encounter when you play. A trap effect that incorporates damage along with nondamaging effects should have a lower damage number, reducing the damage to that of a lower-level trap.

Stress Traps: A stress trap is like a no-damage trap except that it threatens damage and might eventually follow through on that threat if the characters fail to take the necessary actions. A room filling with water or one that has a slowly descending ceiling is a stress trap. This kind of trap might work better as a skill challenge, but see the water-filling chamber and crushing walls room traps on the following pages.

TOP TEN TRAPS TO AVOID

10. Traps without Cause: Traps should guard something specific or be useful to their makers in combat. Traps that have no apparent reason for being there can annoy players.

9. Traps Out of Scope for the Trap Setters: If the stone-axe-wielding grimlock warren has a repeating crossbow trap, there should be a good explanation the characters can discover.

8. Too Many Traps in Expected Places: If you put a trap on a treasure chest in three adventures in a row, you can expect the players to take the next treasure chest they see and toss it down a stairwell to open it. The same goes for statues and doors. Use traps on common objects sparingly to avoid having them get stale.

7. Traps that Counter PC Preparations: The frost giant's palace of ice shouldn't have fire traps. Maybe you can justify it, but instead of explaining why you're making the players unhappy, why not make them feel smart and reward their preparations for cold by giving them exciting ice traps to overcome?

6. Traps in Unexpected Places: It might be "realistic" or effective to put a trap in a surprising place such as the middle of an otherwise unremarkable hallway, but putting traps in places that players take for granted as being safe means they can't do so anymore. If the characters are reduced to testing every square before they walk on it, your game is going to slow to a crawl.

5. Traps Designed to Defeat the Rogue: If your players devote resources to defeating traps, don't punish them by making traps more difficult to overcome. They'll be a lot happier if their choices are meaningful.

4. Traps that Make a Character Sit out the Fight: The greased pit trap in the final encounter room can make a player whose character falls into it bored during what should be the best encounter in the adventure.

3. Traps without Countermeasures: A trap without countermeasures is about as fun as fighting a monster you can't damage. Give the characters multiple means of defeating the trap.

2. Traps that Don't Give Experience: It might feel as though the characters didn't earn their success when they circumvent a trap with a single roll or a clever idea, but not giving XP would be like not giving the players XP for those combats that end in a single round. Sure, they were lucky, but it felt like a great success to them. Allow them to enjoy it.

1. Extremely Deadly Traps: It might make a trap more fearsome to have it cause a lot of damage, but the unseen trap that kills a character is about as fun as walking out your door to find that a falling meteorite has flattened your parked car.

They both use statistics appropriate for elite, ongoing attack, area traps of their level.

3. Assign XP for the Trap: When assigning XP for a trap, you need to know its level and type (single-shot or ongoing, standard or elite). Single-shot traps should be considered minions. Ongoing, no-damage, and stress traps should have the XP of standards or elites.

ELITE AND SOLO TRAPS

You might want a trap to be elite so that it takes up more space or deals more damage than a standard version of the same trap, but it's often more fun just to add another trap. Don't fall prey to thinking that elite equates to more fun or greater danger. It can mean those things, but a trap the characters fail to circumvent and that deals a lot of damage to them could just as easily be less fun than a standard trap. Similarly, if you increase the level of an encounter by adding an elite trap, but then the characters don't trigger that trap, the encounter becomes less of a challenge.

Making a trap elite is similar in many respects to making a monster elite. Use the traps in this chapter and in the *Dungeon Master's Guide* as examples. Options include increasing a trap's attack bonus by 2, increasing its damage, increasing its number of attacks, and increasing the space the trap occupies or the area it can affect.

As for solo traps, you might consider creating such a trap as a skill challenge, and you can also combine different traps to make a solo encounter. The hallmark of a solo encounter is that it keeps all the characters involved, so a solo trap needs to include ways for each character to contribute to either help overcome the trap directly, or at least to mitigate the damage or other effects the party is subject to during the encounter. Similarly, each character should be at risk during an encounter with a solo trap.

STANDARD AND ELITE TRAP STATISTICS*

	Standard	Elite
Initiative bonus	+2	+4
Attack vs. AC**	Level + 5	Level + 7
Attack vs. other defenses**	Level + 3	Level + 5

*If you want to derive statistics such as defenses and AC, see "Damaging Objects" (*Dungeon Master's Guide*, page 65).

**Reduce the attack bonus by 2 for powers that affect multiple creatures.

SAMPLE TRAPS

Each of the trap descriptions below contains a Tactics section that provides some advice and suggestions on using the trap, and many of the traps here also contain sample encounters.

Kissing Maiden	Level 4 Lurker
Trap	XP 175

When a square is entered, a section of floor slides aside and a stone post levers up to hit the creature in the square, pushing it back. The stone post then swings back down to reset the trap as long as the square is empty.

Trap: A square hides a post that deals damage and pushes a creature. The post provides cover while the creature is in the square.

Perception
+ DC 17: A panel in the floor ahead of you is loose, suggesting that it slides to one side.
+ DC 22: Another portion of the floor gives in when pressed down. It might be a trapdoor or a pressure plate.

Trigger
The floor panel slides aside and the post swings up when a creature enters the square.

Attack
Opportunity Action   **Melee**
Target: The creature that triggered the trap
Attack: +7 vs. Fortitude
Hit: 1d10 + 4 damage, and the target is pushed 2 squares in the direction the trap is set to push.

Countermeasures
+ A character standing in the square of a triggered kissing maiden that missed can keep it from resetting by jamming an object in the way of the post or the sliding section of floor that hid the post, requiring a DC 12 Thievery check.
+ A character adjacent to the trap can delay or disable a kissing maiden with a DC 17 Thievery check.

TACTICS

Use a kissing maiden with other traps or terrain powers, so that a pushed PC lands in another dangerous square. Place the kissing maiden in a space the PCs have to cross, so they need to disable it or risk triggering it multiple times. An encounter could include multiple kissing maidens teamed with creatures that fly or hover.

SAMPLE ENCOUNTER

A group of evil dwarves defends a fortified chamber that is rife with traps. The dwarf hammerers use their *shield bash* attacks to push enemies into kissing maidens, while the dwarf bolters position themselves behind the traps.

Level 8 Encounter (XP 1,825)
+ 2 dwarf bolters (level 4 artillery; *Monster Manual*, page 97)
+ 3 dwarf hammerers (level 5 soldier; *Monster Manual*, page 97)
+ 5 kissing maiden traps (level 4 lurker)

Falling Iron Portcullis — Level 7 Minion Obstacle
Trap — XP 75

When a pressure plate is stepped on, a hidden iron portcullis drops from the ceiling, blocking the hallway.

Trap: A portcullis drops into 2 adjacent squares when a 2-square-wide pressure plate is stepped on. A secret panel hides the winch that raises the portcullis.

Perception
- DC 14: The ceiling has a 2-inch-wide slot packed with gray dirt and small stones.
- DC 19: A portion of the floor gives in when pressed down. It might be a trapdoor or pressure plate.
- DC 24: A secret panel in the wall beyond the pressure plate hides the winch that raises the portcullis.

Trigger
A portcullis falls and blocks the passage when a creature steps on a pressure plate.

Attack
Immediate Reaction   Area 2 adjacent squares
Target: Each creature in the area
Attack: +10 vs. Reflex
Hit: 3d8 + 5 damage, and the target is restrained and falls prone. If the target is already prone, it takes no damage, but its turn ends immediately.
Miss: Half damage, and the target is pushed 1 square (roll a d20: 1–10 push forward, 11–20 push back).

Countermeasures
- A character who finds the winch can crank it up with a DC 8 Athletics check.
- A character adjacent to the trap can delay or disable one portcullis or pressure plate with a DC 19 Thievery check.
- A restrained character can use the escape action (DC 19) to free himself, moving 1 square but remaining prone.
- A character not restrained by the portcullis can force it open with a successful DC 24 Strength check.
- A character can attack a portcullis bar (AC 8, Reflex 8, Fortitude 8; hp 45). Destroying a bar opens enough room for a Small or Medium creature to squeeze through with an escape action (DC 14). Destroying two bars allows a Large creature to squeeze through (DC 19), and Small and Medium creatures count the square as difficult terrain.

TACTICS
Place the triggering pressure plate beyond the portcullis so that it can divide the party, then start a combat encounter. Alternatively, have a monster run away from the PCs and trigger the portcullis to fall on the PCs who follow. Use multiple portcullises to isolate the PCs within a room, and have monsters with ranged attacks or insubstantial monsters attack.

SAMPLE ENCOUNTER
An adventurer fell prey to a falling portcullis, was eaten by carrion crawlers, and then rose as a ghost. Now he lures other adventurers to a similar fate, and the carrion crawlers, with their troglodyte handlers, come to investigate the sound of the gate crashing down.

Level 7 Encounter (XP 1,525)
- 2 carrion crawlers (level 7 controller; *Monster Manual*, page 40)
- 1 falling iron portcullis trap (level 7 obstacle)
- 1 trap haunt ghost (level 8 lurker; *Monster Manual*, page 116)
- 2 troglodyte maulers (level 6 soldier; *Monster Manual*, page 252)

Water-Filling Chamber — Level 8 Elite Blaster
Trap — XP 700

When a character moves onto a central square in the room, reinforced iron doors crash down over the exits, and a face carved in the wall opens its jaws to spew water into the room. Each iron door can be opened to prevent accidental entrapment, but each door release has three locks.

Trap: The chamber seals off and fills with water when a pressure plate is stepped on.

Perception
- DC 14: The face carved in the stone walls looks like it has a movable jaw.
- DC 19: A portion of the floor gives in when pressed down. It might be a trapdoor or pressure plate.
- DC 24: A hidden slot is above each doorway. Something might fall out of it.

Initiative +4

Trigger
The trap is triggered when a creature enters the trapped square. When triggered, the iron doors fall into place. Roll initiative. On the trap's initiative count, water begins to pour from the faces in the walls.

Attack
Standard Action   Area the entire room
Target: Each creature in the area
Effect: On the trap's initiative count, the water level in the room rises. The water has the following effects each round.
Round 1—No effect on Medium creatures. The room is difficult terrain for Small creatures.
Round 2—The room is difficult terrain for Medium creatures. Small creatures must swim.
Round 3—All creatures must swim.
Round 4—The room is filled with water. All creatures are considered to be swimming underwater.

Countermeasures
- A character adjacent to the trapped square can delay the trigger with a DC 19 Thievery check.
- A character adjacent to one of the doors can partially prop it open with a DC 24 Thievery check. This causes the room to fill with water in twice as many rounds, using the round 1 result on round 2, the round 2 result on round 4, and so on.
- A character adjacent to one of the doors can use a key to open one of its three locks, assuming the character has the right key.
- A character adjacent to one of the doors can open one of its locks with a DC 19 Thievery check.
- A character adjacent to the carving on the wall can reduce the flow of water into the room for 1 round by partially closing the carving's mouth with a DC 14 Strength check. For each round that the mouth is held partially closed, water still flows in but at a slower rate. For every 3 rounds that the mouth is held partially closed, the water rises as though a single round had passed (see "Effect," above).
- A character adjacent to one of the doors can attempt to break it down with a DC 30 Strength check.
- A character adjacent to one of the doors can attack it in an attempt to break it open (AC 5, Fortitude 10, Reflex 5; hp 80).

TACTICS

Don't worry about the physics here. A water-filling chamber is about a cool scene, not the minutia of water pressure or cubic volume. That said, consider the dungeon design and the location from which the water is flowing. Perhaps setting off this trap allows the PCs to access a previously flooded section of the dungeon.

Crushing Walls Room	Level 11 Elite Blaster
Trap	XP 1,200

When a character moves onto a central square in the room, reinforced iron doors crash down over the exits, and two opposing walls begin to press inward. Each iron door can be opened to prevent accidental entrapment, but each door release has three locks.

Trap: One square in the room is a pressure plate that makes the walls press together when it is stepped on.

Perception
- ✦ DC 16: Slight scratches in the floor and ceiling suggest that the walls can move inward.
- ✦ DC 21: A portion of the floor gives in when pressed down. It might be a trapdoor or pressure plate.
- ✦ DC 26: A hidden slot is above each door. Something might fall out of it.

Initiative +4   **Speed** 1 (consider altering this based on the size of the room)

Trigger
The trap is triggered when a creature enters the trapped square, which is typically in the center of the room. When triggered, the iron doors fall into place. Roll initiative. On the trap's initiative count, the walls move inward.

Attack
Standard Action   **Area** the entire room
Target: Each creature in the area
Effect: On the trap's initiative count, each wall moves inward 1 square. Creatures adjacent to the wall are automatically pushed 1 square. When the crushing walls are 1 square apart, they attack all creatures in the room until all are crushed to death.
Attack: +14 vs. Fortitude
Hit: 3d6 + 5 damage.
Miss: Half damage.

Countermeasures
- ✦ A character adjacent to the trapped square can delay or disable the trigger with a DC 26 Thievery check.
- ✦ A character adjacent to one of the doors can disable it with a DC 26 Thievery check.
- ✦ A character adjacent to one of the doors can use a key to open one of its three locks, assuming the character has the right key.
- ✦ A character adjacent to one of the doors can open one of its locks with a DC 21 Thievery check.
- ✦ A character adjacent to one of the moving walls can prevent its inward movement with a DC 21 Strength check. If the walls are 1 square apart, the DC increases to 26. Any number of characters can aid the one making the check.
- ✦ A character adjacent to one of the doors can attempt to break it down with a DC 25 Strength check.
- ✦ A character adjacent to one of the doors can attack it in an attempt to break it open (AC 5, Fortitude 10, Reflex 5; hp 80).

TACTICS

The danger of this trap depends on the size of the room and the speed of the walls. At least one doorway should be accessible when the walls are still 1 square apart, allowing the PCs a chance to escape.

You could change the trigger to something active, such as a lever that an enemy might pull. This becomes even more interesting if the enemy is still engaged in the fight. Maybe the room has high walls but an open top. Then the villain and his allies can watch from above and attack the PCs, or the PCs can attempt to move out of the trap by going up.

For a double whammy, put the PCs up against this trap and a group of monsters that have phasing. The phasing creatures move into and out of the room through the crushing walls, taking advantage of the space behind the walls for refuge from attacks.

Giant Rolling Boulder	Level 14 Minion Blaster
Trap	XP 250

When tis trap is triggered, a huge rolling boulder is released and crashes through a false wall. It begins rolling down the hall, crushing everything in its path.

Trap: A trigger you define releases a distant boulder that begins rolling toward the trigger area, and it rolls until stopped.

Perception
✦ DC 23: A character near the distant false wall can determine that it is thin and that a large space is behind it.
✦ DC 28: A character realizes that the trigger is in tension and that setting it off releases something.

Initiative +2

Speed 8 (consider altering this based on the length of the roll and the PCs' speeds)

Trigger
The trigger might be an enemy pulling on a lever, a character pressing the wrong button, or someone taking the gem from a statue's eye. When the trap is triggered, roll initiative. On its initiative count, the boulder moves.

Attack
Standard Action | **Area** trample attack in squares
or Immediate Interrupt | entered by the boulder
Trample: Each turn, the boulder moves its speed and enters creatures' spaces. This movement does not provoke opportunity attacks. The boulder can end its move in an occupied space. Creatures in the boulder's space at the start of their turns have cover and can act normally. When the boulder enters a creature's space, the boulder makes a trample attack. If a creature enters a square of the boulder's space, the boulder makes a trample attack as a free action.
Trample Attack: +17 vs. Reflex
Hit: 3d10 + 6 damage, and the target is knocked prone.
Miss: Half damage.

Countermeasures
✦ A character adjacent to the rolling boulder can stop it with a DC 28 Athletics check. Making this attempt provokes a trample attack as an immediate interrupt, and the character's Athletics check fails if the boulder's trample attack hits.
✦ A character adjacent to the trigger (or the location from where the trigger is activated) can delay the trigger with a DC 23 Thievery check.
✦ A character adjacent to the boulder before it begins to roll can disable the trap with a DC 23 Thievery check. The character must have broken through the false wall first (AC 4, Fortitude 12, Reflex 4; hp 30).

Tactics

This trap is straightforward. The big boulder rolls down, crushing all in its wake. Consider how the boulder stops. Does it come crashing to a halt, smash through a wall into an unexplored room, roll up a ramp and reverse direction, or even go careening off a cliff to slam into structures far below? You can combine several boulder traps in a room that has ramps on either side, causing the boulders to roll back and forth across the room. A more complex room might contain boulders with crisscrossing paths, forcing creatures in the room to be constantly moving.

Death Strangler Statue	Level 16 Blaster
Trap	XP 1,400

This statue is of a masked humanoid holding wicked-looking spiked chains in each hand. When a creature approaches, it comes alive, lashing out with its chains.

Trap: When the trap is triggered, this Medium statue lashes its chains at nearby enemies, holding them in place and slowly squeezing the life out of them.

Perception
- ✦ DC 20: Just before a character enters the statue's attack area, the character notices that the statue moves slightly, as if it were ready to pounce.
- ✦ DC 25: The character notices a group of spidery runes carved lightly on the statue's base.

Additional Skill: Arcana
- ✦ DC 25: The character realizes that the statue is made with the help of magic, and it might be dangerous or even animate in nature.
- ✦ DC 28: An Arcana check to detect magic sees an arcane aura that surrounds the trap (5 squares in every direction) and recognizes that this might be a trigger area for an effect.

Trigger
When an enemy enters the magical aura radiating 5 squares around the statue, the statue animates and attacks that creature with the following attack, but as an immediate reaction instead of a standard action. Then roll for the statue's initiative. It acts each round on that turn, until no creature is within its trigger area.

Initiative +2

Attack ✦ Necrotic

Immediate Reaction   Melee 5
or **Standard Action**
or **Opportunity Action**
or **Free Action**

Target: One creature

Attack: +19 vs. Reflex

Hit: 1d10 + 7 damage, and the target is restrained and takes ongoing 10 necrotic damage.

Special: The statue can have only two creatures restrained at one time, and if two are restrained, it cannot make another attack until it releases a creature or a creature escapes. The statue can release a creature from being restrained at any time with a free action.

Countermeasures
- ✦ A restrained character can use an escape action (DC 25 check) to free himself and end the necrotic damage.
- ✦ As a standard action, a creature adjacent to the statue can disrupt the controlling enchantment with a DC 20 Thievery or Arcana check. Doing so renders the statue inert until the start of that creature's next turn and causes the statue to release any creatures it currently has restrained. If this check fails by 5 or more, the statue can instead make the above attack against the creature, but as an opportunity action instead of a standard action.
- ✦ Succeeding on a complexity 1 skill challenge (4 successes before 3 failures) using either Thievery or Arcana successfully disables the statue. The characters disabling the statue must be adjacent to it. Each attempt takes a standard action, and with each failure, the statue can make an attack as a free action against the failing creature (if it already has two creatures restrained, it releases one before making this attack).
- ✦ The statue has AC 10, Reflex 10, Fortitude 28, and hp 200. When it is reduced to 0 hit points, the trap is destroyed.

TOP TEN WAYS TO MAKE YOUR TRAPS MORE FUN

10. Reward the PCs with Treasure: Perhaps the last victim's skeleton is still impaled on the spear trap, including her belt pouch.

9. Reveal a World Detail: Perhaps the falling block from the ceiling reveals the ghoulish carving that represents the true deity of the temple.

8. Encounter the Trap Keeper: The PCs can discover hints about later traps (assuming the clever trap keeper doesn't figure out a way to deceive them).

7. Give an Adventure Tip: The iron portcullis that drops down to seal the PCs in the hall of spinning blades has a representation of the dungeon complex in the pattern of its iron bars. It's a map!

6. Give the Characters Something to Learn: If removing the green gem set off the statue's trap, stepping on the green mosaic in the floor sounded the alarm, and turning the green-handled crank made the bridge turn

sideways, the PCs might think twice about opening that giant green door.

5. Reveal a New Section of the Dungeon: The spiked pit might have an access tunnel so that bodies and valuables can be retrieved without a risky climb into the pit.

4. Team It with Other Traps: A trapped chest is a bit more interesting when it sits on the lap of a fire-breathing statue in a room where poison darts shoot from the wall.

3. Give the PCs Control: The PCs reset the trap and trick their foe into stepping into it.

2. Allow Every PC to Contribute: Maybe the wizard can make an Arcana check to reveal a panel hidden by an illusion. Perhaps the fighter can hold the trap open with a Strength check.

1. Combine It with Combat: A room with pit traps is more interesting if the PCs can push monsters into the pits.

TACTICS

These simple but effective guardians are often found in pairs next to a doorway or looming over a treasure trove. The trap has a glimmer of magically granted intelligence, and it is magically programmed with rudimentary self-preservation. When a creature tries to disable the trap, the death strangler statue typically lets go of other restrained creatures to attack the threat. This glimmer of intelligence also allows the statue to tell friend from foe.

SAMPLE ENCOUNTER

Typically placed by an evil leader or by a creature that values property or solitude, these traps can be accompanied by a number of monsters, but they work best with a mix of controllers, artillery, and even the occasional lurker or skirmisher.

Level 16 Encounter (XP 7,000)
- ✦ 1 bodak skulk (level 16 lurker; *Monster Manual*, page 36)
- ✦ 2 death strangler statues (level 16 blaster)
- ✦ 1 yuan-ti malison disciple of Zehir (level 17 controller; *Monster Manual*, page 270)
- ✦ 1 yuan-ti malison incanter (level 15 artillery; *Monster Manual*, page 269)

Elemental Tiles	Level 16 Obstacle
Trap	XP 1,400

The area is riddled with floor tiles that transform before your eyes. At times, each tile resembles stone that ripples like water; then it transforms to boiling ice. Later the tile dances with a flame-colored mist that crackles before it grows into spikes of lightning. Whatever these tiles are, they don't look stable.

Trap: Each of these traps has eight strategically placed tiles, and whenever a creature enters a tile space, it is attacked by a random form of elemental energy. Also, when creatures are in close proximity to the tiles, every so often a random tile erupts, spewing an area with hazardous elemental energy. This trap has two triggers and two attacks.

Perception
- ✦ No Perception check is needed to notice the tiles, because they are readily apparent.
- ✦ DC 25: The character notices a focus device located in an out-of-the-way place. The device likely controls the magic of the tiles.

Additional Skill: Arcana
- ✦ DC 25: The character realizes that the tiles are channeling the energy of the Elemental Chaos, and each does so in a dangerously unstable way.
- ✦ DC 30: The character recognizes the focus device as a *chaos stone*—the controlling focus for this type of trap—which can be overloaded with the right kind of attacks or through careful manipulation. Successful manipulation requires a character to use the same energy that the tiles spew during the round in which that character attempts to manipulate the focus device.

Trigger 1
A creature enters a square that contains an elemental tile. The trap then makes the following attack.

Attack ✦ Varies
Opportunity Action   Melee 1
Target: The creature that triggered the trap
Attack: +19 vs. Fortitude
Hit: 2d8 + 7 damage of a type determined by a d6 roll (1, acid; 2, cold; 3, fire; 4, force; 5, lightning; 6, thunder damage), and the target is slowed (save ends).

Trigger 2
Once enemy creatures are in the encounter area, roll initiative. On the trap's initiative count, a random elemental tile explodes with primordial energy, making the following attack.
Initiative +2

Attack ✦ Varies
Standard Action   Close burst 5
Target: Each creature in burst
Attack: +19 vs. Reflex
Hit: 1d10 + 7 damage of a type determined by a d6 roll (1, acid; 2, cold; 3, fire; 4, force; 5, lightning; 6, thunder damage), and the target is slowed (save ends). The burst creates a zone of difficult terrain until the end of the trap's next turn. The type of energy also determines the current vulnerabilities of the *chaos stone* (see Countermeasures).

Countermeasures
- ✦ Succeeding on a complexity 1 skill challenge (4 successes before 3 failures) using either Thievery or Arcana disables the trap. The characters disabling the elemental tiles must be adjacent to the *chaos stone* to make an attempt. Each attempt takes a standard action. On a failed check, all the tiles explode in the close burst attack.
- ✦ The *chaos stone* has AC 14, Reflex 14, Fortitude 28, and hp 100. When it is reduced to 0 hit points, the trap is destroyed. When the elemental tiles trap makes a close burst attack, its *chaos stone* focus is especially susceptible to the same kind of attack until the start of the trap's next turn. During that time, a successful attack against the *chaos stone* that deals the same type of damage as the trap's most recent attack automatically scores a critical hit on the *chaos stone*.

TACTICS

The placement of these tiles appears random, but cunning trapmakers have a method to the mad scattering. The tiles are placed to work well with powers that cause forced movement or that cut off flanking and other combat positioning options.

SAMPLE ENCOUNTER

These traps are found in the lairs of elemental creatures or demons, and they work well with those creatures due to their natural resistances to the damage types these unstable tiles spew forth.

Level 15 Encounter (XP 6,600)
- ✦ 2 earth titans (level 16 elite brute; *Monster Manual*, page 122)
- ✦ 1 elemental tiles trap (level 16 obstacle)
- ✦ 2 immoliths (level 15 controller; *Monster Manual*, page 56)

Wind rushes by and coalesces into a ghostly form that has roughly the shape of a large hunting cat. It attacks and then fades into nothingness.

Trap: A phantom hunter fades in and out of existence, and it attacks creatures within a defined area that is normally no larger than an 8-by-8-square section.

Perception
- ✦ DC 20: The character notices that the shadows play strangely in the area, as if ghostly figures move within it.
- ✦ DC 25: The character notices a strange totem tucked away in the area.

Additional Skill: Arcana
- ✦ DC 29: After the characters spot the totem, an Arcana check to detect magic determines that it courses with primal power.

Trigger
When an enemy enters the trap area, the phantom hunter makes the following two attacks on initiative counts 25 and 20. If an enemy is currently adjacent to the trap's focus totem or holding it, the phantom hunter attacks that creature instead of attacking a random enemy.

Attack 1
Standard Action   **Melee** 1
Special: This attack recharges on a roll of 6 on a d6. The phantom hunter uses this attack first during an encounter. Then, on each of the trap's subsequent turns, make a recharge roll before the attack. If the recharge is successful, it uses this attack instead of the one noted below.
Target: One creature
Attack: +23 vs. AC
Hit: 3d8 + 7 damage, and the target is weakened and slowed (save ends both).

Attack 2
Standard Action   **Melee** 1
Target: One creature
Attack: +23 vs. AC
Hit: 2d8 + 7 damage.

Countermeasures
- ✦ Succeeding on a complexity 1 skill challenge (4 successes before 3 failures) using either Nature or Arcana on the totem disables the trap. The characters disabling the phantom hunter must be holding the totem. Each attempt takes a standard action. If the skill challenge results in failure, the totem explodes, making the following attack.

   Immediate Reaction   **Close** burst 5
   Target: Each creature in burst
   Attack: +21 vs. Reflex
   Hit: 3d8 + 7 damage.
- ✦ The phantom hunter does not attack anywhere outside the trap area, unless the totem is taken outside the area. If the latter is true, the phantom hunter attacks only a creature standing adjacent to the totem or holding it.

TACTICS

Both the haunting nature of the phantom hunter and its connection to an area make it optimal for guarding places that have treasure, to protect areas where rituals are performed, or to defend devices and spots of major importance. Craftier trap setters might have the totem focus readily displayed, tempting those trained in Nature or Arcana to attempt to disable it,

knowing that the phantom hunter will harry them until the task is complete.

SAMPLE ENCOUNTER

Dragons and other powerful creatures that have hoards, or those with cluttered lairs, use these traps to guard themselves and their treasures.

Level 20 Encounter (XP 15,400)
- ✦ 1 elder green dragon (level 19 solo controller; *Monster Manual*, page 80)
- ✦ 1 phantom hunter trap (level 18 lurker)
- ✦ 4 ogre bludgeoneers (level 16 minion; *Monster Manual*, page 198)

This highly complicated vault's lock looks like it's a pain to pick . . . and it is, in more ways than one.

Trap: This complex lock takes a skill challenge to unlock, and each wrong move has dire consequences for those attempting to open it as well as those nearby.

Perception
- ✦ No check is necessary to notice that this is a complicated vault-style lock, with numerous devices that need to be picked or disabled before the door can be opened.
- ✦ DC 22: The character notices that some of the lock's devices are adorned with magical runes.

Additional Skill: Thievery
- ✦ DC 22: Six separate locks need to be disabled in the right order before the door can be opened.

Additional Skill: Arcana
- ✦ DC 27: Once the runes are spotted, they can be identified as Abyssal symbols of pain, terror, and death.

Trigger
The trap is a complexity 2 skill challenge (6 successes before 3 failures) that requires a DC 22 Thievery check for each success. With each failed check, the trap makes the following attack. Each attempt to disable a lock takes a standard action. With each success or failure, another attempt to disable a lock must be made before the end of the attempting creature's next turn, or a failure in the challenge is accrued. On the third failure all the locks reset, requiring the skill challenge to be performed anew, but ending the immediate threat.

Attack ✦ Necrotic, Psychic
Immediate Reaction   **Close** blast 5
Target: Each creature in blast
Attack: +21 vs. Fortitude
Hit: 2d6 + 7 necrotic damage, and the target takes ongoing 10 psychic damage and a -2 penalty to ability checks and skill checks (save ends both).

Countermeasures
- ✦ A character can ready a standard action to make a DC 22 Arcana check when someone fails a Thievery check during the skill challenge to open the pain vault. On a successful Arcana check, the failure in the challenge is still accrued, but the succeeding character negates the blast attack.
- ✦ The lock has AC 20, Reflex 20, Fortitude 25, and hp 400. If it is destroyed, the trap is disabled.

TACTICS

Simple, versatile, and effective, the pain vault is a great way to keep intruders away from valuables and sensitive areas. Creatures create or modify a pain vault with triggers that warn nearby monsters or guards when someone fails the first attempt in a skill challenge, which increases the danger at the most inopportune time.

SAMPLE ENCOUNTER

Controllers and soldiers typically guard a pain vault because their control over movement makes the trap's debilitating blast hard to avoid.

Level 21 Encounter (XP 17,600)

✦ 1 death priest hierophant (level 21 elite controller; *Monster Manual*, page 209)
✦ 1 pain vault trap (level 20 warder)
✦ 3 rot harbingers (level 20 soldier; *Monster Manual*, page 223)

Life Eater Haze	Level 22 Obstacle
Hazard	XP 4,150

With a violent hiss, billows of blue-tinged purple gas fill the room. Each gasp of the vile stuff drains your strength and saps your life essence.

Hazard: This strange gas steals the life from those within it.
Perception
✦ It takes no check to see the gas.
Additional Skill: Arcana
✦ DC 24: The character recognizes the life-draining traits of the haze.
Trigger
When a living creature starts its turn in the gas, the gas makes the following attack.
Attack ✦ Necrotic, Poison
Opportunity Action   Area the entire room
Target: Each living creature that starts its turn in the gas
Attack: +23 vs. Fortitude
Hit: 1d10 + 6 poison damage, and ongoing 10 necrotic damage (save ends). *First Failed Saving Throw:* The ongoing damage increases to 15 necrotic. *Second Failed Saving Throw:* The target loses a healing surge.
Countermeasures
✦ Making a close or an area attack that has the radiant keyword nullifies the haze in the affected squares until the end of the attacker's next turn (or, in the case of a zone, until the zone ends). Those who start their turns in nullified areas are not attacked.

TACTICS

Undead use these hazards to obscure places of power and treasure troves because of the obstacle's ability to deal damage to the living. A lich might hide its phylactery in a large field of these mists.

Sample Encounter

Undead lurk within these strange purple mists.

Level 22 Encounter (XP 22,650)

+ 4 abyssal ghoul myrmidons (level 23 minion; *Monster Manual*, page 119)
+ 1 giant mummy (level 21 brute; *Monster Manual*, page 193)
+ 1 life eater haze trap (level 22 obstacle)
+ 2 voidsoul specters (level 23 lurker; *Monster Manual*, page 244)

Far Realm Star Trap	Level 26 Elite Blaster
Trap	XP 18,000

Light bends strangely in the room due to dimensional distortion. Motes that resemble starlight bob up and down in six places throughout the area.

Trap: When a creature enters a square that has a mote of starlight, that light attaches itself to the creature and begins to burn. Each round, another mote is drawn to the afflicted creature; when all six motes are on the creature, the motes explode.

Perception

+ No Perception check is needed to notice the motes, unless they are hidden.

Additional Skill: Arcana

+ DC 26: The character identifies the nature of the starlight motes, and realizes that if all six latch on to the same creature, they'll explode.

Trigger

When a creature enters a square with a mote in it or starts its turn there, the mote makes the following attack. If the attack is successful, the starlight mote latches on. At the start of a creature's turn, if it has at least one mote upon it, the nearest mote moves to enter the creature's space and makes the same attack, attempting to latch on to that creature.

Attack ✦ Radiant

Opportunity Action   **Melee** 1

Target: One creature

Attack: +31 vs. Reflex

Hit: 1d8 + 9 radiant damage, and the mote latches on to the target. While a mote is latched on to a creature, that creature is dazed, and at the start of its turn it takes 1d8 + 9 radiant damage. The mote is removed when it is destroyed (see Countermeasures) or when the target or a creature adjacent to the target succeeds on a DC 20 Athletics check to pull the mote off the target. A mote that is pulled off occupies the target's square, but for every 5 points by which the check result exceeds 20, the creature removing the mote can push the mote 1 square.

Secondary Trigger

When all six star motes latch on to the same creature, they make the following attack.

Opportunity Action   **Close** blast 5

Target: Each creature in blast

Attack: +31 vs. Reflex

Hit: 4d8 + 10 radiant damage, and the target is knocked prone.

Miss: Half damage.

Effect: All the motes are destroyed.

Countermeasures

+ The starlight motes are bound to a particular location, and while that location can be somewhat large, the motes do not pass its boundaries. If a creature with attached motes leaves the area, the motes unlatch at the boundary.
+ A DC 31 Arcana check made as a standard action by a creature sharing the same space with a mote or adjacent to one can calm it for a short time. With a success, the mote unlatches from a creature (if it is attached) and does not move or attack until the end of the next turn of the creature that succeeded on the check.
+ Each mote has AC 33, Reflex 33, Fortitude 30, hp 75, and immune radiant. While attached to a creature, a mote gains a +5 bonus to AC and Reflex.

Tactics

Defeating a Far Realm star trap forces the PCs to split up, take damage, and keep the starlight motes apart. Evil creatures place this trap in areas guarded by lurkers and artillery creatures, where splitting up enemies is optimal.

Sample Encounter

These traps work best with controllers and soldiers that can force movement into the starlight motes, or limit the range of movements and actions, making the motes more dangerous. Since they are things of the Far Realm, they commonly are encountered with creatures from beyond the boundaries of the known universe.

Level 28 Encounter (XP 73,000)

+ 1 Far Realm star trap (level 26 elite blaster)
+ 1 gibbering orb (level 27 solo controller; *Monster Manual*, page 127)

Maddening Mural	Level 29 Warder
Trap	XP 15,000

A seemingly normal landscape is carved into the wall, but the more you look at it, the more you spot strange details. Images of vegetation hide eyes, mouths, and claws, and the shapes themselves start to twist into horrid monstrosities that reach out from the mural, lashing at your sanity.

Trap: This strange painting threatens the sanity of those who wander too close.

Perception

+ No check is needed to notice the painting.
+ DC 19: A character more than 10 squares away sees that the images in the painting twist and writhe. Something is definitely strange about the painting.

Additional Skill: Arcana

+ DC 33: The character identifies the painting as a maddening mural and knows the risks of getting too close to it.

Trigger

The trap is triggered when an enemy ends its turn within 10 squares of the painting. The trap's psychic attack then lashes out at the creature in an attempt to snare and devour its sanity.

Attack ✦ Psychic

Opportunity Action   **Ranged** 10

Target: The creature that triggered the trap

Attack: +32 vs. Will

Hit: 2d8 + 10 psychic damage, and the target's sanity is entrapped within the painting. While the target's sanity is entrapped, the target is dazed and slowed and can spend actions in only the following three ways:

Stumble Away (Move Action): The entrapped creature cannot run.

Fight the Painting (Standard Action): The entrapped creature can make any at-will attack against the painting. The attack deals damage to the painting's physical statistics (see Countermeasures).

Free Itself (Standard Action): A DC 19 Intelligence, Wisdom, or Charisma check frees the creature from the entrapment. When a creature frees itself from the prison, it is still dazed until the start of its next turn.

Countermeasures

✦ An entrapped character who is trained in Arcana or Thievery can use a standard action to attempt to disable the painting. A DC 28 success with Arcana or Thievery gains 1 success on a complexity 1 skill challenge (4 successes before 3 failures). After 4 successes, the painting is disabled. After 3 failures, each entrapped character takes 3d8 +10 psychic damage, and the skill challenge must be started again.

✦ The painting can be attacked. It has AC 20, Reflex 20, Fortitude 30, and hp 300.

TACTICS

Frequently used by the insane or depraved, these paintings are typically placed in grand audience halls or despicable temples. Since it attacks only the enemies of its maker, the painting allows skirmishers and soldiers to position themselves with debilitating effect, and brutes to strike with impunity.

SAMPLE ENCOUNTER

Because this trap is ideal for controlling large areas of the battlefield, it works well with groups that lack a controller. Its strange and disturbing nature lends itself well to the lairs of depraved cults, undead tyrants, devils, and Far Realm monstrosities.

Level 30 Encounter (XP 96,000)

✦ 1 atropal (level 28 elite brute; *Monster Manual*, page 11)

✦ 1 maddening mural trap (level 29 warder)

✦ 5 sorrowsworn reapers (level 27 soldier; *Monster Manual*, page 242)

PULLING IT ALL TOGETHER

A well-crafted combat encounter combines disparate elements—monsters, terrain, traps and hazards, skill checks and challenges, interesting objectives, and atmospheric setting—to create an exciting tactical challenge for the players and their characters. An encounter that features lots of movement, plenty of tough decisions, and abundant opportunities to use clever tactics is a dynamic and entertaining scene in the ongoing story of your game. The final section of this chapter presents a single encounter built using some of the new elements introduced in the preceding pages.

THE PORTAL RITUAL

Encounter Level 14 (5,400 XP)

3 bearded devils (B)
2 chain devils (C)
4 loathsome chanters (L)
Crushing walls room trap
Legion devil hellguards

SETUP

Devils are performing a ritual that will create a yawning portal to the depths of the Nine Hells. They have chosen to perform this ritual in a chamber in the middle of a bustling city in the world. The characters' objective is to interrupt the ritual before the devils complete it. See the Tactics section for more information about what these devils do during the encounter.

When the characters open the door, read:
A low sound like a religious chant drones in your ears as you open the door. A hideous, squat creature draped in a mockery of vestments and emblazoned with the symbol of Asmodeus stands near a smoking brazier. Its open mouth is clearly one source of the chanting you hear. A horrible devil with a beard made of twisting snakes clutches a glaive and snarls at you.

Religion Check
DC 16 *The creature you see chanting is likely one of four. You must destroy all four to interrupt the ritual.*

Perception Check
DC 16 *You hear three other voices chanting—one coming from each passageway leading out of this room.*
DC 21 *The smoke rising from the brazier is dark gray, but it glows with its own inner fire. It drifts in a coherent cloud, though no breeze stirs the air in the room.*

3 Bearded Devils (B)   Level 13 Soldier
Medium immortal humanoid (devil)   XP 800 each

Initiative +10   **Senses** Perception +14; darkvision
Beard Tendrils aura 1; enemies that begin their turns adjacent to
the bearded devil take 5 damage.
HP 129; **Bloodied** 64; see also *battle frenzy*
AC 29; **Fortitude** 25, **Reflex** 22, **Will** 23
Resist 20 fire
Speed 6
⊕ **Glaive** (standard; at-will) ✦ **Weapon**
Reach 2; +18 vs. AC; 2d4 + 5 damage, and the target is marked
until the end of the bearded devil's next turn and takes ongoing
5 damage (save ends).
↓ **Claw** (standard; at-will)
+18 vs. AC; 1d6 + 5 damage.
Battle Frenzy
While the bearded devil is bloodied, it gains a +2 bonus to
attack rolls and deals an extra 5 damage with its melee attacks.
Devilish Teamwork
Allies adjacent to the bearded devil gain a +2 power bonus to
AC.
Alignment Evil   **Languages** Supernal
Skills Intimidate +11
Str 20 (+11)   **Dex** 15 (+8)   **Wis** 16 (+9)
Con 17 (+9)   **Int** 10 (+6)   **Cha** 11 (+6)
Equipment glaive

2 Chain Devils (Kyton) (C)   Level 11 Skirmisher
Medium immortal humanoid (devil)   XP 600 each

Initiative +14   **Senses** Perception +7; darkvision
HP 116; **Bloodied** 58
AC 25; **Fortitude** 22, **Reflex** 24, **Will** 19
Resist 20 fire
Speed 7; see also *dance of battle*
⊕ **Spiked Chain** (standard; at-will)
Reach 2; +16 vs. AC; 2d4 + 7 damage.
↓ **Double Attack** (standard; at-will)
The chain devil makes two spiked chain attacks.
↓ **Chains of Vengeance** (free, when first bloodied; encounter)
The chain devil makes two spiked chain attacks.
↓ **Hellish Chains** (standard; at-will)
+14 vs. Reflex; the target is wrapped in chains and restrained
(save ends). The chain devil can use its chains to restrain only
one creature at a time.
Dance of Battle (minor; at-will)
The chain devil shifts 1 square.
Dance of Defiance (immediate interrupt, when a melee attack
is made against the chain devil; recharges after the chain devil
uses *chains of vengeance*)
The chain devil shifts 1 square.
Alignment Evil   **Languages** Supernal
Skills Intimidate +11
Str 19 (+9)   **Dex** 24 (+12)   **Wis** 15 (+7)
Con 20 (+10)   **Int** 14 (+7)   **Cha** 13 (+6)

4 Loathsome Chanters (L)   Level 11 Minion
Medium immortal humanoid (devil)   XP 150 each

Initiative +6   **Senses** Perception +6; darkvision
HP 1; a missed attack never damages a minion.
AC 27; **Fortitude** 23, **Reflex** 22, **Will** 22
Resist 10 fire, 10 poison
Speed 6, teleport 3
⊕ **Claw** (standard; at-will)
+16 vs. AC; 6 damage.
⤦ **Death's Rebuke** (when reduced to 0 hit points) ✦ **Psychic**
Close burst 2; targets enemies; +14 vs. Will; 6 psychic damage.
Alignment Evil   **Languages** Supernal
Str 14 (+7)   **Dex** 12 (+6)   **Wis** 12 (+6)
Con 14 (+7)   **Int** 10 (+5)   **Cha** 12 (+6)

Legion Devil Hellguards   Level 11 Minion
Medium immortal humanoid (devil)   XP 150 each

Initiative +6   **Senses** Perception +6; darkvision
HP 1; a missed attack never damages a minion.
AC 27; **Fortitude** 23, **Reflex** 22, **Will** 22; see also *squad defense*
Resist 10 fire
Speed 6, teleport 3
⊕ **Longsword** (standard; at-will) ✦ **Weapon**
+16 vs. AC; 6 damage.
Squad Defense
The legion devil hellguard gains a +2 bonus to its defenses when
adjacent to at least one other legion devil.
Alignment Evil   **Languages** Supernal
Str 14 (+7)   **Dex** 12 (+6)   **Wis** 12 (+6)
Con 14 (+7)   **Int** 10 (+5)   **Cha** 12 (+6)
Equipment plate armor, heavy shield, longsword

TACTICS

The bearded, chain, and legion devils interpose
themselves between the PCs and the loathsome
chanters, using all their powers to prevent the ritual
from being disrupted.

The loathsome chanters (minion devils whose sole
purpose is to chant the words of the ritual) must use
a total of sixteen standard actions over the course of
the encounter to complete the ritual. For every four
actions they complete, four legion devil hellguards
arrive in the large entry room to help fight off the
player characters. If the chanters complete the ritual,
the portal is established and the characters must then
deal with the consequences.

FEATURES OF THE AREA

Illumination: Each brazier gives off bright light
in a radius of 10 squares, which is sufficient to illuminate the entire area as long as the loathsome chanters
remain alive.

Braziers: The four braziers the chanters are using
in the ritual produce infernal fumes (page 60). When
the encounter begins, each brazier is surrounded by
a cloud of infernal fumes in a burst 1. Squares filled
with infernal fumes are lightly obscured. The fumes
can move up to 4 squares each round. A creature that
ends its turn in a square of infernal fumes takes 5 fire

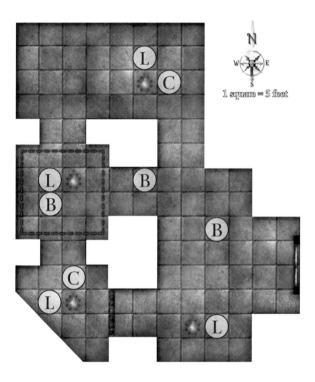

1 square = 5 feet

Infernal Brazier	Single-Use Terrain

These heavy brass braziers smoke with noxious fumes. What's burning in there, anyway?

Standard Action
Requirement: You must be adjacent to the brazier.
Check: Athletics check (DC 23) to push over the brazier.
Success: The brazier spills its contents.
Target: Each creature in a close blast 3 from the brazier
Attack: +16 vs. Reflex
Hit: Ongoing 10 fire and poison damage (save ends).

When a loathsome chanter is killed, its brazier is extinguished and the cloud of infernal fumes associated with that brazier dissipates.

Crushing Walls Room Trap: See page 68 for details of this trap. When the loathsome chanter in the small square room is killed, the trap is activated: Iron doors slam down over all three exits from the room, and the ceiling begins to descend. The room is 4 squares high, and the ceiling moves 1 square per round.

A LONG FIGHT

With a few tweaks, you can turn this encounter into a long encounter with multiple waves of enemies, using some of the suggestions from the "Long Fights" sidebar on page 55.

Instead of legion devil hellguards joining the encounter, add more bearded devils, chain devils, or other devils (the erinyes, gorechain devil, and misfortune devil from *Monster Manual 2* are all of an appropriate level) with every four actions the chanters complete. Create a second encounter and add half of it to the ongoing encounter for every four actions completed. For example, two gorechain devils and two erinyes together form a level 13 encounter (4,400 XP). With every four actions the chanters complete, then, one of each kind of devil appears in the room.

When all four loathsome chanters are killed, the characters can all spend a healing surge and regain the use of one expended encounter power, as a sign of their gods' favor resting upon them.

and poison damage per tier and is dazed until the end of its next turn.

The loathsome chanters are not affected by the damage caused by the fumes, but they are dazed as long as the fumes remain in place around the braziers. However, as soon as more creatures enter the room, the fumes begin to move. Each cloud remains a burst 1 (3 squares by 3 squares) as it drifts through the area. The clouds stay within the confines of their separate rooms.

A character adjacent to a brazier can use it as a weapon, using an Athletics check to gain access to its terrain power. (The chanters can't be damaged by a tipped-over brazier, but the other devils can be.)

DYNAMIC ENCOUNTERS

In addition to trying to make every encounter have some tidbit of story behind it, I'm also learning how to create more dynamic encounters. This is something I've observed from the way Chris Perkins runs his game. There's almost always some kind of twist, surprise, or dynamic element of the encounter. Sometimes it's subtle—after all, if you introduce a surprise every time, it makes each surprise less significant. It could be a trap that springs mid-battle, or a creature that calls another creature to its aid, or the terrain could turn out to be a dangerous slime that grasps at your feet.

Forcing the PCs to adapt to different situations and circumstances encourages them to think outside the box, which in the end, makes the payoff much greater. Providing

subtleties that characters can use to their advantage gives a sense of satisfaction when a player picks up on that detail, and it encourages all the players to pay closer attention to what's going on. Maybe this isn't the best kind of encounter for the hack-and-slash player, but even the hack-and-slash player can enjoy the encounter when he takes advantage of a giant chasm into which he pushes an enemy. These days, I'm thinking about upcoming battles weeks in advance, brainstorming ideas when I'm driving my car or going to bed, trying to think of the next best way to bring originality to an encounter.

–Greg Bilsland, originally posted on Wizards.com staff blogs

CHAPTER 3

SKILL CHALLENGES

SKILL CHALLENGES are a versatile tool in your DM's toolbox, well suited to modeling a wide variety of tasks the player characters might undertake in the course of an adventure. From disabling a complex trap to negotiating peace between warring nations, skill challenges take complex activities and structure them into a simple framework of skill checks. They should never replace the roleplaying, puzzling, and ingenuity that go into players' approach to those situations, but they place that effort into a defined rules structure so you can more easily adjudicate them and players can more easily understand the options available to them.

This chapter supplements the material in the *Dungeon Master's Guide* that introduces the rules for skill challenges. The start of the chapter repeats the fundamental rules for creating and running skill challenges, since they've been updated since the first printing of the *DMG*. From there, the chapter continues with lengthy advice for creating skill challenges that are engaging and exciting for every player at the table.

Here's the content of the chapter in a nutshell:

✦ **Skill Challenge Basics:** The basic rules for skill challenges, updated and all in one place, along with an example of a challenge in play and a discussion of ground rules for creating a compelling skill challenge.

✦ **Skill Challenges in Depth:** This section highlights five key elements of successful skill challenges: time frames, allowing a variety of options, preparing for failure, progressive challenges, and branching challenges.

✦ **Skill Challenge Examples:** A series of examples round out the chapter.

Some of the material in this chapter originally appeared in the virtual pages of *Dungeon Magazine* at www.dndinsider.com. "Ruling Skill Challenges" is a regular feature in *Dungeon*, highlighting advice and examples for DMs wanting to make better use of skill challenges in their games.

VINCENT DUTRAIT

The *Dungeon Master's Guide* lays out the basic rules for skill challenges. This page includes a quick-reference summary of those rules, since they have been updated and clarified.

THE SKILL CHALLENGE FRAMEWORK

To deal with a skill challenge, the player characters make skill checks to accumulate a number of successful skill uses before they rack up 3 failures.

The complexity of a skill challenge determines the number of successful checks the characters must accumulate before failing three checks. In combination with the challenge's level, it also determines how hard the challenge is for the characters to overcome and the XP award they receive for completing it.

SKILL CHALLENGE COMPLEXITY

Complexity	Successes	Failures
1	4	3
2	6	3
3	8	3
4	10	3
5	12	3

A skill challenge's level determines the DC of the skill checks involved. As a general rule, set the challenge's level to the same level as the player characters, and set most of the DCs in the challenge to moderate difficulty. If you use mostly easy DCs, you're probably creating a lower-level challenge, and if you use mostly hard DCs, you're creating a higher-level challenge.

SKILL CHECK DIFFICULTY CLASS BY LEVEL

Level	Easy	Moderate	Hard
1st–3rd	5	10	15
4th–6th	7	12	17
7th–9th	8	14	19
10th–12th	10	16	21
13th–15th	11	18	23
16th–18th	13	20	25
19th–21st	14	22	27
22nd–24th	16	24	29
25th–27th	17	26	31
28th–30th	19	28	33

SKILLS IN A CHALLENGE

When you're planning a skill challenge, think of ways that characters might use skills to achieve the goal of the challenge. Try to come up with as many as seven useful skills (either primary or secondary)—or about as many skills as there are characters in your party, plus two. Know what skills your player characters are trained in, and feature those skills heavily in the challenge. If you use skills the PCs aren't trained in, assign easy DCs. See "Allow a Variety of Options" on page 85 for more about selecting skills.

Primary skills contribute directly to the characters' count of successes in the challenge. They should be the skills most directly and obviously related to achieving the goal of the challenge. Secondary skills are useful in the challenge, but don't always count for successes. See "Primary and Secondary Skills" on page 85 for more information.

A good skill challenge also allows for other actions outside the framework of the skill system to contribute to the party's success. Spending money, using powers or action points, combat encounters, rituals, and the simple passage of time can contribute successes or do any of the things that secondary skill checks can accomplish.

CONSEQUENCES

Whether characters succeed or fail at the skill challenge, the adventure must go on. Of course, there should be consequences for failing the challenge, but those consequences can't bring the adventure to a halt. Penalties for failure in a skill challenge might include the loss of healing surges or some other lingering penalty, making a later encounter more difficult. See "Prepare for Failure" on page 86 for more about the consequences of failure.

When characters succeed on a skill challenge, they receive experience points as though they had defeated a number of monsters of the challenge's level equal to the challenge's complexity. For example, if characters successfully complete a 7th-level challenge with a complexity of 1, they receive 300 XP (the award for a single 7th-level monster). If they complete a 7th-level challenge with a complexity of 5, they receive 1,500 XP (the award for five such monsters).

In addition to XP, characters might earn rewards specific to the challenge (which might simply boil down to the adventure continuing smoothly). They could also gain one or more treasure parcels, bonuses or advantages in future encounters, or information useful later in the campaign.

EXAMPLE OF PLAY

This example shows a DM running "Hunting the Mastermind" (page 90) for five PCs: Aelar (an elf ranger), Baredd (a human paladin), Chenna (a halfling bard), Donn (a human invoker), and Eglath (a goliath warden).

DM: You're left with the last misty remnants of the demonic creature's corpse and a handful of

frightened witnesses. "What was that thing," some-one asks, "and where did it come from?"

Donn: Can I make an Arcana check to see if I know anything about it?

DM: Sure.

Donn: I got a 14.

DM (marking down a success for the characters): OK, you know that the creature was some sort of demon, not native to the world. It was probably summoned here.

Aelar: Can I look around and see if I can tell which way it came?

DM: Sure, make a Perception check.

Aelar: With my keen elven eyes, I get a 17.

DM (marking a second success): Yes, you see a weird-looking tuft of fur that it left behind, but when you breathe on it, it dissolves into mist.

Chenna: I'd like to talk to the bystanders, and see if any of them know where it came from. How about a Diplomacy check—a 13.

DM (marking a third success): Well, everyone here knows about as much as you do about where it came from—they point to the door it came in through. But one woman was standing near the door when it came in—she was the first to raise the alarm—and she says that she heard it whispering as it approached. Something about hunting for "the five."

Baredd: The five? Like it was hunting for the five of us?

DM: Maybe. Make an Insight check.

Baredd: Ugh, only a 10.

DM (marking a fourth success): Good enough. It's looking like someone summoned this thing to hunt for you, and maybe you can follow its trail back to whoever summoned it.

Aelar: Well, then I'll keep searching and see if I can find that trail.

Eglath: I've got a good Perception, too. I'll assist.

DM: OK, another Perception check?

Aelar: Only a 13.

Eglath: You get +2 from me.

DM (marking a fifth success): OK, you head down the stairs in the direction the thing came from, and it looks like the trail's gone cold. But then Eglath points out a pair of feet sticking out from a dark corner—maybe another one of the demon's victims.

Chenna: Surely more people saw it come this way, then. Can I use Streetwise to find out?

DM: Sure.

Chenna: Oh no! A 1! Well, that gives me a 9.

DM (marking down the group's first failure): Well, you find some people to ask—unfortunately, they're a group of thieves in the middle of a crime, and they're not too happy about being interrupted. Why don't you all roll initiative?

A quick combat encounter with a group of halfling thieves interrupts the challenge briefly, but it continues along these lines when the combat is over, with all characters contributing their strengths to the completion of the challenge.

Ground Rules

A skill challenge is fundamentally a kind of encounter, much like a combat encounter. Follow these guidelines to create a skill challenge that's every bit as exciting, engaging, and dangerous to the characters as a combat encounter.

1. Like combat encounters, skill challenges work best when you and the players want one to happen.

Let's say you designed a combat encounter for your next adventure. The characters need to cross a bridge, and there's a big, hungry troll in their way. Time for a fight!

That is, unless the players decide to sneak around the troll or bribe it with a cask of fine ale. A good DM knows that sometimes it's best to take the party's crazy plan and run with it, especially if the players back up their ideas with a few rolls of 20 on Stealth or Diplomacy checks. A good DM thinks on his feet and rewards clever, interesting ideas.

The same logic applies to skill challenges. Is there a chance that a really good idea could completely trump your skill challenge? Don't fret! That's a good thing. D&D is a game about creativity and imagination. If there's only one specific, scripted path to success, you've lost what makes D&D fun. When you build a skill challenge, be prepared for it to head in a direction you didn't anticipate or for the party to fail utterly. That way, the game moves on regardless of what happens with the challenge.

2. As in a combat encounter, if standing in one place and doing the same thing over and over again is the best plan, you need to go back to the drawing board.

A skill challenge is a lot more than a fancy extended skill check. The best ones embrace improvisation and a broad range of skills and abilities. Let's say the characters are trapped in a dungeon when the exit collapses. Is digging their way out a skill challenge?

At first blush, the answer seems like yes. The party has to work as a group to clear the rubble. Athletics and Dungeoneering seem like the perfect skills to measure the PCs' success. Yet in play, such a skill challenge is boring. The characters who excel at those skills make their checks while everyone else hangs back, reluctant to make their own checks because they don't want to be the reason that the group fails the challenge. If your potential skill challenge has a similar bottleneck—in which only one skill does the heavy lifting for the challenge—you need to rethink the challenge.

3. As in a combat encounter, a variety of options makes a skill challenge compelling.

The *DMG* tells you to mix up artillery, soldiers, and the other monster roles in your combat encounters. A mix of beasties makes for a fun fight because it varies the challenge and lets you throw a broad array of abilities at the PCs. Every character has a chance to shine, and the party has to act as a team to answer each threat the monsters pose. Everyone has the same basic goal (blast the monsters), but each character achieves that goal in different ways.

This piece of advice is similar to the second rule, but there's an important distinction here. It isn't enough to pick a wide variety of skills. You need to create a broad range of subchallenges and obstacles within a challenge. A good skill challenge consists of a number of different incremental tasks that combine for a fun encounter. It isn't enough to pull different skills into the challenge. The players should feel as though their characters have a lot of options and important decisions. Otherwise, a skill challenge turns into a boring series of die rolls.

4. Unlike a combat encounter, a skill challenge can cover hours or even days of progress.

Think about how long it should take the party to resolve the skill challenge. If your answer can be measured in minutes, you might be looking at a simple skill check. When you design a skill challenge to cover a day or a week of effort, you open it up to a wide variety of individual hurdles within the challenge as a whole and a broader range of skills.

In the example on the previous page, the dialogue was compressed for the sake of brevity. When this skill challenge plays out in the context of the larger adventure it's a part of, each check making up the challenge might be separated from the others by hours of game time. Only after extended effort over a period of time—interspersed with other activities—do the characters succeed at what they set out to do; the rest of the action in the game world doesn't grind to a halt until the challenge is over.

The time factor is easy to overlook in designing a skill challenge, and that's an error that can turn a compelling challenge into a rote series of die rolls. You know you've lost your group and messed up your design when the players are doing anything but playing the game. The best insurance against this problem lies in spreading a challenge out over multiple scenes, each allowing a different, general approach to the problem. By varying the environment and situation, you keep things fresh even when the group uses the same skills. There's a world of difference between the Diplomacy check against a drunken guard who mistakes the party's half-orc fighter for his best friend and the same check against the nosy shopkeeper who tries to shake down the PCs for a bribe. If you back up each scene with good roleplay and descriptions, the simplest skill challenge becomes an interesting, varied experience.

Extending a skill challenge over a span of time has an important benefit: It lets you plausibly impose radical changes to the challenge without straining the players' suspension of disbelief. For instance, it's ludicrous for the party to run into a long chain of NPCs, each requiring a different skill check to handle, during a 15-minute visit to the local pub. However, if the characters meet those NPCs during an entire day of scouring a city for information, the game makes a lot more sense.

Here are two rules that are related to rule 4. They arise when you embrace the idea of a skill challenge as working on a different time scale compared to a fight.

4a. Each skill check in a challenge should accomplish one of the following goals:

✦ Introduce a new option that the PCs can pursue, a path to success they didn't know existed.

✦ Change the situation, such as by sending the PCs to a new location, introducing a new NPC, or adding a complication.

✦ Grant the players a tangible consequence for the check's success or failure (as appropriate), one that influences their subsequent decisions.

If you think about it, the same situation applies in a battle. If the wizard fries the orc warriors with his *fireball*, the rogue sneaks over to the orc shaman and attacks him rather than leaping to help the fighter. During a combat encounter, the actions taken by each character and monster set the stage for the next person's turn. In a good combat encounter, the situation constantly changes. The same thing applies to skill challenges. The best challenges are those that you can adjust as you react to the players' decisions.

4b. The characters should always be the active party in a skill challenge.

This is a subtle point, but one that can spell the difference between success and failure. Placing the characters into the role of the aggressor means pushing your NPCs into a passive role as blockers, people who stand between the PCs and success and forcing the characters to serve as the catalysts for action. As with a lot of gaming advice, that sounds simple, but implementing it can be tough. It's best illustrated with an example.

The characters need to escape from a group of pursuers. It's easy to default to have the PCs making Endurance or Athletics checks to see if they can stay ahead of the chase, but that situation pushes them into a passive role. The guards are the active party: They chase the PCs, and the PCs make checks to avoid capture.

Instead, set up the challenge so that the PCs are the aggressors. They should make checks to foil the pursuit, such as by throwing obstacles in the guards' way, taking a path that discourages pursuit (climbing up a building and running across the rooftops), sparking a brawl between two gangs, or starting a fire that serves as a distraction.

In this example, you might allow PCs to make checks to outrun the guards, but that should be one option among many. Even then, it's best to flavor that option with a sense that the PCs are the ones creating obstacles that the guards can't overcome. An Athletics check doesn't mean the PC is simply running really fast. Instead, it represents a character dodging through a crowded street with ease while the guards struggle to push through.

Placing characters in the active role has an important effect on your design, your presentation, and the players' engagement. It forces the players to step up and make plans rather than sit back and react to your NPCs. It also compels you to create multiple paths and options. When the PCs are the passive group in a challenge, it's too easy to allow logic to dictate that one repeated skill check is the best way to plow through the challenge.

ALTERNATIVES TO SKILL CHALLENGES

If a skill challenge isn't the right tool for the job, you can use other mechanics to bring skills to bear in specific situations.

A group check can be an effective way to resolve a situation when everyone is making checks using the same skill. For example, if your party is sneaking up on some bandits, there's no skill challenge involved in their stealthy approach. All that matters is a single skill, Stealth, and the time frame of the situation is only a few minutes of movement. You could play this scene as a simple collection of individual skill checks, with a single poor roll ruining the party's chance of surprising the bandits. As an alternative, though, you can make it a group skill check: Everyone rolls, and if at least half the party beats the bandits' passive Perception score, the group achieves surprise.

A simple skill test, requiring some number of successful checks but with no penalty for failing 3 checks, can be a good way to model certain situations in the game. For example, traps are a more significant challenge if they require more than a single Thievery check to disable. You could decide that a trap requires 2, 3, or 4 successful checks to disable. To avoid keeping the rogue or warlock tied up for several rounds while the rest of the party fights the monsters, though, make sure that multiple characters can contribute to the effort to disable the trap. That can be as simple as declaring that hitting the trap with an attack counts as a successful check.

The following section highlights some key points about designing and running skill challenges, including a short example to illustrate each point.

TIME FRAME

Ground rule 4 says that skill challenges can take hours or days of game time. That's not always the case—some skill challenges take place in the middle of a combat encounter and on the same time scale (see "In-Combat Challenges," below). But a challenge that has depth and a variety of options works best if it's spread out over a longer period of time. In fact, a skill challenge can be a great way to boil down what for the characters are long or tedious days of exploration, investigation, or just slogging through the swamp into an encounter that plays fast at the table, carries real rewards for success and penalties for failure, and livens up your game session.

IN-COMBAT CHALLENGES

When a skill challenge occurs in a combat setting, it effectively replaces one or more monsters in the encounter. (In terms of XP, it's worth a number of monsters of its level equal to its complexity.) Don't create challenges of complexity 3 or higher that you intend to take place in the midst of combat—there won't be enough monsters to keep the characters busy, or the challenge will take up too much of the party's attention. Think of a simple challenge (complexity 1 or 2) as one type of objective you can use to add interest to a combat encounter, as described in Chapter 2. In fact, several of the sample objectives described on pages 40-41 could include skill challenge elements.

+ **Make Peace:** The characters must use interaction skills to convince their opponents to stop fighting.

+ **Retrieve an Object:** The characters must open a locked chest, disable a ward, or activate the power of the object with a simple skill challenge.

+ **Sneak In:** You might structure this encounter as a skill challenge using Stealth, Bluff, and other skills, with combat encounters resulting from the characters' failed checks. If they fail the challenge, the alarm is raised.

In an in-combat skill challenge, each skill check needs an associated action type—standard, move, or minor. Using move or minor actions for skill checks can make it easier for the characters to fight and pursue the challenge at the same time.

Before using an in-combat skill challenge, make sure it wouldn't work better as just a single skill check. The danger of using a skill challenge is that it can tie up a single character for multiple rounds while everyone else is "having fun" in combat. Don't make the rogue spend the whole fight disabling traps in a skill challenge in which only Thievery is useful. Involve as much of the party as you can, or else make the activity a single skill check.

"Closing the Portal" on page 89 is a good example of an effective in-combat challenge.

ENCOUNTER CHALLENGES

An audience with the duchess, a room full of traps, or a magically warded door are challenges that feel like encounters—they present a straightforward obstacle the characters must overcome, and they might even appear in a dungeon room just as a typical combat encounter does. These challenges are encounters in their own right, which probably means they're complexity 4 or 5. They must involve the whole party—otherwise some characters would have nothing to do for an entire encounter. See "Getting Everyone Involved" on page 86.

The time required in the game for the characters to complete an encounter challenge is up to you. A skill check in such a challenge might represent a standard action's worth of work, a minute of effort, or several minutes of focused activity.

"Opening the Ninth Ward" on page 90 is an example of an encounter challenge.

STRUCTURE CHALLENGES

A skill challenge that takes place between other encounters gives structure to a part of the game that would otherwise be exploration time. A challenge of this sort is clearly an abstraction—it distills large amounts of unstructured activity down into a number of skill checks.

You might consider using skill challenges for these kinds of activity:

+ **Investigation:** When the characters are trying to solve a mystery, boil down the clues into the results of skill checks. "Hunting the Mastermind" on page 90 is an example of this technique.

+ **Overland Travel:** Use a skill challenge to represent the obstacles and hazards the characters face as they cross a desert or a swamp, navigate a river, or pilot a *planar dromond* through the Astral Sea. See "The Rushing River" on page 94 for an example.

+ **Gathering Information:** As the characters range through town looking for rumors or question ancient spirits about the dangers that lie ahead, you can build a skill challenge in which the number of successes they achieve determines how much information they get. See "The Restless Dead" on page 93 for an example of this kind of skill challenge.

You can even use a structure challenge as the framework for a whole section of an adventure, or even the entire adventure. Rather than using a flowchart to determine the course of events in an event-based adventure (see the *Dungeon Master's Guide*, page 115), you can use a skill challenge in multiple stages, with the successes and failures the characters accrue determining when events occur and what happens. As with encounter challenges, the time frame of a structure challenge is up to you to determine. A check might represent anything from a few minutes to a day or a week of activity.

See "Moving through Suderham" on page 98 for an example of a structure challenge.

ALLOW A VARIETY OF OPTIONS

Remember ground rule 3: Just as a combat encounter with a mix of monster roles is more interesting than a fight against five of the same monster, a variety of skills, a broad range of subchallenges and obstacles, and a series of different, incremental tasks can make a skill challenge much more interesting. Even more important, this mix of skills and obstacles helps each player feel that his or her character has a lot of options and the possibility of making important decisions.

As a starting point, build a long and diverse list of relevant skills for the challenge. First (as mentioned earlier), aim for a number of skills equal to the number of characters in the party plus two. If there are more PCs than useful skills, you're potentially leaving a few characters without any way to make a meaningful contribution outside of using aid another actions.

Athletics is a great skill for challenges because of its nature—it can have an effect on almost any form of physical activity—and because twelve of the eighteen classes in the game to date have it on their class skill lists. Nature and Perception seem like obvious choices for many challenges, but far fewer classes have ready access to them (only six of the eighteen). Aim for at least half of the relevant skills to come from the following selection that six or more classes feature on their class lists:

Arcana	History
Athletics	Insight
Diplomacy	Intimidate
Dungeoneering	Nature
Endurance	Perception
Heal	Religion

Here's a summary of the "rare" skills, those offered by only three to five classes:

Acrobatics	Streetwise
Bluff	Thievery
Stealth	

Of course, a skill isn't rare in your game if most of the characters in your party has it, and a common skill isn't going to help your party if no one took training in it. If every character in your group has a class from *Player's Handbook 2*, you might have a lot of PCs trained in Nature, but no one who can pull off a decent Streetwise check. Know what skills your player's characters are good at, and tailor your challenges to those skills.

One way to help ensure that everyone in a party has a way to get involved in a skill challenge is to make sure you choose skills that are common to characters of each of the four roles. The list below gives the skills that are common to most of the classes that share each role.

Controller: Arcana, Diplomacy, History, Insight
Defender: Athletics, Endurance, Heal, Intimidate
Leader: Arcana, Diplomacy, Heal, History
Striker: Acrobatics, Athletics, Endurance, Intimidate, Perception

PRIMARY AND SECONDARY SKILLS

Once you have a list of the skills you want to be relevant for the challenge, break them down into primary and secondary skills. Aim for two or three secondary skills, with the rest primary. Primary skills give the characters successes (and failures) toward the ultimate goal of the challenge. Secondary skills don't always directly contribute to the group's success, but they can have other important effects. For example, a successful check with a secondary skill can accomplish one of the following effects:

✦ Cancel out a failure with another skill.
✦ Give one or more characters a bonus to a check with a primary skill.
✦ Allow a character to reroll another skill check.
✦ Open up the use of another skill in the challenge.
✦ Increase the maximum number of successes that a primary skill can contribute to the party's total.

GROUP CHECKS

One way to make sure every character is involved in a skill challenge is to require group checks. In a group check, everyone makes a specified skill check, and the group scores a success if at least a certain number of characters beats the set DC. For example, you might call for a group Endurance check, with the group succeeding if at least half the characters succeed, figuring that those who succeed on their checks can help out those who fail. Or you might call for a group Perception check, but if even just one character succeeds, the group gets a success because of the one sharp-eared member.

"Traveling through Gorgimrith" on page 92 and "Moving through Suderham" on page 98 are examples of how to use group checks in the context of a skill challenge.

ALLOW OPTIONS BESIDES SKILLS

Give some thought to things the characters might do aside from using skills—and be ready when you run the skill challenge to account for the things players try that you could never have anticipated. Characters can use powers and sometimes rituals in the midst of a skill challenge, and plenty of other tactics (such as bribery and combat) might alter the circumstances of a skill challenge, sometimes dramatically.

A good rule of thumb is to treat these other options as if they were secondary skills in the challenge. You might let a character negate a failed Diplomacy check by greasing an NPC's palm. Using an encounter power that's not directly relevant to the challenge might give the character a bonus to a subsequent skill check. You might allow a character to spend an action point to reroll a failed skill check.

Some categories of actions, though, are significant enough to earn an automatic success in the challenge. A character who performs a relevant ritual or uses a daily power deserves to notch at least 1 success toward the party's goal.

Here are some options you might want to account for in designing a skill challenge.

- ✦ Spending money (at least one-tenth the purchase price of a magic item of the character's level).
- ✦ Dealing damage to a creature or object.
- ✦ Voluntarily taking damage (in a combat situation) or sacrificing a healing surge.

GETTING EVERYONE INVOLVED

It can be tempting for some players to let the rest of the party handle the work of a skill challenge. In fact, at times it doesn't make sense, statistically speaking, for a character to even attempt a check, because the character's chance of success is so small and failure has such a negative consequence for the whole group.

If you include a wide variety of skills—and more specifically, select skills that you know the characters in your party are good at—this shouldn't be a huge problem. Just as in a combat encounter, everyone in the group should have a meaningful way to contribute to the group's success in the challenge, even if it's just making the same skill check a few times in a row.

Maximum Number of Successes: Even if you make sure that every character can contribute in a skill challenge, some players will resist taking part unless they have to contribute in order for the group

to succeed. If the wizard can move the group through the challenge with a series of Arcana checks, there's no need for anyone else to take part. You can force the rest of the group to participate by limiting the number of successes that any particular skill can contribute. A good maximum is equal to the complexity of the challenge. Once the wizard has achieved 3 successes with Arcana, she has done all she can do, and it's time for someone else to step up to the plate.

Aid Another: You don't want the fighter with a +0 Intelligence modifier and no training in Arcana to feel as though his best option in a skill challenge is aiding the wizard's Arcana check. If a skill the fighter is trained in is relevant to the challenge and the wizard's use of Arcana is limited to a maximum number of successes, the fighter almost certainly has better things to do.

If you think that the situation justifies doing so, you can limit the amount of aid characters can receive from their allies in the midst of a challenge. For instance, it could be that there's only so much assistance that a character making a Diplomacy check can receive—perhaps the person the group is talking to shouts, "Enough of this chatter! Let me speak to just one of you." Also, a skill challenge might require the group to split up so that characters at different locations can't aid each other. Allow reasonable use of the aid another action in skill challenges, but rein it in if the characters start to abuse the privilege.

PREPARE FOR FAILURE

The outcome of a skill challenge should always keep the game moving. It should be possible for the characters to fail the challenge, but the adventure must go on regardless—the characters just have to deal with the consequences of the failed challenge in addition to the other threats the adventure poses. Make sure you prepare for the possibility of failure as you're designing a skill challenge. Don't set up a challenge in which success means the characters unlock the door and failure means the door stays locked. Instead, if the characters fail, they unlock the door just as the guards come into view.

In other words, make sure that failure still leaves the characters with something to do. If the characters must get past the ninth ward before they can move onto the next part of the adventure, then the challenge should assume that they do get past the ward. If you're creating a skill challenge to move the PCs through this part of your story, the point of the challenge should be to determine how quickly they get past the ward, or whether they alert the monsters on the other side of the ward, or whether they get through it with all their healing surges intact. In short, the skill challenge doesn't really measure whether they succeed or fail; it measures how well they succeed.

Also, be sure to distinguish between what the characters find desirable and what the players enjoy. The characters probably don't like being attacked by drow assassins in the middle of the night, but the players will probably have fun playing out the encounter. Failing a skill challenge can create plenty of problems for the PCs, but the best kinds of problems are the ones that lead to additional fun encounters.

Consider these options as consequences for failure in a skill challenge:

✦ Increase the difficulty of the characters' next encounter, or throw an encounter at them that's a clear result of the failure.

✦ Assess the characters one or two healing surges each.

✦ Impose a lingering effect, such as a disease or a curse that works like one, that hinders the characters for some time.

✦ Impose story-related consequences: The characters are too late to save the captives, they lose the duke's favor, or they fail to gain some key information to help them in the adventure.

✦ Require the characters to attempt the skill challenge again.

STAGES OF FAILURE

An effective way to make a skill challenge lively is to provide immediate consequences for each failed check in the challenge—such as a brief combat encounter, or more opponents appearing in the midst of an ongoing combat. Each time the characters fail, the consequences become gradually worse, climaxing in the termination of the skill challenge after 3 failures. See "Hunting the Mastermind" on page 90 for an example of this technique.

Aside from combat encounters or combatants, here are some penalties you can assess in response to failed checks in a challenge:

✦ The character who failed the check loses a healing surge or (in a combat context) takes damage.

✦ The characters must spend time or money making up for the failure.

✦ For the rest of the challenge, no character can achieve a success using the same skill that was used for the failed check.

✦ If the challenge takes place in a combat situation, the character who failed the check is dazed or even stunned until the end of his or her next turn. Or, an opponent is angered and gains a +2 bonus to its next attack roll.

ZOLTAN BOROS & GABOR SZIKSZAI

◆ The next check using a specified skill takes a penalty. For example, if a character fails an Intimidate check in the midst of a complex negotiation, the next character who attempts a Diplomacy check takes a -2 penalty.

STAGES OF SUCCESS

One way to account for the possibility of failure is to construct a skill challenge in which each success moves the characters partway toward their goal—so that even if they fail, they still have some of what they need. This method works well, for example, in a challenge whose goal is to extract information from a hostile or wary NPC: With each success, the characters get some tidbits of information. The most valuable information comes last (when they achieve the target number of successes for the complexity of the challenge), but even 1 success followed by 3 failures gives the characters some tidbits they can use to keep the adventure moving. See "The Restless Dead" on page 93 for an example of this technique.

Perhaps the characters undertake a skill challenge to weaken a vampire lord before they finally face him in combat. Each success (or every 3 successes) removes some protective ward or special defense the vampire lord possesses, so even if the characters fail the challenge—and are thrust into combat with the vampire—they've still weakened him a little, and the fight is measurably easier than if they had achieved no successes at all.

PROGRESSIVE CHALLENGES

Like a combat encounter, a skill challenge is much more interesting if it changes and evolves as the characters progress through it. A good way to think about the party's progress through the challenge is to break it into three sections. For a skill challenge with a complexity of 5 (12 successes), each stage can last for 4 successes. For a challenge with a complexity of 1 (4 successes), the middle stage might start after they achieve their first success and last until they get their third—or you might break the challenge into just two stages.

The three stages of a skill challenge are not that different from the parts of a story (see page 8), except that the denouement comes after the skill challenge is complete. The first stage, the introduction, sets up the skill challenge, makes it clear what the goal is, and lays the groundwork for the first few skills or options for the characters. Then comes the rising action, when the challenge becomes more complex and urgent. Then in the climax, the characters successfully complete the challenge (or not) and the encounter is over.

Different skills might be useful in different stages of the challenge. For example, in the first stage of a challenge involving overland travel, the characters are hacking through the woods using skills such as Athletics, Endurance, and Nature. In the second stage, they join up with a caravan as guards, making skills such as Perception and Insight more important.

Try to make sure that the characters' actions and successes or failures in each stage of the challenge have consequences in the next stage. If the characters decide to rely heavily on Intimidate in their first meeting with an important NPC, that individual might throw more obstacles in their way in the later stages. Or if the characters fail two History checks in the middle of a challenge, they might not get a chance to talk to the sage who could have helped them in the final stage.

A progressive challenge is long and complex by its nature. See "The Rushing River" on page 94 for an example of one.

Triggers: Counting the number of successes the characters have achieved is one way to measure their progress through the stages of a challenge. In effect, this treats each stage as a miniature skill challenge requiring a smaller number of successes to complete, but with a shared tally of failures among the three stages. An alternative, though, is to use more specific triggers to move from one stage to the next.

TRANSPARENCY AND SKILL CHALLENGES

Sometimes, it makes sense to tell the players that they face a skill challenge. Other times, signaling that you're using the mechanic jars the players out of the moment, reminding them that they're playing a game rather than negotiating with a green dragon for their lives. A skill challenge brings a structure to the game. When you decide whether to tell the players they are in a skill challenge, what you're really choosing is whether to let them know they are in that structure.

Tell the players they are in a skill challenge when that structure helps them handle the situation and understand what is going on. If they're adrift, stuck in neutral in the face of a bewildering array of options, then a skill challenge is a good way to focus their attention. They see what skills they can use and understand that they need successes while avoiding failures. As the players make skill checks, they can begin to understand the situation in a way that informs how they play their characters, allowing them to immerse themselves in the action.

Keep the skill challenge on your side of the DM's screen, not telling the players, when they clearly understand their goal and know what their options are. In this case, the players can engage the situation as their characters. Their PCs know what to do. Reminding the players that they are in a skill challenge introduces a layer of artificiality to the situation that breaks the drama and shatters the scene's immersive nature.

—Mike Mearls

When a specific triggering event occurs, something happens in the context of the skill challenge to change the challenge in a noticeable and interesting way. Consider the following trigger ideas:

✦ The characters get a success (or a failure) with a particular skill.

✦ The characters reach a certain number of accumulated failures.

✦ The characters seek out a specific character to talk to, location to visit, or otherwise initiate their own change of scene.

✦ Each player has had a chance to take one turn in the skill challenge.

✦ Some amount of time has passed.

A changing situation in a skill challenge introduces new opportunities for the characters, giving them the chance to use new skills or presenting new ways they can apply their skills. For example, a character who makes a successful Insight check while talking to the duchess might notice her eyebrow raised in interest when matters of history come up, opening the possibility for PCs to use History checks to impress her.

BRANCHING CHALLENGES

Sometimes you might want to construct a skill challenge in which the characters can succeed in one of two ways, making use of different skills or otherwise taking different approaches to the resolution of the challenge. When the possible outcomes include a variety of possible successes, you can create a branching challenge.

For example, in a diplomatic talk, failure in the challenge might mean the breakdown of the talks, leading to violence (and a series of combat encounters). Success, however, can mean one of two possible outcomes—one favoring each party involved in the negotiations. Over the course of the skill challenge, individual characters might contribute toward the success of one side or the other, or the group might coordinate effectively to ensure victory for one side.

In a branching challenge, each possible successful outcome has a target number of successes depending on the challenge's complexity. Each time a character scores a success with a skill, that success counts toward one of the two possible outcomes. The target that is reached first determines the outcome of the challenge.

A branching challenge can be a great way to allow for some conflict within the party of player characters, without that conflict growing too disruptive. The characters can disagree on the approach to take or the goal to pursue while still working together to avoid failing the challenge entirely. However, if you expect the characters to split their efforts between two goals, it's best not to set the complexity of the challenge higher than 3. Otherwise, you're asking the characters to achieve too many successes, assuming that they get more or less the same number of successes toward each goal.

"Chasing the Bandits" on page 91 and "War by Other Means" on page 96 are examples of branching challenges.

SKILL CHALLENGE EXAMPLES

The rest of this chapter includes examples—mostly drawn from published adventures—that illustrate the finer techniques of skill challenge design.

CLOSING THE PORTAL

—Shawn Merwin, from *Dungeon Delve*

In the midst of a combat encounter against a demonic solo monster, the PCs must close a portal to the Abyss to prevent an army of demons from entering the world. They can attempt to complete this in-combat skill challenge (see page 84) either before or after they defeat the monster. Closing it afterward is easier, because the monster is no longer present, but closing it beforehand reduces the creature's power.

Choose an appropriate creature for the encounter. The skill challenge as it appeared in the *Dungeon Delve* supplement used an abyssal spitter, similar to the mordant hydra in the *Monster Manual*. You might apply the Demogorgon cultist or Orcus blood cultist theme (see Chapter 4) to an adult dragon or a fen hydra, or use a group of demons of an appropriate level. Each monster in the encounter gains this additional power:

Portal Energy
As long as the portal remains open, the monster deals 2 extra damage on each of its attacks.

Level: 11 (XP 600).
Complexity: 1 (requires 4 successes before 3 failures).
Primary Skills: Arcana, History, Thievery.
Arcana (DC 16, standard action): The PC bends the magic of the portal to his or her will, slowly closing it off. A character must be within 5 squares of the portal to attempt this check.
History (DC 16, minor action): The character recognizes the arrangement of runes around the portal as something he or she has read about before. This recollection provides a clue about the energy powering the portal.

This skill can be used to gain 1 success in this challenge. No character can attempt this check more than once, and this check cannot be retried if the PCs fail to complete the skill challenge on their first try.

Thievery (DC 21, standard action): The character manages to weaken the magical energy feeding the portal. A character must be adjacent to the portal to attempt this check.

Success: If the PCs get 4 successes, the portal closes permanently. The monsters lose the benefit of their *portal energy* power.

Failure: If the characters accumulate 3 failures and any demon is still alive within 10 squares of the portal, a barlgura (*MM* 53) appears in the portal and attacks the PCs. The PCs must begin the skill challenge again from scratch; each additional failed challenge brings one more barlgura than the previous failed challenge (two for the second one, three for the third, and so forth).

Even if the PCs can't close the portal, as long as all the demons in the vicinity are defeated, the portal can't get any stronger, and thus can't disgorge its army. However, from time to time additional abyssal denizens might slip into the world through this portal.

OPENING THE NINTH WARD

To reach the villain's sanctuary or the repository of a mighty artifact deep in a dungeon, the characters must bypass a powerful magical ward that binds the doors.

This encounter challenge (see page 84) operates in 10-minute turns. Each character in the party can make one skill check each turn, and each character must also make one Endurance check every turn.

Level: Any.

Complexity: 4 (requires 10 successes before 3 failures).

Primary Skills: Arcana, Endurance, History, Perception.

Arcana (moderate DC by level, 10 minutes): A character can use Arcana to sense the presence of magic and identify the nature of the ward. Additional successes indicate a breaking of the ward through arcane means. This skill can be used to gain 4 successes in this challenge.

Endurance (moderate DC by level, no action, group check): As soon as the characters begin investigating the ward, it starts to give off necrotic energy. Each 10 minutes, the characters must make a group Endurance check to measure how well they weather the life-draining energy. If at least half the group succeeds, they earn 1 success.

History (moderate DC by level, 10 minutes): A character can use History to recall a mention of the ward in an ancient text, indicating a useful step to take in bypassing the ward. Since the ward has a certain notoriety, this skill can be used to gain 4 successes in this challenge.

Perception (moderate DC by level, 10 minutes): A character using Perception notices very fine lines traced in the doorway and hears the faintest of vibrations when hands are moved over the door in a certain way. This skill can be used to gain 4 successes in this challenge.

Secondary Skills: Religion, Dungeoneering, Thievery, special.

Religion (moderate DC by level, 10 minutes): A character's knowledge of religious texts that mention the ward in passing can give one character a +2 bonus to the next Arcana or History check that character makes.

Dungeoneering (hard DC by level, 10 minutes): The character has heard of similar wards, and can either give one character a +2 bonus to the next Perception check that character makes, or change one character's failed Endurance check (as part of the group check) into a success.

Thievery (moderate DC by level, 10 minutes): The character's skill at fine manipulation helps a character with Arcana to undo the ward, giving a +2 bonus to the next Arcana check.

Special: Performing the Knock ritual gives the characters 1 automatic success. The ritual can be used only once for this purpose.

Success: If the characters achieve 10 successes, the ward is opened without harm and they can move into the next room of the dungeon.

Failure: If the characters get 3 failures, the ward erupts in necrotic energy that drains two healing surges from each character. The characters can still pass through, but creatures in the next room might be alerted or empowered by the sundering of the ward.

HUNTING THE MASTERMIND

—James Wyatt, adapted from the EBERRON *Campaign Guide*

A demonic creature called forth by a mysterious ritual has attacked the characters, and now they need to find out where it came from. In this skill challenge, the characters make use of their deductive powers (Perception and Insight), their ability to navigate the streets and denizens of the city (Streetwise, Diplomacy, and Intimidate), and their knowledge of or research about the demon itself (Arcana). The characters must assemble what clues they have into a coherent picture of the threat that faces them as they make their way down to the lowest levels of the city to find the source of that threat.

Level: 1 (XP 500).

Complexity: 4 (requires 10 successes before 3 failures).

Primary Skills: Arcana, Diplomacy, Insight, Intimidate, Perception, Streetwise.

Arcana (DC 10): A character who makes a successful Arcana check identifies the creature as a demon that must have been summoned into the world. A second successful check reveals no lingering magical energy in the area of the demon's attack, implying that it was not summoned directly to that location. This skill can't grant any further successes until the characters have achieved 9 successes, but at that point it allows a character making a successful Arcana check to pinpoint the magical energy emanating from the villain's base. This skill can be used to gain a maximum of 3 successes in this challenge.

Diplomacy or Streetwise (DC 10): The character coaxes useful information from a witness at the scene or near the scene of the attack: either an indication of which way the demon came or a description of its haunting whisper as it moved through the city, which includes words pertinent to its purpose in attacking the characters.

After the characters have achieved 5 successes, they're close enough to the villain's base that they can learn more about his activities in the area. Witnesses in the area describe the villain's suspicious activity and physical appearance, and also mention the strange lights and sounds emanating from a townhome in the neighborhood.

Insight (DC 10): The character pieces together some of the information the group is learning. Characters can't attempt two Insight checks in a row; after a successful Insight check, the party must score a success with a different skill before anyone can attempt another Insight check. With a successful check, the character synthesizes information toward a more coherent picture of the threat they face: The demon made its way toward them from somewhere in a specific neighborhood, explicitly searching for them and apparently knowing where they were with some degree of accuracy.

Intimidate (DC 15): A character can use Intimidate as a substitute for Diplomacy to extract information from witnesses. Intimidate effectively substitutes for Diplomacy, although at a higher DC.

Perception (DC 15): The demon left some traces of its passing as it moved from the villain's base to the site of the attack. The character can use Perception to follow this trail. With a success, a character might find a wisp of fur that dissolves into mist when touched, a corpse tossed in a dark corner, or a witness describing the creature's passage. Such witnesses can then be the subjects of Diplomacy or Intimidate checks.

Success: If the characters earn 10 successes, they find their way to the villain's base. When they enter the tower, they start a combat encounter with the villain or his minions.

Failure: This skill challenge uses the principle of stages of failure (see page 87). Each time the characters fail a skill check, they have a brief combat encounter. The city can be a dangerous place, and asking the wrong questions or poking into dark corners can quickly get characters into trouble. Each time the characters fail a skill check as part of this challenge, they have a minor combat encounter. Build easy encounters worth between 300 and 400 XP—not even a full level 1 encounter. They'll be over quickly so characters can get back into the skill challenge.

If the characters fail their first skill checks, you can choose to wait until the characters have moved beyond the scene of the last encounter before presenting them with these complicating encounters.

If they fail three checks, you can let them continue until they achieve 10 successes, throwing combat encounters at them with each additional failure, or simply bring them to the villain's base right away. Either way, the villain's agents are on the lookout for their arrival, and the encounter at the tower is more challenging.

Chasing the Bandits
—Robert Donoghue and James Wyatt

The characters are chasing a small group of bandits across the countryside. In this branching challenge (see page 89), the characters have a choice of two paths to success. They can decide to move as quickly as possible, hoping to catch the bandits before they meet up with reinforcements. Or they can put a greater emphasis on stealth, hoping to get the drop on the bandits when they catch up to them. Each character can make one skill check for each day of the challenge, and the skill chosen determines which goal the success counts toward.

Although some of the skill checks in this challenge are individual efforts that seem to allow a particular character to gain an advantage that his or her companions don't enjoy, a certain amount of abstraction is necessary in how the challenge plays out. For instance, a PC who succeeds on an Endurance check to run fast doesn't actually outdistance his friends; the group still stays together, so that everyone is present when the challenge comes to a conclusion.

Level: Any.

Complexity: 2 (requires 6 successes of either sort before 3 failures).

Primary Skills: Athletics, Endurance, Nature, Stealth, Streetwise.

Athletics (moderate DC by level): The character pushes through obstacles with physical strength, leaping over gullies and climbing up cliffs in an attempt to catch the bandits as quickly as possible. A success with this skill counts toward the speed goal.

Endurance (moderate DC by level): The character concentrates on running as fast and long as possible. A success with this skill counts toward the speed goal.

Nature (moderate DC by level): The character uses knowledge of geography and the terrain of the region to choose the best course—either the quickest route to intercept the bandits, or one that provides good cover for the characters when they approach the bandits. A success with this skill counts toward the goal of the character's choice.

Stealth (moderate DC by level): The character opts for a slower but quieter approach, hiding in forested terrain so the bandits aren't aware they're being followed. A success with this skill counts toward the stealth goal.

Streetwise (moderate DC by level): As the party passes through farmsteads and villages, the character makes sure that no one runs ahead of them to warn the bandits. A success with this skill counts toward the stealth goal.

Success (Speed): The characters intercept the bandits before they meet up with reinforcements, so the resulting combat encounter is easier than it would otherwise be.

Success (Stealth): The characters get the jump on the bandits, gaining a surprise round in the combat encounter against them. However, the bandits have reinforcements, so the encounter is a little tougher.

Failure: The characters still catch up with the bandits, but the bandits have gained reinforcements. To make matters worse, they're alert to the characters' approach and set up an ambush, so the bandits get a surprise round in the encounter.

TRAVELING THROUGH GORGIMRITH

—Bruce Cordell, Chris Tulach, and Bill Slavicsek, from *Kingdom of the Ghouls*

In this challenge, the adventurers must travel through twisting tunnels inside a great mountain fortress for at least six hours to reach the other side. This is a structure challenge (see page 84) that boils a long underground journey down into six to eight group checks representing the party's ability to bypass and overcome obstacles that arise in their way. The challenge uses triggers (see page 88) to mark the changing environment as the group progresses, with each stage of the challenge calling for one group check.

Each hour of the journey, every character must make a skill check using a specific skill. If at least half the characters succeed on the check, the group earns 1 success toward their goal. Otherwise, they earn 1 failure. If they succeed on 6 checks in a row, they reach the far end of the tunnels in just 6 hours, but each failure adds an hour to the journey. At the end of the trip, they face a combat encounter.

Because much of the challenge involves avoiding the monsters that haunt these tunnels, each failed group check along the way results in a combat encounter (see "Stages of Failure" on page 87). Build encounters appropriate to the setting, aiming for relatively easy encounters 2 or 3 levels below the party. If

the party fails an Endurance check (in hour 4 or hour 7), each character also loses a healing surge.

Level: 25 (XP 14,000).

Complexity: 2 (requires 6 successes before 3 failures).

Primary Skills: Athletics, Dungeoneering, Endurance, Perception, Religion, Stealth.

Hour 1, Dungeoneering (DC 26, group check): The characters find a safe path through the tunnels, realizing that the right direction lies in the tunnels that lead downward, away from the top of the mountain.

Hour 2, Stealth (DC 26, group check): The characters quietly work their way past a pack of monsters, remaining undetected.

Hour 3, Athletics (DC 17, group check): The characters easily climb over hazardous recesses in the tunnel and jump over black, foul-smelling eruptions to progress deeper into the mountain.

Hour 4, Endurance (DC 17, group check): The characters stave off the effects of the terrible smell, the hard travel over soft ground, the hot, humid air, and the lingering miasma that permeates the tunnels.

If the party fails this check, each character loses a healing surge.

Hour 5, Perception (DC 26, group check): The characters spot a roaming pack of monsters and avoid a battle.

Hour 6, Religion (DC 31, group check): The characters use their observations while traveling within the tunnels and their knowledge of Gorgimrith and undead to avoid a particularly dangerous area of unstable surfaces and necrotic cysts. You can replace this check with a different skill if the environment or the creatures that inhabit it suggest a better choice.

Hour 7, Endurance (DC 26, group check): The characters stave off the effects of the terrible smell, the hard travel over soft ground, the hot, humid air, and the lingering miasma that permeates the tunnels in their seventh hour of travel.

If the party fails this check, each character loses a healing surge.

Hour 8, Athletics (DC 26, group check): The characters easily climb over hazardous recesses in the tunnel and jump over black, foul-smelling eruptions to progress deeper into the mountain.

Success: If the characters earn 6 successes, they find their way to the final exit from the tunnels in good time and without further incident.

Failure: Each time the characters earn a failure, adjust the outcome of the hour's activities from that described above and run a combat encounter. After their third failure, you can either run a combat encounter immediately, or add monsters to the encounter the characters have when they emerge from the tunnels.

If the characters get 3 failures, the trip through the tunnels takes the characters longer than anticipated. They still reach the final exit, but each character loses a healing surge along the way.

THE RESTLESS DEAD

−Richard Baker and Mike Mearls,
from *Thunderspire Labyrinth*

This structure challenge (see page 84) involves gathering information from the spirits of a trio of adventurers who were slain years ago when they attempted to cleanse the demonic influence from an ancient stronghold. They managed to recover the four items needed to open the door to the inner sanctum, but they were then killed by the green dragon (called the Guardian) that serves as sentinel over the sanctuary.

The spirits can speak but are otherwise unable to affect the world. When the characters enter the area, the spirits manifest, greet the characters in Common, and ask what they seek in this place. Over the course of the challenge, the spirits attempt to determine the characters' intentions. If the characters can convince the spirits of their trustworthiness and that their cause is just, the spirits describe what the characters must do to reach the inner sanctum. Otherwise, the characters must stumble their way through the challenges in the subsequent encounters without any aid.

Level: 5 (XP 1,000).

Complexity: 5 (requires 12 successes before 3 failures), though the PCs gain some information even if they fail this challenge.

Primary Skills: Arcana, Athletics, Diplomacy, Dungeoneering.

Arcana or Dungeoneering (DC 12): The characters impress Mendara with their knowledge of mystic lore and dungeon environments.

Athletics (DC 12): As a cleric of Kord, Valdrog applauds feats of strength or athletic prowess. This skill can provide a maximum of 2 successes.

Diplomacy (DC 17): The PCs use the Diplomacy skill to convince the NPCs of their good intentions. However, the spirits believe that actions speak louder than words, so this is a hard check.

Secondary Skills: Bluff, Intimidate, Insight.

Bluff (DC 17): A character who has any ill intentions can use Bluff in place of Diplomacy to attempt to convince the spirits that his or her intentions are good.

Intimidate: The spirits cannot be intimidated, for they are beyond harm. Using this skill results in an automatic failure, and the PC who made the Intimidate check takes a -2 penalty to all other skill checks in this challenge.

Insight (DC 17): During the conversation, Mendara makes outrageous claims about the trio's exploits. If a character succeeds on this Insight check, that PC realizes she is lying. If the character questions Mendara and attempts to learn why she is lying, the PCs gain a success. Only 1 success can be gained in this way.

Conclusion: The PCs receive information based on the total number of successes achieved. Whether the PCs succeed or fail, the slain adventurers can finally rest in peace; they have attempted to help a group avenge their loss. Once the challenge ends, the NPCs say farewell (or they warn of impending death if the encounter went poorly) and fade from view.

Success: If the PCs attain 12 successes, the slain adventurers hail them as allies. The group provides all the information below.

Failure: If the PCs earn 3 failures, the spirits provide information based on the PCs' number of successes up to that point, as shown below (and see "Stages of Success" on page 88).

The following information is provided as read-aloud text that the spirits relay to the PCs after the skill challenge comes to a conclusion. Alternatively, you can dole out this information gradually over the course of the challenge, each time the characters reach a new threshold of successes.

0-1 Successes: *This place is the Proving Grounds, a testing place for worshipers of the demon lord Baphomet. You must find four items: a knife, a mask, a bell, and a book. You must place each of these items on one of four circles of runes found in this complex. The items must be placed on the runes at the exact same time.*

2-3 Successes: *The knife, the mask, and the bell are held within chambers built to test Baphomet's worshipers. You can find these chambers to the north, west, and south of where we now stand, through these eastern double doors and then through another set of double doors that leads to the west.*

THE SLAIN ADVENTURERS

Valdrog the Brute: Valdrog appears as a male human with a thick, black beard. His spectral chainmail is ripped apart because the Guardian killed him by tearing him in half. Valdrog was a cleric of Kord, and he speaks with a booming voice. He is rude, aggressive, and quick to challenge the PCs' bravery; he respects demonstrations of strength and wants to help a worthy group.

Sir Terris: This dwarf was a paladin of Pelor and served as the group's valiant defender. Terris wears plate armor and keeps his helm's faceplate closed. He was slain when the Guardian crushed his skull with a single bite. Sir Terris

is wise and kind, though he is also judgmental. He asks many questions, seeking to trap the PCs in a contradiction or a lie. He is quick to make accusations and slow to trust. The PCs must prove their good intentions to win his support.

Mendara the Mystic: The group's wizard, Mendara is an elf who died by the dragon's breath. She wears green robes and carries a staff. Mendara is eager to recruit someone who has the intelligence and acumen to overcome the challenges that lie ahead. She lies to the PCs, hoping to expose their greed. She is haughty and talkative.

4-5 Successes: *The fourth item, the book, is on an altar in a small shrine to the east.*

6-7 Successes: *To the east of the Proving Grounds is the inner sanctum. Its door opens only when the proper ceremony is completed. The items used for the ceremony disappear if you try to remove them from the Well of Demons, and upon completion of the ceremony, they return to their former locations.*

8-9 Successes: *Completing this ceremony summons the terrible Guardian and activates several traps in the area. The Guardian is a green dragon imprisoned here. It can swoop past its prey and attack. It emerges from a great pit in the center of the complex.*

10-11 Successes: *Each of the chambers in this complex has a magical trap designed to harass intruders. The central corridor is the fastest way to move around, but it also has its own trap: a crushing sphere of magical force that rolls along its length.*

12 Successes: *There is a treasure hidden beneath the altar in the chamber south of here.*

THE RUSHING RIVER

–Logan Bonner, from the
Worldwide D&D Game Day adventure
Journey Through the Silver Caves

At the exit to the cave, you come to a stream that rushes over a small waterfall and joins up with a bigger river that stretches far into the distance ahead.

Near the stream is a raft. You see a few sloppy axe cuts. It looks like the orc you saw escaping made a hasty attempt to sabotage it as he ran out.

This skill challenge is a structure challenge (see page 84) that models the characters' attempt to navigate a twisting, bizarre river—a difficult task, especially for those who haven't made the trek before. The challenge uses stages of success (see page 88) to reflect the characters' progress along the course of the river, measured by the total number of successes they have accumulated so far. Some skills are useful in every stage, while others are useful only in the specific circumstances of certain stages of the journey.

YOU'RE SWIMMING? REALLY?

This challenge assumes the characters are using the raft provided in the cave. If they don't, every character needs to make a DC 15 Athletics group check at the start of the challenge. If at least half the characters succeed, the party gets 1 success. Otherwise, they get 1 failure. Give the characters a chance to get a watercraft after stage 1, such as a canoe sitting near the river they can steal. If they continue swimming, they make group checks to swim for each section; the DC is 20 during stage 2 and stage 5. They can't gain any more successes for swimming, but can gain failures.

The challenge assumes that the characters are following an orc who is escaping in a canoe, and that the orc damaged the raft the characters are using.

Level: 5 (XP 1,000).

Complexity: 5 (requires 12 successes before 3 failures).

ENTIRE CHALLENGE

These skills can be used at any point during the challenge, unless otherwise noted.

Primary Skills: Nature, Perception, Thievery.

Nature (DC 12): The character helps navigate the twisting, branching sections of the river. After the characters have a total of 7 successes, it's too late to use this skill.

Perception (DC 17): The character spots the orc's canoe up ahead, and is able to follow his course. This skill can be used to gain 1 success in each stage. An individual character can use Perception to contribute only 1 success to the entire challenge.

Thievery (DC 12): The character works to repair the damage the orc did to the raft. This skill can be used to gain 1 success in this challenge.

Secondary Skills: Endurance.

Endurance (DC 12): The character stays alert despite the rigors of the journey. This doesn't give any successes, but the character can reroll one failed skill check later in the challenge. A character can use this skill in this way only once in the challenge.

STAGE 1: WILDERNESS

This is the first stage of the journey, right after the characters leave the cave.

Primary Skills: History, Nature.

History (DC 17): The character recalls a map of this section of the river, which helps the PCs choose a path among the twisting branches. If the group gains 2 successes with this skill, the characters remember that rapids lie ahead, and each character gains a +2 bonus to Acrobatics or Athletics checks to avoid falling off the raft at the start of stage 2.

Nature (DC 7): It's easier to navigate here, where the character can see the sky. Use this DC instead of the one in the "Entire Challenge" section.

STAGE 2: RAPIDS

After 3 successes, the characters enter a channel where imposing stone cliffs rise up on all sides, then come upon a twisting, rocky patch of rapids. Read:

All around you, the water begins to churn, becoming white with foam. It comes out of nowhere: You couldn't even see the rapids until they were right upon you. As waves of rough water crash against the jagged rocks all around you, ephemeral voices fill the air, screaming in rage. It's as though the water itself wants to drag you to a watery grave.

When the characters enter this area, each makes an Acrobatics or Athletics check (DC 17, or DC 22 if the raft hasn't been repaired). A character who fails this check falls in the water. This check doesn't give any successes or failures, but sets up the skills for this part of the challenge.

Primary Skills: Acrobatics, Athletics, Endurance.

Acrobatics (DC 12): A character on the raft can make Acrobatics checks to keep the raft on course and stay balanced. This skill can be used to gain 2 successes in this challenge.

Athletics (DC 17): A character who has fallen into the water can swim to get back onto the raft or get through the rapids safely. Each character who has fallen in the water can gain up to 1 success in the challenge this way.

Endurance (DC 17): Any character can attempt this skill to weather the rapids, and each can gain up to 1 success doing so.

Secondary Skills: Diplomacy.

Diplomacy (DC 12): The PC speaks to the raging voices in the river, calming them. This gives no successes, but lowers the DCs for Athletics and Endurance checks by 5 for this stage of the challenge.

STAGE 3: RESPITE

After 6 successes, the river returns to normal. The characters can use the skills noted above in "Entire Challenge" during this stage, but the respite is brief–as soon as they achieve 1 more success, they move on to the next stage of the challenge.

During this stage, the characters also find an old, wrecked boat at the end of the rapids. It might hold a treasure parcel, a combat encounter, or both.

STAGE 4: THE GUARDIAN GHOSTS

This stage occurs after the PCs have gained a total of 7 successes. Two guardian spirits, former arcanists of the empire of Nerath, stop the party just before the river enters a series of stone tunnels leading back underground. Read:

You stop in midstream, and it seems you've been transported to a different place. The air around you blurs and ripples, and at the bottom of the river you see the dead

---

ROLEPLAYING THE GUARDIANS

The river guardians are stoic and difficult to read. If they see a token of passage from Nerath, they allow the travelers to pass with no questions asked. Otherwise, they ask only that the characters convince them they aren't dangerous. They don't care if the travelers are altruistic or noble, only that they aren't going to cause trouble for the (now-defunct) empire. The guardians are unaware of Nerath's fall, and they don't accept evidence to the contrary.

---

bodies of many travelers. In front of you, two ghostly humans in robes appear and address you. "We are guardians of this river. Present a token of passage, or prove you deserve to travel this waterway."

Navigating is useless in the arcane realm the PCs currently occupy, so the Nature skill can't contribute to the group's success beyond this point.

Primary Skills: Arcana, Bluff, Diplomacy, Intimidate.

Arcana (DC 12): The character discusses magic with the guardians, showing a dedication to and respect for the arcane arts.

Bluff (DC 17): The character describes a noble purpose that the characters aren't actually pursuing.

Diplomacy (DC 12): The character offers evidence that the characters are noble and trustworthy.

Intimidate (DC 17): The guardians are not easily intimidated, and only characters who have obvious magical power that might be capable of banishing them can achieve a success with this skill.

Secondary Skills: History, Insight, Thievery.

History (DC 12): The character recalls that the fallen empire of Nerath sometimes used tokens of passage as authorization for travelers to pass along certain roads or waterways. A successful check allows a character to use Thievery as described below.

Insight (DC 12): The character realizes that the guardians are practitioners of arcane magic from the empire of Nerath. This gives no successes, but gives a +2 bonus to all further skill checks against the guardians.

Thievery (DC 17): Once a character has made a successful History check, the same or a different character can use Thievery to create a quick forgery of the token of passage the guardians ask for. A successful check lets the characters immediately move on to the next stage of the challenge if they choose, while failure gives them a -2 penalty to all further checks made in this segment.

STAGE 5: UNDERGROUND

When the characters have 10 successes, the river guardians allow them to pass into the stone tunnels near their destination. Read:

The river descends underground, and you soon reach a lake that splits off into seven paths. Nothing you've heard so far indicates which path is the correct one.

The characters can't use Nature to navigate here.

Primary Skills: Arcana, Dungeoneering, Perception, Religion.

Arcana (DC 12): By detecting the presence of residual magical energy, the character narrows the number of possible paths. This skill can be used to gain 1 success in this challenge.

Dungeoneering (DC 12): The character watches the currents and figures out which path is least likely to be a dead end.

Perception (DC 17): The character spots the orc's canoe heading down one of the passageways. This gives 2 successes (thereby ending the challenge).

Religion (DC 12): The character seeks guidance from a deity. If the character specifically called upon Avandra or Melora, the DC is reduced to 7, and succeeding on this check grants 2 successes instead of 1.

ENDING THE ENCOUNTER

After the skill challenge is over, the party travels into a long, curving (but placid) tunnel that deposits them in the expansive underground cavern in which their next encounter takes place.

Success: The characters successfully reach their destination.

Failure: The characters go off course, crash and are separated, or whatever makes sense based on the checks they failed at. Traveling on foot or on the wreckage of the raft, they get to the next encounter late and weakened. If the characters were speaking to the river guardians when they failed, they have to shield themselves from the guardians' arcane powers. Whenever they fail the challenge, each character loses a healing surge.

WAR BY OTHER MEANS

—Robert Donoghue

The town of Parsain has long been contested ground between the Duchies of Hallber and Yranes, with each having a list of historical reasons for their claim. Until recently, the town had been under threat from nearby monsters, and neither was willing to press their claim and get entangled in local matters. However, after a group of heroes (perhaps the player characters) freed the town from the threat that loomed over it, both have taken an interest in reestablishing old claims. Each has sent a representative and a body of militia intent on making that happen, and tense negotiations have begun.

This skill challenge represents the player characters' efforts to oversee and perhaps influence the negotiations as they try to keep matters from devolving into violence. It works best if the characters have a strong interest in the fate of the town (perhaps because they were the ones who freed it from the monsters' yoke), but good reasons to support both sides of the conflict. In this branching challenge (see page 89), the characters can contribute their successes to either side of the negotiation, with the intent of either helping one side achieve its goals or finding a balanced and equitable resolution.

The negotiations stretch over a number of days. Each day, each player character can attempt one skill check as part of the challenge.

Hallber's Representative: Hallber is represented by Sir Anders Petrus, a soldier in the duke's service. He's a large, burly man with a great black beard, a booming voice, and a brash demeanor that makes it easy to overlook the fact that a cunning tactical mind lies behind those eyes. He views Parsain as a military holding, a place to secure a weak point on the duchy's border.

Before negotiations begin, or sometime during the first day of the talks, Anders approaches one or more of the characters who appear to be neutral or willing to favor Hallber and attempts to gain their support. The offer is this: Support Hallber throughout the negotiations, and if Hallber decisively wins the challenge (which means Hallber wins and Yranes gets fewer than 3 successes), the character will receive a reward—a magic weapon or implement of the character's level. If Anders is called out, he will of course deny that any such offer was made, and if the character acts against Hallber, the deal is off.

Yranes's Representative: Yranes is represented by Dame Venna Las, a half-elf wizard who has the practiced polish of a long-time diplomat and the well-concealed heart of a snake. Parsain is a commercial interest to her, and she has an eye on building some roads to and through the town.

Before negotiations begin, or sometime during the first day, Venna approaches one or more of the characters who seem to be neutral or willing to favor Yrane and attempts to gain their support. The offer is this: Support Yranes throughout the negotiations, and if Yranes decisively wins the challenge (which means Yranes wins and Hallber gets fewer than 3 successes), the character will receive a reward—a neck slot or arm slot magic item of the character's level. If Venna is called out, she will of course deny that any such offer was made, and if the character acts against Yranes, the deal is off.

Level: Any.

Complexity: 2 (requires 6 successes before 3 failures).

Primary Skills: Diplomacy, Dungeoneering, History, Intimidate, Stealth.

Diplomacy (moderate DC by level): A character can step in as an advocate for either side and argue on that side's behalf. A failed check suggests that the character didn't do very well at this task.

Alternatively, a character can use Diplomacy to try to keep negotiations on an even keel. If the character generates a success with this use of the skill, he or she can save it rather than applying it immediately to the skill challenge. At the end of a day of negotiations, the character can assign the success to whichever side has fewer successes. If the two sides are tied,

the character might choose either side to receive the success, or choose not to apply the success at all.

Dungeoneering (moderate DC by level): One of Hallber's main arguments is that Parsain needs better defenses. The character can take the day to plan out defenses and make a case that Hallber's reinforcements are unnecessary, or use this study to underscore Hallber's arguments. A failed check means the character's disagreements with other experts leaves the issue muddied and tempers frayed.

History (moderate DC by level): The character makes a historical case for one side or the other. These arguments are well treaded, but a successful check brings some fresh detail to light. A failed check means the character's point does not hold up to examination and opens the door to a more devastating counterpoint. Each time this skill adds a success to one side or the other, the History DC for adding another success to that side increases by 5.

Intimidate (hard DC by level): Openly threatening the diplomats might not be the best approach, but there are more subtle ways to use this skill. The character whispers in the ears of the diplomats of one side, reminding them of the recent dangers facing this town and the likelihood that they'll return, perhaps making it seem a less desirable prize. A failed

roll means the diplomats see through the character's actions.

Stealth (moderate DC by level): The character spends time eavesdropping on one side and shares that information with the other side. A failed check indicates that the character passed on misinformation.

Secondary Skills: Endurance, Nature, Religion.

Endurance (moderate DC by level): The stakes are high, and when matters are most heated, the negotiations stretch into the wee hours of the night. When a day's negotiations end with the two parties either tied in successes or with 2 failures accumulated, the characters must make a group Endurance check. If at least half the group succeeds, the characters' ability to stay in control of their faculties serves them well as fatigue shortens tempers and frays nerves, and the characters can negate 1 accrued failure. If less than half the party succeeds, someone has snapped, perhaps even one of the characters, and the side represented by most of the characters who failed their checks accrues another failure.

Nature (moderate DC by level): Haggling over discrepancies in their respective maps, both parties agree on the third day of negotiations to send out a surveying team to iron things out. If a character who is trained in Nature has not antagonized either side, the character is offered the opportunity to lead the expedition. If that character makes a successful Nature check, he or she can subtly influence the readings to favor one side or the other, granting that side a success. If the character does not choose a side, the side with fewer successes gains a success. On a failure, the mission reaches no consensus, and tensions run that much higher. The party can attempt only one Nature check in the course of the challenge.

Religion (moderate DC by level): On the second day of the negotiations, the town celebrates a holiday, and the townsfolk ask one of the characters who is trained in Religion to offer a few words at the ceremony. A successful Religion check can add 1 success to either side by couching subtle nods to that side's position in the address, or a speech on the virtues of understanding and fellowship can negate 1 accrued failure from either side. The party can attempt only one Religion check in the course of the challenge.

Success: If Hallber accumulates 4 successes, the negotiations end up favoring that duchy, and it lays claim upon the town. On the other hand, if Yranes accumulates 4 successes first, then the duchy of Yranes gains the town.

The winner gets ownership of the town, but the more successes the loser has, the more concessions it can demand. If Hallber has at least 3 successes, it earns the right to leave a garrison in town. If Yranes has at least 3 successes, it sets up warehouses and a mercantile post in town. Ultimately, the town will benefit most from the fairest arrangements.

If the arrangement is particularly equitable (which is to say the other side got its concession), the town thrives in the future, and the characters can expect to have a safe haven there. If the arrangement is imbalanced, then the winning duchy eventually absorbs the town completely, and the citizens will have no great reason to remember these events fondly.

Failure: If negotiations break down, war is the only option left on the table. If either side has fewer than 3 successes when the challenge ends, fighting breaks out immediately. Otherwise, the negotiators withdraw and the war proceeds more formally. In either case, the town of Parsain suffers as the battlefield for this conflict.

MOVING THROUGH SUDERHAM

−Mike Mearls

Level: 9 (XP 2,000).
Complexity: Special.

This complex skill challenge stretches the definition of a skill challenge to an extreme, showing how you can use the basic framework of a skill challenge to structure an entire adventure. It's a structure challenge (page 84) that uses the choices of the characters as triggers (page 88) to move into different stages of the challenge. However, it turns some of the basic assumptions and rules of skill challenges on their head and incorporates a set of random events that respond to the failures of the characters as the challenge progresses.

The challenge represents the difficulty that characters face as they travel around Suderham, a city ruled by a band of foul slave traders known as the Slave Lords. The characters might need to enter the city to free someone from the Slave Lords' clutches, slay a particularly powerful villain, or otherwise take an active step to disrupt an evil plot. Use this skill challenge whenever the characters need to move through town.

There are four quarters in the city: the military quarter, the wealthy quarter, the thieves' quarter, and the official quarter. Regardless of where they are, the characters have four basic kinds of activity they can attempt: travel within their current quarter, travel to a different quarter, find directions, or gather information. In addition, if they find themselves chased by guards or facing conflict they would rather avoid, they can attempt to evade pursuit.

Whatever kind of activity the characters are attempting, each member of the party must make an effort to keep a low profile and contribute to the group's success. When the characters attempt one of these kinds of activity, or other some other activity defined as part of a random event, each character makes a check using one of the skills allowed by the activity. Different characters can use different skills. You can also allow a PC to improvise the use of a skill. Use DC 14, 19, or 24, depending on how clever and feasible the idea is.

In addition to making his or her own check, each character can aid another character's check. If at least half the characters succeed on their checks, the group is successful. A failed check adds 1 failure to the group's accumulated failures in the challenge, but the challenge does not end at 3 failures.

Travel in Their Current Quarter: The characters can move through a quarter with a group check using Athletics, Stealth, or Streetwise. Their current location determines the skill check DCs (see the Traveling Through Suderham table, below). Using this option takes 2d10 minutes. Success on this check means the characters arrive at their destination (assuming they know where they are going).

Travel to a Different Quarter: Moving between quarters is tricky, because the borders between quarters are heavily patrolled and long, wide avenues between them make sneaking or leaping from rooftop to rooftop difficult. Moving between quarters requires a group check using Diplomacy, Intimidate, or Streetwise, using the higher of the DCs for the two quarters the characters are traveling between. Traveling between quarters takes an additional 1d10 minutes (3d10 altogether). Failing this check counts as 2 failures in the challenge.

Find Directions: The characters can take a chance on finding directions. They spend 2d10 minutes asking around (or finding someone who knows where their destination is). They make a group check using Diplomacy or Streetwise. If they succeed, they learn how to get to their destination and arrive there if it is in their current quarter. Otherwise, they need to ask someone else.

Gather Information: The characters can spend some time ferreting out rumors, making a group check using Bluff, Diplomacy, or Streetwise. Success allows them to learn a rumor. It takes an hour to hit the local pubs and find any rumors.

Evade Pursuit: The characters make a group check using Athletics (to outrun their pursuers), Bluff (to create a disguise), Stealth (to hide), or Streetwise (to find a shortcut or other difficult-to-follow route), using the appropriate DC for the quarter. If they succeed, they escape. Otherwise, the PCs are cornered and must fight their pursuers. Failure on this check does not count as a failure in the skill challenge. Use the guidelines given below for the guard random encounter to determine the repercussions of a fight.

Suderham's Quarters

Each of the city's four quarters has a distinct flavor stemming from the kinds of businesses found there and the people who live there. The quarter the characters are moving around in determines the DCs for skill checks they make in that quarter.

Military Quarter: The military quarter features barracks, armories, and slave quarters. It lacks any taverns, inns, and similar establishments. Folk here keep to themselves. They are either laborers at work or guards on or off duty. The PCs are likely to land in trouble faster here, but most people leave them alone.

Guards here are usually off duty and looking to avoid trouble. Taking a gentle approach with Diplomacy is the best route. Intimidate checks are likely to be taken as a challenge.

Official Quarter: The official quarter is home to government buildings, temples, and warehouses that store trade goods. The guard maintains heavy patrols in this area, and the guards are on high alert, making Stealth and Bluff difficult skills to use. Athletics is relatively easy, since the tallest, most ornate buildings in town are found here.

Thieves' Quarter: The guards rarely enter the squalid thieves' quarter. Crumbling old buildings, flophouses, run-down taverns, and other seedy establishments dominate this quarter, along with tenements filled to overcrowding. The thugs and criminals of this quarter have little use for social niceties, so Diplomacy works poorly here. The Streetwise skill offers easy access to dives that the guards avoid, side alleys, and other ways to keep out of sight.

Wealthy Quarter: The slave lords and other rich merchants of the city make their homes in this quarter. It is the second most heavily patrolled area, after the official quarter. The wealthy quarter hosts sprawling mansions with well-tended grounds, high-end taverns and inns, and other establishments that cater to the upper class. The broad boulevards have plenty of trees, gardens, statues, and other decorations.

Streetwise offers little utility here, since the broad avenues and sprawling estates make this quarter of the city the least urban in character of all Suderham's quarters. In comparison, a group that uses Stealth has an easy time of it. The guards make frequent patrols, but the mansions provide many hiding spots. Many of them are walled, surrounded by lush gardens, and ornamented with other flourishes that offer plenty of ways to avoid notice.

TRAVELING THROUGH SUDERHAM

	Military Quarter	Official Quarter	Thieves' Quarter	Wealthy Quarter
Athletics	DC 19	DC 14	DC 19	DC 19
Bluff	DC 19	DC 24	DC 19	DC 19
Diplomacy	DC 14	DC 19	DC 24	DC 19
History	DC 24	DC 19	DC 19	DC 19
Insight	DC 19	DC 19	DC 19	DC 19
Intimidate	DC 24	DC 19	DC 19	DC 19
Stealth	DC 19	DC 24	DC 19	DC 14
Streetwise	DC 19	DC 19	DC 14	DC 24

Success and Failure

This challenge does not follow the normal rules for skill challenges. Successful skill checks help the characters accomplish relatively minor goals but don't accrue toward a final goal for the challenge. Likewise, failures don't determine the end point of the challenge; they simply measure how much attention the characters draw to themselves over the course of their time in the city. The challenge ends when the characters accomplish whatever other goals they're pursuing in the city, which should be the object of one or more quests. The challenge defines the context for the characters' other activities in the city.

When the characters fail skill checks, they draw some amount of attention to themselves and put the town watch on a higher level of alert. Armed patrols increase in strength and frequency. The secret police send out agents to track down the characters. Eventually, if the characters are foolish or unlucky, Suderham becomes an armed camp in which it's impossible for the characters to move around safely.

Keep track of the failures the characters accrue over the course of the challenge. Each time they fail a check, consult "Effects of Failure," below. The characters suffer all the consequences shown for the number of failures they've accrued and for all lesser number of failures. For example, when the characters have failed five checks, the consequences noted for 5 failures, 4 failures, and 3 failures are all in effect in the city.

In addition, in the big, interconnected social web of a city, failure breeds failure. Each time the characters accrue a failure, also roll on the random events list.

If the characters lie low, staying out of sight or even leaving the city, the city slowly returns to normal. Each day that passes without the characters accruing any failures (whether because they succeed on all their checks or because they don't attempt checks), roll a d20. On a 10 or higher, subtract 1 failure from their accrued total.

At the end of the adventure, when the characters have finished their business in Suderham, award them 400 XP each for overcoming this 9th-level challenge.

Effects of Failure

Three or more failures: The town guard schedules more patrols. Increase the DC of all Athletics and Stealth checks by 2.

Four or more failures: The secret police become more active in questioning townsfolk. Increase the DC of all Diplomacy and Streetwise checks by 2.

Five or more failures: The guard reserves are called into duty. Random encounter results of 6-10 become guard patrols in the military, wealthy, and official quarters (as if you had rolled a 15-20).

Six or more failures: The guards and secret police become more active. Increase all check DCs by an additional 2.

Seven or more failures: The city is on a high level of alert, with guards actively searching from house to house. Each time the characters attempt to take a short rest in a building or alley in town, roll a d20. On a 16 or higher, the characters encounter a guard patrol (as a random event result of 15-20). If they try to take an extended rest, a guard patrol encounter occurs on a roll of 10 or higher.

Eight or more failures: The town is in a state of combat readiness. All DCs increase by an additional 4, and all random events are guard encounters.

Random Events

Life in the big city is full of surprises, and Suderham is no exception. Whenever the PCs take an action as part of this skill challenge (except evading pursuit), roll a d20 and consult the following list of events. If the characters are in the official quarter, add 5 to the roll. The characters might avoid any complications, they might take a penalty (or a bonus) to the skill check made as part of the challenge, or they might need to make a few checks to avoid a potentially dangerous situation.

If the PCs fail a check made as part of a random event, they do not suffer a failure for the skill challenge unless the event states otherwise.

1-5: No event.

6: The PCs encounter a merchant who offers them 2 gp each if they'll help him unload his cart. To help, the characters must make a group Athletics check (DC 19) to unload his fragile goods. If they succeed, the merchant offers them a ride. Once, at a time of their choosing, they can arrange to travel from this quarter to any other without making skill checks.

7: A spy seeking to help free a slave notices the characters. With a successful group Diplomacy check (DC 24), the group gains access to the network of liberators in the city. The Streetwise DC for this quarter is reduced by 5. If the characters fail, the spy suspects them of being turncoats. Roll a d20 twice and take the higher result when rolling for random events in this quarter.

8: A group of slaves tries to escape. The characters can help them with a group Stealth check (DC 19) to avoid detection, help capture them with a group Athletics check (DC 19), or do nothing. If the characters assist the slaves and succeed, the next time they fail a check to travel in the city, a group of slaves who heard of the characters' valor provide a distraction and cancel the failure. If the characters fail to help them, they accrue a failure. If the characters capture the slaves, they gain a +2 bonus to all skill checks involving guard patrols if they succeed but take a -5 penalty to all checks involving slaves and those sympathetic to them whether they succeed or fail.

9: A gang of hobgoblin mercenaries picks a fight with a guard patrol on the street in front of the characters. The characters can jump into the fight or do nothing. If they help one side or the other, then for the next week, any guard patrol made up of the group they help ignores them on a d20 roll of 15 or higher. However, the characters take a -5 penalty to skill checks against patrols of the other side for the next week. Killing any combatants gives the characters 2 failures in the skill challenge.

10: A group of drunken off-duty soldiers tries to pick a fight with the characters. A successful group check using Bluff or Intimidate (DC 19) scares them off. On a failed check, the guards attack. If the characters defeat the guards, they gain a +2 bonus to all Intimidate checks in this quarter. If the characters kill any guards, they immediately accrue 3 failures in the challenge. Beating the guards unconscious brings no ill consequences (brawls are common here; the guards end up in the brig).

11: A cart loaded with goods topples over, blocking the street. The characters must make another check to travel through this quarter.

12: A thief runs past the characters, with a shopkeeper close behind. The characters can stop the thief with a group Athletics check (DC 19) or ignore him. If they ignore him, the shopkeeper curses at them and attracts a guard patrol. If they catch the thief, the shopkeeper covers them with praise, and the next time the characters are pursued by guards in this quarter, they can hide in the shopkeeper's business and automatically escape detection.

13: The characters come across an old building. A group check using History or Religion (DC 19) allows them to realize it was once a temple of Tiamat, the god of greed, and should have a secret meeting chamber in the back. If the characters are chased in this quarter, they can make Stealth checks with a +5 bonus by hiding in that chamber.

14: A horde of rats emerges from a nearby sewer grate, throwing the street into chaos. Each character must attempt an individual Athletics check (DC 19) to avoid the rats. A character who fails this check takes 1d10 + 5 damage. A character who inspects the grate sees that, although it is too narrow for a humanoid to fit through, it does open to a wide tunnel. A successful group check using History or Streetwise (DC 19) allows the characters to find a nearby entrance to the sewer tunnels. From now on, the characters can use the tunnels to travel in this quarter without making skill checks. Each time the characters use the tunnel, though, one character must make an unaided History check (DC 19) to plot a usable path to the party's destination. If this check fails, the characters encounter monsters that lurk in the sewers.

15-20: The characters run into a guard patrol and must make a group check to avoid the guards. Roll a d20 to determine what type of patrol they encounter and what skills they can use to evade the patrol.

1-9: 1d6+1 hobgoblin soldiers (*Monster Manual*, page 139). The group check can use Athletics (DC 14), Bluff (DC 19), Diplomacy (DC 24), Intimidate (DC 19), or Stealth (DC 14). These hobgoblin mercenaries are poorly paid and undisciplined. They are eager for a fight (thus the high Diplomacy DC) but are inattentive as they patrol (allowing low Athletics and Stealth DCs).

10-20: 2d4 human guards (*Monster Manual*, page 162). The group check can use Athletics (DC 19), Bluff (DC 14), Diplomacy (DC 19), Intimidate (DC 24), or Stealth (DC 19). An Insight check (DC 19) reduces the DC for either Diplomacy or Intimidate by 5 (determine at random) as the character notes the guards' moods—either eager to move on or easily cowed. The human guards are thorough in their work but seek any excuse to avoid a fight. They are well paid, and dead men can't spend their gold at the local pub.

Failure: If the PCs fail their group check to avoid the guards, they accrue 1 failure in the challenge, and the guards try to arrest them. The characters can fight or flee. If the PCs fight, they accrue 3 additional failures if they kill any guards. At the end of each round of combat, roll a d20. On a result of 16 or higher, another guard patrol arrives on the scene. On each round after the first, apply a cumulative +2 modifier to this check.

CHAPTER 4

CUSTOMIZING MONSTERS

THE MONSTER *Manual* books offer hundreds of enemies to include in your encounters, but you can further customize these monsters, to tailor them to fit the feel and flavor of your campaign. This chapter adds more elements to your DM's toolbox by expanding the options from the *Dungeon Master's Guide* and adding a new tool: monster themes.

This chapter includes the following sections:

✦ **Monster Themes:** Each monster theme provides a suite of powers you can draw upon to add to existing monsters or use when you create new monsters. You then create thematic links across encounters, even when using monsters that might not normally be associated with each other. The section also details nine themes drawn from D&D lore.

✦ **Templates:** First introduced in the *Dungeon Master's Guide*, this section on templates includes more than a dozen new monster templates, as well as class templates for each of the nine classes from *Player's Handbook 2* and the FORGOTTEN REALMS® *Player's Guide*.

✦ **Creating Monsters:** Updated guidelines for how to create your own elites, solos, and minions.

GEORGI SIMEONOV "CALADER"

MONSTER THEMES

Many of the iconic monsters of D&D come in themed groups or varieties, from packs of slavering gnolls to the deceptive rakshasas. These creatures share not only physical traits, but also tactics and even powers. Encounters with these creatures take on a distinctive flavor because of these shared characteristics.

Using the monster themes presented here, you can add that same distinctive flavor to any array of creatures. Each theme provides story-based and mechanical changes that modify existing monsters to better fit the flavor you've chosen. For example:

✦ A troglodyte curse chanter whispers a blasphemous prayer to Demogorgon and brings madness to her enemies.

✦ The proximity of Telven Vale to the Feywild imbues many of its denizens—including a tribe of ogres—with powers of stealth and trickery.

✦ Kobolds dedicated to Tiamat ignore the streams of acid that drip from the ceiling of their accursed temple . . . and unleash their own acidic breath upon unwary intruders.

Each monster theme begins with an explanation of the theme, then presents a suite of options for customizing your monsters. These options include story-based changes—such as alterations to a monster's appearance or behavior—as well as mechanical adjustments in the form of new powers and skill modifications. Finally, each theme includes a sample stat block showing how you can customize an existing monster by using the theme.

You can use these themes to modify existing creatures, to tweak your own creations, or to serve as the nucleus of an entirely new monster. Most of the advice here concerns modifying existing monsters. See the sidebar "Designing Your Own Themed Monsters" for how to use this concept in conjunction with creating your own monsters from scratch.

USING THEMES

Applying a monster theme is a straightforward procedure. You don't need to rebuild the monster's stat block—you can run the monster with a few extra notes jotted in the margin that detail its new powers.

Step 1. Choose a Theme: If you're thinking about this idea, you've probably already picked out a theme that works for your campaign. But if you don't see one that fits, you can craft one easily. See "Designing Your Own Themes" for details.

Step 2. Choose a Monster: After you've selected the theme, pick the monster you want to modify.

Some themes work better with particular kinds or roles of monsters, and within the theme each power describes the roles it fits best. For example, the Demogorgon theme works well with brutes, because many of the new powers described in that theme are designed to fit those monsters. You can choose to modify a lurker or a soldier with one of these powers, but keep in mind that the modified monster is going to end up feeling a bit like a brute. This doesn't change the monster so much that it can't fulfill its original role, so you shouldn't change its role.

One exception: If you give a monster a leader power, the monster gains the leader role.

Step 3. Choose Story Changes: A theme is more than a menu of new powers. It also has a story template that you can use to turn a mundane creature into a unique opponent.

It's easy to forget about description and story elements when assembling a monster's statistics and powers, but story plays an important role in how a monster functions in a game. A monster without a good story is merely a pile of numbers, and that frequently leads to forgettable encounters or adventures.

When adding a theme to a monster, note how its appearance or behavior changes. These changes should reflect not only the monster's altered powers, but also its new allegiance to a specific deity, primordial, or other villainous master.

This step could just as easily occur after choosing the new powers. In fact, some powers might suggest particular story alterations, and vice versa, so you might jump back and forth between these two steps.

Step 4. Choose Powers: After selecting the theme, the monster, and any story-based changes, you need to choose the powers to add.

Choose one attack power and one utility power from the theme and add those to the monster's stat block. You can also apply some or all of the skill modifications in a theme description, though this isn't necessary.

Attack Powers: Each theme includes a number of different attack powers. Some are new at-will attack powers, while others are per-encounter or recharge-based enhancements to the monster's existing basic attacks. In some cases, powers in this category don't include an attack, but instead enhance the monster's offensive prowess in other ways.

Utility Powers: In addition to attack powers, each theme also includes options that don't involve attack rolls or directly deal damage, such as beneficial auras, healing powers, special movement options, situational benefits, and so on.

In most cases, adding a utility power doesn't alter a monster's core identity or tactics as drastically as adding a new attack power.

THEMED GROUPS

When first experimenting with themes, try to limit yourself to no more than one or two themed monsters in any given group. This helps you deal with the added complexity more gradually, and it also helps spotlight these "new" monsters for your players.

For instance, debuting a full tribe of Demogorgon-themed troglodytes is exciting, but allowing the players to meet these new troglodytes gradually enhances the unique nature of the monsters. Players can become inured to special monsters if you overuse them, so dole them out with care . . . that is, until you unleash a whole pack of Demogorgon-themed zombies with *lashing tentacles* and *carnage* in a big, climactic encounter!

Within a themed group, strike a balance between uniformity and variety. It's fine if all the themed monsters in an encounter display the same "new" at-will power, but in that case their encounter and utility powers should have more variety.

When themed monsters appear repeatedly in an adventure—a good thing, by the way, since it draws attention to the importance of the theme—use the same combination of monster plus changes so that your players start learning the connections.

For example, if the opening encounter of your adventure features a pair of Legion of Avernus dwarf hammerers with *inspiring death*, make sure the dwarf hammerers in the fourth encounter use the same power. Players feel rewarded when they figure out even the simplest of puzzles, and even though "dwarf hammerer plus *inspiring death*" doesn't seem like a puzzle to you, from the other side of the screen that realization can feel like an epiphany.

DESIGNING THEMES

If your campaign includes a particularly notable master villain, cult, or thematic element, consider creating a monster theme tied to that story element. Doing so is easier than crafting new monsters from scratch, but it has a similar effect: enemies with a unique feel that stand out from the everyday foes.

A theme is composed of two main parts: the story elements and the mechanical elements (the powers). When these two parts work well together, you and your players will remember the encounters featuring the themed monsters.

Start with the story of your theme to form an idea of where your theme is going. The answers to these two questions can point you in the right direction.

What's the basic concept? This first step points the way for everything to come. For example, are you modeling monsters on your archvillain, are you detailing an organization, or are you positing a regional influence on the monsters?

How do the monsters visibly demonstrate the theme? These visible cues help players understand what they face. Do your themed monsters wear a different style of clothing? Are they physically misshapen? What do their new powers look like in use?

After you have the story basics, move to the mechanical elements of attack and utility powers. In many cases, your story choices point toward particular powers. For example, if you intend to create a monster theme based on the Prince of Frost and his Winter Fey (see *Manual of the Planes*), you already know that cold-themed powers are a good choice.

Aim for two to five new powers in each new category. If you use too small a range of powers, all your themed monsters start feeling the same. Use too many, and it becomes hard for players to recognize the theme when they see it.

Link the powers strongly to the theme, avoiding generic effects that any monster could have. Ideally, a player encountering one of these monsters should identify it as belonging to the theme: "Hey, those zombies have tentacles for arms . . . keep your eyes open for a priest of Demogorgon around here somewhere!"

Also, as you can see from the themes presented here, it's fine to reuse (or adapt) existing monster powers. That's particularly true when the theme you're creating is linked to or based on that monster.

Attack powers include anything that deals damage or adds offensive punch to an attack. Damaging auras, harmful conditions, and extra-damage conditional effects all count as attack powers.

Utility powers include anything that isn't an attack. Healing effects, ally boosts, special movement, and defensive benefits are all examples.

When crafting a power, you might have to scale its effect by level or tier. See the examples in this chapter for guidance.

THEMES FOR MINIONS

Using a theme with a group of minions can be a great way of showcasing the theme, since its effect is multiplied over several monsters. However, when a theme power mentions an amount of damage or an amount of healing, halve that value (rounding down) when you give the power to a minion.

For dice of damage or healing, convert the value to half the average result. For example, a kobold minion with *dragon breath* would deal 2 damage to enemies in the blast (rather than 4.5, which is the average result of a 1d8 roll).

This method keeps a big group of minions from having too great an impact on combat.

DEMOGORGON CULTIST

One of the mightiest of demon lords, Demogorgon is a two-headed fiend who embodies madness and absolute destruction. The Prince of Demons commands his followers to engage in wanton destruction, laying waste to all that they find.

Demogorgon finds most of his adherents among troglodytes, kuo-toas, ogres, and other savage humanoids given to mindless, destructive violence. His human cults arise in times of chaos, when brute strength and blood lust allow even the weakest peasant to survive and, in the madness of battle, flourish. Other creatures that might align themselves to Demogorgon's cause include ettins, trolls, giants, titans, the occasional aberrant monster, and of course, demons. Worshipers of Demogorgon keep beasts such as drakes or otyughs as pets, and particularly vicious magical beasts—even rare dragons—might throw in with a cult dedicated to this demon prince.

Brutes, controllers, and skirmishers make the best Demogorgon-themed monsters. Some powers in this theme upgrade the monster's melee prowess, while others exemplify the madness inherent in the Demon Prince's cultists.

Creatures of this theme display bestial, even inhuman characteristics, such as forked tails or even tentacles instead of (or in addition to) arms. Extraordinarily dedicated followers sometimes boast two heads.

Demogorgon appears in *Monster Manual 2*, along with a number of related monsters.

Skill Modification: +2 bonus to Intimidate checks.

ATTACK POWERS

Demogorgon's cultists favor overwhelming force, preferably delivered quickly, to defeat their enemies. His priests enjoy magic that twists and turns their enemies' minds.

DEATH FURY

Death fury turns melee-oriented monsters into ravening terrors of pure damage. The power is ideal for a brute or a soldier and is well suited for monsters with few other attack powers. You might try giving it to a troglodyte mauler so that it can mark multiple characters each round while bloodied even as it accelerates its own demise by drawing more attacks.

Death Fury (minor; usable only while bloodied; encounter)
Until the end of the encounter, this creature can make two melee basic attacks as a standard action, each with a -2 penalty to the attack roll. After this creature uses *death fury*, the only attack powers it can use until the end of the encounter are basic attacks.

DOMINATING GLARE

This power is ideal for a controller or a creature that enjoys being surrounded by enemies. An oni night haunter, for example, might dive into battle before unleashing a *dominating glare*.

Dominating Glare (standard; recharge ⚅⚅) ✦ **Psychic**
Close blast 3; targets enemies; level + 3 vs. Will; the target is dominated until the end of this creature's next turn.

LASHING TENTACLES

When added to a melee-based monster, this aura slightly increases its damage output. For a monster that favors ranged attacks, *lashing tentacles* serves as an incentive for enemies to keep their distance. Try applying this power to artillery, brutes, or controllers. An ogre warhulk with *lashing tentacles* growing from its shoulders makes for an imposing—and potent—foe, particularly as it wades into the middle of the party to subject multiple characters to the aura.

Lashing Tentacles (Fire) aura 1; any enemy that enters the aura or starts its turn there takes 2 fire damage.
Level 11: 4 fire damage.
Level 21: 6 fire damage.

MADDENING STRIKE

Maddening strike works best for brutes and controllers that are likely to be in the thick of melee. An immolith can use its reach to deliver a *maddening strike* against one character adjacent to another.

Maddening Strike (standard; encounter)
This creature makes a melee basic attack. If the attack hits, the target makes a melee basic attack as a free action against a creature of this creature's choice.

UTILITY POWERS

These powers favor large groups of melee combatants.

CARNAGE

Give this power to brutes, skirmishers, or soldiers that fight in teams, allowing them to grant the bonus to each other. Kuo-toa guards that have *carnage* can seize the PCs' attention when they gang up on the characters.

Carnage
This creature gains a +1 bonus to melee attacks if one or more of its allies are adjacent to its target.

DEMONIC FRENZY

A monster that has *demonic frenzy* should spend plenty of time in the middle of combat. Pair it with multiple brutes or soldiers (specifically leaders) to maximize the effect. An ogre warhulk with *demonic frenzy* surrounded by a bunch of ogre savages makes a tough encounter.

> **Demonic Frenzy** aura 5; any bloodied ally within the aura gains a
> +1 bonus to attack rolls.

DUAL BRAIN

Though useful for any monster, *dual brain* is particularly helpful for elite and solo monsters—or any monster with a low Will—since it prevents them from being taken out of the fight for long by mental effects. This feature manifests physically as a second, mostly vestigial head sprouting from the monster's shoulders. Two-headed barlguras with *dual brain* are tough to slow down with mental effects.

> **Dual Brain**
> At the end of this creature's turn, it saves against dazed and
> stunned conditions and charm effects.

THREATENING REACH

A Large or Huge brute or soldier can influence a wider swath of the battlefield with this power. This ability typically manifests as long, sinewy limbs that look like tentacles. A squad of ogre thugs with *threatening reach* can create an effective wall between the characters and a villain.

> **Threatening Reach**
> This creature can make opportunity attacks against any enemy
> within the reach of its melee basic attack.

Ettin Spirit-Talker of Demogorgon — Level 12 Elite Controller (Leader)

Large natural humanoid (giant)   XP 1,400

Initiative +6   **Senses** Perception +17

Demonic Frenzy aura 5; any bloodied ally within the aura gains a +1 bonus to attack rolls.

Lashing Tentacles (Fire) aura 1; any enemy that enters the aura or starts its turn there takes 4 fire damage.

HP 252; **Bloodied** 126

AC 28; **Fortitude** 27, **Reflex** 21, **Will** 26

Saving Throws +2

Speed 6

Action Points 1

⊕ **Club** (standard; at-will) ✦ **Weapon**

     Reach 2; +17 vs. AC; 1d8 + 7 damage, and the target is pushed 1 square.

⤳ **Curse of Shattered Bone** (standard; at-will)

     Ranged 10; +15 vs. Will; the next time the spirit-talker hits the target with a melee attack, the attack is treated as a critical hit and deals 1d12 extra damage. The curse lasts until the end of the ettin spirit-talker's next turn.

↞ **Spirit Call** (standard; recharge ⚄ ⚅) ✦ **Necrotic**

     Close burst 5; +15 vs. Fortitude; 2d6 + 6 necrotic damage, and the target slides 3 squares.

Double Actions

     At the start of combat, the ettin spirit-talker makes two initiative checks. Each check corresponds to one of the ettin spirit-talker's heads, and the ettin spirit-talker takes a turn on each initiative count. The ettin spirit-talker has a full set of actions on each of its turns, and its ability to take an immediate action refreshes on each turn.

Dual Brain

     At the end of each of its turns, the ettin spirit-talker saves against dazed and stunned conditions and charm effects.

Alignment Chaotic evil   **Languages** Giant

Skills Intimidate +10, Religion +12

Str 25 (+13)   **Dex** 10 (+6)   **Wis** 23 (+12)

Con 22 (+12)   **Int** 13 (+7)   **Cha** 15 (+8)

Equipment hide armor, 2 clubs

ENCOUNTER GROUP

An ettin spirit-talker leads a disparate war band of cultists devoted to the two-headed demon prince. They roam the countryside, destroying all in their path.

Level 13 Encounter (XP 4,200)

✦ 1 ettin spirit-talker of Demogorgon (level 12 elite controller)

✦ 1 hill giant (level 13 brute; *Monster Manual*, page 121)

✦ 2 kuo-toa marauders (level 12 skirmisher; *Monster Manual*, page 172)

✦ 1 mezzodemon (level 11 soldier; *Monster Manual*, page 58)

The denizens of the Feywild are known for their stealth and trickery. From the wily gnome to the graceful eladrin, these creatures display abilities that allow them to elude attack and escape pursuit.

The Feywild Denizen theme allows you to add elements of these iconic creatures to other monsters. Whether you want to craft the perfect pet for an eladrin hunting party or build a singularly elusive squad of enemies to frustrate your characters, this theme offers a variety of options to suit your tastes.

This theme appears commonly among fey and natural creatures. Any type of creature might have the Feywild Denizen theme, from humanoids such as elves or gnolls to animates such as a shambling mound. Skirmisher, controller, and lurker abilities mesh well with the powers provided by this theme.

You can add this theme to creatures that already have fey-themed powers (such as eladrin or gnomes) to enhance their fey nature, or layer it onto other creatures—deathjump spiders, vine horrors, or wights—to create a connection to the plane. Such creatures might be natives unusual to the plane or might have taken on fey properties due to the Feywild's influence on their home region.

Creatures of the Feywild Denizen theme appear more lithe and agile than their unmodified counterparts. They might have luminous, pupilless eyes, melodic voices, or faintly glowing auras.

Origin: The creature's origin becomes fey.

Skill Modifications: +2 bonus to Acrobatics, Bluff, Nature, and Stealth checks.

ATTACK POWERS

Creatures that have the Feywild Denizen theme favor attacks that harass and frustrate foes. The powers available in this theme favor monsters that like to keep enemies at bay or launch ambushes.

BEFUDDLING SHOT

This power gives the allies of artillery, controller, or lurker monsters combat advantage and the chance to move away from the target without provoking opportunity attacks. An ettercap webspinner can use *befuddling shot* with its *web net* so that its fang guard allies can deliver *spider bites* with combat advantage.

> ⤳ **Befuddling Shot** (standard; encounter)
> This creature makes a ranged at-will attack. If the attack hits, the target is dazed until the end of its next turn.

BEGUILING STRIKE

Controllers and lurkers like this power because they have melee attacks but dislike being attacked in return. Don't use this power for brutes or soldiers,

because they're supposed to be attacked. A specter that pops up in the middle of the party and unleashes its *beguiling strike* can cause a cascade of opportunity attacks against the target.

> ⟊ **Beguiling Strike** (standard; encounter) ✦ **Charm**
> This creature makes a melee basic attack. If the attack hits, the target is beguiled (save ends). While the target is beguiled, it makes an opportunity attack against any one of its allies that attacks the creature that used *beguiling strike* on it.

DISTRACTING ILLUSION

An at-will attack that can slow multiple characters is great for any artillery or controller monster that favors ranged and area attacks, because it keeps the characters at a distance. It also prevents characters from breaking away from a combat to pursue another foe. A cyclops impaler that has *distracting illusion* uses it to prevent the PCs from evading its cyclops warrior allies.

> ✳ **Distracting Illusion** (standard; at-will) ✦ **Illusion**
> Area burst 2 within 10; level + 5 vs. Will; the target is slowed and can't shift until the end of this creature's next turn.

SURPRISE ATTACK

Add this power to an artillery or a lurker that has a good Stealth modifier or an invisibility power. An elf

VINCENT DUTRAIT

archer with *surprise attack* takes on a strong lurker flavor, using its Stealth skill to become hidden before launching a longbow attack.

> **✝ or ➶ Surprise Attack** (standard; usable while this creature is hidden; recharge ⚄ ⚅)
> This creature makes a melee or ranged at-will attack that deals 1d8 extra damage.
> *Level 11:* 2d8 extra damage.
> *Level 21:* 3d8 extra damage.

UTILITY POWERS

Feywild creatures are known for their stealth and trickery, and these powers reflect those qualities.

CHANGE SHAPE

This power is great for keeping characters from knowing what they're facing until it's too late. Only humanoid monsters can use this power. A medusa archer's snaky hair gives its identity away–unless it has *change shape*.

> **Change Shape** (minor; at-will) ✦ **Polymorph**
> The creature can alter its physical form to appear as an attractive humanoid of its size and any race or gender (see "Change Shape," *Monster Manual 2*, page 216).

FADE AWAY

Fade away performs double duty as a defensive power and as a way for an artillery monster, a lurker, or a skirmisher to gain combat advantage for its next barrage of attacks. Don't use it for monsters that are supposed to draw attention (including brutes and soldiers). A stirge with *fade away* that grabs a character becomes harder to kill, since you can hit it only once before it turns invisible for a round.

> **Fade Away** (immediate reaction, when this creature takes damage; encounter) ✦ **Illusion**
> The creature becomes invisible until it attacks or until the end of its next turn.

FEY STEP

This power gives an artillery monster a quick escape, allowing it to keep launching ranged attacks from a safe distance. It also works well for skirmishers and soldiers, particularly those that benefit from positioning on the battlefield (such as flanking). A macetail behemoth with *fey step* can teleport into the middle of a group of enemies to use *tail sweep*–much easier than moving normally!

> **Fey Step** (move; encounter) ✦ **Teleportation**
> This creature teleports 5 squares.

FEYWILD POSITIONING

This power can change a combat significantly, bringing a controller's or skirmisher's allies from vulnerable positions into superior ones. Use it to set up (or escape from) flanks, converge on a bloodied character, or slip away through difficult terrain. A gnoll claw fighter can use *Feywild positioning* to allow its allies to shift adjacent to a foe, so it can deal extra damage with *pack attack* in the next round.

> **Feywild Positioning** (minor; encounter)
> Each fey ally within 5 squares of this creature can shift 2 squares as a free action. The creatures ignore difficult terrain during the shift.

Fey Bodak Skulk	**Level 16 Lurker**
Medium fey humanoid (undead)	XP 1,400

Initiative +16   **Senses** Perception +10; darkvision
Agonizing Gaze (Fear, Gaze, Necrotic) aura 5; each creature within the aura that makes a melee or a ranged attack against the bodak skulk takes 5 necrotic damage before the attack roll is made and takes a -2 penalty to the attack roll.
HP 124; **Bloodied** 62
AC 29; **Fortitude** 29, **Reflex** 27, **Will** 29
Immune disease, poison; **Resist** 15 necrotic; **Vulnerable** 5 radiant; a bodak skulk that takes radiant damage cannot weaken a target until the end of its next turn.
Speed 6
⊕ **Slam** (standard; at-will) ✦ **Necrotic**
+21 vs. AC; 1d6 + 5 damage plus 2d6 necrotic damage, and the target is weakened until the end of the bodak skulk's next turn.
✝ **Surprise Attack** (standard; usable while the bodak skulk is hidden; recharge ⚄ ⚅)
The bodak skulk makes a melee at-will attack that deals 2d8 extra damage.
➶ **Death Gaze** (standard; encounter) ✦ **Gaze, Necrotic**
Ranged 10; targets a living creature; +19 vs. Fortitude; if the target is weakened, it drops to 0 hit points; otherwise, the target takes 1d6 + 6 necrotic damage and loses a healing surge.
Spectral Form (standard; at-will)
The bodak skulk becomes invisible and gains insubstantial and phasing. It can do nothing but move in its spectral form, and it can return to its normal form as a free action.
Change Shape (minor; at-will) ✦ **Polymorph**
The bodak skulk can alter its physical form to appear as an attractive humanoid of its size and any race or gender (see "Change Shape," *Monster Manual 2*, page 216).
Skills Stealth +14
Alignment Evil   **Languages** Common
Str 21 (+13)   **Dex** 19 (+12)   **Wis** 15 (+10)
Con 22 (+14)   **Int** 6 (+6)   **Cha** 23 (+14)

ENCOUNTER GROUP

A ruthless eladrin uses a couple of bodak skulks infused with fey powers as bodyguards and also to hunt his enemies.

Level 17 Encounter (XP 8,400)
- ✦ 2 fey bodak skulks (level 16 lurker)
- ✦ 1 bralani of autumn winds (level 19 controller; *Monster Manual*, page 102)
- ✦ 2 firebred hell hounds (level 17 brute; *Monster Manual*, page 160)

The prolific, ill-tempered creatures known as goblins—including their hobgoblin and bugbear cousins—live in nearly every corner of the world. By extension, then, they live near almost every kind of creature in the world. From time to time, these tribes adopt, enslave, or domesticate nongoblins. Some of these creatures serve the goblins, while others live alongside them or even lead them.

Whatever their place in the tribe, these creatures inevitably learn new tricks from the goblins around them. Hobgoblins teach military tactics and discipline, while bugbears share their predatory, bullying ways. And of course, you can't live in a goblin tribe without picking up basic methods of sneaky survival.

Common goblin-friends include pets such as wolves, worgs, and drakes. Ogres, ettins, and other big humanoids find work as guards in goblin society. Some hobgoblin tribes welcome devils in their midst, and in rare instances a truce between goblins and a rival humanoid tribe (such as lizardfolk) might lead to a sharing of traditions. Of course, goblins of all kinds also learn tricks from each other, so the sight of bugbears learning hobgoblin discipline or tough goblins learning to bully the smaller among them are quite common.

Although physical changes aren't common to monsters that have this theme, such creatures bear particular symbols of the tribe. These might take the form of crude icons painted onto armor, garish tattoos, or simple brands.

If your campaign features more than one notable goblin tribe, differentiate them by choosing dissimilar pets and allies (or powers) for each tribe. For instance, if the mighty Red Hand tribe is known for its drakes and ogres, perhaps the lowly Broken Spear clan favors wolves and enslaved kobolds.

Skill Modifications: +2 bonus to Athletics checks or Stealth checks. The Athletics bonus represents hobgoblin-style military training, while the Stealth bonus is picked up from hanging around with goblins and bugbears.

ATTACK POWERS

This selection includes options flavored for all three of the main kinds of goblins.

MINION SACRIFICE

This power works best in the hands of an artillery monster, a controller, or a lurker that leads minions from a distance. Effectively, it turns each minion into a one-use ranged attack. A goblin hexer feels little remorse when ordering its goblin cutter minions to throw themselves onto the swords of its enemies.

With its *incite bravery* power, it can even maneuver them into the ideal position.

Minion Sacrifice (standard; at-will)
Area burst 1 within 10; targets one enemy adjacent to this creature's minion ally; level + 7 vs. AC; the target is dazed until the end of this creature's next turn. One minion ally adjacent to the target drops to 0 hit points.

PREDATORY EYE

Give this power to a brute, a lurker, or a skirmisher that can achieve combat advantage easily. Some bugbears teach this trick to their dire wolf pets.

Predatory Eye (minor; encounter)
This creature deals 1d6 extra damage on the next attack it makes against a creature granting combat advantage to it. It must apply this bonus before the end of its next turn.
Level 11: 2d6 extra damage.
Level 21: 3d6 extra damage.

TACTICAL OPPORTUNITY

This power draws melee attacks from adjacent goblin allies to this creature. Thus, a soldier monster that has this power pairs well with any goblin that doesn't like to be attacked (which includes most goblins). With his reach, the human guard can make excellent use of this power (since he doesn't have to be adjacent to the triggering attacker).

Tactical Opportunity (immediate reaction, when an enemy misses an ally and that ally uses *goblin tactics*; at-will)
This creature makes a melee basic attack against the triggering enemy.

TACTICAL ORDERS

From sneaky goblins to tactical hobgoblins to predatory bugbears, virtually all goblin brutes, controllers, and soldiers (leaders are best) benefit from good positioning. A hobgoblin commander who has *tactical orders* can turn a rabble of goblin cutters, blackblades, and sharpshooters into a deadly threat by enhancing their existing benefits from combat advantage.

Tactical Orders aura 5; any bugbear, hobgoblin, or goblin ally within the aura deals 1d6 extra damage to a creature granting combat advantage to it (or 1 extra damage if the ally is a minion).

Utility Powers

Most of these powers are designed to benefit groups of allies, from the great numbers favored by *bullying demeanor* to the hobgoblin allies required by *phalanx soldier* and *rallying cry*.

Bullying Demeanor

This power works best when you give it to a brute or a soldier that has the most hit points in the group and surround it with lower-level allies (or even minions). A bugbear warrior with *bullying demeanor* brings along a dozen goblin cutters to make him feel tough.

Bullying Demeanor
> This creature gains a +2 bonus to melee attack rolls while its allies (including itself) outnumber its enemies. While no ally is within sight, this creature takes a -2 penalty to all defenses.

Goblin Tactics

This power works well for artillery, lurker, and skirmisher monsters both as an escape maneuver and as a positioning trick (to flank a foe). Goblin tribes sometimes train gray wolves in *goblin tactics*, allowing the beasts to take up the flanking positions they and their goblin masters enjoy.

Goblin Tactics (immediate reaction, when missed by a melee attack; at-will)
> This creature shifts 1 square.

Phalanx Soldier

A minion or a soldier that has this power needs hobgoblins around to benefit from it, so use it in groups. A bugbear warrior trained to fight in an orderly fashion alongside its hobgoblin allies can become a dangerous foe.

Phalanx Soldier
> This creature gains a +2 bonus to AC while at least one hobgoblin ally is adjacent to it. This creature also counts as a hobgoblin for the purpose of other creatures' *phalanx soldier* ability.

Rallying Cry

Thanks to *hobgoblin resilience*, this power, which works well with a brute or a soldier, is likely triggered during most combats, as long as the creature stays near its hobgoblin allies. A bugbear warrior (perhaps trained by hobgoblin commanders) appreciates this power, particularly when it teams up with a bunch of hobgoblin grunts.

Rallying Cry (immediate reaction, when a hobgoblin ally within 2 squares of this creature saves; encounter)
> This creature gains temporary hit points equal to 3 + its level.

Young Blue Dragon Goblin Ally   Level 6 Solo Artillery
Large natural magical beast (dragon)   XP 1,250

Initiative +5   **Senses** Perception +10; darkvision
Tactical Orders aura 5; any bugbear, hobgoblin, or goblin ally within the aura deals 1d6 extra damage to a creature granting combat advantage to it (or 1 extra damage if the ally is a minion).
HP 296; **Bloodied** 148; see also *bloodied breath*
AC 23; **Fortitude** 24, **Reflex** 21, **Will** 21
Resist 15 lightning
Saving Throws +5
Speed 8, fly 10 (hover), overland flight 15
Action Points 2
ⓣ **Gore** (standard; at-will) ✦ **Lightning**
 Reach 2; +11 vs. AC; 1d6 + 5 plus 1d6 lightning damage.
ⓣ **Claw** (standard; at-will)
 Reach 2; +9 vs. AC; 1d4 + 5 damage.
† **Draconic Fury** (standard; at-will)
 The dragon makes a gore attack and two claw attacks.
↗ **Breath Weapon** (standard; recharge ⚄ ⚅) ✦ **Lightning**
 The dragon targets up to three creatures with its lightning breath; the first target must be within 10 squares of the dragon, the second target within 10 squares of the first, and the third target within 10 squares of the second; +11 vs. Reflex; 1d12 + 5 lightning damage. *Miss:* Half damage. This attack does not provoke opportunity attacks.
↗ **Bloodied Breath** (free, when first bloodied; encounter)
 Breath weapon recharges, and the dragon uses it.
↞ **Frightful Presence** (standard; encounter) ✦ **Fear**
 Close burst 5; targets enemies; +11 vs. Will; the target is stunned until the end of the dragon's next turn. *Aftereffect:* The target takes a -2 penalty to attack rolls (save ends).
✵ **Lightning Burst** (standard; at-will) ✦ **Lightning**
 Area burst 2 within 20; +11 vs. Reflex; 1d6 + 4 lightning damage. *Miss:* Half damage.
Phalanx Soldier
 The young blue dragon gains a +2 bonus to AC while at least one hobgoblin ally is adjacent to it. The dragon also counts as a hobgoblin for the purpose of other creatures' *phalanx soldier* ability.
Alignment Evil   **Languages** Common, Draconic
Skills Athletics +20, Insight +10, Nature +10
Str 20 (+8)   **Dex** 15 (+5)   **Wis** 14 (+5)
Con 18 (+7)   **Int** 12 (+4)   **Cha** 13 (+4)

Encounter Group

Hobgoblins enjoy raising fierce pets, and what creature fits that description better than a dragon?

Level 9 Encounter (XP 2,066)
- ✦ 1 young blue dragon goblin ally (level 6 solo artillery)
- ✦ 1 hobgoblin commander (level 5 soldier; *Monster Manual*, page 140)
- ✦ 7 hobgoblin warriors (level 8 minion; *Monster Manual*, page 138)

Of the many vast armies that have marched across the fiery plains of the Nine Hells, none is as well known to mortals as the infamous Legion of Avernus. Named for the uppermost layer of the Hells, this army theoretically owes its allegiance to the pit fiend Bel. In reality the legion has no one ruler, since its teachings and influence have long since spread beyond the astral dominion of the devils.

Today, splinter groups calling themselves the Legion of Avernus exist across the world and even on other planes. These groups frequently serve as mercenaries for anyone willing to meet their high price. They care little for the cause and are willing to kill anyone, anywhere . . . with one exception: Some say that no legionnaire will ever knowingly battle another, even if they belong to different platoons bearing no alliance other than their shared origin.

Veterans of the legion invariably bear scars both physical and mental from their inhumanly intense training regimen. Their loyalty to one another bears no question; to the last member, every unit lays down its life for the legion.

Though the group was once entirely made up of devils, humanoids now compose the largest section of the Legion of Avernus. Humans and hobgoblins are common among the legion, but many tieflings, dwarves, dragonborn, and half-orcs find the legion to their liking as well.

The legion trains mighty beasts such as rage drakes, owlbears, and dire wolves to fight alongside its soldiers.

Most members of the legion are (or soon become) evil; it's just too hard to engage in emotionless slaughter without turning dark inside, and the legion has no room for sensitive souls. However, chaotic evil creatures lack the discipline to survive long in the legion.

Particularly infamous legion platoons include the Broken Fangs (a squadron of hobgoblins and low-level devils, with several dire wolves and a young red dragon), and the Infernal Infantry (a group of azers and legion devil veterans led by a fire giant forge-caller named the Crimson General).

Skill Modifications: +2 bonus to Athletics, Endurance, and Intimidate checks.

ATTACK POWERS

The attack powers of the Legion of Avernus reward good positioning and tactics.

FIRE SHIELD

This power adds a bit of damage-dealing ability to a melee-based monster, or provides stay-away incentive when fighting more fragile foes. A tiefling heretic's *fire shield* gives PCs a good reason to stand back.

> **Fire Shield** (Fire) aura 1; each enemy that enters the aura or starts its turn there takes 2 fire damage.
> *Level 11:* 5 fire damage.
> *Level 21:* 8 fire damage.

INFERNAL WOUND

Give this power to a soldier that otherwise lacks the ability to mark PCs. A squad of hobgoblin warriors with *infernal wound* keeps the PCs' attention away from the hobgoblins' leaders.

> **Infernal Wound** (standard; recharge ⚄ ⚅)
> This creature makes a melee basic attack. If the attack hits, the target is marked and takes ongoing 5 damage (save ends both).

INSPIRING DEATH

This power works best in the hands of any minion or soldier likely to die before its comrades do. Legion devils of any level are proud to offer their platoon an *inspiring death*.

> **Inspiring Death** (when this creature drops to 0 hit points)
> One ally within 2 squares of this creature gains a +2 bonus to the next attack roll and damage roll it makes before the end of that ally's turn.

MINION SACRIFICE

A minion ordered by an artillery, a controller, or a lurker monster to throw itself onto the blade of a PC is sure to call attention to itself, so make sure you have plenty of legion devil minions of the appropriate level. A tiefling darkblade with *minion sacrifice* can throw minion after minion at the characters while hidden, setting up its other allies to take advantage of the dazed targets.

> **Minion Sacrifice** (standard; at-will)
> Area burst 1 within 10; targets one enemy adjacent to this creature's minion ally; level + 7 vs. AC; the target is dazed until the end of this creature's next turn. One minion ally adjacent to the target drops to 0 hit points.

UTILITY POWERS

The following powers represent both tactical training and physical hardening.

FIRE RESISTANCE

Pair a fire-resistant creature with fire-using allies for maximum effect. A cambion hellfire magus doesn't need this resistance . . . but the rakshasa warriors serving it appreciate the protection from its *soulscorch* power.

TRIUMPHANT SURGE

This power works best when its owner, a brute or a soldier, can survive late into the battle. Most ogres don't have the discipline for the legion, but the rare ogre warhulk that doesn't wash out gains great effect from *triumphant surge*.

Triumphant Surge (whenever this creature bloodies an enemy or reduces an enemy to 0 hit points)
  This creature gains temporary hit points equal to one-half its level.

Hobgoblin Legionnaire of Avernus	Level 5 Soldier (Leader)
Medium natural humanoid	XP 200

Initiative +8   **Senses** Perception +5; low-light vision
HP 64; **Bloodied** 32
AC 21; **Fortitude** 21, **Reflex** 18, **Will** 19; see also *squad defense*
Speed 5
⊕ **Spear** (standard; at-will) ✦ **Weapon**
  +12 vs. AC; 1d8 + 5 damage. If the hobgoblin commander hits with an opportunity attack, it shifts 1 square; see also *lead from the front*.
↤ **Tactical Deployment** (minor; recharge ⚄ ⚅)
  Close burst 5; allies in the burst shift 3 squares.
Infernal Wound (standard; recharge ⚄ ⚅)
  The hobgoblin commander makes a melee basic attack. If the attack hits, the target is marked and takes ongoing 5 damage (save ends both).
Lead from the Front
  When the hobgoblin commander's melee attack hits an enemy, allies gain a +2 bonus to attack rolls and damage rolls against that enemy until the end of the hobgoblin commander's next turn.
Hobgoblin Resilience (immediate reaction, when the hobgoblin commander becomes subject to an effect; encounter)
  The hobgoblin commander rolls a saving throw against the triggering effect.
Squad Defense
  The hobgoblin commander gains a +2 bonus to all defenses while adjacent to a legion devil or any creature that has the Legion of Avernus theme.
Alignment Evil   **Languages** Common, Goblin
Skills Athletics +14, Endurance +7, History +10, Intimidate +9
Str 20 (+7)   **Dex** 14 (+4)   **Wis** 16 (+5)
Con 16 (+5)   **Int** 12 (+3)   **Cha** 10 (+2)
Equipment scale armor, heavy shield, spear

Fire Resistance
  This creature gains resist 10 fire.
  Level 11: Resist 20 fire.
  Level 21: Resist 30 fire.

LEGION INITIATIVE

This power benefits monsters that want to choose where the fight occurs, whether by charging at PCs before they can react or by moving to a more defensible position. Bearded devils with *legion initiative* can win initiative more easily, exposing PCs to their *beard tendrils* aura when the characters' first turn comes up.

Legion Initiative
  This creature gains a +5 bonus to its initiative check if at least one ally is within sight.

SQUAD DEFENSE

Obviously, this power requires appropriate allies to have any effect, so pair a controller, a minion, or a soldier with legion devils or other creatures of this theme. A line of hobgoblin soldiers with *squad defense* becomes nearly unbreakable.

Squad Defense
  This creature gains a +2 bonus to all defenses while adjacent to a legion devil or any creature that has the Legion of Avernus theme.

ENCOUNTER GROUP

Many hobgoblins find the Legion of Avernus to their liking. Those who rise to positions of command lead small platoons of devils into battle.

Level 6 Encounter (XP 1,330)
✦ 1 hobgoblin commander (level 5 soldier)
✦ 10 legion devil grunts (level 6 minion; *Monster Manual*, page 64)
✦ 2 spined devils (level 6 skirmisher; *Monster Manual*, page 66)

The vile and sinister drow serve their Spider Queen with a mixture of loyalty and fear. Priests rule with ruthless authority, and those who show promise receive special blessings from their divine ruler.

Although drow, driders, and spiders are the most common creatures to become Lolth's Chosen, the Spider Queen's gifts can seem unexplainable to mortals. Many monsters considered to be of the "servant class" receive these gifts as well, from goblins and ettercaps to grimlocks and rage drakes. Powerful allies such as demons and vampires are also occasionally chosen by the Spider Queen.

Lolth has need of both foot soldiers and specialists, so her chosen include creatures of all roles from minion to controller. Each one knows its place in the hierarchy, never daring to question those above it in status.

Chosen drow typically wear an ornate platinum spider embossed or embroidered on their clothing as an emblem of their status. Lesser creatures of this theme instead bear tattoos or brands in the shape of a spider. Some also grow spidery limbs or fangs, and compound eyes are a common mutation as well.

Skill Modifications: +2 bonus to Dungeoneering and Stealth checks.

ATTACK POWERS

These powers include options derived from existing drow. All work well with drow tactics and allies.

DARKFIRE

Combat advantage is useful to any creature, but this power shines when an artillery, a lurker, or a skirmisher monster (or its allies) relies on combat advantage for additional effects. A bugbear strangler with *darkfire* can set up its own strangle attack without needing to flank or ambush the enemy.

Darkfire (minor; encounter)
Ranged 10; level + 1 vs. Reflex; until the end of this creature's next turn, the target grants combat advantage and can't benefit from invisibility or concealment.

LOLTH'S AUTHORITY

Though normally the purview of drow priests, the authority of Lolth is sometimes granted to other beings judged worthy of leading her "children." Controllers and soldiers (specifically leaders) can make best advantage of this power. An ettercap fang guard uses *Lolth's authority* to enhance its deathjump spider allies.

Lolth's Authority aura 5; each drow or spider ally within the aura gains a +1 bonus to attack rolls and a +2 bonus to damage rolls.

POISON WEAPON

Encountering the drow's poison in the hands of another creature, such as a controller or lurker, is a great way to foreshadow the appearance of drow later in an adventure. A squad of grimlock ambushers hints at the group's secret master's identity when their poisoned weapons find the mark.

Poison Weapon (minor; recharge ⚅⚅) ✦ **Poison**
The next time this creature hits a creature with a weapon attack, it makes a secondary attack against that creature. *Secondary Attack:* +16 vs. Fortitude; the target takes a -2 penalty to attack rolls (save ends). *First Failed Saving Throw:* The target is weakened (save ends). *Second Failed Saving Throw:* The target is knocked unconscious (save ends; the target takes a -5 penalty to this saving throw).

VIRULENT POISON

Give this power to a spider or similar creature that has a poison attack to impart additional punch to that attack. A squad of drow warriors with *virulent poison* can open with a devastating volley of attacks.

Virulent Poison (standard; encounter)
The creature makes a melee basic attack. The attack gains the poison keyword, and if the attack hits, the target takes ongoing 5 poison damage (save ends). If the attack already deals ongoing poison damage, increase that value by 5.

UTILITY POWERS

Drow and spider characteristics are mixed here, offering abilities to Lolth's Chosen that are both useful and unsettling.

BLESSING OF THE SPIDER QUEEN

Give this power to any creature allied to a drow, or to those that have special powers affecting drow or spiders. Bugbear warriors with *blessing of the Spider Queen* can deliver devastating attacks to enemies enveloped by a drow's *cloud of darkness*, and they also benefit from a drow priest's *Lolth's authority* aura (see above).

Blessing of the Spider Queen
This creature is not blinded while within a *cloud of darkness*, nor does that power block this creature's line of sight. This creature is considered a drow and a spider for the purpose of the effects of allies' powers.

CLOUD OF DARKNESS

This power lets an artillery monster, a lurker, or a skirmisher attack with combat advantage or slip away from adjacent enemies without provoking opportunity attacks. Some flameskulls crafted from the heads of drow spellcasters retain the ability to create a *cloud of darkness* to disguise their escape.

↞ **Cloud of Darkness** (minor; encounter) ✦ **Zone**

Close burst 1; the burst creates a zone of darkness that lasts until the end of this creature's next turn. The zone blocks line of sight for any creature except this one. Any creature except this one is blinded while within the zone.

SCUTTLING ESCAPE

This power is best in the hands of a leader, an elite, or a solo monster—the kind of enemy you expect to last until the retreat is sounded. Of course, the commander leaves all nondrow and nonspider allies behind to "guard the escape route." A drow blademaster with *scuttling escape* can last long enough to turn a potential rout into a chance for its comrades to fight another day.

Scuttling Escape (move; encounter)

This creature and each drow or spider ally within 5 squares of it can shift 4 squares as a free action.

SPIDER CLIMB

This power lets a monster reach a defensible position, escape enemies, or even just look extra creepy. A drow arachnomancer scuttling across the wall alongside its spider allies is sure to send a shiver down the PCs' spines.

AMELIA STONER

Spider Climb

This creature gains a climb speed equal to its normal speed, and can use its climb speed to move across overhanging horizontal surfaces (such as ceilings) without making Athletics checks.

Chosen Mezzodemon	**Level 11 Soldier**
Medium elemental humanoid (demon)	XP 600

Initiative +9   **Senses** Perception +13; darkvision
HP 113; **Bloodied** 56
AC 27; **Fortitude** 25, **Reflex** 22, **Will** 23
Resist 20 poison, 10 variable (2/encounter)
Speed 6

⊕ **Trident** (standard; at-will) ✦ **Weapon**
Reach 2; +18 vs. AC; 1d8 + 5 damage.

↓ **Skewering Tines** (standard; requires a trident; at-will) ✦ **Weapon**
Reach 2; +18 vs. AC; 1d8 + 5 damage, and the target is restrained and takes ongoing 5 damage (save ends both). While the target is restrained, the mezzodemon can't make trident attacks.

↞ **Poison Breath** (standard; recharge ⚄ ⚅) ✦ **Poison**
Close blast 3; targets enemies; +16 vs. Fortitude; 2d6 + 3 poison damage, and ongoing 5 poison damage (save ends).

Poison Weapon (minor; recharge ⚅) ✦ **Poison**
The next time the mezzodemon hits a creature with a weapon attack, it makes a secondary attack against that creature. *Secondary Attack:* +16 vs. Fortitude; the target takes a –2 penalty to attack rolls (save ends). *First Failed Saving Throw:* The target is weakened (save ends). *Second Failed Saving Throw:* The target is knocked unconscious (save ends; the target takes a –5 penalty to this saving throw).

Blessing of the Spider Queen
The mezzodemon is not blinded while within a *cloud of darkness*, nor does that power block this creature's line of sight. The mezzodemon is considered a drow and a spider for the purpose of the effects of allies' powers.

Alignment Chaotic evil   **Languages** Abyssal
Skills Dungeoneering +10, Intimidate +11, Stealth +9
| **Str** 20 (+10) | **Dex** 15 (+7) | **Wis** 16 (+8) |
| **Con** 17 (+8) | **Int** 10 (+5) | **Cha** 13 (+6) |
Equipment trident

ENCOUNTER GROUP

Mezzodemons that have the Lolth's Chosen theme are special gifts from the Spider Queen to her most trusted servants.

Level 12 Encounter (XP 3,800)

✦ 1 drow arachnomancer (level 13 artillery; *Monster Manual*, page 94)
✦ 2 drow warriors (level 11 lurker; *Monster Manual*, page 94)
✦ 3 chosen mezzodemons (level 11 soldier)

ORCUS BLOOD CULTIST

Known as the Demon Prince of the Undead, Orcus rules from the palace of Everlost, deep within the Abyss. From there, his influence spreads across his realm of Thanatos and into the world in the form of countless undead servants as well as scattered cults that gather in graveyards and similar locations.

Such cults invariably include undead among their number, from the lowly skeleton or zombie to mummies and liches. Many of these creatures manifest new powers as a mark of their allegiance to the Blood Lord.

Humanoids also serve Orcus, from death-crazed acolytes to dark hierophants. Cult leaders share the Demon Prince's corpulent physique, while rank-and-file members might be gaunt and skeletal, or they might even encourage rotting wounds to fester in their flesh. The most "blessed" among them teeter on the brink between life and undeath.

As one of the most powerful denizens of the Abyss, Orcus also counts demons among his faithful. These demons take on aspects of undeath, and some bear ram's head brands deep in their flesh.

Monsters of all roles find service in the cults of Orcus, though the Prince of Undead favors brutes, controllers, and lurkers.

Skill Modification: +2 bonus to Religion checks.

ATTACK POWERS

The attack powers detailed here run the gamut of flavors of undeath, including both ranged and melee options.

AURA OF IMPENDING DEATH

This power is great in the hands of an artillery monster or a brute that has lots of hit points, but it also helps keep characters away from more fragile monsters. An ogre warhulk with *aura of impending death* draws a lot of attention, since characters must struggle to defeat it before the aura kills them.

Aura of Impending Death (Necrotic) aura 2; while this creature is bloodied, each enemy that enters the aura or starts its turn there takes necrotic damage equal to one-half this creature's level (minimum 1).

BLOODSTAINED STRIKE

This power is appropriate for any brute, lurker, skirmisher, or soldier, but it works best in the hands of a monster that can easily maneuver to reach a chosen target. A group of dark creepers with *bloodstained strike* can quickly converge on a bloodied character.

Bloodstained Strike (standard; recharge ⚁ ⚂) ✦ **Necrotic**
This creature makes a melee basic attack against a bloodied target. This creature gains a +2 bonus to the attack roll and deals extra necrotic damage equal to one-half its level.

PENUMBRA OF DOOM

Combine artillery, lurker, and soldier monsters (specifically leaders) that have this power with multiple undead allies. A troglodyte impaler with *penumbra of doom* can make an unfortunate character into an excellent target for its honor guard of boneshard skeletons.

Penumbra of Doom (standard; at-will)
Ranged 10; level + 5 vs. Fortitude; the target is weakened until the end of this creature's next turn. Also, this creature's undead allies deal 1d6 extra damage until the end of this creature's next turn (2 damage if the creature is a minion).
Level 11: 2d6 extra damage (4 damage if the creature is a minion).
Level 21: 3d6 extra damage (6 damage if the creature is a minion).

ROTTING STRIKE

A creature that has this power needs to survive until characters are bloodied, so it either needs good hit points or the ability to stay safe until the right moment. Brutes, lurkers, and skirmishers make excellent candidates for this power. Zombies become a more significant threat when they unleash *rotting strikes* midway through the fight.

> **Rotting Strike** (free, when this creature hits with a melee basic attack during its turn; encounter) ✦ **Necrotic**
> The target takes ongoing necrotic damage equal to 2 + one-half this creature's level (save ends).

UTILITY POWERS

These powers bestow a strong essence of undeath on any creature.

THE DEAD RISE

This power is appropriate only for monsters of 16th level or higher. The more creatures that are around one that has this power, the more chances a monster with this power gets to use it, so be sure to include plenty of foes in the encounter. Don't give this power to more than one creature in a fight—it's just too confusing to keep track of all the dead rising. A dracolich gets extra value from its rakshasa warrior allies thanks to this power.

> **The Dead Rise** aura 6; one dead nonminion creature within the aura at the start of this creature's turn rises as an abyssal ghoul hungerer to fight at this creature's command.
> *Level 26:* The dead creature rises as an abyssal ghoul myrmidon instead.

DEATH'S EMBRACE

Give this to a creature you expect to be in the middle of combat. If you put this aura on multiple creatures, spread them out to cover the entire battlefield. A swarm of abyssal ghoul hungerers with *death's embrace* ensures that PCs won't ignore them in favor of the ghouls' master.

> **Death's Embrace** aura 5; each enemy within the aura takes a -2 penalty to death saving throws.

NECROTIC BURST

Any brute, controller, or soldier (preferably leader) in a team of undead can benefit from a timely *necrotic burst*. A battle wight with *necrotic burst* can make his zombie hulk servants even more durable.

> **Necrotic Burst** (minor; encounter)
> Each undead ally within 5 squares of this creature gains temporary hit points equal to 2 + this creature's level.

SPIRIT OF UNDEATH

This power makes any creature feel like one of the undead, rewarding good player character tactics as well as augmenting appropriate monster powers. A deathlock wight that employs human guards that have *spirit of undeath* can bring them back from the dead with its *reanimate* power.

> **Spirit of Undeath**
> The creature gains resistance to necrotic damage equal to 5 + one-half its level, and it gains vulnerability to radiant damage equal to half that value. This creature is considered undead for the purpose of the effects of allies' powers.

Zombie Hulk of Orcus		Level 8 Brute
Large natural animate (undead)		XP 350

Initiative +2   **Senses** Perception +3; darkvision
Death's Embrace aura 5; each enemy within the aura takes a -2 penalty to death saving throws.
HP 88; **Bloodied** 44; see also *rise again*
AC 20; **Fortitude** 23, **Reflex** 17, **Will** 18
Immune disease, poison; **Resist** 10 necrotic; **Vulnerable** 10 radiant
Speed 4
⊕ **Slam** (standard; at-will)
    Reach 2; +12 vs. AC; 2d8 + 5 damage.
† **Zombie Smash** (standard; recharge ⚄⚅)
    Reach 2; targets a Medium or smaller creature; +12 vs. AC; 4d8 + 5 damage, and the target is knocked prone.
Rotting Strike (free, when the zombie hulk hits with a melee basic attack during its turn; encounter) ✦ **Necrotic**
    The target takes ongoing 6 necrotic damage (save ends).
Rise Again (the first time the zombie hulk drops to 0 hit points)
    The zombie hulk makes a new initiative check. On its next turn, the zombie hulk rises (as a move action) with 44 hit points.

Alignment Unaligned		**Languages** –
Str 21 (+9)	**Dex** 6 (+2)	**Wis** 8 (+3)
Con 18 (+8)	**Int** 1 (-1)	**Cha** 3 (+0)

ENCOUNTER GROUP

Zombie hulks of Orcus frequently serve priests of the Demon Prince of Undead, working alongside other undead servants.

Level 7 Encounter (XP 1,700)

- ✦ 1 deathpriest of Orcus (level 9 controller; *Monster Manual*, page 210)
- ✦ 3 wraiths (level 5 lurker; *Monster Manual*, page 266)
- ✦ 2 zombie hulks of Orcus (level 8 brute)

The *Monster Manual* details several human snaketongue cultists, but by using this theme you can create an endless variety of devotees of Zehir. Regardless of the original creature's form, after transformation into a snaketongue it becomes a loyal disciple of the god of poison.

The yuan-ti prefer human cultists, because these servants can pass for normal in society. However, Zehir welcomes evil humanoids from all races and backgrounds, from tieflings and hobgoblins to savage lizardfolk and corrupt eladrin. The snaketongue cult also includes serpentine and reptilian creatures of all sizes, including snakes, wyverns, drakes, and hydras. You can also enhance existing snaketongue cultists and even yuan-ti with these powers.

The powers common to the snaketongue cult are appropriate for all roles, since the cult welcomes all to the service of Zehir. The yuan-ti deem minions, brutes, and soldiers expendable, but they prize lurkers and controllers for their key talents of assassination and battlefield leadership.

All snaketongue cultists bear minor reptilian traits. In some cases, these traits are readily visible: scaled skin, sharp claws, or slitted eyes. Other cultists display more subtle transformations, including forked tongues or unusually sinuous limbs. Least common of all are the massive bodily transformations, such as a cobra's hood or a snakelike body in place of legs.

Skill Modifications: +2 bonus to Bluff checks and Stealth checks.

ATTACK POWERS

Unsurprisingly, most snaketongue attack powers are related to poison use—either that of the cultist or of its allies.

SERPENT'S WORDS

Although useful in many situations, this power is best when the wielder (a controller works well) has allies that gain benefits from combat advantage. A hobgoblin warcaster allied with plenty of goblin blackblades and sharpshooters can use *serpent's words* to great effect.

> **Serpent's Words** (standard; at-will)
> Ranged 5; targets a nondeafened creature; level + 5 vs. Will; the target is dazed until the end of this creature's next turn.

SNAKETONGUE POISON

Any weapon-wielding creature can benefit from this power, but it's even better if the creatures can expect to survive long enough to recharge the power. A doppelganger assassin can deliver a *snaketongue poison* attack, then use *cloud mind* to hide until it recharges.

> **Snaketongue Poison** (minor; recharge ⚅⚅) ✦ **Poison**
> The next time this creature hits with a weapon attack, the target of the attack takes ongoing poison damage equal to one-half this creature's level (save ends).

TOUCH OF ZEHIR

A creature that has this power need not be able to deal ongoing poison damage, as long as it's paired with creatures that can. Artillery and controller monsters make the best use of this power. A medusa archer with *touch of Zehir* can use the power in concert with its own or any of its snaketongue allies' poison attacks.

> **Touch of Zehir** (standard; at-will) ✦ **Poison**
> Ranged 10; targets a creature that has ongoing poison damage; level + 5 vs. Fortitude; the target takes poison damage equal to its ongoing damage, and it is dazed until the end of this creature's next turn.

VENOM ENHANCEMENT

This power is most effective for a monster, preferably a leader, that stands in the thick of the fight, and the monster should have plenty of allies who deal ongoing poison damage. Rumors of a massive yuan-ti breeding project bent on releasing thousands of deathrattle vipers with *venom enhancement* into the wild are the product of overactive imaginations . . . perhaps.

> **Venom Enhancement** aura 2; each enemy within the aura that has ongoing poison damage takes a –2 penalty to all defenses and saving throws.

CHIPPY

UTILITY POWERS

Snaketongue utility powers lend themselves to tactics of defense and escape, which plays on the yuan-ti's tendency to slip away rather than fighting to the death.

CHAMELEON DEFENSE

This power is good for discouraging ranged attacks. It can protect fragile monsters from ranged attacks, or it can encourage characters to stay close to dangerous melee monsters. Give this power to an entire group of snaketongues to protect them from being picked off at range.

Chameleon Defense

This creature has concealment against enemies that are more than 3 squares away.

SERPENT FORM

This power is appropriate only for monsters of 5th level or higher. It can grant formidable melee capabilities, or provide a way to escape a fight. After expending its encounter powers, a greenscale marsh mystic transforms into a serpent to bring the battle directly to its enemies.

Serpent Form (minor; at-will) ✦ **Polymorph**

The creature transforms into a deathrattle viper. Any equipment the creature is carrying merges with the new form. The creature uses the deathrattle viper's statistics instead of its own, except for hit points. Reverting to its true form is a minor action.
Level 9: The creature becomes a crushgrip constrictor.
Level 16: The creature becomes a shadow snake.

SERPENTINE BODY

This power is fun to unleash on a party that favors immobilizing and restraining attacks, but don't overdo it. A guardian naga that has *serpentine body* becomes nearly impossible to pin down.

Serpentine Body

This creature gains a +5 bonus to saving throws against being immobilized or restrained, and a +5 bonus to checks made as part of an escape action. This creature can also stand up from prone as a minor action.

SLITHER AWAY

Give this power to artillery, lurker, or skirmisher monsters that move around during combat to maximize its benefit. An iron gorgon's *trample* becomes more dangerous when its speed and defenses increase.

Slither Away (while bloodied)

This creature gains a +2 bonus to speed and a +2 bonus to all defenses.

Snaketongue Wyvern	Level 10 Skirmisher
Large natural beast (mount, reptile)	XP 500

Initiative +10   **Senses** Perception +12; low-light vision
Venom Enhancement aura 2; each enemy within the aura that has ongoing poison damage takes a -2 penalty to all defenses and saving throws.
HP 106; **Bloodied** 53
AC 24; **Fortitude** 24, **Reflex** 20, **Will** 19
Speed 4, fly 8 (hover)
⊕ **Bite** (standard; at-will)
   Reach 2; +15 vs. AC; 1d8 + 7 damage.
⊕ **Claws** (standard; usable only while flying; at-will)
   +15 vs. AC; 1d6 + 7 damage, and the target is knocked prone.
ǂ **Sting** (standard; at-will) ✦ **Poison**
   Reach 2; +15 vs. AC; 1d6 + 4 damage, and the wyvern makes a secondary attack against the same target. *Secondary Attack:* +13 vs. Fortitude; ongoing 10 poison damage (save ends).
ǂ **Flyby Attack** (standard; at-will)
   The wyvern flies 8 squares and makes one melee basic attack at any point during that movement. The wyvern doesn't provoke opportunity attacks when moving away from the target.
Aerial Agility +2 (while mounted by a rider of 10th level or higher; at-will) ✦ **Mount**
   While flying, the wyvern grants its rider a +2 bonus to all defenses.
Slither Away (while bloodied)
   The wyvern gains a +2 bonus to speed and a +2 bonus to all defenses.

Alignment Unaligned		**Languages** –
Skills Stealth +10		
Str 24 (+12)	**Dex** 17 (+8)	**Wis** 15 (+7)
Con 18 (+9)	**Int** 2 (+1)	**Cha** 8 (+4)

ENCOUNTER GROUP

Some yuan-ti breed wyverns to display serpentine characteristics. These foul beasts frequently guard lairs of snaketongue cultists.

Level 9 Encounter (XP 2,150)
✦ 1 snaketongue celebrant (level 11 controller; *Monster Manual*, page 273)
✦ 6 snaketongue zealots (level 12 minion; *Monster Manual*, page 272)
✦ 1 snaketongue wyvern (level 10 skirmisher)

Strange, alien entities press at the boundaries of the cosmos. Their horrid, unknowable forms burrow endlessly at the walls of creation, desperate to break through the wards and barriers that keep them at bay, eager to destroy all that lives as they turn the planes into their feasting grounds. These beings are the denizens of the Far Realm, a place beyond nightmare and outside all mortal and divine reason. In the Far Realm, the rules and laws that bind the cosmos together break down into utter chaos.

The alien beings of the Far Realm press against the borders of the cosmos and project their minds into the world to twist, subvert, and control the creatures that would be their prey. The entities of the Far Realm use their powers to rend the minds of mortal creatures. Their corrupted victims call themselves Those Who Hear, because the entities of the Far Realm appear within their minds first as helpful voices that urge them toward achieving their personal desires. Soon the voices change, pushing Those Who Hear to engage in blasphemous rites that call forth Far Realm entities. The voice's desires become the victim's, and in time the unfortunate soul is a puppet controlled by his or her Far Realm masters.

A creature contacted by a Far Realm being becomes a member of a cult centered on the acquisition of esoteric knowledge and forbidden lore. The first creature contacted by the Far Realm serves as the cult's leader. The leader uses innate charm, promises of power, and borrowed magical abilities to gather more cultists to him. Power-hungry mages might also join the cause, along with druids and heretical priests who are disillusioned with the world and who seek new paths to power. Those Who Hear promise not only power, but a fast, easy path to attaining it. This pledge is a siren's lure to the young, ambitious, and reckless. The greatest tragedy of these cults is that many of their members realize the group's true nature only when it is too late to turn against it.

Those Who Hear typically gather in cities and towns, hiding in bastions of civilization. The secrets they need rest in libraries and temples, while they effectively recruit from among young and impressionable apprentices, disaffected youth, and frustrated, petty nobles. Sometimes these cults gather in dungeons and other forgotten corners of the world, particularly if the dungeon hides some secret tied to the Far Realm.

Members of a Far Realm cult typically have a tattoo inscribed over their hearts to mark their membership, or they could have a glyph or other strange symbol hidden beneath their clothing. Although a cult's membership consists primarily of humans, elves, tieflings, and dragonborn, its leaders also call aberrant creatures to their side. Foulspawn, gricks, grells, and carrion crawlers serve the cultists as allies.

Cultists range from unaligned to chaotic evil, moving more and more toward chaos and madness as they delve into the cult's deepest mysteries.

Skill Modifications: +2 bonus to Arcana, Endurance, and Perception checks.

ATTACK POWERS

The attack powers of Those Who Hear allow them to subvert and control their enemies. Some of their abilities transform them into hideous beings of the Far Realm for short periods of time.

AURA OF MADNESS

This aura is great for sliding enemies into flanking situations or moving allies into defensive positions. Controllers or leaders can also push characters into areas of difficult terrain in which they can't shift. A foulspawn berserker's allies use this power to push enemies into its *berserker aura*.

> **Aura of Madness** (opportunity, when a creature starts its turn within 3 squares of this creature)
> This creature slides the triggering creature 1 square.
> *Level 11:* 2 squares.
> *Level 21:* 3 squares.

FAR REALM MANIFESTATION

This power horrifies the players while keeping their characters rooted in place. Soldiers are great beneficiaries of the power. The dragonborn soldier loves the ability to mark adjacent enemies. When this power is combined with the dragonborn's *impetuous spirit* and *martial recovery*, characters have a rough time disengaging from it.

> **Far Realm Manifestation** (minor 1/round; usable only after this creature is first bloodied; at-will)
> Close burst 1; targets enemies; level + 3 vs. Reflex; the target is slowed until the end of this creature's next turn. *Effect:* The target is marked until the end of this creature's next turn.

MIND TWIST

This power works well for a creature that already has abilities that can manipulate its enemies' positions. A tiefling heretic can lure characters into melee, use *cloak of escape* to evade them, and then unleash this power on the closely grouped characters.

> **Mind Twist** (standard; recharge ⚄ ⚅) ✦ **Charm**
> Ranged 10; level + 3 vs. Will; the target makes an at-will attack against one of its allies. The creature that uses *mind twist* chooses the attack and its target. In addition, the target makes opportunity attacks against its allies (save ends).

PSYCHIC SCREAM

A well-placed *psychic scream* ruins the PCs' plans and forces them to confront enemies they would rather avoid, such as minions that have *seed of madness* (see below). This power works well for controllers and soldiers. The foulspawn berserker loves to use this power to force enemies to remain close to it.

Psychic Scream (standard; recharge ⚅⚅) ✦ **Psychic**
Close blast 5; targets enemies; level + 3 vs. Will; 1d8 + one-half level psychic damage. The target is dazed and during its turn, the target must attack the enemy nearest to it at the start of its turn (save ends).

SEED OF MADNESS

This power transforms minions into walking land mines. Though it has a low attack bonus, each minion killed is one more chance for the cultists to control a character. Mobs of human rabble that have this attack are great from a story perspective, since they represent the hapless victims recruited into the cult, and they can serve as living shields that protect the cult's leaders.

Seed of Madness (when an enemy reduces this creature to 0 hit points) ✦ **Charm**
This creature makes the following attack against the triggering enemy: Ranged 20; level + 1 vs. Will; the target is dominated until the end of its next turn. The creature that used *seed of madness* still chooses the dominated creature's action, even if it is dead or unconscious.

UTILITY POWERS

These powers represent the ways that creatures are transformed by their exposure to Far Realm energy.

FAR REALM ACTION

An extra action point is insurance against a missed attack, allowing the creature to use an at-will power again. It can also set up a combination attack with its own abilities. Any creature that deals extra damage with combat advantage, such as the foulspawn mangler, loves an action point. It turns a round of powerful attacks into a devastating flurry.

Far Realm Action
This creature gains 1 action point.

MIND OF MOVEMENT

Artillery, controller, and leader monsters can make excellent use of this power. Pair them with minions and creatures that gain benefits from flanking. For example, a gnome arcanist loves to use this ability to pull its allies into its aura of illusion.

Mind of Movement (minor; recharge ⚄ ⚅)
Each ally within 5 squares of this creature can shift 2 squares as a free action.

PSYCHIC FEEDBACK

Another minion booster, this feature is a great addition to all the members of the cult to create the feel of a hive mind. Creatures that are low-level compared to the PCs and minions make the most of *psychic feedback*.

Psychic Feedback (when this creature drops to 0 hit points) ✦ **Psychic**
Each enemy adjacent to one or more creatures that have *psychic feedback* takes 2 psychic damage.

Crazed Human Rabble	Level 2 Minion
Medium natural humanoid	XP 31

Initiative +1   **Senses** Perception +1
HP 1; a missed attack never damages a minion
AC 15; **Fortitude** 13, **Reflex** 11, **Will** 11; see also *mob rule*
Speed 6
⊕ **Club** (standard; at-will) ✦ **Weapon**
+6 vs. AC; 4 damage.
Aura of Madness (opportunity, when a creature starts its turn within 3 squares of the human rabble)
The human rabble slides the triggering creature 1 square.
Psychic Feedback (when the human rabble drops to 0 hit points) ✦ **Psychic**
Each enemy adjacent to one or more human rabble takes 2 psychic damage.
Mob Rule
The human rabble gains a +2 power bonus to all defenses while at least two other human rabble are within 5 squares of it.

Alignment Unaligned		**Languages** Common
Str 14 (+3)	**Dex** 10 (+1)	**Wis** 10 (+1)
Con 12 (+2)	**Int** 9 (+0)	**Cha** 11 (+1)

Equipment club

ENCOUNTER GROUP

A mob of cultists teaches the PCs that the press of numbers sometimes outweighs their skill at arms, particularly when they face the power of the Far Realm. The gnome and the mage are the cult's priests, the guards are bodyguards clad in ornate armor, and the scout is a spy who works for the cult.

Level 4 Encounter (XP 967)
- ✦ 1 elf scout (level 2 skirmisher; *Monster Manual*, page 106)
- ✦ 1 gnome arcanist (level 3 controller; *Monster Manual*, page 134)
- ✦ 2 human guards (level 3 soldier; *Monster Manual*, page 162)
- ✦ 1 human mage (level 4 artillery; *Monster Manual*, page 163)
- ✦ 7 crazed human rabble (level 2 minion)

Since ancient times, many cults dedicated to Tiamat have borne the bloody insignia of the Red Hand. These cults typically arise behind a powerful, charismatic leader; when the world is fortunate, they fall not long after at the hands of bold heroes. But the influence of the Queen of Evil Dragonkind never disappears from the world, and the cycle continues.

Tiamat's cults can include any sentient creatures seeking wealth and power, from humans or lizardfolk to ogres or giants. Although one incarnation of the Red Hand might be linked to a particular race—such as the hobgoblins of Kulkor Zuul who sought to establish a new empire in the smoking ruins of Elsir Vale some years ago—the next might include members of a dozen races working side by side for the common cause.

Whatever the primary membership of the Red Hand, it invariably includes creatures of draconic descent. Dragons and evil dragonborn flock to Tiamat's banner, eager to serve their dark queen, and dragonspawn and drakes walk alongside the armies as well.

Most creatures belonging to the Red Hand display their loyalty with the group's symbol painted on a tunic or shield: a crimson hand, its five fingers pointed upward. Some also display draconic characteristics, such as scales, fangs, or claws.

Skill Modifications: +2 bonus to Intimidate checks and Perception checks.

ATTACK POWERS

These powers call to mind the most formidable weapons of the dragon: fear and destruction.

BLOODIED RECHARGE

This power makes any creature feel like a dragon by allowing it to reuse a key power when it becomes bloodied. A bodak skulk with *bloodied recharge* can unleash an extra and unexpected *death gaze.*

Bloodied Recharge (free, when first bloodied; encounter)
> One of this creature's encounter attack powers recharges, and this creature uses it.

DRAGON BREATH

A single monster that has *dragon breath* might not make much of an impression . . . but a horde of such monsters does. Use this power with brutes, controllers, skirmishers, and soldiers to achieve the best result. Kobold dragonshields with *dragon breath* keyed to the dragon they serve can use this power without worrying about damaging each other.

✦ **Dragon Breath** (minor; encounter) ✦ **Varies**
> Close blast 3; level + 1 vs. Reflex; 1d8 damage. Choose acid, cold, fire, lightning, or poison when a creature receives this power. This power deals damage of that type.
> *Level 11: 2d8 damage.*
> *Level 21: 3d8 damage.*

FRIGHTFUL PRESENCE

This is a great opening attack for controllers, lurkers, and soldiers because it leaves characters reeling while the monster's allies pour in. Add this to a wyvern and keep its enemies on their toes.

✦ **Frightful Presence** (standard; encounter) ✦ **Fear**
> Close burst 3; targets enemies; level + 3 vs. Will; the target is stunned until the end of this creature's next turn.

TIAMAT'S WILL

Dragons often keep a trusted servant (preferably a leader) that has this power nearby, usually safely out of melee. An elder red dragon might be accompanied by a pair of fire giant forgecallers blessed with *Tiamat's will.*

➢ **Tiamat's Will** (standard; encounter)
> Ranged 10; targets one dragon or dragonborn that has *breath weapon* or *dragon breath*; the target's *breath weapon* or *dragon breath* recharges.

CHIPPY

UTILITY POWERS

The utility powers of Tiamat's Red Hand support the teamwork and loyalty common among her cults.

CHROMATIC BOON

Give this to any brute, skirmisher, or soldier likely to be caught in an ally's burst or blast (such as *dragon breath*). A team of dragonborn soldiers with *chromatic boon* can use *dragon breath* without fear of including their allies in the blast.

Chromatic Boon (immediate interrupt, when an enemy hits or misses this creature; encounter)

The creature gains resist 5 acid, resist 5 cold, resist 5 fire, resist 5 lightning, or resist 5 poison until the end of the encounter.

DEVOUR MINION

A big brute, controller, or soldier that has this power and plenty of minions around changes the tenor of battle; now, those minions aren't just annoyances. A young white dragon can use *devour minion* on its large supply of kobold minions for a boost during combat.

Devour Minion (minor; recharge ⚃ ⚄ ⚅)

This creature reduces one adjacent minion ally that is smaller than it to 0 hit points. This creature gains temporary hit points equal to 5 + the minion's level.

FOR THE MASTER

The more monsters that have this power the better, so give it to a bunch of minions or brutes for maximum effect. For example, when they are not being devoured by their young white dragon master, a horde of kobold minions that have *for the master* can prove daunting.

For the Master

This creature gains a +1 bonus to attack rolls while it is within 5 squares of a dragon. This creature is considered a dragon and a dragonborn for the purpose of the effects of allies' powers.

TELEPATHIC WARNING

Primarily a story element, this power doesn't affect combat . . . unless, of course, the dragon master is near enough to join the fray. Having a few well-placed kobold slyblades with *telepathic warning* throughout a dragon's lair can ensure that their master isn't taken by surprise.

Telepathic Warning (standard; encounter)

This creature sends a short message to a dragon that is up to 1 mile away. This creature can also use this power as a free action when it drops to 0 hit points, even if has already expended the power.

Dragonborn Gladiator of Tiamat	Level 10 Soldier
Medium natural humanoid	XP 500

Initiative +9   **Senses** Perception +6
HP 106; **Bloodied** 53; see also *dragonborn fury*
AC 24; **Fortitude** 23, **Reflex** 20, **Will** 21
Speed 5

⊕ **Bastard Sword** (standard; at-will) ✦ **Weapon**
+15 vs. AC (+16 while bloodied); see also *lone fighter*; 1d10 + 5 damage.

⊹ **Finishing Blow** (standard; at-will) ✦ **Weapon**
Target must be bloodied; +15 vs. AC (+16 while bloodied); 2d10 + 5 damage, and the dragonborn gladiator's allies gain a +2 bonus to attack rolls until the end of the dragonborn gladiator's next turn.

↩ **Dragon Breath** (minor; encounter) ✦ **Fire**
Close blast 3; +12 vs. Reflex (+13 while bloodied); 1d6 + 4 fire damage.

↩ **Frightful Presence** (standard; encounter) ✦ **Fear**
Close burst 3; targets enemies; +10 vs. Will; the target is stunned until the end of the dragonborn gladiator's next turn.

Chromatic Boon (immediate interrupt, when an enemy hits or misses this creature; encounter)
The dragonborn gladiator gains resist 5 acid, resist 5 cold, resist 5 fire, resist 5 lightning, or resist 5 poison until the end of the encounter.

Dragonborn Fury (only while bloodied)
A dragonborn gains a +1 racial bonus to attack rolls.

Gladiator's Strike
When a dragonborn gladiator hits an enemy with an opportunity attack, the target is knocked prone.

Lone Fighter
The dragonborn gladiator gains a +2 bonus to melee attack rolls while adjacent to only one enemy.

Alignment Unaligned   **Languages** Common, Draconic
Skills Athletics +15, History +7, Intimidate +17, Perception +8
Str 21 (+10)   **Dex** 15 (+7)   **Wis** 12 (+6)
Con 18 (+9)   **Int** 10 (+5)   **Cha** 16 (+8)
Equipment scale armor, bastard sword

ENCOUNTER GROUP

These dragonborn have thrown their lot in with the Queen of Evil Dragonkind and frequently are found in the company of her spawn.

Level 10 Encounter (XP 2,900)
✦ 3 dragonborn gladiators of Tiamat (level 10 soldier)
✦ 2 redspawn firebelchers (level 12 artillery; *Monster Manual*, page 88)

A template adds features to a monster, making it more powerful in a number of ways—it increases a monster's hit points, its saving throws, and the number of powers it has, its action points, and, in the case of a class-based template, its defenses. Frequently it grants battlefield functionality and story considerations the monster didn't have before.

Typically, you give a template to a monster when you want it to have a special impact in your game. Monsters with templates can serve as elite guards, spies, favored beasts, chief lieutenants of major villains, or just about anything out of the ordinary.

The two types of templates are functional templates and class templates. A functional template allows you to customize a creature to fulfill a story or combat role. Some functional templates allow you to change some aspect of the creature's nature (for instance, the terrifying haunt template transforms a living creature into an undead one) while others provide a number of abilities that allow the creature to epitomize a certain monster theme. A functional template can work well with a monster theme (discussed in the earlier part of this chapter), and you can use one to create an elite or a solo monster that serves as a "boss" monster or generate a powerful creature within the theme.

A class template grants a creature a limited number of feature and powers from a class, allowing you to flavor the creature to that class without having to treat it like a player character. With the release of the FORGOTTEN REALMS® Player's Guide and Player's Handbook 2, nine new classes have been added to the game. Toward the end of this section, you'll find templates for the classes from these two books.

APPLYING A TEMPLATE

Full details for applying templates to creatures are provided starting on page 175 of the *Dungeon Master's Guide*. The basic procedure is outlined below.

Templates work best when you apply them to a creature that is not a minion, elite, or solo creature. When you apply a template to a standard creature, the template upgrades the creature to elite. Follow these steps when applying a template to a standard creature.

✦ Make sure the monster meets the prerequisite of the template.

✦ Change the creature's role to the one specified in the template entry.

✦ Change the creature's type and origin, if applicable, and add any keywords specified in the keyword entry.

✦ Go through the template line by line and add all the new features and powers given in the template entry.

✦ If a monster has a vulnerability and the template grants a resistance of the same type, combine them and apply the difference. For example, a creature that has vulnerability 5 fire and is granted resist 10 fire by a template would now have resist 5 fire.

✦ If the template grants an encounter power the monster has already, the monster gains two uses of that encounter power.

You can apply two templates to a standard monster, or apply a template to an elite monster and thereby make it a solo creature, but do so with care. In many cases, finding or designing a solo creature can serve your purposes better than constructing one through a template. If working with a template (or two) is a better option for the situation, apply the template or templates, but do not change the monster's defenses, hit points, saving throws, and action points. Then make the following adjustments.

✦ Don't add the hit points that the template specifies to an elite creature to make it solo. Instead, double the creature's hit points, or, if the elite creature is 11th level or higher, multiply its hit points by 2.5.

✦ Class templates also provide defense bonuses to the creature. When applying a class template's bonuses to defenses to a creature that has two class templates, apply only the higher bonus to each defense rather than stacking the bonuses.

✦ A solo creature's bonus to saving throws becomes +5.

✦ Solo creatures have 2 action points.

Beast of Demogorgon

Functional templates allow you to add story and combat hooks to your monsters. Many functional templates allow the monster to work more smoothly with monster themes, such as the ones presented earlier in this chapter, or with the less implicit themes that already exist in the various *Monster Manuals* and other game supplements. A functional template might grant leader powers to an ordinary creature, or make it a unique and truly fearsome foe.

Like all templates, each of the following functional templates transforms the modified creature into an elite monster—a force to be reckoned with on the game table.

BEAST OF DEMOGORGON

Blindly destructive and insanely bloodthirsty, these two-headed mutants are revered as the "blessed" of the demon lord by the insane cults that serve him. In most cases, a cult of Demogorgon creates these odd two-headed mutants by using torture and agonizing rituals. Other times, the evil forces of the Abyss warp these creatures and thrust them out into the world. No matter the method of their creation, these creatures are the focus of fear, awe, and reverence among the demented worshipers of the demon lord, and they hold a place of honor . . . though they are frequently bound to that place by chains and other protections until the beast is needed for its master's work.

When you apply this template, the subject of the template gains an extra head.

Prerequisite: A one-headed beast or magical beast.

Beast of Demogorgon	Elite Brute
	XP Elite

Senses All-around vision
Hit Points +8 per level + Constitution score
Saving Throws +2, +4 against fear
Action Points 1
‡ **Double Bite** (standard; at-will)
   If the creature this template is applied to already has a bite melee basic attack, it can make two of those attacks with a standard action. If it does not have a bite melee basic attack, it gains the following attack:
⊕ **Bite** (standard; at-will)
   Level + 3 vs. AC; 1d8 + Strength modifier.
   Level 11: 2d8 + Strength modifier.
   Level 21: 3d8 + Strength modifier.
Rage of Demogorgon (when first bloodied; encounter) ✦ **Healing**
   The beast of Demogorgon gains regeneration 5 and scores a critical hit on a roll of 18-20 until it is no longer bloodied or drops to 0 hit points.
   Level 21: Regeneration 10.

CHAMPION OF BANE

When Bane sends his followers marching on the world, he puts one of his special champions in the lead. These fierce warlords epitomize the devotion to pure tyranny and carnage that Bane desires. They can resist the effect of fear-based attacks, and inspire that same emotion among their troops. These soldiers become tougher the closer they are to the brink of death, and they fight on even after receiving a mortal wound.

Prerequisite: Humanoid or magical beast.

Champion of Bane	Elite Soldier (Leader)
Humanoid or magical beast	XP Elite

Tyrant's Blessing aura 3; each bloodied ally within the aura deals 1d6 extra damage with melee attacks.
Hit Points +8 per level + Constitution score
Saving Throws +2, +4 against fear and charm effects
Action Points 1
Last Command (immediate interrupt, when an ally within 10 squares of the champion of Bane drops to 0 hit points; at-will)
   The triggering ally can make a melee basic attack as a free action with a +2 bonus to the attack roll.
↞ **Inspiring Carnage** (minor; recharge ⚅)
   Close burst 3; targets allies; the target can make a melee basic attack as a free action.

CHAOS WARRIOR

Chaos can destroy. It can also corrupt. When chaos corrupts a creature, the creature becomes a killing machine infused with elemental energy. These corrupted creatures are known as chaos warriors.

Chaos warrior

EVA WIDERMANN

Chaos warriors sometimes gain this strange boon from a primordial or a powerful servant of one. Mere contact with the Elemental Chaos or a part of the world touched with intense elemental energy can transform a creature. Whatever the source of the boon, a chaos warrior not only takes on some of the powers of its elemental masters, including an elementally charged breath weapon, but it also adopts the destructive behavior and entropic desires that mark primordials and their servants.

Prerequisite: Humanoid.

Chaos Warrior	Elite Brute
Humanoid	XP Elite

Destructive Wake aura 5; each enemy within the aura takes a –5 penalty to saving throws against ongoing damage.
Hit Points +10 per level + Constitution score
Resist 5 variable (1/encounter)
  Level 11: 10 variable (1/encounter)
  Level 21: 15 variable (2/encounter)
Saving Throws +2
Action Points 1
Devastating Assault
  Whenever a chaos warrior hits with a charge attack or hits a creature granting combat advantage to it, the attack also deals ongoing 5 damage (save ends).
  Level 11: Ongoing 10 damage.
  Level 21: Ongoing 15 damage.
↞ **Destabilizing Breath** (standard; encounter) ✦ **Varies**
  Close blast 5; level + 3 vs. AC; 2d6 + Constitution modifier cold, fire, lightning, or thunder damage, and the target takes ongoing 5 damage of that type and a –2 penalty to AC and Fortitude (save ends both).
  Level 11: Ongoing 10 damage.
  Level 21: 3d6 + Constitution modifier damage and ongoing 15 damage.

CURSED GUARDIAN

Although some guardians are willing servants, others are pressed into service by strange magic, and through that magic they can sometimes gain terrifying powers.

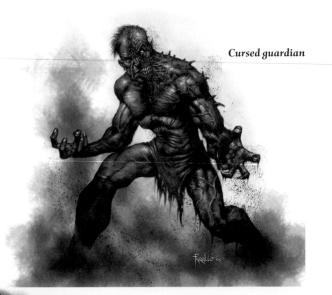

Cursed guardian

Creatures with this template can have varying origins and be affected by it in different ways. The following template has a Far Realm theme, but by slightly changing to its recharge attack power, you can create a different application for this template. For instance, by changing the ongoing damage of *soul siphon* to fire, you can make the modified creature into an infernal-themed cursed guardian.

Prerequisite: Humanoid or magical beast.

Cursed Guardian	Elite Soldier
Humanoid or magical beast	XP Elite

Soul Void aura 1; each enemy that starts its turn within the aura can't spend action points until the end of its next turn.
Hit Points +8 per level + Constitution score
Saving Throws +2; +4 against fear and charm effects
Action Points 1
⤳ **Beckoning Gaze** (minor 1/round; at-will) ✦ **Gaze**
  Ranged 3; level + 5 vs. Will; the target is pulled 3 squares and marked (save ends).
Caged Mind
  A cursed guardian that is dominated is instead dazed for the same duration that the dominated effect would have.
Soul Siphon (free, when the cursed guardian hits an enemy with a ranged attack; recharge ⚄ ⚅) ✦ **Psychic**
  That enemy takes ongoing 5 psychic damage and is dazed (save ends both).
  Level 11: Ongoing 10 psychic damage.
  Level 21: Ongoing 15 psychic damage.

DRAGONTOUCHED DESTROYER

A dragontouched destroyer is fused with the power of dragons to make a rampaging scaly machine of death that serves among the hosts of those who follow Tiamat.

Some dragontouched destroyers are created from corrupted dragon eggs that produce these hybrid creatures instead of true dragons. Others are shaped by agonizing rituals performed by the priests of Tiamat on those who dared to steal from the Queen of Evil Dragonkind or her faithful.

A dragontouched destroyer is a brute in mind and body. Cowed and trained to follow the orders of a commander, be that a warlord of the Red Hand, a priest of Tiamat, or anyone else in a position of leadership, the destroyer wades through its foes with claw, tooth, and its dangerous spewing breath. It fights ferociously until it or its commander is dead.

Prerequisite: Beast, humanoid, or magical beast.

Dragontouched destroyer

Grizzled Veteran

A grizzled veteran is a survivor—rough around the edges, tough as nails, and both deadly and decisive. When the going gets dangerous, a grizzled veteran is someone you want on your side. Often, though, a veteran's survivalist nature comes into conflict with the idealism that drives adventurers. When you are always looking out for number one, everyone else is a potential enemy.

Unlike other more villainous templates, the grizzled veteran works best when applied to an NPC the PCs have worked with before or have even learned to trust. Its tough and tricky nature makes the NPC's betrayal that much more painful.

Prerequisite: Humanoid.

Grizzled Veteran	**Elite Skirmisher**
Humanoid	XP Elite

Hit Points +8 per level + Constitution score
Saving Throws +2
Action Points 1
⚔ **Dirty Trick** (minor 1/round; at-will)
 No attack roll; the target grants combat advantage to the veteran until the end of the veteran's next turn.
⚔ **Veteran's Retort** (immediate reaction, when an enemy misses the grizzled veteran with a melee attack; at-will)
 The grizzled veteran makes a melee basic attack against the triggering enemy.
Veteran's Luck (minor; encounter)
 The grizzled veteran makes a saving throw against each effect on it that a save can end.
Combat Advantage
 A grizzled veteran deals 1d6 extra damage against any target granting combat advantage to it, and after the attack, the grizzled veteran can shift 2 squares as a free action.
Skills The grizzled veteran gains training in Bluff.

Hellbound Soldier

Although many creatures take on pacts with the powers of the Nine Hells for their own benefit, some beings make deals with devils to avoid death or defeat. Warriors who are on the verge of death or generals who are about to lose everything sometimes call upon infernal powers to save their lives or the day on the battlefield. Those who take this path serve as hellbound soldiers, powerful pawns in the armies of the Nine Hells.

Hellbound soldiers are pitiful beings who vocally lament their service and choice with each swipe of their blade. They are powerless to resist the will of their diabolical masters.

Prerequisite: Nondevil humanoid.

Dragontouched Destroyer	**Elite Brute**
Beast, humanoid, or magical beast	XP Elite

Senses Darkvision
Hit Points +10 per level + Constitution score
Saving Throws +2
Action Points 1
⚔ **Bite** (standard; at-will)
 Level + 2 vs. AC; 1d8 + Strength modifier damage, and ongoing 5 damage (save ends). If the modified creature already has a bite basic attack, increase the damage of this template's bite attack or the creature's original bite attack (whichever deals more damage) by one die step.
⚔ **Claw** (standard; at-will)
 Level + 2 vs. AC; 1d6 + Strength modifier damage, and the target is knocked prone. If the modified creature already has a claw attack, increase the damage of this template's claw attack or the creature's original claw attack (whichever deals more damage) by one die step.
⚔ **Destroyer's Breath** (standard; encounter) ✦ **Varies**
 Close blast 3; level + 2 vs. Reflex; 2d10 + Constitution modifier damage. Choose acid, cold, fire, lightning, or poison when a creature receives this power. This power deals damage of that type.
 Level 11: 3d10 + Constitution modifier damage.
 Level 21: Close blast 5, and 4d10 + Constitution modifier damage.
Bloodied Breath (free, when first bloodied; encounter)
 Destroyer's breath recharges, and the destroyer uses it.

Hellbound Soldier — Elite Soldier
Humanoid — **XP Elite**

Hit Points +8 per level + Constitution score
Resist 5 fire
  Level 11: Resist 10 fire.
  Level 21: Resist 15 fire.
Saving Throws +2
Action Points 1

⸸ Devilish Mark (minor; at-will) ✦ **Fire**
  The target is marked until the end of the hellbound soldier's next turn. If the marked target makes an attack that does not include the hellbound soldier, it takes 5 fire damage.
  Level 11: 10 fire damage.
  Level 21: 20 fire damage.

Agonizing Smite (free, when the hellbound soldier hits a target it has marked with a melee attack; recharge ⚄ ⚅)
  ✦ **Fire**
  The attack deals ongoing 5 fire damage, and the target is dazed (save ends both). *Aftereffect:* The target takes ongoing 5 damage (save ends).
  Level 11: Ongoing 10 damage.
  Level 21: Ongoing 15 damage.

Devil's Pawn
  When a devil adjacent to the hellbound soldier takes damage, that damage is reduced by 10, and the hellbound soldier takes 10 damage.

Mad alchemist

MAD ALCHEMIST

Alchemists can be a little off kilter by nature, but years of pondering esoteric formulas and inhaling or imbibing the results of one too many experiments gone wrong can send even the sanest alchemist over reason's edge. Though they are masters of their craft, mad alchemists dabble in unstable and bizarre formulas that explode with strange effects. Sometimes even they are surprised by the mad effects they create with their admixtures, elixirs, and concoctions.

Prerequisites: Humanoid or magical beast, Intelligence 12.

MAD ALCHEMIST AND ALCHEMY

If you have access to *Adventurer's Vault,* you can customize the mad alchemist by swapping out the *alchemist fire* power with another volatile alchemical item of its level or near it. If you want a more complicated mad alchemist, you could even give one two different types of volatile alchemical items to throw during combat.

Hellbound soldier

Mad Alchemist — Elite Artillery (Leader)
Humanoid or magical beast — XP Elite

Hit Points +8 per level + Constitution score
Resist 5 poison
Level 11: Resist 10 poison.
Level 21: Resist 15 poison.
Saving Throws +2; +4 against fear and charm effects
Action Points 1

✳ **Alchemist Fire** (standard; at-will) ✦ **Fire**
Area burst 1 within 10; level + 3 vs. Reflex; 2d6 fire damage. *Miss:* Half damage.
Level 11: 3d6 damage.
Level 21: 4d6 damage.

Toughening Concoction (minor; recharge ⚅⚅)
Close burst 3; targets allies; the target gains 1d6 temporary hit points (roll once and apply the temporary hit points to all allies) and a +2 bonus to AC and Fortitude until the end of the mad alchemist's next turn.
Level 11: 2d6 temporary hit points.
Level 21: 3d6 temporary hit points.

Unstable Admixtures
Each time the mad alchemist scores a critical hit with its *alchemist fire* (or any swapped alchemical power; see the sidebar), or grants temporary hit points to three or more allies with *toughening concoction*, it gains another random effect from its power. Roll a d6 and consult the following table. The effect applies to one enemy hit by the *alchemist fire* power, or one enemy within the burst of the *toughening concoction* power. If multiple targets are available, the alchemist chooses which target is affected.

Roll Effect
1 The target is dazed (save ends).
2 The target takes 5 ongoing poison damage (save ends). Increase the ongoing damage by 5 per tier.
3 The target gains vulnerable 5 cold, fire, lightning, poison, or thunder (mad alchemist's choice) (save ends). Increase the vulnerability by 5 per tier.
4 The target is immobilized (save ends). *Aftereffect:* The target is slowed (save ends).
5 The target is blinded (save ends).
6 The target is polymorphed into a frog (save ends). While in this form, it is slowed and dazed, and cannot make attacks or use powers.

SLITHERING IDOL

The corrupt and degenerate yuan-ti are fervent followers of Zehir, the god of poison and serpents. When a cult or cabal of these snake-worshiping mutants is blessed by their dark god, they are served and protected by a slithering idol—a physical manifestation of Zehir's favor. Powerful, nimble, and able to calm the violent urges of enemies around them, these snake hybrids can take many forms, but the one they prefer is that of a giant snake. Many yuan-ti revere these creatures as walking gods, and the zealous lay down their lives in an instant to protect the existence of a slithering idol.

Prerequisite: Beast (reptile), humanoid, or magical beast.

Slithering Idol — Elite Skirmisher (Leader)
Beast (reptile), humanoid, or magical beast — XP Elite

Senses Low-light vision
Slither Blessing aura 5; each ally within the aura ignores difficult terrain when shifting.
Hit Points +8 per level + Constitution score
Resist 5 poison
Level 11: Resist 10 poison.
Level 21: Resist 15 poison.
Saving Throws +2
Action Points 1

↗ **Hypnotic Eyes** (minor 1/round; at-will) ✦ **Charm**
Ranged 5; level + 5 vs. Will; the target can't make opportunity attacks (save ends).

Slither Shift (move; at-will)
The slithering idol shifts 3 squares, ignoring difficult terrain.

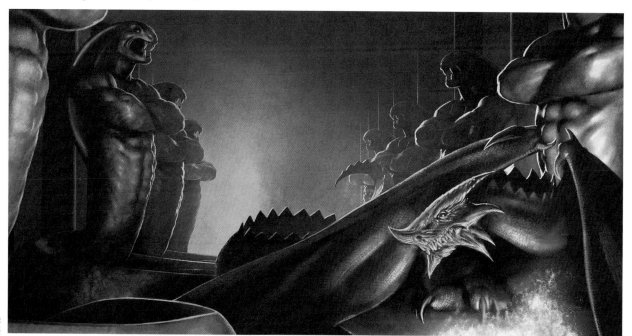

Slithering idol

Spectral Assassin

Skillful killers move with the stealth of a ghost, and the best take on the aspect of one. Through an ancient ritual, mystical training, or the blessing of a dark power, spectral assassins gain the ability to walk through walls and avoid enemy attacks by turning into a whiff of insubstantial mist. Worse still, when they manifest, their weapon's strike is murder.

Prerequisite: Humanoid.

Spectral Assassin	Elite Lurker
Humanoid	XP Elite

Initiative +4 (or +2 if the modified creature is a lurker)
Hit Points +6 per level + Constitution score
Saving Throws +2
Action Points 1
Assassin's Fading (immediate interrupt, when an enemy makes a melee or ranged attack against the spectral assassin; recharge ⚅ ⚇) ✦ **Illusion**
  The spectral assassin becomes invisible until the end of its next turn, and it can shift 1 square as a free action.
Combat Advantage
  A spectral assassin deals 2d6 extra damage against any target granting combat advantage to it.
  Level 21: 3d8 extra damage.
Invisible Killer
  While invisible, a spectral assassin scores a critical hit on a roll of 19-20 and deals 1d10 extra damage with a critical hit.
Skills Stealth +4

Spiderblessed Spinner

Lolth, Queen of Spiders and Mistress of Intrigue, is known for blessing those whom she finds worthy with an aspect of the arachnids that she holds dear. Transformation into a drider is one such blessing typically reserved for her favored drow agents; the spiderblessed spinner is another that Lolth applies more freely to those who follow her. In a painful transformation process, the host grows extra eyes, six spiderlike appendages, and spinnerets on another part of their body—usually the host's natural hands. The creature uses these new tools to control and wreak havoc on the battlefield, where it binds foes in webs and pushes those who dare approach toward the sword point of other agents of the Queen of Spiders.

Prerequisites: Humanoid or magical beast, level 11.

Spiderblessed Spinner	Elite Controller
Humanoid or magical beast	XP Elite

Senses All-around vision; darkvision
Hit Points +8 per level + Constitution score
Saving Throws +2; +4 against poison effects
Action Points 1
Repelling Legs (standard; at-will)
  Close burst 1; targets enemies; level + 3 vs. Fortitude; 2d6 + Strength modifier damage, and the target is pushed 3 squares.

Poison Web of Lolth (standard; encounter) ✦ **Poison**
  Area burst 2 within 10; level + 3 vs. Reflex; 3d10 + Constitution modifier poison damage, and the target is grabbed. The target takes a -4 penalty to attempts to escape the grab.
Spider's Escape (immediate interrupt, when hit with a melee attack; recharge ⚅)
  The spiderblessed spinner shifts 4 squares and can move through enemy spaces during the shift.

Terrifying Haunt

Ghosts can come in many forms. Some are cursed to roam until a past sin is righted, or a wrong undone. Others are merely the animus of hate, raging eternally in undying terror. A terrifying haunt is a particularly hateful and enduring form of ghost. These ghosts can take any shape, but one thing is common to every one of them—it hates the living and uses its powers to spread fear and death to any living creature that dares cross its path.

Terrifying Haunt	Elite Controller
(undead)	XP Elite

Senses Darkvision
Terrifying Presence (Fear) aura 3; each enemy within the aura takes a -2 penalty to saving throws and all defenses.
Hit Points +4 per level + Constitution score
Resist insubstantial
Saving Throws +2; +4 against fear effects
Speed fly 6 (phasing)
Action Points 1
Haunting Gaze (minor 1/round; at-will) ✦ **Fear, Gaze**
  Ranged 5; level + 4 vs. Will; the target can make only one saving throw at the end of its turn (save ends).
Howling Terror (standard; recharge ⚅) ✦ **Fear, Psychic**
  Close burst 3; level + 2 vs. Will; 2d6 + Charisma modifier psychic damage, and the terrifying haunt slides the target 4 squares. *Miss:* Half damage, and the terrifying haunt slides the target 1 square.

Terrifying haunt

CHIPPY

Victim of the Mad Dance

The korred (see *Manual of the Planes*, page 135) are masters of ecstatic dance. Their music is so enchanting that some who stumble upon their heathered hills dance themselves to death. Others become deeply enthralled and enslaved by the maddening rhythms, and they take on the savage ways of the korred and other deadly fey.

A victim of the mad dance has embraced its plight, embodying the deadly jig of the korred and other fey enraptured by the dancing lunacy of the Feywild.

Victim of the Mad Dance	Elite Skirmisher
	XP Elite

Hit Points +8 per level + Constitution score
Saving Throws +2; +4 against charm effects
Action Points 1
Mad Dance (standard; recharge ⚄ ⚅)
　The victim of the mad dance shifts its speed and makes a melee basic attack.
Insane Resolve (minor; recharge ⚅)
　The victim of the mad dance makes saving throws against each effect on it that a save can end.
Combat Advantage
　A victim of the mad dance knocks prone any target granting combat advantage to it when it hits with a melee attack.

CLASS TEMPLATES

These templates feature the classes from *Player's Handbook 2* and the Forgotten Realms *Player's Guide*. Follow the normal method for applying a template, and choose powers for the monster from the class. Here are general guidelines on how to do this.

✦ **At-Will Attack Powers:** Typically you'll pick one. Sometimes you might want to choose more, but do so sparingly. Pick two when you apply the druid template, since druids split their at-will attacks between their normal form and beast form.

✦ **Encounter Attack Powers:** Choose one power of a level equal to or lower than the monster's level. For monsters of 21st level or higher, choose one additional encounter power. You can't take two powers of the same level.

✦ **Daily Attack Powers:** Choose one power of a level equal to or lower than the monster's level. For monsters of 21st level or higher, choose one additional daily power. You can't take two powers of the same level.

✦ **Utility Powers:** Choose one power of a level equal to or lower than the monster's level. For monsters of 11th level or higher, choose one additional utility power. For monsters of 21st level or higher, select a third utility power. You can't have more than one power of the same level.

The possible downside to applying a class template is that you'll end up with a complicated monster that has a potentially overwhelming number of powers. Sometimes this is fine, because these templates work best for memorable elite monsters that should be harder to beat and have more resources available to them. At the same time, don't be afraid to simplify these monsters when you can. If a single utility power is enough to make your frost giant warden interesting, don't feel as though you have to use the other features of the warden template.

Avenger

Power Source: Divine.

Avenger	Elite Skirmisher

Defenses +1 Fortitude, +1 Reflex, +1 Will
Saving Throws +2
Action Points 1
Hit Points +8 per level + Constitution score
Weapon Proficiency Simple melee, military melee, simple ranged
Armor Proficiency Cloth
Trained Skills Religion, plus one other skill from the avenger class skills list
Class Features Avenger's Censure, Channel Divinity, *oath of enmity*
Implements Holy symbols

Barbarian

Power Source: Primal.

Barbarian	Elite Brute

Defenses +2 Fortitude
Saving Throws +2
Action Points 1
Hit Points +10 per level + Constitution score
Weapon Proficiency Simple melee, military melee
Armor Proficiency Cloth, leather, hide
Trained Skills One skill from the barbarian class skills list
Class Features Feral Might, *rage strike*, Rampage

Bard

Power Source: Arcane.

Bard	Elite Skirmisher (Leader)

Defenses +1 Reflex, +1 Will
Saving Throws +2
Action Points 1
Hit Points +8 per level + Constitution score
Weapon Proficiency Simple melee, longsword, scimitar, short sword, simple ranged, military ranged
Armor Proficiency Cloth, leather, hide, chainmail, light shield
Trained Skills Arcana, plus two other skills from the bard class skills list
Class Features Bardic Training, Bardic Virtue, *majestic word*, Skill Versatility, *words of friendship*
Implements Wands

Druid

Power Source: Primal.

Druid	Elite Controller

Defenses +1 Reflex, +1 Will
Saving Throws +2
Action Points 1
Hit Points +8 per level + Constitution score
Weapon Proficiency Simple melee, simple ranged
Armor Proficiency Cloth, leather, hide
Trained Skills Nature, plus one other skill from the druid class skills list
Class Features Primal Aspect, Ritual Casting, *wild shape*
Implements Staffs, totems

Invoker

Power Source: Divine.

Invoker	Elite Controller (Leader)

Defenses +1 Fortitude, +1 Reflex, +1 Will
Saving Throws +2
Action Points 1
Hit Points +8 per level + Constitution score
Weapon Proficiency Simple melee, simple ranged
Armor Proficiency Cloth, leather, hide, chainmail
Trained Skills Religion, plus one other skill from the invoker class skills list
Class Features Channel Divinity, Divine Covenant, Ritual Casting
Implements Rods, staffs

MONSTER-MAKING TIPS

Creating new monsters brings risks. Look out for these pitfalls when creating monsters and encounters.

Effects that Take Away Actions: The dazed and stunned conditions (and to a lesser extent, immobilized and restrained) should be used sparingly.

Effects that Reduce Damage Output: The weakened condition and monsters with insubstantial or swarm traits can be interesting problems for characters to deal with, but being weakened for the majority of a fight just isn't fun! Make sure you use these abilities only in diverse monster groups, so the PCs aren't *all* dealing low damage.

Too Much Healing: Monsters shouldn't have a strong ability to heal themselves, especially not in large amounts (such as a healing surge). It can make a fight drag, or even turn it into a stalemate.

Repetitious Resistances: Remember what damage types your PCs use, and use a variety of resistances. If your group has a fire wizard, don't throw the group against only azers for several encounters in a row.

Stealing Resources: Avoid monsters that take away or turn off the PCs' resources, such as healing surges, limited-use powers, or magic items.

—Logan Bonner

Shaman

Power Source: Primal.

Shaman	Elite Skirmisher (Leader)

Defenses +1 Fortitude, +1 Will
Saving Throws +2
Action Points 1
Hit Points +5 per level + Constitution score
Weapon Proficiency Simple melee, longspear
Armor Proficiency Cloth, leather
Trained Skills Nature, plus one other skill from the shaman class skills list
Class Features Companion Spirit, *healing spirit, speak with spirits*
Implements Totems

Sorcerer

Power Source: Arcane.

Sorcerer	Elite Artillery

Defenses +2 Will
Saving Throws +2
Action Points 1
Hit Points +6 per level + Constitution score
Weapon Proficiency Simple melee, simple ranged
Armor Proficiency Cloth
Trained Skills Arcana, plus one other skill from the sorcerer class skills list
Class Features Spell Source
Implements Daggers, staffs

Swordmage

Power Source: Arcane.

Swordmage	Elite Soldier

Defenses +2 Will
Saving Throws +2
Action Points 1
Hit Points +8 per level + Constitution score
Weapon Proficiency Simple melee, military light blades, military heavy blades, simple ranged
Armor Proficiency Cloth, leather
Trained Skills Arcana, plus one other skill from the swordmage class skills list
Class Features Swordbond, Swordmage Aegis, Swordmage Warding
Implements Any light blades or heavy blades

Warden

Power Source: Primal.

Warden	Elite Soldier

Defenses +1 Fortitude, +1 Will
Saving Throws +2
Action Points 1
Hit Points +8 per level + Constitution score
Weapon Proficiency Simple melee, military melee, simple ranged
Armor Proficiency Cloth, leather, hide, light shield, heavy shield
Trained Skills Nature, plus one other skill from the warden class skills list
Class Features Font of Life, Guardian Might, Nature's Wrath

CREATING MONSTERS

More art than science, monster creation can be tricky—and it's about more than just the numbers.

Monster Manual 2 introduces a few tweaks to monster creation, particularly for elites, solo monsters, and minions. Use the following information to supplement what's presented on page 184 of the *Dungeon Master's Guide*.

CREATING NEW ELITES

Elites no longer gain additional bonuses to all defenses. Instead, follow the same rules as for standard monsters. If you want to adjust an older monster to use the same scale, dropping all its defenses by 2 can work in a pinch (but might be a bit generous to the PCs).

CREATING NEW SOLOS

The creation of solo monsters has changed in three major ways.

Hit Points: Multiply hit points by 4. Monsters of 11th level or higher no longer have quintuple hit points.

Defenses: Solos no longer gain extra bonuses to all defenses. Use the same defenses as for a standard monster.

Better When Bloodied: This type of change isn't as straightforward. When a solo monster is bloodied, it should become more dangerous and more mobile. Add a couple of abilities from the following list to reflect this advantage.

✦ Recharge one or more limited powers, and possibly use one right away (such as a dragon's *bloodied breath* power).

✦ Gain an at-will attack that deals more damage, or deal more damage with all attacks while bloodied.

✦ Gain an extra attack per round (as a minor action, part of a multiple attack power, or a larger area or close power).

✦ Gain a damaging aura.

✦ Move after becoming bloodied, or gain a new movement power. Movement might include shifting, teleportation, flight, or phasing—anything to keep the fight from becoming static.

These guidelines are intended to make the monster feel more deadly, but without allowing the fight to get too long. Therefore, don't give a monster additional hit points or higher defenses when it's bloodied.

CREATING NEW MINIONS

Expendable fodder, minions appear in big groups with the sole purpose of dying quickly and making the PCs feel cool. They should have simple mechanics to match, and they also have roles to make it easier to determine the types of combat tactics they use.

You can create a new minion from scratch, or remove abilities from a standard monster to make a simpler minion. Most steps in creating a minion (including setting defenses and attack bonuses, as well as determining its role) are the same as for a standard monster, with the following exceptions.

1. Adjust Hit Points: All minions have 1 hit point, and a missed attack never damages a minion.

2. Keep It Simple: Minion abilities shouldn't require record-keeping. For instance, a minion's attack shouldn't have an effect that a save can end, nor should it have recharge abilities (and probably not encounter abilities). Immediate action powers are also rare. Some exceptions, though, are fine: A goblin minion might have the immediate action *goblin tactics* power so that it still feels like a goblin.

3. Set Damage for Attacks: Use the Minion Damage by Level table to set damage amounts for a minion's attacks. Remember that minions don't use dice for damage, just flat values. Minion damage is roughly half of a standard creature's damage.

MINION DAMAGE BY LEVEL

Level	Standard Damage	Brute Damage
1st–3rd	4	5
4th–6th	5	6
7th–9th	6	7
10th–12th	8	10
13th–15th	9	11
16th–18th	10	12
19th–21st	11	13
22nd–24th	13	16
25th–27th	14	17
28th–30th	15	18

Artillery minions deal 25% less damage on multitarget and melee attacks. At the heroic tier, four minions are equivalent to one standard monster. Five minions are equivalent to one standard monster at the paragon tier, and six at epic. Design encounters at the paragon tier with five minions of a given type instead of four, and at the epic tier with six minions instead of five.

ADVENTURES

CHAPTERS 6-8 of the *Dungeon Master's Guide* cover creating and running adventures, weaving them into campaigns, and rewarding players. This chapter expands on the information presented in that book. The range of topics presented here can help you create exciting, immersive stories and epic campaigns for your players' enjoyment.

✦ **Alternative Rewards:** Sometimes player characters appreciate rewards that are less tangible than a magic item or monetary reward. This section discusses divine and legendary boons and grandmaster training, which function like magic items but allow you to tell different stories in your game.

✦ **Item Components:** As an alternative to simply handing out magic items, you can require characters to gather the ingredients of an item and assemble it to earn their treasure.

✦ **Artifacts:** Building on the four artifacts presented in the *Dungeon Master's Guide*, this section further discusses how to use artifacts and presents seven new artifacts. Unique artifacts in this section include a few designed to benefit a whole party of characters and one intended to remain relevant for an entire campaign.

✦ **Organizations:** This section discusses how to add depth to your campaign with organizations, such as villainous groups, rivals to the player characters, and friendly organizations that might be patrons to the characters.

✦ **Campaign Arcs:** The chapter concludes with four example campaign arcs—broad storylines for campaigns that take characters from levels 1-30. This section gives special emphasis to the paragon tier, leading into the paragon campaign material presented in the next chapter.

RALPH HORSLEY

Brother Allwen pushed the ogre's corpse from atop the altar to Kord. How could this chapel have remained hidden in the dungeon depths for so long? As he pulled out his holy symbol to begin the ceremony of consecration, a voice roared out, "Truly you are the worthiest of my clerics! Accept this boon of strength and might!"

Nerrida dashed past Grissom as the dragon died, reaching for the iron flask she kept on her belt. With just a few drops of the beast's boiling blood, she could imbue her staff with the spirit of the seventh fire.

The old gnome whom Sherrek had rescued from an orc prison treated Sherrek like a snot-nosed beginner rather than a seasoned adventurer, but he seemed to have skills to teach. "You hold that dagger like a blind kobold. And I don't want to start on how you dodged those arrows. You're lucky you don't have one dangling out of your eye socket. I, Vallario Seven-Cuts, shall teach you the fine art of the blade."

In a D&D game, rewards can take on a wide variety of forms. Your players might most appreciate piles of gold coins and glimmering magic weapons, but characters in books, movies, and comics rarely receive such rewards. Who wants to always read about a boring miser who counts his coins or a brute who believes his magic sword makes him the greatest warrior in the world?

Stories and characters do draw on such themes, but for your game, consider those themes the exception rather than the rule. In D&D campaigns, DMs can award treasure as a pat on the back for a job well done. Treasure acts as a reward that boosts power in addition to that gained with a new level. A hard-fought, tense victory over a troll horde feels greater if the trolls' treasure chest contains magic armor a PC desires.

Yet not every fight plays out as a tense, life-or-death affair, and not every treasure chest contains items the PCs want. This section discusses variant rules for treasure, with a focus on more story-focused rewards that can increase the sense of mystery and wonder in your game. Players might find it more interesting if, instead of treasure, you hand out a boon from the gods or an offer of training from the world's greatest fencing master.

OVERVIEW

The alternative rewards presented in this section share the following rules characteristics:

✦ An alternative reward replaces a magic item. When you place treasure parcels, you can use an alternative reward in place of an item.

✦ You can use alternative rewards alongside traditional magic items. Without additional changes to the rules, you should replace one magic item per level with an alternative reward. Optional rules later in this section explain how to make alternative rewards more prevalent.

✦ These rewards occupy the same mechanical space as magic items. They balance on the same power curve and aim at the same place within the body of a character's abilities.

✦ An alternative reward lasts for five levels of play and then fades. This rule applies because characters normally sell or replace items as they gain levels. Alternative rewards occupy the same space in the game, so a similar process applies to them. However, see "Decide on Duration" on page 138 for exceptions to this rule.

REWARD TYPES

This section describes three types of alternative rewards: divine boons, legendary boons, and grandmaster training. These reward categories reflect three iconic stories of how and why characters earn such rewards.

DIVINE BOONS

Individuals who aid a deity's holy cause receive wondrous, divine gifts. A particularly blessed character, or one who earns a deity's gratitude, can gain a divine boon.

LEGENDARY BOONS

Great deeds can confer wondrous powers on individuals. A character could earn a legendary boon by bathing in the blood of an ancient dragon, reading a tome of esoteric knowledge, or solving the riddle of an immortal sphinx.

CHOOSING REWARD LEVELS

To make alternative rewards feel special, use them to replace the highest-level magic items you would otherwise give out. If you plan to give 10th-level characters two alternative rewards and two items, use rewards to replace parcels 1 and 2 (a level 14 item and a level 13 item), and use items for parcels 3 and 4 (the level 12 and level 11 items). Over time, the characters acquire items of a higher level than their alternative rewards. In the short term, this approach makes alternative rewards feel appropriately weighty.

GRANDMASTER TRAINING

The absolute master of a craft, such as an archmage or the greatest living swordmaster, can teach techniques and abilities that transcend a character's normal limits.

HOW REWARDS WORK

An alternative reward works the same as a magic item, except it doesn't take up a item slot or require a character to hold it, because it isn't a physical object. In addition, characters can't buy, sell, or disenchant a reward. (They might be able to "enchant" an alternative reward using a ritual comparable to the Enchant Magic Item ritual; see "A Reward-Based Game" on page 138 for more details.)

Alternative rewards never grant enhancement bonuses. Characters must still rely on magic items to gain enhancement bonuses to attack rolls and damage rolls, AC, and other defenses. An alternative reward can replicate any other property or power granted by a magic item, including item bonuses. If you use a magic item property that gives an item bonus as an alternative reward, the bonus still counts as an item bonus. Do not associate the alternative reward's bonus with a physical item, and don't stack the alternative reward's item bonus with other item bonuses to the same statistic.

Otherwise, treat a reward the same as you would an item. Using an alternative reward's daily power works the same as using a magic item's daily power, and it counts against a character's limit of item daily power uses between milestones.

CREATING A REWARD

An alternative reward replaces a magic item the characters would otherwise find. Pick the magic item parcel you want to replace, and use the item's level as the reward's level. Then follow these four steps to create an ideal reward for your characters and your campaign.

1. Create the Story: Choose one of the types of rewards detailed in this section and use the advice included for it to create a story and other background details for the reward.

Don't underestimate the importance of this step. A reward shares the same basic mechanics as a magic item. Without a good story to back it up, a reward might seem like merely a magic item that the characters can't sell or trade. Read over the advice given for each type of reward, and think about how to create a compelling experience for the players.

Alternative rewards offer you a chance to bring your world to life. They connect a player's desire for magic loot with your desire to create a vivid, entertaining story and game world.

2. Plant the (Story) Seeds: A reward works best when it is woven seamlessly into the story, especially if the characters have to work hard to gain it or make use of it. The characters might hear about the reward and seek it out, or they might stumble across it and immediately realize its importance. You could craft the story and background of your campaign so that the characters know the importance and value of the reward before they find out about its mechanics.

3. Choose Powers and Effects: You can create the powers and properties of a reward by borrowing the mechanics of a magic item of the same level. This advice comes with a caveat, though: Players who are familiar with the game and who know how items work place extra pressure on the DM to use story and background elements to make the reward seem distinctive and compelling. If the players figure out you simply used *bracers of mighty striking* to define the property of the reward you call *blessing of the Sword Lord*, the reward might lose its mystery, wonder, and uniqueness.

Start by finding an item that has effects that connect with the flavor and story of the reward you want to create. If you know the level of the reward you want to create, you should limit your search to items of that level; alternatively, you can find an appropriate item and use its level as the level of your reward.

If you find more than one appropriate item, you could use a property from one item and a power from another one. This approach helps to conceal your source when you draw on existing material. You must still ensure that the potency of the resulting reward corresponds appropriately to its level.

Since story plays an essential role in a reward's design, concoct a basic description of how the reward manifests and what happens when a character uses it. The blessing of a deity might cause an image of the deity's holy symbol to appear on the character's hand. A specific description of how a character executes a special attack breathes life into a new technique a character learned by training with a master.

APPLYING BOONS TO ITEMS

For your own convenience, you can transform mundane items, such as weapons or armor, into magic items by imbuing them with divine and legendary boons. When Ivella the tiefling fighter pierces the dying dragon's heart with her broadsword, the fiery blood of the ancient wyrm transforms her sword into a *flaming weapon*. When Uldane the halfling paladin performs a great service for Avandra, she transforms his +5 *magic short sword* into a *holy avenger*.

Using boons in this manner offers you another way of giving magic items as treasure. This approach has more flavor than hiding an item under a monster's bunk or buying or creating the items, and it remains firmly in the realm of the standard D&D reward system.

4. Decide on Duration: A reward typically fades after the character gains about five levels. This rule exists to enforce the same sort of turnover that occurs with normal magic items. A paladin eventually replaces his +2 *plate armor* with +3 armor. A *casque of tactics* (see *Adventurer's Vault*) might give way to a *clockwork cowl*.

You can design rewards with different durations. A reward might last for as little as one level or as many as ten. A legendary boon might last until the character takes an extended rest (useful if you want to draw characters into more encounters between rests; see "Drawing Characters Onward" on page 54). A divine boon might be equivalent to a consumable magic item—Avandra grants a character the ability to reroll three saving throws, and then the boon expires. If you use future treasure parcels to increase the power of a type of grandmaster training instead of giving a new item or reward, the benefit could be permanent and grow in power as the character gains levels.

Don't overload the characters with temporary rewards, and don't rob them of rewards they use frequently unless you design the reward as a short-term enhancement.

Weigh the duration of an alternative reward against the normal useful life of a comparable item. If you make the duration shorter, give more rewards to compensate, or don't count the rewards against the treasure the party receives. If you make the duration longer, use future rewards to improve the item, instead of giving new rewards or items.

A REWARD-BASED GAME

You can remove magic items from the game entirely and replace them with alternative rewards. Doing so results in a game that feels different from traditional D&D and might help you create a particular tone you want for your campaign.

In a campaign with no magic items, magic holds less value. Your players might dislike the lack of variety, but it allows you to create a story-driven campaign—rather than one driven by mechanics—that gives magic a rare and wondrous feel.

Don't ditch magic items without thinking it over. Discuss your decision with your players, so they understand what your campaign would entail. Players might appreciate the added layer of customization that items offer, and losing that feature could reduce their enjoyment of the game.

More important, without magic items as an easy reward, the pressure on you increases to provide a compelling story that propels the PCs forward. This option works best if you have experience as a DM and have already run several successful campaigns. You can use the following suggestions to replace magic items in your campaign.

AC, Defense, Attack, and Damage Bonuses: Without magic items, the PCs' attacks, defenses, and damage lag behind. You can solve this problem by giving the PCs flat bonuses as they advance in level. These bonuses stack.

Attack and Damage: All characters gain a +1 bonus to attack rolls and damage rolls at 2nd, 7th, 12th, 17th, 22nd, and 27th level.

Defenses: All PCs gain a +1 bonus to AC, Fortitude, Reflex, and Will at 4th, 9th, 14th, 19th, 24th, and 29th level.

Parcels: Remove the highest- and lowest-level magic item parcels from each level of treasure you hand out. You can dole out fewer magic items because the PCs do not need those items to boost their attacks and defenses.

Masterwork Armor: Give characters masterwork armor as treasure in addition to the rewards and monetary treasure you give. Treat masterwork armor as a magic item of a level equal to the lowest-level magic armor made from that type of masterwork armor. For example, a suit of crysteel armor (see *Adventurer's Vault*) has a minimum enhancement bonus of +4. A suit of +4 *magic armor* is a 16th-level magic item, so treat the masterwork armor as a 16th-level item as well.

Use Rewards: Replace the remaining magic item parcels with rewards designed using this section.

The rewards you use affect your campaign. Divine rewards reflect a world where the deities take an active role in mortal affairs. If you create a world where people consider magic a scarce or dangerous tool, you should rely on grandmaster training rewards. Legendary rewards fit a campaign that features magical vistas and bizarre locations where people still view magic as a mysterious and mistrusted source of power.

Spending Money: In a standard D&D campaign, characters find heaps of gold partly so they can buy or enchant magic items they choose. If you eliminate magic items from your campaign, think about what else characters can do with their monetary treasure.

You could allow characters to spend their money on rituals that grant them boons, effectively restoring an amount of player control over character customization. Replace the Enchant Magic Item ritual with three distinct rituals: Implore Divine Boon, Invoke Legendary Boon, and Grandmaster Training. These rituals might have special requirements beyond the Ritual Caster feat and the expenditure of gold—perhaps characters can perform Implore Divine Boon only at a significant temple and must be in their deity's good graces. Otherwise, the rituals function the same as Enchant Magic Item and allow characters to acquire a boon of their choice of their level or lower.

Allowing characters to buy alternative rewards can diminish the specialness of those rewards in players' eyes. You could instead reduce monetary treasure drastically to account for the fact that characters no longer need to buy as much stuff. If you cut monetary rewards in half, characters would still have enough money to purchase rituals and consumable items, as well as support their standard of living.

DIVINE BOONS

Although the deities in the D&D world do not have omniscient powers, they do take an active interest in important events. A character might gain a divine boon as a reward for doing something that directly aids a deity or harms a deity's enemies.

An adventurer's typical activities fall into that definition. A divine boon comes into play when the gods take a personal interest in an event, such as a character performing a task worthy of drawing the gods' attention. Killing orcs that attack a temple does not deserve a divine boon. Slaying the high priest of Tiamat as he attempts to rally an army to conquer an entire continent in the Dragon Queen's name–now, that accomplishment deserves a divine boon.

DIVINE BOONS IN THE CAMPAIGN

Divine boons can come into play when the characters perform a great deed for a deity. Alternatively, a boon might come out of nowhere, and its appearance kicks off the next story arc in your campaign. The boon might come with a quest, or the character who receives the boon could draw the attention of the deity's enemies. Perhaps the boon comes from the rival of the character's chosen deity.

In any event, make receiving a divine boon a major affair in a campaign. A deity has just taken notice of a character!

A divine boon is a good reward for one of the following activities:

✦ Avenging the death of a deity's beloved servant.
✦ Rediscovering a long-lost temple.
✦ Foiling a major plot by the deity's enemies.
✦ Saving one of the deity's favorite servants from danger.

You might also bestow a divine boon as a preemptive reward, a gift handed out before the characters undertake a perilous quest. Bahamut might appear to a paladin the night before an adventure, providing advice for the coming quest and granting the paladin a boon to aid him or her in a future encounter.

Boons never occur in a vacuum. When the deities meddle in the world, the other deities (and other entities, such as primal spirits) might involve themselves. If Bahamut grants his champion a boon, Tiamat might target that champion for death or create a dark prophet of her own to oppose him.

The actual mechanics of the boon take one of two forms. You can duplicate the effects of a magic item, or you can use one of the following sample divine boons, designed to correspond with the deities of the D&D pantheon. A boon effect equates to an item of its level and feels like a divine gift.

5

Sample Divine Boons

Avandra's Boon of Escape — Level 3+

Gambits that rely on luck and crushing blows against oppressors draw boons from Avandra. Individuals blessed by her are impossible to corner.

Lvl 3	680 gp	Lvl 18	85,000 gp
Lvl 8	3,400 gp	Lvl 23	425,000 gp
Lvl 13	17,000 gp	Lvl 28	2,125,000 gp

Divine Boon

Property: If you start your turn with two or more enemies adjacent to you, you can shift 2 squares as a move action.
Level 13 or 18: Shift 3 squares.
Level 23 or 28: Shift 4 squares.

Power (Daily ✦ Teleportation): Move Action. Teleport 2 squares.
Level 8: Teleport 3 squares.
Level 13: Teleport 4 squares.
Level 18: Teleport 5 squares.
Level 23: Teleport 6 squares.
Level 28: Teleport 7 squares.

Bahamut's Protective Ward — Level 3+

Bahamut grants his boon to heroes who shield the weak from the strong. Individuals who fight in Bahamut's name are beacons of hope and protection.

Lvl 3	680 gp	Lvl 18	85,000 gp
Lvl 8	3,400 gp	Lvl 23	425,000 gp
Lvl 13	17,000 gp	Lvl 28	2,125,000 gp

Divine Boon

Property: Gain a +1 item bonus to opportunity attack rolls.
Level 13 or 18: +2 item bonus.
Level 23 or 28: +3 item bonus.

Power (Daily): Minor Action. Until the end of your next turn, enemies adjacent to you provoke opportunity attacks from you if they make attacks that do not include you as a target.
Level 8: Gain a +1 bonus to these attacks.
Level 13: Gain a +2 bonus to these attacks.
Level 18: Gain a +3 bonus to these attacks.
Level 23: Gain a +4 bonus to these attacks.
Level 28: Gain a +5 bonus to these attacks.

Corellon's Boon of Arcane Might — Level 3+

Corellon brought arcane magic to the world. Mortals who please him gain access to powers that otherwise take years of study to master.

Lvl 3	680 gp	Lvl 18	85,000 gp
Lvl 8	3,400 gp	Lvl 23	425,000 gp
Lvl 13	17,000 gp	Lvl 28	2,125,000 gp

Divine Boon

Property: Choose an at-will power from an arcane character class. You can use that power as an encounter power.

Power (Daily): Choose a 1st-level encounter power from an arcane class. You can use that power as a daily power.
Level 8: Choose an encounter power of 3rd level or lower.
Level 13: Choose an encounter power of 7th level or lower.
Level 18: Choose an encounter power of 13th level or lower.
Level 23: Choose an encounter power of 17th level or lower.
Level 28: Choose an encounter power of 23rd level or lower.

Erathis's Beacon — Level 3+

The first cities were carved from the wilderness in the name of Erathis. With her boon, the same sense of teamwork allows you and your allies to overcome any obstacle.

Lvl 3	680 gp	Lvl 18	85,000 gp
Lvl 8	3,400 gp	Lvl 23	425,000 gp
Lvl 13	17,000 gp	Lvl 28	2,125,000 gp

Divine Boon

Property: When you use the aid another action, you grant your ally a +4 bonus rather than +2.

Power (Daily ✦ Healing): Minor Action. An ally within 5 squares of you can spend a healing surge. That ally also gains a +1 bonus to his or her next attack roll.
Level 8: The ally regains 1d6 additional hit points.
Level 13: The ally regains 1d6 additional hit points and gains a +2 bonus to his or her next attack roll.
Level 18: The ally regains 2d6 additional hit points and gains a +2 bonus to his or her next attack roll.
Level 23: The ally regains 2d6 additional hit points and gains a +3 bonus to his or her next attack roll.
Level 28: The ally regains 3d6 additional hit points and gains a +3 bonus to his or her next attack roll.

Ioun's Revelation — Level 3+

Ioun rewards study and the relentless pursuit of knowledge. Supporters who earn her favor gain the ability to master any task, no matter how daunting.

Lvl 3	680 gp	Lvl 18	85,000 gp
Lvl 8	3,400 gp	Lvl 23	425,000 gp
Lvl 13	17,000 gp	Lvl 28	2,125,000 gp

Divine Boon

Property: Gain a +2 item bonus to skill checks.

Power (Daily): Minor Action. Until the end of the encounter, you and your allies gain a +1 bonus to skill checks with a single skill of your choice.
Level 8: +2 bonus.
Level 13: +3 bonus.
Level 18: +4 bonus.
Level 23: +5 bonus.
Level 28: +6 bonus.

Kord's Mighty Strength — Level 3+

Kord lends his strength to followers who prove their mettle in battle against his enemies.

Lvl 3	680 gp	Lvl 18	85,000 gp
Lvl 8	3,400 gp	Lvl 23	425,000 gp
Lvl 13	17,000 gp	Lvl 28	2,125,000 gp

Divine Boon

Property: Gain a +2 item bonus to Athletics checks and a +5 item bonus to Strength checks made to break objects.

Power (Daily): Minor Action. Until the end of the encounter, you gain a +1 item bonus to melee damage rolls.
Level 8: +2 item bonus.
Level 13: +3 item bonus.
Level 18: +4 item bonus.
Level 23: +5 item bonus.
Level 28: +6 item bonus.

Melora's Storm Blessing — Level 3+

Individuals who please Melora gain the ability to walk upon the air, soaring over their enemies and obstacles placed before them with ease.

Lvl 3	680 gp	Lvl 18	85,000 gp
Lvl 8	3,400 gp	Lvl 23	425,000 gp
Lvl 13	17,000 gp	Lvl 28	2,125,000 gp

Divine Boon

Property: If an enemy uses a forced movement effect against you, you can shift 1 square as a free action at the end of the forced movement.

Power (Encounter): Move Action. You fly 5 squares.
Level 8: You fly 6 squares.
Level 13: You fly 7 squares.
Level 18: You fly 8 squares.
Level 23: You fly 9 squares.
Level 28: You fly 10 squares.

Moradin's Blessing of Iron — Level 3+

Moradin grants the strength of the mountain and the toughness of iron to followers who win his favor. His blessing augments both body and mind, instilling bravery and toughness in his chosen.

Lvl 3	680 gp	Lvl 18	85,000 gp
Lvl 8	3,400 gp	Lvl 23	425,000 gp
Lvl 13	17,000 gp	Lvl 28	2,125,000 gp

Divine Boon

Property: If an enemy pushes you, you can reduce the distance you are pushed by 2. If an enemy pulls you and that pull leaves you adjacent to that enemy, you can make a melee basic attack against that enemy as an opportunity action.

Power (Daily): Immediate Interrupt. *Trigger:* You take damage. *Effect:* Reduce the damage you take by 5.
Level 8: Reduce the damage by 8.
Level 13: Reduce the damage by 10.
Level 18: Reduce the damage by 15.
Level 23: Reduce the damage by 20.
Level 28: Reduce the damage by 25.

BOONS OF EVIL DEITIES

What happens when an evil deity grants a character a boon? The sample divine boons here cover the good, lawful good, and unaligned deities presented in the *Player's Handbook*, but not the more sinister deities detailed in the *Dungeon Master's Guide*. Plenty of circumstances exist in which the characters might receive a blessing from a deity who has no sample boon presented here. Unaligned player characters might worship Bane, Tiamat, or even Vecna, or at least perform deeds that advance the cause of those deities without qualifying as evil deeds. The characters might also aid an evil deity when faced with a greater evil—a demon prince or primordial, for example.

Use the sample boons presented here as a model for the divine boons of evil deities, or use the guidelines on page 137 to create an appropriate divine boon based on a magic item. Bane's boon might be similar to Bahamut's, for example, or it could have the same power as a *terror weapon*.

Pelor's Sun Blessing — Level 3+

The undimmed light of Pelor shines from individuals who champion his cause. They drive evil before them and bring solace to companions who fight alongside them.

Lvl 3	680 gp	Lvl 18	85,000 gp
Lvl 8	3,400 gp	Lvl 23	425,000 gp
Lvl 13	17,000 gp	Lvl 28	2,125,000 gp

Divine Boon

Property: If you deal damage to a target that has vulnerability to radiant damage, you deal extra damage equal to your Wisdom or Constitution modifier, whichever is higher.

Power (At-Will): Minor Action. You emit bright light in a 5-square radius. As a minor action, you can stop emitting light.

Power (Daily ✦ Healing): Minor Action. An ally within 5 squares of you can spend a healing surge, and that ally gains a +1 item bonus to saving throws until the end of the encounter.
Level 8: The ally gains a +2 item bonus to saving throws.
Level 13: The ally regains 1d6 additional hit points and gains a +2 item bonus to saving throws.
Level 18: The ally regains 1d6 additional hit points and gains a +3 item bonus to saving throws.
Level 23: The ally regains 2d6 additional hit points and gains a +2 item bonus to saving throws.
Level 28: The ally regains 2d6 additional hit points and gains a +4 item bonus to saving throws.

KEREM BEYIT

ALTERNATIVE REWARDS

5

CHAPTER 5 | *Adventures*   141

The Raven Queen's Shroud — Level 3+

The Raven Queen cloaks her champions in a shroud of darkness, a halo of divine magic that aids them in enforcing the dictates of fate.

Lvl 3	680 gp	Lvl 18	85,000 gp
Lvl 8	3,400 gp	Lvl 23	425,000 gp
Lvl 13	17,000 gp	Lvl 28	2,125,000 gp

Divine Boon

Power (Encounter): Minor Action. Choose a target within 10 squares of you. That target gains the mark of the Raven Queen until the end of the encounter. On your turn, you can reroll the result of one damage die against that target. This reroll does not alter the damage for other targets hit by an area or close attack.

Power (Daily ✦ Teleportation): Minor Action. You teleport adjacent to the target that bears the mark of the Raven Queen.

Level 8: You gain a +1 power bonus to attack rolls against the target until the end of your next turn.

Level 13: You gain a +1 power bonus to attack rolls and a +2 power bonus to damage rolls against the target until the end of your next turn.

Level 18: You gain a +1 power bonus to attack rolls and a +4 power bonus to damage rolls against the target until the end of your next turn.

Level 23: You gain a +2 power bonus to attack rolls and a +4 power bonus to damage rolls against the target until the end of your next turn.

Level 28: You gain a +2 power bonus to attack rolls and a +6 power bonus to damage rolls against the target until the end of your next turn.

Sehanine's Mark of the Dark Moon — Level 3+

The priests of Sehanine speak of the dark moon, an invisible celestial object that casts protective shadows upon Sehanine's followers. As her favored one, you are shielded from harm by the dark moon.

Lvl 3	680 gp	Lvl 18	85,000 gp
Lvl 8	3,400 gp	Lvl 23	425,000 gp
Lvl 13	17,000 gp	Lvl 28	2,125,000 gp

Divine Boon

Property: If a creature cannot see you, you take half damage from its attacks that hit you and no damage from its attacks that deal damage on a miss.

Power (Daily ✦ Teleportation): Immediate Reaction. *Trigger:* You take damage. *Effect:* You teleport 2 squares.

Level 8: You teleport 3 squares, and you can make a Stealth check as a free action to hide if you end this teleport in cover or with concealment.

Level 13: You teleport 4 squares, become invisible until the end of your next turn, and can make a Stealth check to hide as a free action.

Level 18: You teleport 6 squares, become invisible until the end of your next turn, and can make a Stealth check to hide as a free action.

Level 23: You teleport 8 squares, become invisible until the end of your next turn, and can make a Stealth check to hide as a free action.

Level 28: Immediate Interrupt. *Trigger:* You take damage. *Effect:* You teleport 8 squares, become invisible until the end of your next turn, and can make a Stealth check to hide as a free action.

LEGENDARY BOONS

A character gains a benefit from a legendary boon when he or she completes a specific act, such as slaying a powerful beast or visiting a site of untold power. Legendary boons, like divine boons, fill a similar role to that of magic items.

You might need to sell the idea of a legendary boon to your players. Use story and flavor elements to prevent the boon's mechanical effects from seeming dull and rote.

A legendary boon could kick off a quest or otherwise push the PCs to acquire the boon. The wizard in the party might hear about the library of a great archmage hidden in a dungeon. If the wizard reaches the library and studies its contents, he or she could gain a greater mastery over magic. Of course, a fearsome lich (perhaps a continuing villain from your campaign) guards the place. Even worse, the characters last saw the map to the library's location in the hands of a cleric of Bane.

Characters should have strong motivations to seek out legendary boons. Dangle a boon in front of the PCs like a carrot, but guard it with powerful monsters and other obstacles that require planning and fighting to overcome. The word "legendary" holds critical importance here. You want your players to feel that the mighty forces they confront have a strong root in the campaign world and the story.

It doesn't hurt to lay the groundwork for a legendary boon early in the campaign. Ask the PCs what items they want, and turn those items into legendary boons.

To make a legendary boon more interesting, you can incorporate any of the following features.

✦ **A Legendary Story:** Drinking the waters from the first spring to erupt after the deities created the world grants untold power.

✦ **A Powerful Figure in Myth or Legend:** Bathing in the blood of the dragon Festergrim, slayer of King Algus and ravager of the forest of Lorem, grants a character immunity to fire. The blood of an unnamed dragon just stains a character's favorite hauberk.

✦ **A Place in the Larger Story:** Reading the Book of Five Truths gives a character a legendary boon and provides a map showing the resting place of the artifact the characters need to cure the deadly green plague.

Similar to other alternative rewards, a legendary boon lasts about five levels. At higher levels, the characters can seek more powerful versions of the boon, or you can tie them to the ongoing story of your campaign. For example, the wizard Fenstern gains the *silver hands of power* at the pool of Ralyar. Later in the campaign, when Fenstern and his companions defeat

the cambion mage Gallrak, the *silver hands* absorb Gallrak's arcane power and grow even more potent. In game terms, you just handed the PC a higher-level version of the boon, replacing a treasure parcel as appropriate. In the story, Fenstern reclaims the power that Gallrak once stole from the pool. As an alternative, perhaps Fenstern must return to the pool after defeating Gallrak, and place the cambion's heart in the pool to improve the boon of the *silver hands.*

SAMPLE LEGENDARY BOONS

Book of Five Truths — Level 8+

Scribes recorded five truths on scrolls at the start of the Dawn War and then scattered the scrolls throughout the planes of existence. Each scroll grants its reader essential insight into the nature of being.

Legendary Boon

The First Truth   Lvl 8   3,400 gp
Property: Gain a +2 item bonus to Insight checks and Perception checks.

The Second Truth   Lvl 13   17,000 gp
Property: Gain a +1 item bonus to Wisdom ability checks and Wisdom-based skill checks (but not Wisdom attacks).
Power (Daily): Immediate Interrupt. *Trigger:* You are hit by an attack that targets your Will. *Effect:* You gain a +5 power bonus to Will against the attack.

The Third Truth   Lvl 18   85,000 gp
Property: When performing a ritual, roll twice and take the better result.

The Fourth Truth   Lvl 23   425,000 gp
Property: Gain a +2 bonus to Will.
Property: Gain a +5 item bonus to initiative checks.

The Fifth Truth   Lvl 28   2,125,000 gp
Property: Gain darkvision and a +6 item bonus to Insight checks and Perception checks.
Power (Daily): Minor Action. You can see invisible creatures as if they were visible. *Sustain Minor:* The power remains in effect.

Fortune's Nod — Level 3

Lidda's luck was uncanny. When all hope seemed lost and she was sighing her last breath, fortune smiled on her. She rose to her feet, drove her sword into the young dragon's eye, and smiled.

Legendary Boon   680 gp
Power (Daily): No Action. Gain a +2 power bonus to a saving throw you just rolled; use the new result.

Heartblood of Festergrim · Level 19+

Bathing in the blood of the slayer of King Algus and ravager of the forest of Lorem might not make you immune to fire, but it helps.

Lvl 19	105,000 gp	Lvl 29	2,625,000
Lvl 24	525,000 gp		

Legendary Boon
Property: Gain resist 10 fire.
Level 24 or 29: Resist 15 fire.
Power (Daily): Immediate Interrupt. *Trigger:* You are hit by a fire attack. *Effect:* You and each ally within 5 squares of you gain resist 20 fire until the start of your next turn.
Level 24 or 29: Resist 30 fire.

Quickening Waters · Level 22

The fey spring that feeds the gleaming Sehalandria River, which rushes from the Feywild to the world, grants preternatural speed to anyone who drinks from it.

Legendary Boon 325,000 gp
Property: Gain a +2 item bonus to speed.
Power (Daily): Minor Action. Take a move action.

Silver Hands of Power · Level 14 or 19

The pool of Ralyar glows with arcane power. When the wizard Fenstern dips his hands into the pool, he shrieks in pain. In exchange for this power, Fenstern accepts the momentary agony of the pool transforming his hands into living quicksilver.

Legendary Boon Lvl 14 21,000 gp
Power (Daily): Free Action. *Trigger:* You are hit with a daily power. *Effect:* You can use an at-will power.
Lvl 19 105,000 gp
Power (Daily): Free Action. *Trigger:* You score a critical hit using an encounter power or a daily power. *Effect:* That power is not expended.

GRANDMASTER TRAINING

Garras had traveled for weeks across the fire-blasted Plains of Iron to find this simple thatch hut that belongs to Davros Elden, the finest swordfighter the world has ever known. Garras throws his cloak over his shoulder and adjusts his armor as he strides toward the door.

As Garras raises his hand to knock, a middle-aged male human wearing a frayed robe throws open the door. His gut hangs over his belt, and his right hand grasps a tankard of ale.

"First, you took too long to arrive. Second, you have terrible balance, and I doubt I can teach you anything. Third, that cloak is ugly. Return in a year, and show me you've improved. Maybe then I'll take you in."

The door slams shut. Garras turns, and his back stiffens as shame, anger, and defeat rush over him. He reaches down to the flask at his belt, and the door flies open again.

"Do I smell Barovian whiskey? Maybe you're not as stupid as you look. Bring that flask over here, and let's talk."

As an unmatched warrior, spellcaster, trickster, or priest, the grandmaster writes the texts and creates the disciplines that others follow. A character who displays persistence, luck, or determination could earn the chance to study at the feet of such a master and learn techniques beyond the normal limits of mortal achievement.

Similar to divine boons and legendary boons, grandmaster training gives characters access to magic item powers without the need to own those items. In this case, a character masters a new ability through hours of focused, intense training. This training requires more than rote practice; it involves study with an expert in armed combat or magecraft.

Make your grandmaster more than a faceless NPC who bestows powers on characters who visit him or her. Why replace magic items with grandmaster training if the net result in play remains the same? Build the grandmaster as a living, breathing, active NPC in the campaign. A character who studies under a grandmaster equates to a novice apprenticed to an expert artisan. The character can expect the master to assign tasks that range from the trivial (cleaning the master's home) to the daunting (venturing into the mountains and slaying the high priest of Baphomet's cult).

You might use the stereotypical grandmaster– the elderly martial arts master who takes the young student under his wing, interspersing the student's training with menial jobs and verbal (and physical) abuse. The master has too little time and too much talent to bother with a gentle approach. Either his students learn, or they can seek out a lesser, easier master.

You might find the stereotype fun to play with, or you could explore other options. A grandmaster might be a stern parental figure who offers insight and advice to the characters and never seems satisfied with their work. She could be an old drunk who, unknown to the characters, once held the title of greatest wizard in the city. If the characters sober her up, she recovers enough of her skills to impart them to the characters. A grandmaster could be a deva on the brink of divine ascension, or a deity cloaked in mortal form.

Most important, flavor a grandmaster NPC with interesting quirks, and have him or her participate actively in the characters' lives. Again, this approach falls flat unless you instill the master NPC with interesting details. You want your PCs to remain in the master's training despite the tasks he expects them to perform, the complications he causes, or his meddling in their lives.

A grandmaster comes to life if you incorporate the following features:

✦ **A Vivid Personality:** This key trait, played at maximum volume, outperforms a number of subtle traits. You want your players to associate the grandmaster's personality with his or her name.

✦ **Goals and Desires:** Grandmasters have their own objectives; they assign tasks that help their cause.

✦ **A Place in the Larger Story:** The characters' enemies might kidnap the grandmaster, or the grandmaster might play a direct and pivotal role in developing the story of the campaign.

The training provided by a grandmaster gives a PC the equivalent benefit of a magic item. The PCs might find an item for the master or complete an assigned task to earn their training, which takes the place of an appropriate treasure parcel. It might take a few days or a week for the master's training to sink in.

Obviously, masters provide great ways to drive adventures. A master might require his paladin pupil to go on a quest to prove his dedication to the deity they both worship. A wizard's master could send her into a dungeon to recover a set of lost books. And a master might betray her pupil or reveal that the party's sworn enemy was once her greatest student.

SAMPLE GRANDMASTER TRAINING

Davros Elden's Defensive Step — Level 7

The fencing master's first lesson adjusted Garras's position in a duel, maximizing defense.

Grandmaster Training 2,600 gp
Property: When you shift, you gain a +1 item bonus to AC and Reflex until the end of your next turn.
Power (Encounter): Minor Action. Shift 2 squares.

Davros Elden's Hasty Resurgence — Level 9

When Garras returned for a second lesson, he learned to steady himself when an enemy wore him down.

Grandmaster Training 4,200 gp
Power (Daily): Minor Action. Use this power when you are bloodied to gain temporary hit points equal to your healing surge value.

Davros Elden's Blinding Strikes — Level 11

On Garras's third visit, he learned the technique of making two hasty strikes in blinding succession.

Grandmaster Training 9,000 gp
Power (Daily): Standard Action. Make two melee basic attacks, each with a -2 penalty to the attack roll.

Davros Elden's Aerial Step — Level 13

When Garras returned a fourth time to the master's hut, he learned that Davros Elden had more skill than he let on.

Grandmaster Training 17,000 gp
Property: You take no damage from a fall and always land on your feet.
Power (Daily): Move Action. Fly a number of squares equal to your speed. At the end of your turn, you float down to the ground if you aren't already there.

ALTERNATIVE REWARDS

5

CHAPTER 5 | *Adventures*

145

Sometimes, you might want to strike a middle ground between magic items and mechanics. The concept of item components replaces the flavor of magic items but retain the mechanics, and components allow you to add more background to an item.

The idea behind item components is simple. To ultimately obtain a magic item, the characters must find specific objects or ingredients and perhaps gain the help of an NPC or access a magical location.

Mechanically, an item component replaces a magic item treasure parcel with a number of elements that, when combined, form the item.

For example, you could replace treasure parcel 4 in a set of rewards for a 12th-level party with the components needed to create a level 13 magic item, such as a +3 *assassin's short sword* (see *Adventurer's Vault*, page 63). In this case, the characters need to collect a shard of obsidian from the grand altar to Bane, the poison gland from a venom-eye basilisk, and water drawn from a cistern in the black ore mines. The characters can make the sword when they retrieve these components.

To incorporate the idea of item components into your game, use the following steps:

1. Pick a Parcel: Choose a magic item treasure parcel you want to divide into components and pick an item to fill it.

2. Determine the Components: Divide the selected item into three components. Such an arrangement gives the characters a sense of starting the process of gathering the item's parts, making progress, and then finishing it, without making the process either too simple (two parts) or too involved (four or more parts).

The actual components you devise depend on your campaign. Some or all of them might fit into one or more of the following categories.

Help from an NPC: The characters might need help from an NPC to complete the item. Maybe a priest must bless a sword to make it holy, or a character might need a dryad to kiss a staff to enhance its charm powers. The characters can gain a component of this sort by helping the NPC, by roleplaying the interaction, or by succeeding on a skill challenge.

Harvested Ingredients: Rare herbs, organs taken from slain monsters, or metals or objects taken from special locations fall into this category. The characters might need to hunt down and defeat a certain kind of monster, or they could have to find a rare plant.

Forbidding Sites: Gaining an item component might require the characters to travel to a distant location and use a magic forge, or perhaps they must craft a portion of the item within a certain area of the Elemental Chaos.

3. Place the Components: Think of the components as three miniature treasures. The PCs uncover the final piece at around the same time when they would have found the treasure parcel you replaced. You might include specifics about what the PCs must do to create the item as part of the game's overall plot or a secondary story that comes into play when the PCs attempt to assemble or create the item.

The characters can learn of the components in a number of ways. Have them find the first component, as well as directions explaining the initial step to making the item. The characters could also discover notes on creating the item in an old journal or learn of the process from a mentor. Or the components might pose a mystery: The PCs know they can make an item by assembling the components, but they don't know what the item does.

4. Upgrade or Replace? An item created using these guidelines could replace an old item. Or the process could impart a new power to an existing item, upgrading it to a higher level. If the components improve an existing item, consider augmenting another treasure parcel with gold equal to 20% of the older item's value. Because PCs likely sell older items when they receive upgrades, the extra gold makes up for the loss of those items to sell.

5. Decide How Characters Make the Item: Once the characters have the components, what do they need to do to assemble or create the item? Do they have to follow a specific set of steps to complete the process? You might want to require the PCs to complete a ritual, but avoid requiring the PCs to pay gold to do so. After all, the components fuel the making of the item.

You might require a skill challenge, but if failure means that the PCs ruin the item, you risk frustrating the players. Instead, use a skill challenge to serve as a backdrop during a battle or some other encounter that occurs while the PCs make the item. The skill challenge might determine the number of undead creatures the PCs awaken while they complete the item. If the characters fare poorly in the challenge, they have to fight their way past a deadly encounter to escape, or maybe the party must divide, some fighting fight waves of undead while others finish making the item. If the characters succeed on the skill challenge, the undead leave the PCs alone as they finish the item.

In such a skill challenge, Arcana, Religion, and Nature can reflect the knowledge needed to bind the item's magic. Athletics and Endurance checks represent the physical labor of forging a weapon or some other object. Fine detail work, such as runes etched into a stone, uses Thievery.

At a fundamental level, artifacts are magic items whose role in the game has far more to do with the story of your adventure or campaign than it does with the actual game effects of the item. Characters might buy, sell, enchant, and disenchant any of the hundreds of magic items found in the *Player's Handbook* and *Adventurer's Vault* volumes. They might even quest after those items. But when an artifact enters the characters' lives, the story of the campaign revolves around the artifact for a time.

Artifacts are completely under your control. It's up to you when you introduce an artifact to your game, and it's up to you when the artifact leaves the characters' hands. Ownership of an artifact is the one element of a character's capabilities that the character's player has no control over—it rests entirely in your hands. Use that power for good—the good of your campaign story.

This section introduces seven new artifacts to supplement the ones that appear in the *Dungeon Master's Guide*, and it leads off with some tips to help you incorporate these special items into your game.

Use Artifacts at Any Level: An artifact's overall power level isn't what makes it special. Magic items appear at every level, and there's nothing inherently more special about a level 30 item than there is about a level 1 item. Artifacts are different. There are artifacts appropriate for heroic-level characters as well as epic-level characters, and even the lowliest artifacts are significantly different from ordinary magic items of roughly the same level—not necessarily more powerful, but definitely more significant. So, go ahead

and use artifacts even in your heroic tier game. Introducing an artifact at low levels helps the players see the grand scope of the story they're involved in.

Tie Artifacts to Campaign Themes: Use artifacts to reinforce the story you want to tell in your campaign. If you want to explore themes of how power corrupts those who wield it, introducing the *Eye of Vecna* into your campaign can help reinforce that story. If your campaign involves fighting an oppressive ruler or exploring the cost of freedom, then the *Invulnerable Coat of Arnd* can help expound on those themes.

Recast Stories and Goals: Add details from your campaign to the origin story for an artifact, or alter its goals to strengthen its ties to the themes of your campaign. Does a powerful eladrin villain play an important role in your campaign? Perhaps he is a descendant of Ossandrya, and knowledge of the *Emblem of Ossandrya* is part of his family's lore.

Wait Until Players Have Bought In: Hold off on introducing an artifact into your campaign until after the characters have completed an adventure or two and the players are fully invested in the story of the campaign. They should already know what's at stake and have at least a hint of the nature of the major villain in the story. With that groundwork laid, an artifact's arrival carries the appropriate weight. The players will appreciate the *Invulnerable Coat of Arnd* all the more after they understand the nature of the tyrant they have to overthrow.

Sometimes introducing an artifact can also serve to introduce the villain or theme of a campaign. If you plan to take your campaign in a dramatic new direction in the paragon tier as a major war breaks out in your campaign world, for example, you could introduce the conflict by having the *Standard of Eternal Battle* fall into the characters' hands.

Allow for Conflict: Make sure there's potential for characters to come into conflict with the goals of an artifact. The *Axe of the Dwarvish Lords* seeks to be an inspiration to honorable people. What if the characters discover that there's an easier way to achieve their goals (and the *Axe*'s goals) using deceit and dishonor? Do they take the easy route and displease the artifact, or stick to the *Axe*'s lofty principles and follow a harder road? A decision like this enriches your story and reinforces the idea that player choices matter in the game.

Allow Time for Goodbye: When it's time for an artifact to move on, if the characters are in good standing with it, make the occasion appropriately solemn. Let the characters participate in the artifact's departure, perhaps seeking out appropriate successors or returning it to a special location where it can be found when it's needed again. Give the players a chance to say goodbye to this member of your supporting cast.

"1 CHOSE YOU"

You might decide to introduce an artifact into your campaign in one of two basic ways: Either the characters seek out the artifact, or it falls into their hands—possibly even seeking the characters out. Which approach is better for your campaign depends on the extent to which the players understand what's at stake in the campaign.

If the players understand the stakes and are already determined to pursue the story to its conclusion, then it's fine to send them on a quest to find and acquire an artifact that can help them achieve that goal. This approach can also help you reinforce campaign themes of heroic choice and consequences, particularly if deciding to use the artifact clearly helps the characters accomplish one goal, but might prove a hindrance in other ways.

On the other hand, if your campaign includes the idea that characters are born to a heroic destiny, you can reinforce that idea by having an artifact seek them out. Arthur didn't go on a quest to find *Excalibur* so he could become king; the fact that he was destined to be a great and heroic king led to the artifact coming into his possession.

ADAMANTINE HORSE OF XARN

The *Adamantine Horse of Xarn* is appropriate for mid-heroic-level characters.

Adamantine Horse of Xarn	Heroic Level

At first glance, this artifact appears as an adamantine plate-barded warhorse of particularly powerful build, but further inspection reveals that the entire horse is made of metal and is powered by gears and hidden arcane devices. Due to the genius of its craftsmanship, its noble form moves naturally despite its unyielding material.

Wondrous Item

Property: The *Adamantine Horse of Xarn* is a construct in the form of a warhorse that serves as a mount for its owner. Its statistics depend upon its concordance with its owner.

ADAMANTINE HORSE OF XARN LORE

Arcana or History DC 16: Unlike most other artifacts that are held, worn, or wielded, the *Adamantine Horse of Xarn* is meant to be ridden. The artifact is coveted by warriors who serve the cause of good and who struggle against greed, injustice, and destruction, especially that caused by chromatic dragons.

Arcana or History DC 21: Tales say that Bahamut gave the *Adamantine Horse* to the legendary dragonslayer Xarn, a champion of the young human race. Xarn had already proved his worth against a champion of Tiamat, but he went on to ride the *Adamantine Horse* into battle against one of Tiamat's

aspects. Xarn disappeared from history after that battle, but tales of great heroes who waged war against the Dragon Queen with the help of the artifact are scattered throughout history.

GOALS OF THE ADAMANTINE HORSE

✦ Serve as a mount for a hero devoted to the tenets of law and good.

✦ Protect the weak and uphold justice for the innocent.

✦ Fight against tyranny and greed, especially that perpetrated by chromatic dragons.

ROLEPLAYING THE ADAMANTINE HORSE

If it is owned by a character who shares its philosophy and helps it to achieve its goals, the *Adamantine Horse of Xarn* is a stalwart companion, providing timely aid to its owner. The *Adamantine Horse* can be extremely stubborn, however, with a character who is less perfectly aligned with its goals. The *Adamantine Horse* can't communicate with its rider verbally, but it understands Draconic, Common, and Supernal, and it makes its desires known with a gentle (or not so gentle) nudge, a derisive whinny, or the placement of its metal body to block or reroute passage.

CONCORDANCE

Starting Score	5
Owner gains a level	+1d10
Owner is lawful good	+2
Owner is a paladin, warlord, or avenger	+1
Owner has the Mounted Combat feat	+1
Owner finishes a quest that fulfills the *Adamantine Horse's* goals	+1
Owner defeats an evil dragon (maximum 1/day)	+1
Owner acts in a way contrary to the *Adamantine Horse's* goals	-2
Owner disregards the *Adamantine Horse's* desires	-1

PLEASED (16–20)

"On the battlefield, we move and fight as one."

The *Adamantine Horse of Xarn* is proud to serve its owner as a steed and ally in battle, and it shares its magical power with its owner's allies as well. The *Adamantine Horse's* statistics reflect its pride and confidence.

Property: While you are mounted on the *Adamantine Horse*, any mounted ally within 20 squares of you gains a +2 power bonus to his or her mount's speed and a +5 bonus to damage rolls with charge attacks.

Property: While you are mounted on the *Adamantine Horse*, you gain a +4 bonus to all defenses against opportunity attacks.

Property: The *Adamantine Horse* becomes a 10th-level creature with the following statistics:

Pleased Adamantine Horse of Xarn	Level 10 Brute
Large animate beast (construct, mount)	XP 500

Initiative +6   **Senses** Perception +12; low-light vision
HP 136; **Bloodied** 68
AC 22; **Fortitude** 24, **Reflex** 21, **Will** 22
Speed 10
⊕ **Kick** (standard; at-will)
+13 vs. AC; 1d10 + 8 damage.
↯ **Trample** (standard; at-will)
The *Adamantine Horse of Xarn* can move up to its speed and enter enemies' spaces. This movement provokes opportunity attacks, and the *Adamantine Horse* must end its move in an unoccupied space. When it enters an enemy's space, the *Adamantine Horse* makes a trample attack: +11 vs. Reflex; 1d10 + 8 damage, and the target is knocked prone.
Adamantine Charge (while mounted by a friendly rider of 7th level or higher; at-will) ✦ **Mount**
The *Adamantine Horse* grants its rider 10 extra damage on charge attacks.

Alignment Unaligned	**Languages** Understands Common, Draconic, and Supernal
Str 24 (+12)	**Dex** 12 (+6)	**Wis** 14 (+7)
Con 26 (+13)	**Int** 4 (+2)	**Cha** 10 (+5)

SATISFIED (12–15)
"Together, we shall find glory through our actions!"

Satisfied with its owner's deeds and devotion to the ways of good, the *Adamantine Horse of Xarn* grants its owner and all mounted allies additional powers.

Property: While you are mounted on the *Adamantine Horse*, any mounted ally within 20 squares of you gains a +5 bonus to damage rolls with charge attacks.
Property: The *Adamantine Horse* becomes an 8th-level creature with the following statistics:

Satisfied Adamantine Horse of Xarn	Level 8 Brute
Large animate beast (construct, mount)	XP 350

Initiative +5   **Senses** Perception +11; low-light vision
HP 115; **Bloodied** 57
AC 20; **Fortitude** 22, **Reflex** 19, **Will** 20
Speed 9
⊕ **Kick** (standard; at-will)
+11 vs. AC; 1d8 + 7 damage.
↯ **Trample** (standard; at-will)
The *Adamantine Horse of Xarn* can move up to its speed and enter enemies' spaces. This movement provokes opportunity attacks, and the warhorse must end its move in an unoccupied space. When it enters an enemy's space, the warhorse makes a trample attack: +9 vs. Reflex; 1d8 + 7 damage, and the target is knocked prone.
Adamantine Charge (while mounted by a friendly rider of 7th level or higher; at-will) ✦ **Mount**
The *Adamantine Horse* grants its rider 10 extra damage on charge attacks.

Alignment Unaligned	**Languages** Understands Common, Draconic, and Supernal
Str 23 (+10)	**Dex** 12 (+5)	**Wis** 14 (+6)
Con 25 (+11)	**Int** 3 (+0)	**Cha** 10 (+4)

NORMAL (5–11)
"This union has potential for greatness, but valor must be proven."

The *Adamantine Horse of Xarn* is content to allow its owner to use it as a mount.

Property: The *Adamantine Horse* becomes a 7th-level creature with the following statistics:

Adamantine Horse of Xarn	Level 7 Brute
Large animate beast (construct, mount)	XP 300

Initiative +4   **Senses** Perception +10; low-light vision
HP 105; **Bloodied** 52
AC 19; **Fortitude** 21, **Reflex** 18, **Will** 19
Speed 8
⊕ **Kick** (standard; at-will)
+10 vs. AC; 1d8 + 7 damage.
↯ **Trample** (standard; at-will)
The *Adamantine Horse of Xarn* can move up to its speed and enter enemies' spaces. This movement provokes opportunity attacks, and the warhorse must end its move in an unoccupied space. When it enters an enemy's space, the warhorse makes a trample attack: +8 vs. Reflex; 1d8 + 7 damage, and the target is knocked prone.
Adamantine Charge (while mounted by a friendly rider of 7th level or higher; at-will) ✦ **Mount**
The *Adamantine Horse* grants its rider 10 extra damage on charge attacks.

Alignment Unaligned	**Languages** Understands Common, Draconic, and Supernal
Str 23 (+9)	**Dex** 12 (+4)	**Wis** 14 (+5)
Con 25 (+10)	**Int** 3 (–1)	**Cha** 10 (+3)

UNSATISFIED (1–4)
"The horse has a mind of its own about our purpose."

The *Adamantine Horse of Xarn* still accepts its owner as a rider, but it ignores its owner's commands unless they directly serve the artifact's goals. The *Adamantine Horse* holds back from granting its owner its full power.

Property: The *Adamantine Horse* becomes a 7th-level creature with the statistics shown above, but it doesn't grant its *adamantine charge* ability to its owner.

ANGERED (0 OR LOWER)
"I am unworthy to ride this steed."

Property: The *Adamantine Horse of Xarn* tries not to let its owner mount it. If its owner does somehow mount it, the *Horse* doesn't move.

MOVING ON
"The steed has other fights to join."

The *Adamantine Horse of Xarn* gallops off to other adventures. If it has normal concordance with its owner, it walks off into the sunset the next time the character gains a level, never to be seen again. If it's satisfied or pleased with its owner, it leaves behind a celestial charger (*Monster Manual*, page 159) that serves the *Adamantine Horse*'s former owner faithfully. If the artifact is angered or unsatisfied, it leaves its owner at an inconvenient time to emphasize its disappointment and displeasure with the character's actions.

Amulet of Passage

The *Amulet of Passage* is appropriate for heroic-level characters.

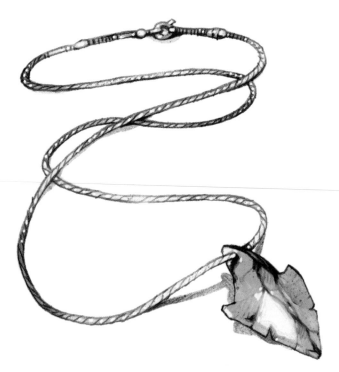

Amulet of Passage	Heroic Level

This fine silver chain is unassuming, bearing a single arrowhead-shaped jewel. While you wear this amulet, it stirs thoughts of legendary battles and heroic deeds.

The *Amulet of Passage* is a +2 magic amulet with the following properties and powers.

Item Slot: Neck

Enhancement: Fortitude, Reflex, and Will

Property: You gain a +2 item bonus to Acrobatics and Athletics checks to escape, and to Thievery checks to open locks.

Power (At-Will): Standard Action. You attune an ally to the *Amulet*. While attuned and within 10 squares of you, an ally can use the *Amulet's* powers (but not its enhancement bonus or properties) as if he or she were wearing it.

Power (Daily ✦ Teleportation): Move Action. You and each attuned ally can each use this power once per day. You teleport a number of squares equal to your speed.

Amulet of Passage Lore

Religion DC 16: An ancient tale describes how Asmodeus, seeking to thwart the power of fate, placed obstacles in the paths of those mortal beings with the greatest destinies. To counter this affront, the Raven Queen crafted the *Amulet of Passage* to guide the greatest mortal heroes back to the path that fate had laid out for them.

Religion DC 21: Another legend claims that Avandra made the *Amulet* to help heroes pursue their own dreams and goals. The *Amulet* grants extraordinary powers of movement—not just to its owner, but to its owner's allies as well.

Goals of the Amulet of Passage

✦ Find those that could become legendary heroes and guide them toward their destined paths.

✦ Continue to move through the world in search of new heroes.

Roleplaying the Amulet of Passage

When the *Amulet of Passage* first comes into a character's possession, it resents the task set before it and must be convinced that its new owner truly is destined for greatness. As its owner continues to succeed, the artifact begins to believe that the character is worthy of his or her destiny.

The *Amulet of Passage* doesn't communicate verbally or telepathically, but it does instill emotional states in its owner, depending on its concordance. It will use feelings of courage and confidence to encourage its owner to push forward without an extended rest (see "Drawing Characters Onward" on page 54).

ARTIFACTS FOR MULTIPLE PLAYERS

This book introduces artifacts that identify themselves with more than one character in the party. Such artifacts might grant powers or properties to two or more characters, as the *Amulet of Passage* does. Other artifacts have concordance based on the actions of each party member, rather than just the artifact's owner, as the *Standard of Eternal Battle* does. Some can be used by multiple characters simultaneously, such as the paired sets of boots *Rash* and *Reckless* or the *Cup* and *Talisman of Al'Akbar*. The *Emblem of Ossandrya*, on the other hand, allows only one owner at a time to use it, but it can be passed from character to character without loss of concordance.

These artifacts can help you reward your players for working well together as a team, or encourage them to think more as a team if they're selfishly inclined. The artifacts can also have the opposite effect if you're not careful, leading to conflict among your players over the "right" way to use the artifact. If conflict does arise, remember that artifacts make their own wishes known to their owners.

VINCENT DUTRAIT

CONCORDANCE

Starting Score	**5**
Owner gains a level	+1d10
Owner reaches three milestones in one day	+2
Owner completes a major quest (maximum 1/day)	+1
Owner's ally dies	-1
Owner stays in the same region for 2 weeks without reaching a milestone	-1

PLEASED (16–20)

"Soon we will accomplish the stuff of legend. Everything we've done so far is just a prelude to what lies ahead."

The *Amulet of Passage* is pleased and impressed with its owner, and it instills a sense of courage, confidence, and destiny in that character. It urges its owner to ever greater achievements.

> **Property:** The *Amulet's* item bonus to Acrobatics and Athletics checks to escape, and to Thievery checks to open locks, increases to +5.
>
> **Power (Daily ✦ Reliable, Teleportation):** Standard Action. You or an attuned ally can use this power. Make an attack: Close burst 10; targets one creature; Intelligence +3, Wisdom +3, or Charisma + 3 vs. Will; on a hit, the target disappears from its location (save ends). While the target is gone from its location, it can't take actions and can't be targeted. On a save, it reappears in the space it last occupied (or in the nearest unoccupied space of its choosing if that space is occupied).

SATISFIED (12–15)

"Our destinies are intertwined as we walk together on the road of adventure."

The *Amulet of Passage* appreciates its owner's drive and encourages that character to achieve more. It instills a sense of restlessness, dissatisfaction, and urgency in its owner, trying to drive the character toward still greater actions.

> **Power (Encounter ✦ Teleportation):** Move Action. You and each attuned ally can each use this power once per encounter. You teleport 10 squares into a space adjacent to an ally who is wearing or attuned to the *Amulet*.

NORMAL (5–11)

"I say we go that way."

The *Amulet of Passage* is noncommittal when it first comes into its owner's possession, waiting to see whether the character will live up to the artifact's expectations. It does encourage the owner to be more decisive, to keep on the move, and to seek adventure and heroic deeds whenever an opportunity presents itself.

UNSATISFIED (1–4)

"If you don't step over the mountain ridge, the scenery never changes."

The *Amulet of Passage* is disappointed in its owner, who clearly lacks the drive or ability to accomplish great things. The character might experience the *Amulet's* displeasure as a nagging feeling of longing, or as thoughts of wanting something more out of life and the need for a change of scenery.

> The *Amulet's* enhancement bonus decreases to +1.

ANGERED (0 OR LOWER)

"We are all lost, and so is this cause."

The *Amulet of Passage* despairs of ever goading its owner to great deeds, and that despair rubs off on the character. The owner feels as if he or she will never achieve great things or accomplish anything of lasting import.

> The *Amulet's* enhancement bonus decreases to +1. The owner can no longer use any of the *Amulet's* powers, and all allies lose their attunement to the *Amulet*.
>
> **Property:** The *Amulet's* item bonus to Acrobatics and Athletics checks to escape, and to Thievery checks to open locks, is negated.

MOVING ON

"I have shown you the path, but you must take the first steps on your own."

After the *Amulet of Passage* has guided its owner and his or her allies onto the path of their destinies, it moves on to find its next owner. Before it leaves, it provides the characters one last passage, typically a teleportation of some great distance (perhaps even across worlds), to where their next great adventure will begin.

CUP AND TALISMAN OF AL'AKBAR

The *Cup* and *Talisman of Al'Akbar* are appropriate for paragon-level characters.

Talisman of Al'Akbar	Paragon Level

This eight-pointed star of hammered platinum hangs on a chain of gold and pearls. Each point of the star is tipped with a diamond, and elaborate patterns of gold inlay cover its surface.

The *Talisman of Al'Akbar* is a +3 magic holy symbol with the following properties and powers.

Implement (Holy Symbol)
Enhancement: Attack rolls and damage rolls
Critical: +3d6 damage per plus
Property: Whenever you make a Heal check, you can roll twice and use either result.
Property: Whenever you use a healing power on an ally, that ally regains 1d10 additional hit points.
Power (Daily ✦ Healing): Free Action. *Trigger:* You reduce an enemy to 0 hit points with an attack power using this holy symbol. *Effect:* You or one ally within 5 squares of you gains regeneration 5 until the end of the encounter.

Cup of Al'Akbar	Paragon Level

Twelve great gems form a ring around the rim of this large gold chalice, which requires two hands to carry. The chalice glows with a faint golden light.

Wondrous Item
Power (Daily): Standard Action. You drink from the *Cup* of *Al'Akbar* and make an Endurance check against a disease affecting you, using the disease's improve DC. If you succeed, you're cured. If you fail, the disease doesn't get any worse while it affects you.
Power (Daily ✦ Healing): Using this power takes 10 minutes. You create one *potion of Al'Akbar* (see below). If you use the *Cup* together with the *Talisman of Al'Akbar*, you can instead create up to three *potions of Al'Akbar*. A potion created in this way reverts to plain water if it isn't consumed within 24 hours.

When filled with water, the *Cup of Al'Akbar* can create a *potion of Al'Akbar*. A creature that drinks one of these potions gains a healing benefit. The potion can't be disenchanted.

Potion of Al'Akbar	Paragon Level

This golden liquid contains great healing magic.

Potion
Power (Consumable ✦ Healing): Minor Action. Drink this potion and spend a healing surge. Instead of the hit points you would normally regain, you regain 30 hit points and make a saving throw.
   If you have no healing surges when you drink this potion, you instead gain 15 temporary hit points.

CUP AND TALISMAN LORE

Religion DC 22: The *Cup* and *Talisman of Al'Akbar* are divine relics with great healing powers. Legend says that they were gifts from Pelor, given to mortals to help the world recover from a time of terrible devastation.

Religion DC 27: After the artifacts were first used to care for the injured and sick, conflicts arose over the ownership of the *Cup* and *Talisman*. Some sought to use the items for good, while others wanted to support armies of conquest, and skirmishes raged over their possession until the artifacts disappeared.

GOALS OF THE CUP AND TALISMAN

✦ Prevent death and eliminate disease.

✦ Avoid creating conflict because of the artifacts' allure.

✦ Atone for the past pain and bloodshed the artifacts have caused.

ROLEPLAYING THE CUP AND TALISMAN

Though each item is a powerful artifact in its own right, the *Cup* and *Talisman of Al'Akbar* appear in histories and lore only as a pair. Likewise, both items think and speak as one entity when in close proximity, echoing one another's words. When separated and in the hands of a good soul, each item comments frequently that it must be reunited with its other half.

The items are altruistic and expect their owner to be as well. They seek only owners who have good intentions and avoid anyone who pursues glory or profit above good deeds. Any owner who uses the *Cup* and *Talisman* directly for profit earns their distrust. A character using the artifacts can reap the normal treasure—and even pay—from adventuring. Forcing the sick or wounded to buy the *Cup's* healing is unacceptable, as is raising someone from the dead because that person is wealthy or powerful rather than worthy or innocent.

Though they're great artifacts of healing, the *Cup* and *Talisman* have also caused much bloodshed among ambitious individuals who sought the items' power. The artifacts still fear their own power and try to escape notice.

AL'AKBAR'S CURSE

The *Cup* and *Talisman of Al'Akbar* were created in a time of great need—some say it was a great plague created by evil deities or demon lords, while others believe it was a war in which great heroes were grievously wounded and killed. Once that time had passed and the artifacts were no longer crucial to survival and victory, their very presence led to hostilities. All sought to own the artifacts, including their owners' enemies, neutral parties who sought their power, and even the owners' allies. At that point, the *Cup* and *Talisman* disappeared. Since that time, they have surfaced when they were needed, but only long enough to accomplish their goals before disappearing again to avoid creating more conflict. The *Cup* and *Talisman* worry that they do more harm than good.

The *Cup and Talisman* are supernaturally alluring and can cause even old allies to turn against one another. The dangers of the artifacts' allure to the characters the longer they hold them should be foreshadowed. At first it could be petty rulers who seek to own the artifacts, but later the situation could escalate to conflicts and dissension among the characters themselves.

Concordance

The *Cup* and *Talisman of Al'Akbar* share one concordance score, but each attitude grants different powers to each item.

CONCORDANCE

Starting Score	5
Owner gains a level	+1d10
Owner is devoted to Pelor	+1
Owner reunites the *Cup* and *Talisman*	+2
Owner completes a quest for worshipers of Pelor	+1
Owner uses the *Cup* or *Talisman* for profit (this includes selling a *potion of Al'Akbar*)	-2
Owner is attacked as a result of owning the item	-2
An ally or innocent dies in the owner's presence (maximum 1/day)	-2

Pleased (16–20)

"We have atoned for the blood spilled over us in the past, but we fear our renown grows too great."

The *Cup* and *Talisman of Al'Akbar* sense that the time to depart is coming soon and feel they have now contributed more good to the world than suffering. It won't be long before the items move on.

The *Talisman's* enhancement bonus increases to +4.
Talisman Critical: +4d6 damage per plus
Talisman Power (At-Will ✦ Healing): Minor Action, 1/ round. One ally you can see can spend a healing surge.
Cup Power (Daily ✦ Healing): Standard Action. You choose a creature (or portion of a creature) within 5 squares of you that died less than 5 minutes ago. That creature returns to life and regains hit points as if it had spent a healing surge.

Satisfied (12–15)

"Our work has saved many lives, but so many still live in need."

You have furthered the artifacts' goals and behaved in a manner approved by their creator. The items trust you and will stay with you for a time.

Talisman Property: Whenever you use a healing power on an ally, that ally regains 2d10 additional hit points.
Cup Power (Daily): Free Action. *Trigger:* You start to perform the Raise Dead ritual. *Effect:* You use the *Cup* and perform the ritual with no component cost. The raised creature doesn't take a -1 death penalty.

Normal (5–11)

"So many call out in pain. We must heal their tortured bodies and ease their suffering."

Special: If you have only one of the artifacts, that artifact encourages you to find the other artifact and drops cryptic hints to lead you to it (or more explicit instructions once it trusts you).
Special: If you have both artifacts, they request that you find and heal those in need. They also emphasize discretion, not wishing for their whereabouts to be discovered.

Unsatisfied (1–4)

"Are my motives pure? Do I truly serve the will of the gods?"

The *Cup* and *Talisman of Al'Akbar* consider you untrustworthy. They don't believe that you truly work for good and are worried that your self-interest is interfering with their altruistic motives. They force you to heal indiscriminately.

Special: You gain no benefit from drinking a *potion of Al'Akbar*.
Property: Whenever you heal an ally and that ally regains additional hit points through the *Talisman*, each enemy within 3 squares of the ally also regains hit points equal to the additional hit points.

Angered (0 or lower)

"The legacy of the Cup and Talisman remains shameful, and I've done nothing to repair it."

You have been actively working against the artifacts' interests, and they wish to find a more worthy owner.

Property: Whenever you spend a healing surge or use a healing power, you reduce the hit points regained by 1d10 (to a minimum of 1 hit point regained). This effect applies even if you're only carrying the *Talisman*.

Moving On

"It's too dangerous to remain here. We must disappear from the face of the world once again."

The *Cup* and *Talisman of Al'Akbar*, eager to avoid too much attention, want to become "lost" once again. This might happen because their owners have revealed the artifacts' presence to too many people and caused conflict (likely if concordance is low), or because the items are fearful that their owners' prominence and success will cause strife in the future (likely if concordance is high).

The artifacts might both move on at once, or one might leave before the other. This second situation usually happens if the two artifacts wish to be far apart and difficult to find to prevent them from falling into the wrong hands.

EMBLEM OF OSSANDRYA

The *Emblem of Ossandrya* is appropriate for paragon-level characters.

Emblem of Ossandrya	Paragon Level

This medallion, shaped like a shield and glowing with soft golden light, bears Corellon's star symbol in its center.

Wondrous Item

Property: You gain resist 10 poison.

Property: You gain a +1 item bonus to saving throws.

Property: You gain a +2 item bonus to Acrobatics, Athletics, and Diplomacy checks.

Power (Encounter): Minor Action. You transfer the *Emblem of Ossandrya* to an ally within 5 squares of you. That ally gains the powers and properties of the artifact, using your concordance to determine them.

Power (Daily): Free Action. *Trigger:* You make an attack roll or skill check and dislike the result. *Effect:* You reroll the attack or check and must use the second result.

EMBLEM OF OSSANDRYA LORE

History DC 22: The legendary eladrin Ossandrya wore this emblem during the Last Battle of the Spiral Tower, when forces loyal to Corellon drove the wicked drow from the Feywild. Since then, it has appeared in times of great crisis, when good must stand strong against the powers of treachery and evil.

History DC 27: The *Emblem of Ossandrya* is far more devoted to the cause of justice and good than even Corellon. It drives its owner to pursue the highest ideals of heroic valor.

GOALS OF THE EMBLEM OF OSSANDRYA

✦ Nurture a group of heroes so that they can begin their epic destiny.

✦ Spread the story of those heroes and help their legend grow among the people of the world.

✦ Encourage daring acts, bold action, and clever stratagems.

ROLEPLAYING THE EMBLEM OF OSSANDRYA

When a character first touches the *Emblem of Ossandrya*, it telepathically asks if the character and his or her allies seek glory for their heroic deeds. With an affirmative answer, the *Emblem* attaches itself to that character's armor or clothing, above and to the left of the character's heart. The *Emblem* is friendly and encouraging, but quickly grows impatient with those who are slow to seek adventure.

The *Emblem* can communicate telepathically and through speech. It speaks Common, Draconic, Dwarven, Elven, Giant, Goblin, and Supernal. The *Emblem* loves to relate the lore of other heroes to which it has been attached. It eagerly listens to any tales told by the heroes, and encourages them to tell such tales to others.

CONCORDANCE

Starting Score	5
Owner gains a level	+1d10
Owner completes a major quest	+2
Owner is trained in Diplomacy	+1
Owner is an eladrin	+1
Owner fails to complete a major quest	-2
Owner or an ally attacks a good or lawful good creature (maximum 1/encounter)	-2

PLEASED (16–20)

"Friends, tales of our deeds shall find a fitting place among the legends of our world."

The characters have proven their worth, and the *Emblem of Ossandrya* accepts them as truly great heroes of grand stature.

Property: You gain resist 20 poison.

Property: You gain a +4 item bonus to Acrobatics, Athletics, and Diplomacy checks.

Power (Encounter ✦ Healing): Immediate Interrupt. *Trigger:* An ally within 5 squares of you is reduced to 0 hit points or fewer. *Effect:* You transfer the *Emblem* to the triggering ally. That ally can spend a healing surge.

SATISFIED (12–15)

"Did you see the baron's face when we told him of our battle at the chasm bridge? Truly, that will be a difficult tale for us to top . . . but we will!"

The *Emblem of Ossandrya* appreciates the valor and daring of its owner and his or her allies, encouraging them to ever greater adventures.

Property: You gain resist 15 poison.
Property: You gain a +3 item bonus to Acrobatics, Athletics, and Diplomacy checks.
Power (Encounter): Immediate Interrupt. *Trigger:* An ally within 5 squares of you fails a saving throw. *Effect:* You transfer the *Emblem* to the triggering ally. That ally can reroll the failed saving throw.

Normal (5–11)

"*My friends, we are destined for greatness.*"

The *Emblem of Ossandrya* has high hopes for its owner and his or her allies, and it gladly seeks their success and glory.

Unsatisfied (1–4)

"*I cannot shake the feeling that we are meant for bigger things than recounting our exploits to tavernkeepers and besotted patrons.*"

The *Emblem of Ossandrya* distrusts its owner's abilities, often wondering telepathically if the character and his or her allies are really trying hard enough.

Property: You take a -1 penalty to attack rolls. When you hit an enemy, the penalty is negated until you take a short rest or an extended rest.

Angered (0 or lower)

"*Perhaps we should explore a lucrative career purveying woolen goods.*"

The *Emblem of Ossandrya* is disgusted with the cowardice or incompetence (or both) of its owner and his or her allies. It stops encouraging bold stratagems and won't remain with its owner much longer.

Property: You take a -1 penalty to attack rolls. When you hit an enemy, the penalty is negated until you take a short rest or an extended rest.
Property: You take a -2 penalty to saving throws instead of the +1 bonus the *Emblem* normally grants.

Moving On

"*We have secured our legend; now others must secure theirs.*"

The *Emblem of Ossandrya* senses that it can no longer help to improve the party's legend, and that other legends-to-be hang in the balance. The next time its owner gains a level, the *Emblem* disappears from the character's armor or clothing, destined to reappear in another place where it's needed more. If the *Emblem* is at least satisfied, it leaves behind a replica of itself for its owner and each of his or her allies. While this item is worn, it grants a +1 item bonus to saving throws but doesn't occupy an item slot.

It's possible that the *Emblem* might request the heroes' help in finding suitable replacements.

Rash and Reckless

Rash and *Reckless* are artifacts appropriate for a pair of paragon-level characters.

Rash and Reckless	Paragon Level

These broad-cuffed black boots suggest an attitude of daring and panache. The two pairs are identical in every detail.

Item Slot: Feet
Property: You can use your Dexterity modifier in place of your Strength modifier to make melee basic attacks with a weapon.
Property: You gain a +2 item bonus to Acrobatics checks and Athletics checks.
Power (Daily): Minor Action. Until the end of the encounter, each enemy adjacent to the ally wearing the other pair of these boots grants combat advantage to you.
Power (Daily): Standard Action. You shift your speed and then make a melee basic attack.

Rash and Reckless Lore

History DC 22: *Rash* and *Reckless* are the individual names of two artifacts, each a pair of boots, meant to be worn by two allies. They originally belonged to a pair of scoundrels who spent their lives in revelry and adventure in the capital city of Nerath years ago. The artifacts allow their owners to work in concert to perform masterful feats of acrobatics and athleticism.

History DC 27: The original owners of *Rash* and *Reckless* were an inseparable pair of adventurers who began their professional life as acrobats in a traveling carnival. They extended the acrobatic training, teamwork, and entertainer's panache that they learned from the sideshows to their adventuring career. Everything else about this duo's life is a matter of conjecture, legend, and tall tale. To this day, no one is sure of their gender or race, where they were born, or the details of their adventuring career. Even their names are lost to history, replaced by the names of the artifacts they left behind as their legacy.

Goals of Rash and Reckless

✦ To perform deeds of daring action and adventure worthy of the stories told of the artifacts' original owners.

✦ To help their owners pursue legendary adventures with flair and boldness.

✦ To lead their owners to riches and renown.

Roleplaying Rash and Reckless

Rash and *Reckless* don't speak, instead communicating through flashes of empathic resonance. A character wearing one of the artifacts is prone to surges of energy, often so great as to make the character leap to his or her feet, overwhelmed with the desire to move around. The artifacts inspire mischievous thoughts and spur the concoction of elaborate plots.

They might suggest a certain course of action—always one that is brash and unconventional. Even limited as they are, the artifacts' communications advance their goal of bringing more daring action and excitement into the world.

Rash and *Reckless* share a friendly sense of competition. Each pair of boots seeks to goad its owner into the greatest, most flamboyant and foolhardy deeds. This competitiveness rubs off on the owners of the items, leading to characters who constantly seek to outdo each other in performing outrageous stunts. The artifacts reward this type of behavior with increased concordance.

CONCORDANCE

Each pair of boots has its own concordance with its owner. Much of the artifacts' concordance depends on the wearer accomplishing outrageous stunts. Maneuvers that are daring but not quite brilliant can increase the artifact's concordance with its owner by 1, while a truly legendary act (as determined by the DM) might increase it by 3.

CONCORDANCE

Starting Score	5
Owner gains a level	+1d10
Owner is a rogue or a bard	+2
Owner is trained in Acrobatics and Athletics	+1
Owner pulls off a maneuver with great panache	+2
Owner rushes into danger (maximum 1/encounter)	+1
Owner falls due to a failed Athletics check	-1
Owner expresses caution	-1
Owner flees from a combat encounter	-2

PLEASED (16–20)

"I know! Let's sneak into the baron's keep to find out what he's up to!"

"And we can steal his scepter while we're there!"

The artifact is delighted with its owner, who displays the kind of behavior that the boots approve of. It encourages thoughts of daring adventures and reckless behavior, which it knows its owner will pursue.

> **Power (Daily):** Move Action. You shift your speed.
> **Power (Encounter):** Free Action. *Trigger:* You score a critical hit. *Effect:* The target is dazed until the end of your next turn.

SATISFIED (12–15)

"Caution be damned!"

"Twice damned, I say!"

The artifact sees encouraging signs that its owner is capable of truly legendary acts and gently urges the character to pursue a course of foolhardy action.

> **Property:** You gain a +2 bonus to Bluff checks while using a disguise.

Property: Whenever you shift, you can move into spaces occupied by creatures, but you can't end your movement in an occupied square.

NORMAL (5–11)

"I feel like doing something . . . crazy."

"Something wild!"

The artifact initially stirs vague longings in its new owner, trying to goad the character into more daring and extravagant behavior.

UNSATISFIED (1–4)

"I don't want to let my life be ruled by fear."

The artifact is displeased with an owner who is either too cautious or too incompetent to accomplish deeds worthy of its original owner. The character feels the artifact's dissatisfaction and longs to find an untapped reserve of bravery. Until the artifact's concordance improves, it grants no powers, but its properties still apply.

ANGERED (0 OR LOWER)

"These boots are slowing me down!"

The artifact despises its owner, believing the character to be incapable of greatness and unworthy of its aid and attention. The artifact grants no powers, and its normal properties no longer apply.

Property: At the start of each encounter, you're slowed (save ends).

MOVING ON

"The show must go on."

Rash and Reckless have a sense of the dramatic and a hunger for helping new performers play to new crowds. They rarely stay with heroes for more than a few adventures (a couple of levels). When it's time for them to move on, they look for a way to make a dramatic exit, preferring to vanish in a flash of light and a puff of smoke after their owners (ideally, working in concert) have accomplished a truly great stunt worthy of engendering a new legend.

If the artifacts are unsatisfied or angered with their owners, they leave at an inopportune time, perhaps disappearing from their owners' feet during an audience with a baron (or a hearing before a judge) to cause embarrassment to their failed owners.

Some stories tell that *Rash and Reckless* will sometimes return to their favorite heroes for a reunion performance and one final adventure.

ROD OF SEVEN PARTS

The renowned *Rod of Seven Parts* is appropriate for characters of any level. Unlike most artifacts, it's designed to come into play early in a character's career and play an important part in adventures through the epic tier.

The *Rod* consists of seven individual segments, each one between 4 and 15 inches long. Reassembled into a whole, they form a slender rod 5 feet in length.

Rod of Seven Parts	Heroic to Epic Level

This short segment of lusterless black metal looks like a single part of a larger whole.

A single segment of the *Rod of Seven Parts* is a +1 magic rod. Each additional segment joined to the first increases the *Rod's* enhancement bonus by 1 to a maximum of +7. The *Rod's* properties and powers depend on how many segments are assembled together.
Implement (Rod)
Enhancement: Attack rolls and damage rolls
Critical: +1d6 damage per segment, or +1d10 damage per segment against elemental creatures
Property: Whenever you use a healing power, one target of the power can make a saving throw.
Property: You gain a +1 item bonus to Diplomacy, Intimidate, and Religion checks per segment.

If all seven segments of the *Rod of Seven Parts* are assembled together, they gain the following additional property:

Property: You can use the *Rod* as a simple melee weapon. You add its enhancement bonus to attack rolls and damage rolls of melee weapon attack powers, and it deals +7d6 critical damage, or +7d10 against elemental creatures. Used as a melee weapon, the *Rod's* proficiency bonus is +2 and its damage die is 1d10.

ROD OF SEVEN PARTS LORE

Religion DC 28: The *Rod of Seven Parts* was forged during the Dawn War that raged at the beginning of time between the gods and the primordials. It was crafted by the Wind Dukes of Aaqa, a group of seven angels that served Bahamut, with the assistance of one of Moradin's exarchs. Forged for use against Miska the Wolf-Spider, a demonic primordial of terrible power, it was ultimately driven through Miska's body, shattering into seven parts as it came into contact with the Wolf-Spider's chaotic energy.

Religion DC 33: As the *Rod* shattered, Miska was cast through a planar breach (see page 185) and lost on an unknown plane, and the seven fragments of the *Rod* were scattered throughout the cosmos. The *Rod* hasn't been reassembled since, despite the best efforts of forces aligned with both sides of the cosmic war.

Goals of the Rod of Seven Parts

✦ Be reunited into a whole item once again.

✦ Establish the divine rule of law in the world and the cosmos, taming the Elemental Chaos and destroying the remaining primordials.

✦ Seek out and destroy Miska the Wolf-Spider once and for all.

Roleplaying the Rod of Seven Parts

It's best for the PCs to find the smallest part of the *Rod of Seven Parts* first. Each individual segment of the *Rod* is capable of guiding its owner toward the next larger segment. If a character holds any portion of the *Rod* and thinks of it as part of a larger item, the character feels a vague sense of where the next largest piece lies, getting a clear sense of direction, but no indication of distance or circumstance.

As soon as two or more pieces of the *Rod* are joined together, the *Rod*'s owner feels its urgent desire to be reassembled. Without being consciously aware of the *Rod*'s influence, its owner also becomes aware of its goals. The character becomes inclined toward order and regulation, feeling a sense of revulsion when confronted by disorder, lawlessness, or anarchy.

Concordance

The primary way to increase the concordance of the *Rod of Seven Parts*, and through that its power, is to seek out additional segments and join them to the first segment found. Regardless of other conditions, the number of segments joined together determines the *Rod*'s maximum concordance, as shown on the second table below.

CONCORDANCE

Starting Score	5
Owner gains a level	+1d10
Each segment of the rod joined to the first	+2
Owner defeats an elemental (maximum 1/day)	+1
Owner defeats a primordial	+4
Owner or an ally attacks an immortal (maximum 1/encounter)	–1
Owner flouts laws or codes of conduct	–2

Number of Segments	Maximum Concordance
One	5
Two	7
Three	9
Four	11
Five	14
Six	17
Seven	20

Pleased (16–20)

"Through us, order will be restored to creation!"

The *Rod of Seven Parts* is mostly or entirely complete, and it hums with life and excitement that rub off on its owner. The *Rod* is actively seeking Miska the Wolf-Spider or another primordial to destroy, and its owner knows the *Rod*'s full purpose.

Property: Whenever you use a healing power, each target of the power can make a saving throw.

Power (Daily ✦ Fear, Psychic): Standard Action. You cloak yourself in a fearsome aura of awe-inspiring divine presence, which enables you to make the following attack: Close burst 3; targets enemies in the burst; Intelligence or Wisdom or Charisma vs. Will; on a hit, the attack deals 2d10 + 5 psychic damage, pushes the target 3 squares, and immobilizes the target (save ends).

Satisfied (12–15)

"Fear me, spawn of Chaos—and fear the Rod I wield!"

With at least five segments assembled, the *Rod of Seven Parts* manifests potent powers in pursuit of its goals. Its owner knows that the *Rod* seeks to destroy primordials and punishes lawless behavior.

Power (Encounter): Move Action. You fly your speed.

Power (Daily): Standard Action. You create a gust of wind: Close blast 5; targets all creatures; Intelligence or Wisdom vs. Fortitude; on a hit, the attack deals 2d10 + 5 damage and pushes the target 3 squares.

Normal (5–11)

"There is more to this Rod . . . I can feel it!"

When a segment of the *Rod of Seven Parts* first comes into a character's possession, the artifact communicates a vague sense of a greater purpose or destiny, but little else. The character is aware of the *Rod*'s properties and knows that finding additional segments of the *Rod* will increase its power.

Unsatisfied (1–4)

"I don't think this thing likes me."

The *Rod*'s owner is either flaunting laws or waging war on angels or devils, and the *Rod* is displeased. It makes its displeasure known, with subtle influence and a vague sense of unease.

Property: The *Rod*'s item bonus to Diplomacy, Intimidate, and Religion checks is negated.

Property: You take a –2 penalty to Bluff checks.

Property: You take a –1 penalty to attack rolls against immortal creatures.

Angered (0 or lower)

"Why am I so tired all the time?"

The *Rod of Seven Parts* is severely displeased and punishes its owner until the character's behavior improves or the artifact decides to move on.

The *Rod*'s enhancement bonus is reduced by 1, and its extra damage on a critical hit is reduced by 1 die.

Property: The *Rod*'s item bonus to Diplomacy, Intimidate, and Religion checks is negated.

Property: You take a -5 penalty to Bluff checks.

Property: You take a -2 penalty to attack rolls against immortal creatures.

Property: After each extended rest, you lose one healing surge.

MOVING ON

"What happened to the Rod?"

The *Rod of Seven Parts* shatters into its component parts, and each segment teleports to a random location across the planes. It might break apart and scatter after its owner uses a daily power from the *Rod*, or after slaying a powerful opponent. If it's displeased with its owner, it might shatter in the instant before the character tries to use it as a weapon or implement. If the *Rod* is pleased with its owner, it might grant a legendary boon (see page 142) in its place.

ADVENTURES WITH THE ROD OF SEVEN PARTS

The *Rod of Seven Parts* was the focus of a super adventure written in 1996 (for the 2nd Edition of the D&D game) by Skip Williams. This truly epic campaign leads the characters on several shorter adventures in pursuit of individual segments of the *Rod*, while encounters with various minions of Miska and the Queen of Chaos, as well as agents of the Wind Dukes of Aaqa, occur at intervals over the course of many levels of play.

A series of adventures involving the *Rod of Seven Parts* could have the characters stumble upon one piece of the *Rod* initially, and then seek out the other six of their own volition. Complicating matters a bit, the characters might discover that forces of chaos also seek the *Rod*, hoping to use it to find and restore Miska the Wolf-Spider to power. The *Rod of Seven Parts* adventure took things one step further, introducing a Wind Duke who sought to restart the ancient war against Chaos by releasing Miska again.

If you introduce the *Rod* to your campaign at low levels, you can include a short quest to find and attach a new segment of the *Rod* once every five levels or so. That way, its enhancement bonus keeps pace with its owner's level. Make sure the artifact stays important to the party in between those adventures by featuring enemies and allies who have an interest in the *Rod*. As the characters assemble more segments, they might get involved with the Wind Dukes, various demonic forces, and ultimately Miska itself.

You can also compress this campaign arc by introducing the *Rod* when the characters are already epic level. Its powers and properties might not be significant to them until they get four or five segments assembled, but the promise of having a +7 rod in hand by the campaign's climax makes the effort worthwhile.

STANDARD OF ETERNAL BATTLE

The *Standard of Eternal Battle* is appropriate for paragon-level characters.

The *Standard* has no single owner, but it considers itself to belong to an entire party of heroes—as if they were a squad of soldiers. Any member of the characters' party can use the powers and properties of the *Standard*, and the actions of the group as a whole determine the artifact's concordance.

Standard of Eternal Battle	Paragon Level

This tattered standard bears the evidence of a dozen great wars and a thousand battles. Dedicated to the spirit of warfare, the banner patiently waits for worthy owners to carry it into combat.

Wondrous Item

Power (At-Will): Minor Action. Any owner of the *Standard of Eternal Battle* can cause it to display any coloration, crest, icon, emblem, or other mark. The chosen symbol remains until an owner uses a minor action to change it.

Power (Encounter ✦ Zone): Standard Action. When you plant the *Standard* in your space or an adjacent square, it creates a zone in a close burst 5. While within the zone, you and your allies gain a +1 power bonus to attack rolls and saving throws.

In addition, while the *Standard* is planted, any of its owners within 5 squares of it can use its powers.

These effects last until the end of the encounter or until the *Standard* is removed from the ground.

The *Standard* can be set into any solid surface, even rocky ground or a stone floor. It doesn't occupy the square. Once planted, it can be removed from the ground as a standard action only by one of its owners or by a creature that has reduced one of its owners to 0 hit points or fewer.

STANDARD OF ETERNAL BATTLE LORE

History DC 22: A gift from the god Bane to an ancient hobgoblin conqueror, the *Standard of Eternal Battle* has flown over countless battlefields in every era of mortal history. It shares its creator's love for war, regardless of the cause or purpose of the conflict.

History DC 27: According to legend, the *Standard* can change hands only through violence—it must be won and claimed as a prize in battle.

GOALS OF THE STANDARD OF ETERNAL BATTLE

✦ Aid those whose goal is conquest through war, subduing a rebellious people, or unseating a usurper.

✦ Be carried by worthy owners. Lesser owners must improve or quickly be replaced or destroyed.

Roleplaying the Standard of Eternal Battle

The *Standard of Eternal Battle* is a manifestation of the spirit of warfare and conquest. To that end, it's crafty and suspicious, being a master and survivor of a hundred betrayals.

Arrogant and completely unconcerned for the fates of all who aren't accomplished warriors, the *Standard* issues commands rather than conversing with its owners. It communicates by speaking through nearby characters, its gravelly voice emerging unexpectedly whenever it wishes to make its point. It doesn't care whether it speaks through one of its owners, a nearby NPC, or even an enemy locked in battle with the owners.

CONCORDANCE

Starting Score	**5**
Owning group finds the *Standard*, rather than taking it from previous owners	-2
Each member of owning group gains a level	+1d10
Owning group contributes to the success of a war or major conquest	+4
Member of owning group reduced to 0 hit points or fewer by an enemy	-1
Member of owning group surrenders to an enemy	-2
Owning group participates in losing effort of a war or major conquest	-4

PLEASED (16–20)

"Even death cannot stay our hands! Fight on!"

The *Standard of Eternal Battle* delights in heroes who take part in glorious battle and refuse to bow down to their foes. It grants its owners the power to cheat death so they can fight longer.

> **Power (Daily ✦ Healing):** Immediate Interrupt. *Trigger:* An enemy reduces you to 0 hit points or fewer while you're within the zone. *Effect:* You regain all your hit points and make a saving throw against each effect on you that a save can end.

SATISFIED (12–15)

"We cannot be held back from victory!"

The *Standard of Eternal Battle* enjoys the tastes of glory it receives and hungers for more. Its owners are filled with confidence as it orders them to seek out greater battles.

> **Power (Encounter):** Minor Action. You and each ally within the zone make a saving throw with a +5 bonus, and you each gain combat advantage against the target of the next attack roll you make before the end of your next turn.

NORMAL (5–11)

"Let us prove ourselves worthy of the banner we fight under."

The *Standard of Eternal Battle* is arrogant but vocally supportive of its owners, even while it silently judges the characters' worth in battle.

UNSATISFIED (1–4)

"We have failed. We must put ourselves back on the path to glory."

The *Standard of Eternal Battle*'s owners have faltered in battle, and the artifact begins to throw greater challenges in their way to test their mettle.

> **Property:** At the start of each encounter, if the level of the highest-level owner is equal to or lower than the level of any enemy in the encounter, the owners of the *Standard* take a -5 penalty to initiative checks for that encounter.

ANGERED (0 OR LOWER)

"We have displeased the Standard. We must prove our worth before we perish!"

The owners are failing to live up to the lofty expectations of the *Standard of Eternal Battle*, and it actively seeks their downfall at the hands of more accomplished warriors.

> **Property:** At the start of each encounter, if the level of the highest-level owner is equal to or lower than the level of any enemy in the encounter, the owners of the *Standard* take a -10 penalty to initiative checks for that encounter.

Property: If planted, the *Standard* can be removed from the ground as a standard action by any creature in or adjacent to its square.

Moving On

"Our doom approaches."

The *Standard of Eternal Battle* balances its desire for worthy owners with its need to exercise control over those individuals. Whether the owners prove unworthy or the artifact loses its absolute control, it eventually seeks to divest itself of its current owners.

The *Standard* doesn't move on of its own volition. It instead draws powerful adversaries to it and its owners on a regular basis. These teams of enemies are often stronger than the current owners (2–5 levels higher) and are dedicated to wresting the artifact from its inferior owners. They begin showing up weekly or even daily, always at the most inopportune moments, until the owners are defeated or surrender the artifact.

Some owners see this doom approaching and rid themselves of the *Standard* before it's too late. According to legend, the *Standard* is often found in a forlorn location, a lowly resting place for such a lofty artifact.

DESTROYING ARTIFACTS

As mentioned in the *Dungeon Master's Guide*, destroying an artifact isn't as simple as using the rules for damaging objects. Each artifact has a specific means by which it can be destroyed. The original *Dungeon Master's Guide* (published in 1979) offered the following list of possible means to destroy an artifact:

1. Melt it down in the fiery furnace, pit, mountain, forge, crucible, or kiln in which it was created.

2. Drop it into or bury it beneath (1) the Well of Time, (2) the Abyss, (3) the Earth Wound, (4) Adonais' Deep, (5) the Spring of Eternity, (6) Marion's Trench, (7) the Living Stone, (8) the Mountain of Thunder, (9) 100 adult red dragon skulls, (10) the Tree of the Universe.

3. Cause it to be broken against or crushed by (1) Talos, a triple iron golem, (2) the Gates of Hell, (3) the Cornerstone of the World, (4) Artur's Dolmen, (5) the Juggernaut of the Endless Labyrinth, (6) the heel of a god, (7) the Clashing Rocks, (8) the foot of a humble ant.

4. Expose it to the penetrating light and flame of (1) the Ray of Eternal Shrinking, (2) the Sun, (3) Truth: that which is pure will become Light, that which is impure will surely wither.

5. Cause it to be seared by the odious flames of Geryon's destroyed soul or disintegrated in the putrid ichor of Juiblex's deliquescing flesh.

6. Sprinkle it with/baptize it in the (1) Well of Life, (2) River Styx, (3) River of Flame, (4) River Lethe.

ORGANIZATIONS

Organized groups give your adventurers the chance to interact and form relationships with set collections of enemies and allies throughout ongoing storylines. Villainous organizations connect the dots between encounters. Virtuous groups provide the PCs with support, a sense of belonging, and a reason to venture forth and find trouble. Organizations between the poles of good and evil flesh out the politics of your setting.

Recurring Villainy

Enemy organizations offer a sense of continuity in your story that solitary villains don't provide, because you remove solitary villains from the game world when they're defeated. Antagonists in roleplaying games are more fragile than villains in movies and comic books. An author can dictate that his villain inconclusively engages with the heroes several times before the final confrontation. In the game, though, any encounter between a set of player characters and a primary villain could end in the death of a carefully nurtured antagonist.

When the characters struggle against a malevolent organization, however, the storyline can continue despite a surprise victory. The defeated creature you intended as the main villain is revealed as a pawn of a larger group, allowing you to create another primary villain for later encounters. During the search for the mastermind, the PCs engage in further fights against other cells of the villainous group.

Connecting the Dots

In a political or city-based scenario, organizational ties between sets of opponents can serve as the connecting tissue that links encounters. After the characters overcome a combat encounter or a skill challenge, plant information that leads them to another encounter or challenge to face a new branch of the organization, or give them a clue to the identity of the lead villain.

Just as dungeon room doors can lead to different encounters, you can plant clues that lead in multiple directions, offering players an interesting choice of next steps. Allow players to choose which opponents to tackle next, so they don't feel forced from one scene into another.

The path from one encounter to the next isn't always straightforward. To keep the adventure on track, don't hide information that leads characters to the next encounter. If they fail on a Perception check or a Streetwise check to glean necessary information, don't leave players with no direction. Give them the information they need, and then let them make checks to uncover extra information that helps them

in other ways. For example, if characters succeed on a check with a high roll, they might find one or more of the following kinds of information.

- ✦ Tactical hints that grant an advantage in the upcoming encounter. You could forewarn the party about traps, necessary equipment or ritual components, or a way to surprise their enemies.

- ✦ Facts they can use to achieve personal goals. A player character who swears to expose his evil uncle might find proof of his uncle's membership in the outlaw band the group has been fighting. Or, a character who has an established love interest could discover an enemy group's plans to kidnap and ransom him.

- ✦ Clues leading to additional encounters. Give characters an incentive to follow obvious links and make dead-end paths less enticing.

- ✦ Details about the inner workings of the villainous organization. This kind of information engages explorers and storytellers. The details don't have to relate directly to the goals of the characters or the adventure in order to be meaningful.

POLITICAL COMPLICATIONS

Another set of plot options appears when characters cannot fight their way from one enemy cell to another because the enemy organization is too strong. This strength might translate literally in terms of level and enemy capability. Build the opposing group's leadership from epic tier monsters when the characters have just embarked on their paragon paths, making a combat confrontation with the organization a deadly proposition.

If you want to create a politically untouchable enemy organization, focus on intrigue and interaction. For example, the enemy group advises the local duke, enjoys the protection of an impulsive deity, or secures the loyalty of the people by generously donating gold to favored causes. Although the characters might occasionally spar with the enemy's minions and lackeys, the PCs can't launch physical attacks on the leaders. Instead, the characters embark on a series of fights, skill challenges, and interactions designed to reduce the enemy group's political influence. Characters might pursue the following tasks:

- ✦ Search for proof that the group secretly conspires against its political protectors.

- ✦ Displace the villains in their patron's favor, either through political intrigue or a series of battles.

- ✦ Use treasure liberated from dungeon delving to purchase the goodwill of the populace. (Increase the available treasure from each encounter. The players need the usual amount to enhance their characters, plus a budget for their political operations. Turn off the gold spigot if the players start raiding their political slush fund to buy magic items for themselves.)

RIVALRY

Organizations can stand in the party's way without being villainous. Rival groups hinder the characters and their goals by competing with them. The rivals' methods might be at least as ethical as the player characters' methods. If the characters behave like a selfish pack of irresponsible freebooters, members of a rival organization might annoy and frustrate the characters by acting with high-handed, self-righteous virtue. A rival group that pursues disastrous ends with the best of intentions offers its own tricky challenge. Give the players reasons to sympathize with these troublemakers, even as the characters struggle to compensate for their rivals' actions.

Examine the characters' goals to determine a rival organization's plans. Invent a reason why a different group of characters wants to work against the PCs without descending into villainy. Consider the following challenges that a rival organization might pose to your characters.

- The characters enjoy the patronage of a wealthy and powerful duke, and another group wishes to secure the duke's favor. Or, the rival adventurers could seek to replace the duke with someone they believe is the duke's older brother, and thus is the rightful claimant to the duke's title.

- A particular temple advocates a rigidly moralistic ideology that might, if it took hold among the populace, put characters who use arcane power out of favor.

- Another adventuring party explores the same dungeon and searches for the same artifact or treasure that the characters are seeking. In addition to creating an interesting rivalry, this situation also encourages the characters to push through encounters without stopping for an extended rest (see "Drawing Characters Onward" on page 54).

Because the rules allow characters to fight rivals without killing them (see "Knocking Creatures Unconscious" on page 295 of the *Player's Handbook*), you can stage combat encounters with members of rival organizations who impede the characters' progress.

Players might not expect their characters to face the logical results of antisocial behavior. Warn the players that if they use lethal force against legitimate organizations, they can expect punishment, which could include any or all the following consequences:

- Trouble with the authorities.
- Revenge attacks by other members of the rival group.
- Withdrawal of support by friends, family, patrons, and community leaders.
- Exile from good or unaligned communities.

BELONGING TO AN ORGANIZATION

You can build a campaign around the idea that the player characters belong to an organization rather than, or in addition to, having them fight against a villainous or rival organization. The players might want their characters to join an established group in your campaign.

You can portray the characters' lives between missions through an adventurer organization, if your group enjoys this aspect of play. It allows you to surround the party with a cast of NPCs who can drive plots and subplots by providing information, requiring rescue, or introducing romantic entanglements.

If your group enjoys a DM-directed style of play, the characters' superior or a contact within the organization assigns the characters the next quest to undertake on the organization's behalf. Don't make membership in an organization feel like a job; let

the characters act as powerful free agents. Avoid the temptation to use their superiors in an organization to create dominance over the characters. Few players want to belong to groups that abuse, punish, or threaten their members. Although authoritarian organizations exist, reserve this type of behavior for enemies and rivals.

Players who prefer an open-ended approach to the game might avoid organizations that assign missions or issue orders. An organization that has a loose structure but clear goals can provide enough motivation to set the players on the road to self-defined missions. For example, the characters might be the only local representatives of a far-flung organization dedicated to fighting cults of Those Who Hear (see page 120) and other people and creatures connected to the Far Realm. The characters have a clear reason to investigate when signs of cult activity surface in the area. The characters might also sense that their local problems are part of a larger story without needing to have missions handed to them by an authority figure.

SHIFTING RELATIONSHIPS

The characters' relationships with an organization can shift, perhaps several times over the course of a long campaign. An organization might initially act as a patron for the characters, hiring or rewarding them on an informal basis for performing particular tasks. As the characters complete missions for the patron group, they might identify with the organization and join as official members, or at least informal operatives. Alternatively, they might grow disenchanted with the group, gradually learning that they do not share or support its true agenda.

Shifting relationships can define a story arc for your campaign. These changes could occur gradually, in response to player interaction, or suddenly, when you unveil a plot twist. Consider the following possible developments:

- The player characters disappoint the organization, and it finds a new group of adventurers to do its bidding. Or, maybe the characters decide they don't want to work for the organization anymore. Either way, the characters must now compete against the organization's new representatives.

- A virtuous organization undergoes a factional struggle that results in the ousting of its benevolent members. The new leadership begins advancing an evil plot, and the characters must decide whether to try to restore the group's original leadership from within the organization or leave the organization and fight it from outside.

- After a political change, a villainous organization that the characters previously couldn't touch is now fair game. Or, the opposite could be true: A well-intentioned group that an evil or misguided ruler once outlawed comes into favor when the rulership changes.

✦ A rival or villainous group encourages a partnership with the characters to combat a greater threat to both groups.

✦ The characters' patron (group or individual) betrays them at a pivotal moment. This scenario is a cliché in fiction and gaming, and as such players might feel duped if you throw this sort of plot twist at them. Use the cliché with caution, and try to make the players feel clever and triumphant when they turn the tables on their treacherous ex-allies.

POWER STRUGGLES

Struggles between organizations provide an endless supply of plot hooks. If characters belong to an organization or have one as a client, they might find themselves contending against its enemies. The PCs' superiors might send them on missions to attack or subvert the opposing organization. Alternatively, agents of enemy organizations might try to neutralize the characters or to thwart their assigned objectives. In an environment of clear morality, in which one organization is good and the other evil, the characters might gravitate to the side of virtue. If both groups operate in shades of gray, the characters might have to wrestle with moral issues when deciding which group to back.

When neither contending organization deserves sympathy, the adventurers could enjoy playing the groups against each other. Perhaps the characters are amoral and self-serving, or they might slowly grind both groups down, pretending to maintain the balance of power between the two while they take power for themselves.

FACTIONS AND SCHISMS

You can design a setting for players who thrive on politics and intrigue by adding conflicts within organizations, as well as conflicts between or among them. Multiple factions compose the average organization. Conflict might occur at the highest levels of the organization as different factions compete to direct the organization's agenda or philosophy. Alternatively, the opposing factions might fully agree on the issues that drive the group but divide along lines of loyalty to rival personalities or the specifics of administrative detail. Faction leaders might also pay lip service to the philosophy and goals of the group while pursuing prestige, authority, and control of the group's purse strings.

When the player characters belong to a factionalized organization, they have frequent opportunities for political maneuvering and intrigue. When factional infighting weakens a rival or villainous organization, the characters could exploit that schism and find unlikely allies willing to strike against mutual rivals within the organization.

The characters need not play a central role in struggles between groups. The warring organizations can serve as a background element that explains why certain places are lawless or rich in adventuresome violence. In the city of Sigil, for example (see the next chapter), player characters could either jump into its ongoing, multisided power struggles or keep their heads down and try to stay neutral.

DEFINING THE CONFLICT

When you build power struggles between organizations into your setting, define the nature of the conflict as covert, peripheral, open, multisided, or polarized (or some combination of these types).

Covert struggles occur beneath a society's seemingly placid surface. Secretive organizations vie for control under the noses of an unsuspecting populace. A clandestine struggle for political power ends when one side wins. Fights over obscure or arcane goals could remain concealed, even when the ripple effects transform the community.

Peripheral conflicts interest the participating groups but exert little influence on anyone else. For example, two schools of wizards might vie for possession of an artifact. Although the competition consumes the two groups, no one in the wider community notices it. Victory for one side changes the two groups forever but exerts no measurable impact on a society.

Open struggles pit two or more groups against one another in violent conflict. Two criminal gangs might fight for control of a specific territory, or two merchant houses might compete for dominance over a specific market or trade route. A barony could erupt in civil war when the baron dies and rival groups support different heirs to the throne. Whatever the conflict's nature, it affects everyday life, creating ongoing jeopardy for all. For the characters, any decision they make could instigate a battle.

Multisided conflicts create a web of mutual dependence and hostility as numerous groups pursue their own agendas. The groups switch between rivalry and alliance as circumstances change; sometimes they cooperate on certain issues while opposing each other on others.

Polarized conflicts drive all comers into one of two opposing camps. Opposed beliefs and interests congeal into mutual hatred. Each side regards associating with the other as treachery. Even if conflict occurs on a political level, flaring tempers could lead to periodic explosions of violence.

ORGANIZATION ELEMENTS

Like any detail about your world, your description of an organization might consist of an idea in your head, a few lines of scrawled notes, or large chunks of elegantly written text. The following format can help you shape your ideas about the groups your PCs interact with. Not all of these elements are appropriate to all kinds of organizations.

NAME OF ORGANIZATION

Goal: What the group hopes to accomplish in the short or long term.

Stated Goal: Groups with secret goals maintain cover stories. The goal tells players what the organization claims to strive for, rather than its true intent.

Size: Rather than giving a specific number of members, this entry describes the group's relative size and scope.

Alignment: The prevailing (though not necessarily exclusive) alignment of the faction that drives the group. In an organization that has a secret agenda, this alignment could be at odds with the alignment of the majority of the unsuspecting members.

Philosophy: Why the organization acts as it does. In case of a secret agenda, include notes on the group's outward philosophy.

History: Additional information on the formation and development of the organization.

Leadership: The group's key leader or leaders, including any local leadership.

Headquarters: The location where the group conducts its business and protects its leaders.

Membership Requirements: How player characters can join the organization, if possible.

Structure: The group's organizational structure.

Activities: The group's current actions to advance its agenda.

Enemies: Other groups that the organization openly or violently conflicts with.

Rivals: Political opponents with whom the group engages in peaceful intrigue.

Factions: Any notable factions within the group.

Other Features: Any additional information on the group.

EXAMPLES

The following six example organizations can serve as models for the groups you want to develop for your campaign, or you can use them as presented here. A few of these examples have specific ties to the city of Sigil, which is described in Chapter 6.

BANESONS

Goal: A secret conspiracy of humans promotes the worship of Bane, the deity of war and conquest. Based on the vision of its founder, the group schemes toward a global apocalypse to transform the world into a mirror of the plane of Chernoggar, Bane's Iron Fortress (see *Manual of the Planes*, page 92), and the Banesons into mighty goblin warriors.

Size: Small and local. The Banesons relies heavily on the charisma and devotion of their leader, and the group holds little appeal beyond its leader's reach.

Alignment: Evil.

Philosophy: "Life offers only misery and falsehood. We are strong, but this world of deception keeps us weak. It is better to be the masters of our own fates and bring on a catastrophe we choose, than to toil and suffer in a world that places no value on our inexhaustible bloodlust."

History: The Banesons formed a generation ago after its founder, Eliath Red-Dust, went to the mountains to fast and received an ecstatic vision of blood.

Leadership: The blacksmith Derthad Red-Dust acts meek and subservient, but secretly he burns with the murderous certainty of his father's mission.

Headquarters: Derthad holds small meetings of his inner circle at his forge.

Structure: The group consists of a dozen small cells; each acts autonomously, occasionally taking direct orders from Derthad. The leaders of the cells knew Derthad's late father, and they meet regularly with Derthad to plot global destruction.

Activities: The group raises funds through raids, kidnappings, and highway robbery. It terrorizes the area with murders and attacks on local authorities. Members try to make these attacks resemble the work of goblins.

Factions: Discontented advisors, led by Derthad's uncle Shael, plan to take over the group if the group doesn't make faster progress toward Bane's earthly victory.

Blackhelm Janissaries

Goal: Defend Blackhelm, Sigil's outpost on Chernoggar (see *Manual of the Planes*, page 92), from invasion and conquest.

Size: Tiny. The majority of the group resides in Blackhelm, and a small circle of auxiliaries and financial supporters aid the Janissaries' cause from Sigil and elsewhere across the planes.

Alignment: Unaligned.

Philosophy: "Without us, Blackhelm is nothing but a district of Zoronor, overrun by bladelings or worse. And you can bet Sigil would fall next."

History: Unnamed Cagers founded the Janissaries between one and two hundred years ago.

Leadership: Watch Captain Barald the Bald, a humorless warlord, leads the Janissaries and brooks no insubordination. Barald's lieutenants issue orders to sergeants, who oversee the rank-and-file. Members who challenge a superior's orders are banished to certain death outside Blackhelm's walls.

Headquarters: The Blackhelm Janissaries use the outpost's central strongpoint, called the Dome, as a headquarters.

Membership Requirements: The Janissaries greet travelers who enter Blackhelm from Sigil by pressing them into service, ejecting them back to the City of Doors, or throwing them over the wall into the dangerous streets of Zoronor (see *Manual of the Planes*, page 93).

Activities: Barald and his lieutenants assign patrols to watch the borders of the outpost and rally the entire force to respond to any incursion.

Enemies: The various denizens of Chernoggar, including agents of Bane and Gruumsh, seek to conquer Blackhelm and use it to secure power in Sigil.

Factions: The rogue Amundini instigates dissatisfaction with Barald the Bald, arguing for a looser leadership that recognizes the heroism of every member of the group and gives each member a voice in the governance of Blackhelm.

The Golden Rope

Goal: Increase prosperity for mercenaries, adventurers, and explorers.

Size: Moderate size, concentrated in a local region of a few nearby towns and cities.

Alignment: Unaligned.

Philosophy: "Only through exploration of wild places can we regain the knowledge to rebuild civilization. We kill monsters and redistribute their treasure as a public service, and we should be rewarded as such."

History: The dwarf dungeon delver Kelken Karu founded the Golden Rope ten years ago, shortly before he was hanged for the murder of an earl.

Leadership: Guildmaster Randaha Mohir, a fast-talking dragonborn, currently leads the guild. A six-member council advises the guildmaster and makes policy by majority vote. Council members are elected on a yearly basis, and the council appoints the guildmaster. Guild members can attend the regular meetings of the council and make suggestions for the guild leadership to consider.

Headquarters: The guild council meets every two weeks at the Juggling Bear tavern.

Membership Requirements: Characters can join the Golden Rope by demonstrating to the guild leader's satisfaction that they have explored at least one dungeon complex. The guild collects a "nomination fee" of 15 gp and annual dues of 10 gp per member.

Activities: The Golden Rope lobbies local government on behalf of its members, encouraging the authorities to pay its members for services rendered to help protect and defend communities from

---

START SMALL!

I'm always tempted to design a campaign setting as a world, or at least a continent, and fill in every square mile with swamps and forests and nations divided by borders. I can look at such a map and say monsters live in the swamp, elves dwell in the forest, and this nation clashes with that nation. TSR produced hefty campaign worlds—Wizards of the Coast still does—and I want to develop my worlds in the same rich detail.

However, when you work with such a large scale, all those details end up far away from the PCs.

If I dropped the PCs on a border between two nations simmering at the edge of all-out war, the characters might find adventure. That campaign could be interesting. Maybe a city lies on the border. Maybe its people don't consider themselves members of either nation, and they resent being fought over. And immigrants from both nations live within its walls. That scenario could be a lot of fun.

That setting works because I switched from the big map to a small spot on it. Once I start running that campaign, the forest with the elves and the swamp with the monsters don't matter, at least not until the campaign grows and expands to include them. In the short term, fleshing out the city on the border and its adventure possibilities serves my purposes better than planning what lies half a continent away.

When you start with the small view, you create space for adventure on that micro level. The campaign contains more than the monsters that live in the swamp a hundred miles distant; it involves the PCs in the dangers that threaten their lives and homes. In 4th Edition, the PCs find more danger than safe zones. Adventure is never far away.

–James Wyatt, from
Dungeoncraft Episode 1, Dungeon 151

monsters and other threats. When its members find themselves in legal trouble, the guild advocates for them and attempts to secure a lenient sentence or dismissal of charges. Finally, the guild looks to expand its operations into new towns and cities.

Enemies: The bandit gang Thordar's Hammers preys on adventurers who travel between towns and the surrounding dungeons and ruins. The family of the earl slain by Kelken Karu still holds a grudge against the guild, and it has enough influence to make the guild's life difficult.

THE LEAGUE OF DUE HIERARCHY

Goal: Promote the legalization of slavery in places that currently forbid it and protect the rights of slaveholders in places that allow slavery.

Size: Small but widespread, the majority of its members can be found in towns and cities ruled by tyrants or dominated by evil races. Only nobles can join, and in areas that permit slavery, one must own slaves to be a member.

Alignment: Evil.

Philosophy: "The great civilizations of the past recognized that some people are born greater than others and allowed society's betters to sell the lowly into bondage. As the world rebuilds, mighty empires will emerge among nations that recognize the righteousness and necessity of the fundamental social order."

History: The League (called the Shacklers by its detractors) sprang up when the world began its slow recovery from the disasters of the past.

Leadership: The Shacklers' ideological leader is the scholar-queen Fusane, monarch of a small, prosperous city-state located on a major trade route.

Headquarters: Ostentatious League halls appear in numerous national capitals, situated near the local palace or congress hall.

Activities: Members of the League appear at governing institutions to lobby in favor of slavery proclamations and decrees. Members also undermine attempts to establish egalitarian rule. The League secretly funds harassment, sabotage, and assassinations of prominent enemies.

Enemies: The Fellowship of Free Souls, a political movement opposed to slavery and authoritarian rule, swears to topple the League.

Factions: An increasingly vocal group of slave traders and wealthy merchants argues for full membership regardless of birth status. These individuals want the League to set aside its other political aims and focus solely on promoting slavery.

RAVEN'S WINGS

Goal: Pay homage to the Raven Queen by laying the undead to their final rest.

Size: Large and widespread.

Alignment: Unaligned.

Philosophy: "We show our devotion to the Raven Queen by taking up arms in her name."

History: A ruler of the tiefling empire of Bael Turath founded the order, where it operated as a subversive and secret organization. The small cells of its membership have passed on traditions for hundreds of years.

Leadership: Each cell governs itself, and the cell leaders try to maintain close communication with their nearest neighbors in the order.

Headquarters: The order maintains hundreds of austere barracks spread throughout hostile, dangerous lands.

Membership Requirements: Characters who worship the Raven Queen can apply for admittance as acolytes and accompany more experienced members on missions against the undead. An acolyte earns full membership status after demonstrating courage and capability in combat against the undead.

Activities: The order launches missions to exterminate the undead and punishes anyone who desecrates cemeteries and monuments.

Enemies: The order opposes and seeks to eliminate cults of Orcus.

Rivals: A mercenary organization called the Graveyard Guild suppresses the undead for fees and treasure.

The following campaign arcs take PCs through three full tiers of play. To illustrate general ideas that are dealt with in the next chapter, the paragon tier receives more attention than the other two tiers.

BREACH SMASHERS

This arc highlights planar adventure, a signature element of paragon-level play.

HEROIC TIER: OUT OF THE BREACH

The players create characters around a common theme: All PCs begin their careers as ordinary residents of Restharrow. A peculiar kind of safety has blessed this tiny village, tucked away in a distant corner of the world, for centuries. Bandits, monsters, wars, and kings have all passed it by.

The players envision their characters as humble villagers and then create the 1st-level characters they become in the course of the first adventure.

In the middle of the night, Restharrow's preternatural seclusion comes to an explosive end. A gigantic planar breach (see page 185) appears in a nearby hillside, showering Restharrow with flaming debris. Altered by arcane winds blown from the breach, the characters spontaneously develop their 1st-level powers. They rescue their surviving neighbors from the wreckage and assist with rebuilding efforts. As time passes, creatures emerge from the breach and disrupt these efforts. Invading monsters spread across the countryside, occupying caverns, ruins, and ancient underground complexes.

For the rest of the heroic tier, the characters protect Restharrow by hunting and destroying these planar invaders. You can use the guidelines from "Increasing or Decreasing Level" on page 174 of the *Dungeon Master's Guide* to create lower-level versions of planar enemies, or use the themes in this book.

To maintain the planar flavor, use the monster creation rules to build toned-down versions of otherworldly planar entities the PCs can fight at low levels. Rework standard stat blocks for low-level creatures into planar enemies.

Between encounters, the characters seal off creature hideouts to prevent monsters from reoccupying them and fortify Restharrow against direct attack. Late in the tier, the PCs learn they must close the breach from the inside. As they prepare for the paragon tier, they recruit and train replacements to guard the village, so they can leave to take the necessary next step.

PARAGON TIER: INTO THE BREACH

Now that the characters have increased in power, they can venture into the breach. During the fight marking their shift to paragon tier, they discover a doorway into Sigil (see Chapter 6). The PCs use the City of Doors as their new home base. They wander the planes, piecing together the information they need to seal the Restharrow Breach.

The first few paragon levels are devoted to the characters becoming familiar with Sigil and navigating its various conflicts. Past heroics come back to haunt the PCs when comrades of dispatched enemies pursue the characters, seeking vengeance.

Early in their sojourn in Sigil, the PCs clash with the Red Marauders. The Red Marauders arrive in Sigil hoping to restore a dwindling planar breach. Their village economically relies on its access to Sigil, which imports construction materials from them. In fighting for their community, the Red Marauders pursue an admirable goal, but they stoop to unscrupulous methods to attain victory.

Each nemesis character serves as a foil to a particular PC. The counterparts exaggerate the worst traits of the corresponding PCs. The Red Marauder equivalent of a humble, stalwart paladin might be a domineering champion of a sinister deity. A mischievous rogue's opposite might engage in deadly practical jokes. Keep conflict with the Marauders indirect, taking the form of skill challenges and character interaction. When the two teams fight, give the PCs reasons not to slaughter their enemies.

Seeking information on the origin of planar breaches, the characters learn of a sage named Chi Machiku, who was investigating that topic when she mysteriously disappeared. Following her trail leads the PCs into adventures throughout the planes.

Upheaval in Sigil provides material for occasional change-of-pace episodes. The group's trainees from Restharrow could also show up in Sigil sporadically, leading to various side missions.

After laboriously reconstructing Machiku's movements from plane to plane, the PCs find her in a githyanki prison in the city of Tu'narath (see *Manual of the Planes*, page 111). When they spirit her back to safety after a series of tough encounters, the characters find her to be a gibbering, incoherent shadow of her former self. Machiku protected her mind from githyanki probing by sending portions of her consciousness throughout the planes. To restore Machiku's sanity and coherence, the PCs must embark on a series of quests to gather objects containing pieces of Machiku's consciousness.

During this phase, the PCs periodically notice the Red Marauders in pursuit. Later, the PCs learn that an oracle warned the Marauders about the characters. The Red Marauders believe that if the PCs succeed in their mission, they will destroy the precious planar breach.

The Red Marauders retrieve the final piece of Machiku's consciousness before the PCs do, bringing on a final showdown that ends the Red Marauders' role in the storyline. This encounter launches the PCs into their epic destinies.

Her mind intact again, Machiku lays out the mission that defines the rest of the PCs' careers: The Restharrow Breach is a symptom of a bigger problem.

EPIC TIER: ASTRAL CATASTROPHE

The entire Astral Sea is undergoing a series of turbulent changes. If it is not stabilized, the whole plane will implode, destroying the universe. Over the eons, excess magical energy has built up in the Astral Sea. Every time a deity or an immortal works a mass-scale ritual, the charge increases. Certain plane-spanning artifacts and vehicles also leak magical energy. The Astral Sea must discharge part of this energy before anyone can work great magic safely.

At the same time, conflict continues to escalate on the planes: the Blood War (see *Manual of the Planes*, page 89) has flared up again. When demons and devils are not battling each other, they raid other planes, searching for artifacts that will give them an advantage. The relics the fiends deploy and the plane-spanning modes of travel they use to retrieve the components leak a large amount of dangerous energy into the Astral Sea. Neither evidence nor persuasion convinces either side to disarm, because both evil forces suspect they might come out on top if they are left to their own devices.

To end the threat, the PCs must intervene in the Blood War and deal enough damage on both sides to force the adversaries to back down. The characters must inflict harm on both groups equally. Otherwise, one side could win the Blood War, an outcome nearly as dire as mutual destruction.

PILLARS OF THE STATE

This campaign puts the PCs, fated from birth to be kings and queens, in the center of a political saga.

HEROIC TIER: THE YOUNG HEIRS

Each PC begins as a likely heir to the throne in one of the Six Kingdoms. (You can adjust the number of kingdoms to the size of your player group.) The Six Kingdoms have historical and cultural similarities but act as politically independent nations that share a common coastline. Once great, each kingdom

now exists as a point of light separated from its fellow nations by swaths of lawless, monster-infested territory.

Design a home kingdom for each character appropriate to his or her background. Each PC's race or class should correspond to that of the royal family of his or her kingdom. For example:

People know the nation of Nizh for its trading fleet and ambitious merchant culture. The mining nation of Murisov boasts a long line of warrior-kings. Priests or paladins rule the land of Tarod, the home of numerous universities, cathedrals, and architects. The eerie kingdom of Karakho entrusts its throne only to a master of the arcane. Rulers of Zvetisk swear to protect its ancient forests. The rolling hills of wheat and barley in Mahin Fields make up the breadbasket of the Six Kingdoms.

The heroic tier trains the characters for the rigors of kingship. The regions' future rulers unite to rid their lands of monsters and brigands. In the Six Kingdoms, monarchs don't sit at home, issuing decrees and eating sweetmeats. Instead, rulers use their mighty powers on behalf of the people. So the adventurers might frequently come across their relatives, the current monarchs, while adventuring.

When they are not honing their abilities in the field, the future monarchs reside in their homeland capitals, where they participate in court intrigue. At upper levels of the tier, the player characters detect a conspiracy of subversive courtiers and functionaries. After several adventures that nearly flush these shadowy figures into the open, catastrophe strikes. Simultaneous coup attempts lead to the seizure of all six royal palaces and the deaths of the current rulers.

Paragon Tier: Long Live the Kings

The PCs kick off the paragon tier by destroying the internal conspiracy. How the conspirators slew the elders remains something of a mystery because the conspirators summoned creatures of unknown type and origin to do the dirty work.

The PCs have little time for mourning; they must ascend to their respective thrones. No longer do they perform missions suggested by others. Now, the PCs root out sources of trouble on their own. Skill challenges and character interactions alert the PCs of the various threats against their nations. These discoveries lead to encounters against monsters, internal rebels, and external enemies. The PCs might have to choose between two problems of apparently equal magnitude because they have the ability to address only one at a time. Encourage the PCs to develop long-term agendas for their kingdoms—agendas that suffer when the PCs leave to deal with a short-term crisis.

Require negotiation between the players as the interests of their separate kingdoms conflict. Start with outwardly simple choices. Do they put down goblin cattle raiders in the hinterlands of Mahin or take to the seas against the pirates threatening the Nizhian fleet?

After the PCs master the basic affairs of state, murkier questions arise. Murisovian miners seek permission to establish a guild. Nizhian traders advise against this development, claiming it will increase the price of iron. Do subversive tendencies drive the miners, or will granting their wishes avoid trouble and assure uninterrupted supplies for the kingdoms' forges?

If the sages of Karakho predict an invasion from sinister Feywild creatures unless the characters destroy a sacred grove in Zvetisk, which nation has its way?

Sometimes, the PCs can solve intractable problems by finding secret villains behind the scenes and thrashing them. Further into the tier, the PCs find agitators from the Iron States stirring up more trouble. This collection of city-states, huddled together on the other side of the sea, has never before posed a threat.

During this phase of the campaign, the time scale between levels expands. The rulers unite when major crises strike, though years can separate the monarchs' onstage time. During transitions that feature heavy roleplaying, the rulers perform the personal duties every monarch faces. They marry, have children, and train their heirs as heroic tier adventurers to continue the cycle.

At mid-tier, an invasion fleet from the Iron States arrives to conquer the Six Kingdoms. United by a cruel and militaristic philosophy, the invaders have transformed themselves into the Iron Empire. Under the pitiless Emperor Krek, the empire has already conquered and absorbed other nations on its side of the sea. Now it intends to add the PCs' kingdoms to its collection of vassal states.

Conflicts between kingdoms, once merely a challenge, now become a greater threat because dissension thwarts all attempts to muster against the Iron Empire. The rangers of Zvetisk resist efforts to use wood from their forests to build a fleet. Rivalry between the priestly caste of Tarod and Karakho's wizard schools holds up the construction of magical defenses. The PCs eventually realize they must unify their people into a single force in order to prevail against the Iron Empire. The characters must also decide among themselves whom to appoint as emperor, leaving all the others as regional governors. Finally, the characters must ensure that the virtues of the kingdoms remain untainted during the consolidation of power.

EPIC TIER: EMPIRE MAKERS

Repelling the invasion is a prelude to a greater undertaking. The PCs learn that Krek is one incarnation of a multidimensional entity planning similar invasions on parallel worlds, throughout the planes. If his multiple selves succeed in conquering seven worlds at once, he gains eternal dominion over all reality. Every world and plane will mirror his tyrannical Iron Empire.

He already has six worlds or planes in his grip and is close to conquering several others. The PCs must now export their combat expertise to these other dimensions and push back Krek's hold one world at a time.

BLOOD AND TREASURE

In this military-themed campaign, the PCs rise from humble beginnings to become generals in a war that begins in the world and extends to extraplanar battlefields.

HEROIC TIER: GATHERING HORDE

The PCs begin as impoverished, rootless wanderers in the vast nation of Veratur. Marauding tribes of orcs and goblins have plunged Veratur, once a great civilization, into a dark age of barbarism. The central government is a shell of its former self. The leader, Autarch Ilius IV, cowers in his besieged palace, waiting for the invading tribes to breach the walls. Cut off from the dying central government, the consuls of Veratur's distant citadels must function as independent commanders.

War drives the PCs from peaceful occupations into lives of adventure. If the characters desire a life of servitude, they could sign up as soldiers at a citadel. Or, they could form a free militia, a small band of heroes that skirmishes against enemy forces, defeating them

and looting their equipment. Occasionally, grateful townsfolk reward the militia with treasure and food.

(Like the middle tier of "Pillars of the State," this phase unfolds on an extended time scale, with interludes of months between levels.)

As the characters progress through the tier, their fame spreads. Now battle-hardened veterans, the PCs attract a steady stream of volunteers anxious to fight in the militia. Intersperse encounters against orcs, goblins, and allied creatures with skill challenges in which the PCs direct their private armies against massed forces. Other sequences require the PCs to instill discipline, supply their growing legion, and prevent their own troops from exploiting the terrified citizenry.

To propel the characters into the paragon tier, create a final skill challenge and encounter composed of a large engagement in which the characters must drive besieging forces away from the Veraturi capital.

PARAGON TIER: ON MUDDY BATTLEFIELD

Certain that invaders would soon overrun his citadel, old Autarch hung himself. Atinar, Autarch's inexperienced, good-hearted son, appoints the PCs as the generals of this shattered realm. He charges them with the mission of driving the barbarian hordes from Veraturi soil.

As the PCs continue to fight barbarian leaders, servitors, and summoned creatures, they must also build their private army into a new Veraturi force. Skill challenges revolve around recruitment and training. As the characters move from citadel to citadel, victories allow them to absorb existing forces into their reconstructed national army.

With the local economy devastated, the characters must figure out how to fund and equip their army.

NUDGING

According to long-standing tradition, DMs lose their pacing control when the characters huddle together to make plans. I used to follow this unwritten rule, keeping largely silent when the characters were planning. Yes, the game would often bog down at these points, as players took opposite sides of a moral or tactical issue and then dug in. Interactions between player characters can be enormously fun—provided that the scenes build and go somewhere. The more they resemble the way we argue in real life, the less engaging they become. Actual arguments are extremely repetitive, consisting mainly of points stated and restated.

Eventually I learned to set tradition aside and gently intervene in player deliberations. If—and only if—the discussion starts to circle in on itself, I take on the role of mediator. I restate the various positions and hint toward solutions. Often a good answer is proposed early on, then

quickly abandoned for no good reason. If so, I bring that up again.

The point is never to impose a solution. By nudging, I'm acting as a real-time scene editor, cutting through the repetition to steer the group toward a fruitful—and mutual—solution.

Sometimes the conversation stalls because the huddle was called prematurely, before gathering enough information. Players might be leaping to false conclusions, or trying to plan their way around too many possibilities. With more investigation, they could reduce the number of variables they need to take into account. I used to fret when they didn't have any NPCs to prompt them when they needed information. Now, in DM voice, I suggest right out that they need to go out and learn more.

—Robin Laws

This task provides motivation for change-of-pace encounters, in which the group tackles various other creature threats to earn necessary treasure and equipment.

When the monetary reward from an encounter dovetails with narrative events, create two sets of treasure. One set allows the PCs to find the magic equipment they need for their characters, and the larger set measures their success in the wider storyline.

Throughout the tier, build up a mortal orc/goblin hybrid named Tuszu for the villain role.

In the upper half of the tier, the final earthly battle for Veratur plays out. By now, each PC commands his or her own army.

As the war grows closer to a conclusion, the PCs notice that supernaturally powerful orc and goblin champions lead more of the enemy forces. On the eve of the final battle for Veratur, the PCs learn that the deities of the plane of Chernoggar, Bane and Gruumsh, have put aside their animosity in an attempt to invade and overrun the world. If Veratur falls, the PCs can expect a full-scale attack from Chernoggar.

EPIC TIER: WAR AGAINST WAR

If the PCs defeat their enemies in the war for Veratur, the characters earn epic status, and they have a chance to kill Tuszu. However, their victory will be short-lived unless they take the battle to Chernoggar and defeat its leaders once and for all.

Although the characters' NPC comrades eagerly anticipate the battle, the ordinary soldiers of Veratur want only to rebuild their mangled nation. The PCs must then travel the planes to recruit heroes willing to invade Chernoggar. Gruumsh and Bane learn of the PCs' efforts and send enemies to deter the characters, which offers encounters to fill out the storyline between skill challenges and narrative scenes.

Finally, the PCs begin a close-fought struggle to take and hold the entire plane. The campaign ends with climactic battles against Bane and then Gruumsh. Upon the deities' defeat, Chernoggar transforms into a peaceful land. A golden era of harmony sweeps the mortal worlds—until your next campaign, when bloody conflict again rears its head.

THE MÖBIUS TRIPPERS

This campaign frame takes the PCs on a journey through the time stream.

HEROIC TIER: MACHINE DREAMS

Ever since the PCs can remember, they have had similar dreams. The characters meet up with each other and learn of their shared nighttime visions. These dreams revolve around the search for components of a disassembled machine. The PCs believe they must reassemble the machine and use it for its intended,

albeit unknown, purpose. If the characters fail to complete this task, they cannot achieve their essential destinies, and a disaster will unfold.

The group's heroic tier adventures revolve around the quest for these parts. Creatures guard or control a majority of the pieces, and the PCs could earn a few components as rewards for tasks. A few individual parts have minor magical powers. Perhaps one or two of the items are currently warding off a devastating flood or preserving a farmland's fertility. In these situations, the group might want to compensate for the items' effects to claim them in good conscience. When the device is assembled, it looks like a vehicle.

During this tier, make associations between each PC and a major deity of your setting's pantheon. Clerics and paladins have these parallels built in. For other characters, subtle thematic associations suffice. These chosen deities are referred to hereafter (in the epic tier section) as the spotlight deities.

PARAGON TIER: THE TAPESTRY TORN

The encounter that enables the group to enter the paragon tier provides the final piece they need to construct the vehicle.

In this tier, the PCs embark on a time-hopping journey. They can travel forward and backward in time. Provide them with a history of your world and let them choose their own missions as they travel through it. As the PCs explore the time stream, you can introduce the following story elements that illustrate the laws of time during this campaign.

✦ Actions the characters take in the past can alter the course of history (subject to the following provisions).

✦ However, a law of conservation appears to be in effect: For instance, if you try to eliminate a tyrant from the time stream by killing his father before the tyrant is born, you find a similar cruel leader, of different parentage, on the throne when you return to the present. The ruler looks different from the dictator the group erased, but the overall historical situation remains essentially unaltered.

✦ A barrier separates normal historical time from the mythic realm of the deities. The time vehicle can't penetrate this barrier.

✦ Time travelers can't go to any time period when they have already existed. Attempts to travel to their own pasts, or to other times they have already adventured in, fail.

✦ If the characters attempt to travel into the future, they can do so. The players might deduce that their characters cease to exist in normal time soon after what they consider the present day.

Once the players figure out these precepts, and perhaps tire of self-directed exploration, the adventurers stumble across a rival group of time-trippers. The God-Killers, a conspiracy of wild-eyed arcanists, seek to free the mortal races from the supposed tyranny of deities. The God-Killers have been wreaking havoc throughout the time stream in their quest to penetrate the mythic realm of the deities.

The climactic battle that destroys the God-Killer leadership elevates the PCs to epic tier.

Epic Tier: Ascension

Shortly after achieving this victory, the PCs realize the God-Killers partially succeeded at their plan. They erased the spotlight deities—and Asmodeus—from history.

Wherever the PCs go in their time vehicle, they find a crisis set off by the absence of a spotlight deity. The adventure allows them to solve the localized problem, but another disaster awaits them at each future destination. Eventually, the PCs discover that the God-Killers' partial success rendered the time stream unstable. If it is not eventually rectified, the absence of the spotlight deities will unravel all existence. To prevent this catastrophe, the characters must visit the mythic past by replicating the alterations to the God-Killers' time vehicle that allowed

them to cross the barrier that separates ordinary and mythic time. The changes wrought by the absence of the spotlight deities complicate the mission, which extends through a series of adventures until they reach the upper reaches of the epic tier.

The climactic sequence of the campaign occurs when the PCs reach the beginning of time and find the spotlight deities still missing. The surviving deities cannot begin the myth of creation without the spotlight deities. The PCs piece together the final revelation: They must become the deities and take part in the creation stories. And one PC must doom himself to eternal evil and torment by taking on the role of Asmodeus.

As an epilogue, the players realize what they must do to ensure the integrity of the universe. They must disassemble the machine and scatter its pieces throughout time, so their past selves can discover it, go back to the dawn of time, and become the founding deities. All the PCs' actions were predestined to bring about the creation of the universe.

DUNGEONCRAFT: THE CAMPAIGN ARC

−James Wyatt, from
Dungeoncraft Episode 3, Dungeon 153

When planning your campaign, you don't have to come up with thirty levels worth of adventures before the PCs set foot in their first dungeon. You just need to sketch out the general arc of the campaign. Where does it start, what happens in the middle, and where and how does it end? If you make that outline early on, you might find it easier to plan adventures as the campaign progresses and plant seeds for future adventures as you go.

The decision to start my campaign in the village and dungeons of Greenbrier helped me figure out how to start my campaign, as well. I also figured out the theme and flavor elements I wanted to highlight in the course of the campaign—specifically, aberrations and the influence of the Far Realm. The origin of Greenbrier Chasm inspired me to consider that the epic-level player characters in my game might someday fight a fiery entity that escaped from the chasm. One day, they must either destroy it or return it to its prison. I also considered having the characters explore the chasm in the heroic tier and then return when they reach an appropriate level to fight other aberrations.

The following broad outline sketches out my campaign arc.

Level 1: The characters make their first expedition into Greenbrier Chasm and fight warped goblins and fell taints. Then the warped goblins raid the farms, and the characters return to stop the raids.

Level 10 (approximately): Back into Greenbrier Chasm to fight foulspawn. (The foulspawn in the *Monster Manual* range from levels 8–12.) A level 14 mind flayer would be a good major villain at that point.

Paragon Tier: As the centerpiece of my campaign, I want to run the 1999 adventure *The Gates of Firestorm Peak*. The original adventure targets character levels 5–8, a range too low for the scope of my adventure. Since I want to design all the encounters anyway, I place this adventure in the mid-paragon tier.

Epic Climax: Characters must fight the fiery aberrant creature that escaped from the chasm and burned the forest.

That event starts a campaign arc heavily flavored with aberrations. I see two gaps in this layout. First, I want to involve in the campaign at least one aberration-hunting organization from the 3rd Edition supplement *Lords of Madness*. I can design paragon paths associated with these organizations and present them to my players as options, so I should probably introduce the players to the organizations before they reach 11th level. I decide to place that encounter around the time they return to Greenbrier Chasm. The organizations could send them back to the Chasm, or the PCs could learn about the organizations as they explore the Chasm. Either way works.

Second, I want the characters to delve into Greenbrier Chasm a third time, probably at the high paragon or low epic levels. Aboleths occupy the high paragon levels, so they make an appropriate threat for the deepest reaches of the Chasm.

With these gaps tightened up, I have outlined a grand story: Young characters from the backward village of Greenbrier face aberrations, seal the Vast Gate, shut off the Far Realm influence creeping through the gate, and defeat the aberration that escaped from Greenbrier Chasm.

GETTING ORGANIZED

I sketch out a story that makes fighting aberrations a major part of the campaign. The organizations in *Lords of Madness* impressed me, so I want to use them in my game. The book features three main organizations devoted to fighting aberrations, plus a fourth tradition (the Keepers of the Cerulean Sign) that fills a similar role. I adapt each one to my campaign. The presence of aberrations profoundly influences this region of the world, and these organizations formed to protect civilization from the depredations of aberrations. Because the player characters must ultimately protect civilization from the threats I have in mind, I want these organizations to serve as resources for character development. I can create paragon paths or feats for the characters in my campaign associated with these organizations. These paths and feats allow my players to build characters with traits that help them fight aberrations and immerse their characters in the ages-long struggle that defines the history of this region.

The Circle of the True defends the world from the aberrant forces that corrupt and destroy nature. Its members sometimes have ties to the primal power source or the fey. I then merge the Gatekeepers from Eberron into the Circle of the True. The modern organization practices numerous Gatekeeper traditions, and orcs in the wilds still preserve the pure Gatekeeper way. Gatekeeper orcs have the same negative disposition toward the PCs as other orcs. But this history makes it possible for a player character belonging to the Circle to strike an uneasy alliance with an orc Gatekeeper to seal a Far Realm portal, such as the one in Firestorm Peak.

I convert the Society of the Sanctified Mind into a scholarly society removed from the front lines of the battle against aberrations. However, this organization has an extensive collection of lore about aberrations. The group worships Ioun, who is also the deity of prophecy. The Society's records could detail who bound the aberration, as well as why and where. And the group might protect prophecies regarding the aberration's escape and eventual destruction.

A holy knightly order, the Topaz Order protects the civilized races from aberrant monster races. This religious order venerates Bahamut, Moradin, and Pelor. Based on what I already know about Greenbrier, the Topaz Order influences the village and the surrounding area, and the players likely encounter this organization first.

The Keepers of the Cerulean Sign are lone individuals who oppose the twisted cults that revere aberrations in the shadows of civilized society. I don't want to make these individuals the focus of the campaign. So maybe a cult of aberration worshipers lives in Lake Town, and the characters enlist a Keeper to combat that threat in the city, or the Keeper could recruit them. I used a cabal of mad alienist sorcerers in my 3rd Edition adventure *The Speaker in Dreams*—maybe I can steal elements from that adventure when the time comes.

FILLING THE HOLES

Now I want to add variety to the campaign outline. My players don't want to fight aberrations their entire adventuring careers, and I don't want to limit my adventure and encounter design. I have clear ideas for aberration-themed adventures along the way, and I want to combine those events with adventures unconnected to the main theme.

So next, I look at my campaign map and review my notes. When I sketch out the first circle around the village of Greenbrier, I generate a couple adventure ideas to fill out the first ten levels of my characters' careers.

Tower Watch: After their first forays into Greenbrier Chasm, I let the characters explore the ancient ruins in the south. I start with a straightforward dungeon crawl in the ruins (inhabited by orcs), and then I encourage the PCs to venture into the mysterious tower these ruins are named for.

What if the top of the tower is an observatory? It could plant the seeds for information about the comet that heralds the opening of the Gates of Firestorm Peak. Or the orcs in the ruins could include a wise old Gatekeeper who passes on important information to the characters that could lead them to future, more peaceful, interactions with Gatekeeper orcs. I want this adventure to vary from the main theme of my campaign arc, and I want to connect the two. The characters leave Greenbrier (the village and the chasm) and fight orcs and whatever else I throw at them in the tower. Then, at or near the end of the adventure, the PCs receive a foreshadowing of future events that ties back to the aberrations of the chasm. This glimpse offers the characters their first chance to see a real campaign forming. They have a purpose beyond fighting in

random encounters against aberrant monsters in their first adventure.

Harrows Pass: I haven't placed this location on my map yet—I just like the name. I have vague notions of undead haunting this place. I could make this adventure an "on the way from here to there" encounter, something fun and different that happens to the characters on their journey to their next adventure. In the Greenbrier area, the PCs learn about the weird occurrences near Firestorm Peak and decide to investigate. To reach Firestorm Peak, they must venture through Harrows Pass. That plan could work, but the players might feel this adventure stands in the way of what they want to do—investigate Firestorm Peak. I want to give them another reason to go into the pass, so I can use the adventure in Harrows Pass to plant additional hooks for the Firestorm Peak adventure. Or the Harrows Pass adventure could foreshadow the weirdness arising in the mountains, meaning this adventure could serve as a prelude to the *Gates* adventure at the beginning of the paragon tier.

Epic Levels: Looking at my sketch outline so far, I see a big gap in what the characters do between the end of the Firestorm Peak adventure and the campaign-ending battle with the epic aberration. I could encourage the characters to make their third foray into Greenbrier Chasm, to explore its deepest reaches and fight aboleths. I can extend this adventure into a long Underdark foray. Maybe the characters must travel underground from Firestorm Peak all the way back to Greenbrier Chasm. They emerge from the chasm to retrace the steps of the ancient aberration, find its new lair, and confront it. Looking at the epic-level monsters in the *Monster Manual*, I decide that aberrant monsters, such as swordwings and gibbering orbs, could join the aboleths as enemies on this trek.

At this point, I want to leave those levels sketchy. A lot can happen between now and then, and I want to stay open to possible new directions, subthemes, and my players' desires. So I have the following outline of my campaign arc, filled out from where I started.

Levels 1-3: Greenbrier Chasm (first forays).
Levels 4-5: Tower Watch.
Levels 6-8: Lake Town—*Speaker in Dreams?*
Levels 9-11: Greenbrier Chasm (second foray, fighting foulspawn and mind flayer boss)—introduce *Lords of Madness* organizations.
Levels 12-13: Harrows Pass (single adventure).
Levels 14-20: The Gates of Firestorm Peak.
Levels 21-28: Greenbrier Chasm (third foray: aboleths, swordwings, gibbering orb).
Levels 29-30: Fight the fiery creature that escaped from the chasm and burned the forest.

CHAPTER 6

PARAGON CAMPAIGNS

A PLAYER character's early career likely entails hack-and-slash adventure, descending into near-surface dungeons, and skirmishing with kobolds, orcs, and gnolls. At paragon status, bold horizons unfold before the PCs. They battle in new places and attract adulation and danger in equal measure.

This chapter includes the following sections:

✦ **Paragon Status:** Whether players reach this status level by level or the DM starts characters at the paragon tier, when a campaign reaches 11th level, the stakes change. Paragon tier campaigns might take PCs into the murky depths of the Underdark or across the scarred landscapes of cursed lands. The characters could explore the planar realities of the Astral Sea or the Elemental Chaos. At the paragon tier, PCs are becoming powerful enough to ascend thrones, command armies, and build new empires from the ruins of the old.

✦ **Sigil, the City of Doors:** Introduce plane-hopping, paragon adventurers to the PCs' potential new home base, Sigil. Sigil offers an infinite number of dimensional gateways to other locations. If the PCs fall into disharmony with the city and its residents, they might learn why people also call the city "The Cage."

✦ **A Conspiracy of Doors:** This adventure for 11th-level player characters introduces Sigil to your campaign. If it exists, the saying goes, you can find it in Sigil. But what happens when the supply lines are cut and expected imports don't arrive on schedule? That's when Estavan, the face of the Planar Trade Consortium, seeks out a group of adventurers to trace the supplies back to their source and discover what's causing the holdup. What starts as a minor inconvenience could lead to panic, starvation, riots, or worse (such as the attention of the Lady of Pain) if the supply lines aren't restored.

When player characters make the leap to paragon status, their characters have stepped onto a new plateau. The challenges they face and the fruits that victory brings increase in magnitude. At the paragon tier, the characters' powers increase, and the world takes notice of the PCs' achievements and potential.

When your PCs reach the paragon tier, encourage them to search for new horizons. As players gain levels, their access to more potent powers, rituals, and magic gives them greater influence over the world. Push your players to seek new challenges, whether in the courts of power, within the Astral Sea, or among the eddies of time.

REACHING PARAGON TIER

As the DM, you can choose the way in which the PCs attain the paragon tier. For new players, the leveling approach works best. PCs start at first level and gradually reach the paragon tier as they learn how to play their characters and get a feel for the game. Not only does this approach offer beginning players ample opportunity to become comfortable with their characters, players might also savor the accomplishment of reaching the paragon tier more if they have earned their way up.

Certain campaign concepts work best if you start characters at the paragon tier. Only heroes of paragon level or higher will have the tools to participate in a campaign built around certain subjects, such as:

+ high-level politics.
+ grand-scale military engagements.
+ sustained adventures in the Underdark or similarly hostile locations.
+ world-hopping adventure.

WREATHED IN GLORY

The characters already demonstrated remarkable skills as heroic adventurers. As they progressed, they noticed signs of a greater destiny awaiting them. As the PCs enter the paragon tier, they exhibit their potential for greatness.

By this point in their careers, the player characters have achieved fame. The common folk know the characters' names and have heard exaggerated legends of their deeds. Wandering troubadours sing ballads about the PCs, spreading their fame across the land.

Your players might react to signs of their characters' growing fame with wariness, as a burden or an annoyance that attracts unwanted attention and saddles adventurers with unpleasant duties. Paragon tier characters command respect. Fame shouldn't limit them; it should increase their options.

+ alternate realities.
+ time travel.

This is not to say that you can't run these types of campaigns with PCs who have not yet attained the paragon tier. You can lay the groundwork for paragon tier campaign themes long before your players have reached paragon status. For instance, to set up a political game during the heroic tier, introduce rulers and other members of the elite class as impossibly distant figures of power. As the adventurers gain levels, they move closer to the heart of power through new contacts. When the PCs reach the paragon tier, the inner circle welcomes them.

You could build a growing threat of war during the heroic tier of a campaign. When the adventurers reach the paragon tier, major hostilities commence.

To foreshadow planar campaigns, add denizens of these environments into encounters that heroic-level PCs have in the natural world.

CROWNS AND THRONES

Players who enjoy negotiation, intrigue, and intricate storylines excel in politically based campaigns. These adventurers can use their paragon status to leverage themselves into positions of influence, either behind thrones or on them.

GAINING INFLUENCE

When the characters attain paragon status, they attract the attention of top local leaders. Successful rulers cultivate strong relations with local paragons and treat them as champions and advisors, sometimes assigning them weighty responsibilities. Rulers rely on paragon characters to vanquish enemies, gather information, provide advice, and fill the national coffers with treasure. Rulers might also ask favored paragon characters to wage war for them.

THE BODY POLITIC

Paragon characters with access to higher levels of government will discover much more about the local political situation than they were aware of at heroic tier. A baron or lord most likely controls and protects each village, town, or collection of settlements. Elders, mayors, or councils oversee the cities and towns. The PCs now wield greater influence over the local rulers at all levels, and they are more likely to find themselves in a position where they are required to mediate conflicting interests. Some nobles might treat paragon adventurers as rivals, rebels, or enemies. A town council might appeal to the heroes for help against a corrupt lord. Various factions of merchants might attempt to win the PCs to their cause against the others. In such circumstances, the characters' skills at negotiation can be at least as important as their skills in battle.

JOINING THE ELITE

To add an interesting complication to your campaign, create a nation in which the ruler must balance the interests of competing elites. The landholders might represent a traditional power base, and the growing merchant houses might be threatening to eclipse them. Either of these elite classes could offer the heroes membership in exchange for their support in its intrigues against the other.

Paragon adventurers could buy their way into the banking class with an investment of their treasure. A character might marry into an influential noble family after rescuing an heir. The PCs could gain shares in a merchant house by eliminating a band of outlaws threatening an important trade route. Fulfilling religious obligations through quests could earn a cleric or a paladin elite status in his or her religious hierarchy.

Factions divide every elite circle. The collective group fights to protect its interests while families, companies, sects, guilds, or other units compete to increase their own status and wealth. The adventurers might ally with one such faction and use their status and talents to help that faction undercut its rivals and rise to prominence.

Alternatively, each player character could represent a different elite faction in a society that has competing centers of power. The adventurers would then work toward a common goal of creating a coalition of these rival groups. NPC rivals oppose the PCs, perhaps while posing as allies. If the heroes choose to involve themselves in political intrigue at this level, they could learn the hard way how difficult it can be to distinguish friend from foe.

Adventurers might also act on behalf of a ruler they admire, or work against an unpopular or illegitimate ruler. Maybe the PCs undertake to install a favored NPC on the throne; players who have a taste for intrigue might even attempt to seize it for themselves.

WIELDING POWER

Player characters can exercise power directly. This choice involves the player characters in governing and offers them both authority and the opportunity to play a part in more intricate storylines.

Typically, one character ascends to power and the others join the ruler's retinue. However, this approach introduces a command structure into the game that could create conflicts among the players. Make sure they operate by consensus. Watch for attendance problems: If a player who has a key role frequently misses game sessions, other players might grow frustrated.

To avoid an unequal power distribution, give each player character an equal power base. Make them

POWER IN A D&D WORLD

In a typical D&D world concept, the last great empire or kingdom collapsed about a century ago and a terrible dark age now grips the world. Monsters roam the wilderness, and points of light dot the countryside. People congregate in these havens of civilization, where adventurers can rest and resupply between forays into the untamed wilds.

Democracies as we know them rarely exist in fantasy worlds. Instead, barons respond to the needs of their citizens—or fail to. As popular figures who walk among the people, paragon characters are in a position to interact with the common people and to see what effects the actions of rulers have on the country as a whole.

Within a society, elite classes hold great influence because they control the primary sources of wealth. These elites include landholders, merchants, and financiers, among others. In a fantasy world, membership in the political elite can also derive from divine favor, control of magic artifacts, or alliances with legendary creatures.

Above the nobles and the other elite classes is the king or queen. Paragon characters are more likely to interact with a land's elites and monarchs. At this level, the characters' support for a nation's political system becomes more important. Paragon PCs are in a position to judge whether a leader is fit to rule, and to enforce their judgment.

allied lords who struggle together against an encroaching, overwhelming menace. Run a ruler-level political campaign only if you can comfortably include concurrent cutaway sequences in which the player characters split up to perform equally important tasks.

If you start the game in the paragon tier, you can appoint the adventurers as fixtures of government. Design the available positions as part of your world-creation process, and let the players divvy them up when they build their characters.

Building up to a paragon tier political campaign requires advance preparation in the heroic tier. Establish a path to power for the characters, possibly by designating one player character as heir to a throne. It follows that he or she would appoint companions as trusted advisors.

In a D&D world, ascending to a throne does not end an adventuring career. Slaying monsters and smiting enemies take on higher stakes when the fate of a barony or duchy hangs in the balance. Rulers also have a magical connection to the places they rule. So when plague or pestilence strikes the land, a queen's subjects expect her to ride with her trusted heroes to destroy the source of the curse. If barbarian hordes howl at the gates, the king must challenge their chieftain to personal combat. If the drow invade from below, the ruler plunges into the Underdark, leaving trusted functionaries in charge while he or she conducts a multiyear crusade to save the land and its people.

MASTERS OF WAR

Your paragon tier campaign might feature mighty armies clashing to resolve ultimate battles of good against evil. You can use this approach to extend a campaign in which PCs rule a nation. Your player character rulers and their retinues might lead armies charging headlong into enemy ranks.

If your players want their military engagements unsullied by politics, appoint them as commanders. In this model, they lead the action on the battlefield without entangling themselves in intrigue or the responsibilities of rule. The rank they hold depends on the setting you chose. In a Roman-style empire, the PCs act as generals of a professional army. A medieval setting casts them as knights and nobles commanding a mix of mercenaries and peasant militias. A campaign set in the Dark Ages would have the PCs rove the land as war chieftains supported by loyal barbarians. In any case, the characters must regularly leave their command duties to engage in standard encounters against high-ranking enemies. They engage in these fights in order to:

✦ prove themselves to potential recruits or allies.

✦ open supply lines.

✦ disrupt shipments to the enemy.

✦ raid for supplies or money.

✦ rescue prisoners.

✦ take enemy hostages.

✦ defeat enemy leaders before they take the field.

RESOLVING BATTLES

You can resolve large-scale battles in several ways. Some possible methods are described here, but you are free to establish specific criteria for winning a particular battle. You can use the same method consistently or switch between methods as adventure pacing and dramatic tension demand.

DRAMATIC DECREE

Decide the battle's victor ahead of time. This approach works best in a campaign that mirrors historical events. Use this technique cautiously: If the player characters are not on the winning side, you need to ensure that they are still presented with an achievable goal.

Whether the characters are queens, generals, or legates, they will need a reason to fight in a particular battle, and a clear objective to fight for. For example, as a part of a larger overall battle the PCs might be tasked with capturing and holding a strategic location, with preventing enemy reinforcements from making a flanking maneuver, or with destroying key resources such as stockpiles of food or weapons. Whether the heroes accomplish their objective or fail should have a clear influence on the ongoing war. This way, the PCs can win an encounter even if their side loses the larger battle.

BATTLES AS SKILL CHALLENGES

When the player characters participate in a battle, whether as generals or frontline warriors, they can determine its outcome with a skill challenge. To reflect situations in which the PCs' army has an advantage over the enemy, use low or moderate DCs for related skill checks. In situations in which the tide turns against the heroes, use high DCs and complex skill challenges.

To give skills more influence in battle, start narrating before forces hit the field. The first time you determine a battle's outcome with skill challenges, suggest ways in which the characters can influence the battle with their skills. Treat the following list as a starting point and add to it as players come up with more possibilities.

Prior to battle:

✦ *Bluff:* Sow demoralizing false rumors among the enemy's ranks.

✦ *Diplomacy:* Recruit additional allies; convince mercenaries or poorly motivated enemy allies to desert or defect to your side.

✦ *Dungeoneering:* Run mining and sapping operations to overcome enemy defenses.

- *Insight:* Counter rumors spread by the enemy among your troops.
- *Nature:* Find natural terrain to attack or defend from.
- *Thievery:* Steal a crucial artifact of martial magic.

While in the fray:

- *Acrobatics:* Dart in, around, and through enemy ranks, spreading confusion.
- *Arcana:* Counteract enemy powers and rituals.
- *Athletics:* Bash forcefully through enemy lines.
- *Heal:* Administer aid to the wounded, improve morale, or allow injured troops to rejoin the fight.
- *Intimidate:* Spur beleaguered enemy units to rout.
- *Perception:* Spot weak points in enemy formations.
- *Religion:* Bless your forces or curse the enemy.
- *Stealth:* Maneuver into position undetected.

If the adventurers succeed on the skill challenge, their side emerges from the battle victorious. If they fail, the enemy drives the PCs' forces from the battlefield or captures them, depending on your story.

Combat of Leaders

Have the adventurers fight the enemy's leaders in an honor combat to determine the outcome of the war. To use this approach, you will need to create an encounter that represents a key turning point of the battle. Prior to the start of full-scale battle, allow the PCs to issue an honor combat challenge offering to stake the battle's outcome on the result of a single encounter between the heroes and opposing leaders.

Allow players to control the nature of this encounter to some degree, by letting the adventurers negotiate the terms of the honor combat: location, time of day, weapons, and other such details. If you like, these negotiations can be resolved through a series of skill challenges.

When designing the honor combat encounter, consider the overall state of the war. If the adventurers' army is fighting a superior force, make the encounter one or two levels higher than the PCs' level. If they are fighting an equal or inferior force, set the level of the encounter equal to that of the group.

Noncombat Resolution

For variety, you could allow a battle to be determined by the characters' actions outside of combat. Present the players with the possibility of achieving victory through the accomplishment of a specific goal. This could involve acquiring a mighty artifact, assassinating an enemy leader, or discovering crucial military or political intelligence. If the adventurers succeed, the battle resolves in their favor.

Numerous Battles Make a War

Include multiple battles in an adventure or campaign in which the adventurers wage war, and have the scenario culminate in a final, decisive engagement. Set the encounter up in such a way that the player characters have an opportunity to engage the leaders of the opposing army. The PCs might receive intelligence identifying the enemy's command location, or during battle they might recognize the battle standard of their adversary across the front lines.

In whichever way you set the stage for the ultimate battle, take into account the history of this war. Prior victories should stack the odds in favor of the adventurers: The terrain should work in their favor, the level of the encounter should equal the level of the PCs, and related skill challenges should use low or moderate DCs. Prior losses should influence the final battle in ways less advantageous to the heroes.

When you are designing this encounter, make sure to consider the consequences of both failure and success for the characters. If one of the characters is the ruler of an embattled nation, what are the results if that army is defeated? Will the enemy nation annex important territory? Will barbarian hordes sweep through the nation, pillaging food and valuables and leaving destruction and famine in their wake? Will the PC ruler be deposed?

And what will be the consequences if the adventurers win? The heroes' rewards should be commensurate with the risks they undertook to achieve this final victory.

Down to the Depths

Groups dominated by explorers, power gamers, slayers, and thinkers might test their paragon status during grueling sojourns into the Underdark. They put aside the relative comforts of near-surface dungeoneering for a prolonged crusade in a hostile environment. The prevailing mood might darken as adventurers struggle to survive. They cannot jaunt back to town and sleep in warm beds, shop for supplies, or spend an evening in a tavern. Food and water become precious resources crucial to survival.

Treated as Monsters

Civilized races, including drow, mind flayers, aboleths, and duergar, inhabit the Underdark, and few of them welcome surface folk. The towns and cities of the drow and the illithids pose serious danger to surface dwellers. These races treat intruders as invading monsters. Capable champions of the Underdark scramble to protect their constituents. Others cry out for the watch, militia fighters, and volunteers to join the fray.

What might begin as an encounter against the nearest group of defenders can segue into a daunting skill challenge as the adventurers flee to safety. If the PCs fail, defending races shackle the adventurers,

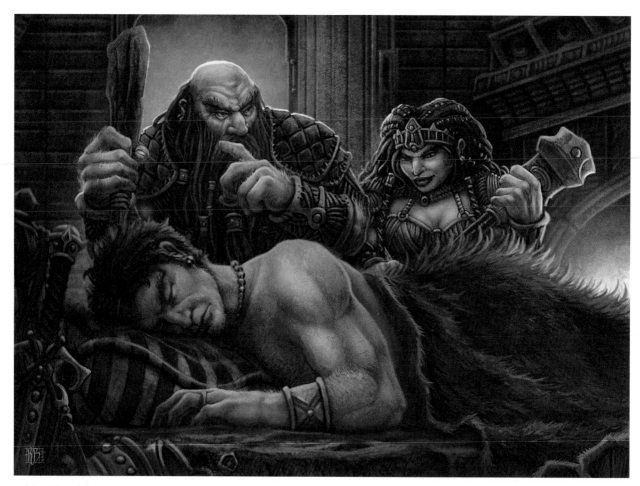

strip them of gear, and imprison them. Once captured, the characters await torture, interrogation, and slaughter. Although the PCs might escape through cunning, luck, or success at a skill challenge, they might find that losing crucial food and equipment is an equally serious threat to their survival.

Unaligned Underdark races, such as dwarves and deep gnomes, also dislike crusading characters and bar them from entering settlements. Adventurers might find these races secretive, ungenerous, and suspicious. Harboring adventurers who attacked neighboring drow, mind flayer, or aboleth settlements would invite reprisals from these formidable enemies. Also, past raiding parties from the surface world have abused dwarf and deep gnome hospitality by stealing food, water, artifacts, and secrets.

Characters should not necessarily trust dwarves and deep gnomes who welcome adventurers into their strongholds. Thieves and slavers run some of these communities, and they bind sleeping guests, strip them of valuable magic, and sell them to drow or fomorian neighbors.

DEPRIVED OF CONTACT

The Underdark limits opportunities for player characters to interact with NPCs. Adventurers can't wander into a settlement and casually engage strangers in conversation. Adventurers might go for weeks without seeing a chatty vendor, a rumor-dispensing bartender, or an informative street urchin. Other explorers and the occasional hermit or madman account for the few communicative, neutral creatures that the group might come across. These circumstances might make exploring the Underdark an unpleasant experience for actors and storytellers.

Without interaction scenes, interludes between encounters shorten in the Underdark, so increase the number of encounters you prepare per session.

LOCATING SHELTER

Characters needing rest in the Underdark face a difficult challenge. The adventurers must make their own safe place here. First, the characters must find a location, within raiding distance of their target, that enemy patrols do not monitor. Few chambers meeting this specification exist. Searching for a suitable base can take days of combat-filled exploration, because no race relinquishes a good base. Creatures of all types covet a cavern capable of providing decent shelter. Explorers should consider taking lairs only from unintelligent or antisocial creatures, since outposts held by civilized races receive regular visitors capable of taking them back.

The original occupants of the adventurers' new base might not return, but other creatures could take up residence in the adventuring group's absence.

Keeping Supplied

Characters will most likely end up scavenging for food and water in the Underdark. Few vendors provide meals here, and the underground environment offers little edible foraging, except for mushrooms and other fungi. Caverns can be dry as deserts or dripping with water contaminated by disease or poison.

You can leave the details of the group's food and water supply abstract. Occasionally tell them that they must replenish their food and water supplies. On the other hand, players sometimes enjoy tracking their in-game resources. If you have this type of player in your group, allow him or her to keep careful records of supply levels at all times.

Adventurers who run low on food or water can find small quantities of the necessary supply by succeeding on Dungeoneering checks with hard DCs. PCs might stumble upon traps or enter difficult encounters while foraging. To acquire significant quantities of supplies, the PCs must win skill challenges or defeat other creatures and take their supplies.

Darkness in the Light

D&D players might regard the Underdark as the classic test of any paragon character's mettle, but players can find regions of equivalent hostility on the surface of the world.

Cursed Lands

During the apocalyptic wars that destroyed the empires of eons past, long-forgotten magic scourged great swaths of the surface world. This magic left behind cursed lands, places where ordinary plants and animals cannot flourish. Strange, venomous animals, warped and twisted by fell magic, prowl across blasted landscapes and through toxic forests. Ghosts and wraiths haunt the buried imperial capitals that lie at the epicenters of these cursed lands. Undead remnants of slaughtered populations wander numbly through the ruins of their obliterated homes. Golems and other automatons constructed by the ancients patrol long-abandoned strongholds, ready to tear intruders to pieces.

Hordelands

Populated by warring tribes of nomadic barbarians, the hordelands contain vast, infertile steppes where natives skirmish constantly. Although adventurers in the heroic tier could overcome individual denizens of the hordelands, only paragon or epic characters dare to explore these realms and face large groups of their inhabitants.

Two or three competing barbarian races dominate the typical hordeland. The term "horde" conjures visions of orcs, goblins, gnolls, ogres, and lizardfolk. Some of these fearsome tribes are made up of humans; others are composed of dwarves, elves, tieflings, or dragonborn. Natives fight from the backs of swift horses and weirder mounts, and tribal folk employ magic vehicles left over from past ages.

Any nation near a hordeland fears the ascension of a great war leader who can rouse the feuding clans to united action. When this happens, the hordes coalesce into seething, bloodthirsty armies and swarm across the land like locusts, leveling every settlement they encounter. When a new chief arises in the hordelands, courageous adventurers must plunge deep into nomad territory to slay this charismatic leader before he or she unites an army.

Kingdoms of Evil

Certain civilized nations, gripped by evil or ruled by monsters, display the same hostility to good or unaligned adventurers as the drow or the mind flayers of the Underdark.

Intelligent, powerful undead sometimes install themselves as leaders of nations and city-states. Vampires, in particular, seek thrones to perch upon, so they can bleed populaces of both blood and money.

Lich kings also seek to rule, so they can sap citizens of their life force and use it to fuel magical experiments. A few of these dusty-veined monarchs dimly remember ruling as mortals in ancient empires. They seek to rediscover the forgotten rituals or sorcerous siege engines that destroyed their original kingdoms.

Ancient dragons might openly declare themselves rulers, but most dragons prefer to manipulate crowned puppets to reign over terrified citizens. Either way, dragons take a direct role in disposing of dissidents by devouring them. Evil dragon rulers tax their populations, demanding a percentage of the population as an offering for consumption.

Devils might take over nations openly, although more seize control through subversion of the existing ruling elite. Asmodeus in particular covets urban settlements. The devilish mania for legalism and bureaucracy infests every aspect of a controlled nation. Networks of spies, functionaries, and guards efficiently maintain order, quickly spotting incursions by foreign paragon characters. Devilish states demand absolute obedience while encouraging people to pursue dark, soul-corroding pleasures.

Undead Armies

A death knight might seize control of a region in order to sate its appetite for battle. One of these skeletal warriors can slaughter the entire population of a town so that it can create a legion of undead with which to pursue its battle against the living. Adventurers might walk into such a town without realizing that its inhabitants are not what they seem.

STREETS OF ANARCHY

The forces of chaotic evil seek conquest without the responsibility of rule. Cities and nation-states overrun by demons and other evil beings devolve into madness and destruction. After the common people flee or die, champions of evil run rampant. Some corrupted subjects remain, furiously defending their shattered turf for reasons they no longer recall. To gain reinforcements, these depraved subjects raid caravans and capture unsuspecting adventurers. Captives must escape or face transformation into demonically controlled minions of the Abyss.

WORLD HOPPING

If you or your group enjoys playing in multiple D&D worlds, a world-hopping campaign means you no longer have to choose between them. You can dip into the epic sweep of a FORGOTTEN REALMS campaign for one story arc and then switch to an EBERRON campaign's pulp-noir fantasy for the next. You can build a world-hopping campaign in an episodic structure or connect the adventures in the various worlds with an overarching continuity in the storyline.

In an episodic campaign, the adventurers move between worlds like rootless wanderers. They might travel a circuit between established worlds or visit a new world with a new story every session, never turning back. The second approach challenges you to create increasingly extreme or distinctive worlds. Don't worry about the depth of detail; focus on a single memorable world concept. Choose a theme for the adventure, and then create a world that expresses that theme in an exaggerated way. World creation and adventure design involve the same process.

You might, for example, create an adventure about the horrors of war. What would a world of incessant warfare look like, and how would its cultures behave? Next, consider what NPCs embody these attitudes. Now, build your encounters from a set of visual images associated with your world concept: a stronghold, a battlefield, and a landscape ravaged by past engagements.

The model of a new world for every adventure also works well for improvised games, where you must constantly create new encounters to suit your players. Improvisation frees you from tracking recurring characters and plot lines, and it allows you a fresh start every few sessions.

Conversely, the adventurers can follow a single storyline as they hop from world to world. They might try to prevent a catastrophe or an invasion that threatens the known spheres of existence. This approach allows your world-destroying villain to take out a few realities and still face defeat in the end. Another take on the concept sends the adventurers to gather pieces of a device that enemies or ancients scattered across multiple realities.

MASTERS OF REALITY

At the paragon tier, situations that embroil the adventurers take on a more fantastic nature. Some of these situations present the possibility of extreme and exotic journeys involving other planes or alternate realities.

PLANAR BREACHES

Denizens of the planes have colonized regions of the natural world in areas known as planar breaches. These places have the physical properties of the inhabitants' home planes. Characters might find adventuring in a breach the same as exploring the related plane, with similar natural properties and similar creatures.

When a breach manifests in the world, it pushes aside the space around it. A breach appearing in the main square of a ruined settlement might cut it in two. The west side of the old city remains intact on one side of the breach. The breach itself forms a newly created buffer between that portion of the city and the rest of the city, which remains intact to the east. Some breaches create peculiar distortions on the borders of the territories surrounding them.

Sometimes a plane overlays the natural world instead of pushing it aside, and the plane and the world mix in strange and unpredictable ways.

Breaches occur in isolated regions. Sages theorize that the psychic energy given off by large masses of intelligent minds acts as a barrier against the materialization of breaches in heavily populated areas.

Breaches can also be created by high-level magic. If a breach is created through magic, a focus object somewhere in the breach maintains a temporary bond between the two planes. Creatures loyal to a breach's creator tenaciously guard these focus objects. Destroying an object initiates the process of the breach's dissipation, giving adventurers just enough time to leap for the borderland before the breach closes.

Most planar breaches are fully contained by the world, but a few create connections between realities, existing in the natural world and in the breach's home plane at the same time. Moving out of the area of the breach could send PCs either back into the world or into the plane.

ALTERNATE WORLDS

You might have your campaign shift between alternate versions of a single reality in order to give your players a change of pace. This approach works best if you spent the heroic tier of your campaign establishing a solid sense of place and a large cast of supporting NPCs.

When the adventurers reach paragon status, they gain the ability to move between alternate worlds. Each new adventure takes them to a recognizable but altered version of the baseline world you established during play in the heroic tier. There, PCs encounter refracted versions of the familiar cast of characters.

These slight changes generate your adventure premises. In one reality, perhaps the heroes' nemesis changes into an ally. In the next, a human they know as a benevolent baroness transforms into a cruel tyrant or leads a resistance movement against the establishment, or maybe she suffers from a mind-sapping curse. Each adventure requires that PCs resolve a narrative involving these altered characters.

Another version of an alternate-worlds campaign includes counterparts for the players' characters whom the characters replace for the duration of the adventure. The alternate-world heroes are significantly different from the PCs in each new world. As part of the information-gathering phase of each adventure, the PCs must work out their context in this new dimension. Do they behave like heroes, cowards, villains, or something in between? Having learned about their alternate selves, the PCs must impersonate them in order to achieve the adventure's final objective.

Once your players assimilate this formula, you can throw them a curve by sending them to an alternate world in which they must face their alternate selves, possibly evil twins.

MASTERS OF TIME

A typical fantasy world's history reaches back tens of thousands of years. Allow the player characters to interact directly with the great events of your setting's past by enabling time travel. Your adventurers can meet legendary figures, fight in classic battles, and witness the birth of the deities. They can journey to the future, encounter their own descendants, marvel at technological wonders, and flee from the death of the world. The PCs might travel using a vehicle, an artifact, or a consistently available ritual. Alternatively, you might make an adventure into the time stream a special, one-time event.

Start by deciding how time travel works in your game. Can characters alter the events of history? If not, allow characters to take only actions that leave known history intact. You could choose a mechanism that protects the fixed nature of time, or you could employ powerful coincidences that prevent characters from affecting history.

You might instead decide to allow actions in the past to change the present as the adventurers know it. If, for example, the characters prevent the pivotal assassination that led to the fall of the great empires, they might return to an altered present day in which those empires cover the entire world.

You can complicate adventures involving time travel by creating consequences for paradoxes. If a change in history prevents the birth of a time traveler, does he or she disappear, or does he or she exist outside the time stream? Can time travelers meet themselves, or do such encounters create a strain on reality of apocalyptic proportions?

As adventurers approach the paragon tier of play, new locations begin to appear on the horizon. These locations are larger than the villages and towns of the heroic tier, grander and more exotic—and often more dangerous. One such location exists at the crossroads of all reality. It is a place of relative peace and rough safety where all kinds of business can take place. This is Sigil, the City of Doors.

Numerous portals connect Sigil to the rest of the multiverse. The planar metropolis exists outside the ordered structure of existence, rising from the interior surface of an immense hollow ring that has no outer side. The residents consider Sigil to be the true center of the multiverse, and visitors have few reasons to contradict this belief.

ORIGIN STORIES

Every collection of lore that touches upon the existence of Sigil has its own unique view of the origin and purpose of the city. Some claim that Sigil is the linchpin that keeps all of existence from flying apart. Many myths and writings from this school of thought associate the city with the legendary proto-entities of old—the predecessors of the gods and primordials. Other scholars believe that the city is a map of all creation, that all that one needs to do to understand the secrets of the universe is to understand the twists

and turns of Sigil. Some see the City of Doors as the easiest, most direct way to get from here to there and back again. And a select few see Sigil as the key to the ongoing battle for the hearts and souls of creation, the place where the literal war of philosophies plays out for good or ill.

Whatever the truth of it, you can find almost anything in Sigil, and almost everyone eventually passes through its portals—either with Sigil as the destination or on the way to someplace else.

THE IMPOSSIBLE PLACE

The City of Doors, named for the many portals that provide the only methods of travel into and out of the city, features impossible topography in an impossible location. The city exists on the inside of a gigantic, hollow ring that has no outer side. It stands apart from the rest of existence. It connects to the Astral Sea and the Elemental Chaos, to the Feywild and the Shadowfell and the natural world, and to a multitude of places beyond imagining, but it isn't a part of any of these. Sigil *is*. For most, that simple fact explains everything.

All the streets and buildings fill the curved interior of the hollow ring. If you look up, and if your view isn't obscured by the persistent rain or fog or smoke from countless chimneys, you can see the

SIGIL FACTS

Sigil is the bustling crossroads of the multiverse, full of portals leading to every known corner of existence.

Population: Approximately 50,000 permanent residents. Representatives of nearly every race and monstrous kind can be found somewhere in the city. A host of transients pass through the city daily, with the result that as many as 250,000 individuals can be present in Sigil at any given time.

Government and Defense: The only being in Sigil who wields any real authority is the mysterious Lady of Pain, the enigmatic guardian and protector of the city. The touch of her gaze causes wounds that spout blood, and her smallest gesture can banish someone or something into an endless maze spawned in a pocket dimension. Her presence is said to prevent gods, demon princes, primordials, and beings of similar power from entering the City of Doors, and the fear of her is sufficient to keep a modicum of order in the streets. Crime is common, but rebellion is unthinkable.

The closest thing Sigil has to a police force is a citizen group called the Sons of Mercy. However, without any official power to make arrests or carry out sentences (though they try all the same), the Sons of Mercy aren't terribly effective in limiting crime. Similarly, the so-called

Sigil Advisory Council might have the city's best interests at heart, but the group lacks real political power.

Inns and Taverns: Sigil's inns and taverns cater to a diverse clientele. Efreets from the City of Brass can find flaming halls of sumptuous luxury. Devils can enjoy a night spent in unthinkable debauchery. A traveler might lodge in an inn whose interior is like a twilit fey grove or a sunless cavern, or eat in a place that's virtually indistinguishable from Fallcrest's Blue Moon Alehouse.

Supplies: The Grand Bazaar, located in the city's Market Ward, is a huge square overflowing into side streets, alleyways, and nearby taverns. It is filled with caravan tents and market stalls. Other marketplaces spring up in many places throughout the city. Most appear during the day, but some surface only at night, such as the Hive's Night Market.

Trade: Because Sigil sits astride all the planes of existence, it enjoys a flow of trade that most other cities would envy if they knew the true measure of its volume. Even with the threat of the Lady of Pain, various nefarious trade routes run through Sigil at any given time.

Temples: Temples to all the gods—including evil gods whose shrines are rarely seen in civilized lands—can be found in the streets of Sigil. Most of them are small, and few claim any significant power in the city's affairs.

buildings across the open hollow overhead. This is a place where the horizon curves up instead of away, where the sky above is always filled with the gray arc of the other side of Sigil's ring. In fact, the horizon in front of you and behind you curves up, so that you are always at the bottom of the ring. Line of sight rarely exceeds more than a few hundred feet due to the concentration of buildings, so the effect isn't prevalent or as disturbing as it could be.

UP AND DOWN

No matter where you stand within the hollow interior ring that Sigil occupies, down is always toward the ground beneath you, and up is in the opposite direction. Flying through the open space between the ring is perfectly possible, but as with most other locations, the danger of falling remains constant. You always fall toward the side of the ring you're closest to. And falling hurts.

DAY AND NIGHT

Sigil has no sun or moon, but it still has a day–night cycle. Each twenty-four-hour period slides from deep darkness to bright light and back again on a regular cycle. The sky gradually fills with a magical luminescence until the light reaches its brightest intensity (the equivalent of noon in the natural world), and then it begins to fade.

At daybreak, the darkness gradually brightens to dawn, with the light increasing in intensity until midday. The light then steadily wanes into a twilight gloom before plunging into blackest night. Unless the night is particularly overcast or foggy, some ambient light shines down from above. This is not the light of distant stars or a moon, since Sigil has none of these. Instead, the fires burning in the streets and buildings above light the night sky with flickering pinpoints of brightness.

The overall cycle provides six hours of bright daylight and six hours of deepest night, each separated by a six-hour period of gloomy twilight.

WEATHER

If it isn't raining when you arrive in Sigil, wait a couple of minutes. A light rain tends to be the usual weather in the City of Doors. The rain falls through the ever-present smoke from the multitude of fires, ranging from a nearly imperceptible mist to a constant drip of cold, greasy water. When it isn't raining (a rarity), the streets fill with fog that can be as wispy as gossamer or so thick as to reduce visibility to a few feet. Even on the brightest days, when the rain stops falling and a breeze blows calmly through the streets, Sigil is cool. At night, when darkness falls, the streets can get uncomfortably cold. And then the rain starts again.

FLORA AND FAUNA

No plants or animals are native to Sigil, but that hasn't stopped life from finding places to thrive in the City of Doors. The most notable vegetation is razorvine. This fast-growing plant aggressively stretches its greasy stalks and knife-edged fronds throughout the city. It grows over everything, climbing walls, entwining statues, and covering pathways with wild abandon. The only thing that keeps it in check is constant pruning and tending. Without such dedicated care, it would choke the place entirely in a matter of months.

Vermin of all kinds have found niches to occupy throughout Sigil. From lowly insects to common rats, nonmonstrous creatures thrive in garbage heaps, dank sewers, and dark corners throughout the city. In addition to more common forms of vermin, giant rats, dire rats, and fearfully intelligent cranium rats can be encountered in the worst parts of the city.

The sewers beneath the city also provide homes for monsters of all descriptions that have found their way through doors to the streets of Sigil.

RAZORVINE

This creeper plant has serrated leaves that unfold from black stems. Razorvine counts as difficult terrain, and a creature entering or starting its turn in a square of razorvine takes 10 damage per tier.

ARCHITECTURE

No natural resources fill the hollow ring, so Sigil has been built with materials brought into the city from somewhere else. Certain locations seem to have sprung into existence out of the nothingness of the hollow ring, but in general the place has been built with imported materials. Every brick, every window, every stick of furniture, was imported from elsewhere—either in finished form or its raw state.

Structures throughout Sigil consist of a wild collection of competing styles from every place—and every time—the city touches. Each era has seen a flurry of construction that mimicked the architectural styles of the period. Because of the nature of Sigil, styles from ages past can still be found, in whole or in part, eons after the originating cultures have disappeared. Sages stalk the back alleys of the city in search of traces of ancient cultures that remain in gables, cornices, domes, and columns.

Today, individuals who want to build a new structure in Sigil or renovate a standing building must either import materials or salvage them from existing structures. An entire shadow profession has grown up around the theft of construction materials. Often the outer structure of a building is more valuable, and more in need of defense from scavengers, than its contents. Sigil's so-called "stone pirates" scuttle out in the night to chip at masonry, saw off boards, and filch metal fittings either for open sale or to fill the order of a wealthy patron.

Architectural styles also provide a telltale hint to the relative status of a street, a neighborhood, or a ward. The well-kept structures of The Lady's Ward bristle with ornamentation, for example, while the shacks and shanties constructed of salvaged, deteriorating materials immediately identify the crowded alleys of the Lower Ward.

PORTALS

The only way to get into or out of Sigil is through a portal. No other form of teleportation or planar travel can penetrate the barriers around the City of Doors. Once you're in Sigil, you can move around the city with teleportation powers, but you can't enter or exit the place except through the portals that dot the cityscape.

A portal, also called a gate, can be any aperture or bounded space. Windows, doors, archways, sewer grates, large crates or chests, pits, trestles, hearths—all these openings and more might be portals in the City of Doors.

Some portals remain constantly active, meaning that all you have to do to use them is to step through one. Many portals, however, require a gate key to operate. Without the proper gate key, a portal is just a space, and a mundane space at that. With the proper gate key, a portal becomes a gateway to someplace else. A gate key usually takes the form of an object, from an actual key to anything else that can easily be carried on your person. Sometimes, however, a gate key might be a spoken word or phrase, a gesture, or a particular state of mind.

DEEPER THAN YOU THINK

Although it's impossible to dig any distance down into the chalky material that makes up the hollow ring of Sigil, the city does have its share of deep basements, catacombs, dungeons, and subterranean passageways. Any travel significantly beneath the surface of Sigil in fact takes you through a door to another reality. Most of the time, travel of this sort leads to tiny pocket realities created expressly for specific purposes by arcane masters of the past. Shop basements, burial chambers for wealthy families, forgotten dungeons, and even Sigil's network of sewers were all created in this fashion in the distant past. Today, rituals permitting these dimensional excavations are not undertaken lightly. Those who can perform such rituals are rare, the rituals themselves are expensive, and such a working is liable to provoke the deadly wrath of the Lady of Pain.

Portals can be permanent, temporary, or shifting. There's something about Sigil that seems to attract randomly occurring portals that wink into and out of existence without any apparent rhyme or reason. These randomly occurring portals can appear anywhere and last momentarily or remain open for days or weeks at a time. An expensive ritual can shield areas from the incursion of random portals, but only the most well-to-do neighborhoods in Sigil can afford to keep such protections in place at all times.

Portals tend to be two-way. If you step through a portal, you can usually step back the way you came. You might need a gate key, but otherwise a door is a door. There are some rare portals that go only one way. Usually, the truth is that a different gate key is required to make the return trip, so it really isn't a one-way door at all. Or the portal winks out or moves before you can step back. But sometimes, you might run into an actual one-way portal—and going through such a portal might leave you in a very bad place indeed.

Permanent Portals

A permanent portal has an opening in Sigil and an opening someplace else (on another plane, in the natural world, or in some pocket dimension) that are always available for use. Every time you step through a permanent portal, you know where you're going to end up. There are no surprises. (Unless, of course, you have no idea where a particular portal connects to.) Permanent portals tend to connect relatively safe and stable locations, such as gate-towns, to Sigil. Many permanent portals are known by someone in Sigil, and the information pertaining to them tends to be valuable currency within the City of Doors.

Temporary Portals

Temporary portals can appear anywhere in Sigil, opening a path between two locations for a short time and then disappearing as though they had never existed. Temporary portals can be as frustrating as they are dangerous—frustrating because if a gate key is needed, you can waste valuable time determining what it is, and dangerous because there might not be any clue about where the portal connects to. In addition, there's often an unpredictable timetable associated with a temporary portal. It might close before your work on the other side is finished, leaving you without a fast and convenient exit back to Sigil.

Shifting Portals

Shifting portals follow a set pattern, although the pattern is rarely obvious or easy to discern. Sometimes the portal in Sigil shifts, sliding from window to doorway to sewer grate throughout the city. Other times, the portal on the other end is the one that moves, bouncing around a particular area of the natural world, or a plane, or even sliding from plane to plane.

These shifts are not random, and the cycle repeats itself so that eventually the portal winds up back in the place it originally began. Enterprising individuals in Sigil make a lot of gold by keeping logs of how the shifting portals work and selling pieces of that information to the right people at the right time. However, there are just as many swindlers as true portal information dealers out there, so a careless adventurer can easily be separated from his or her gold without receiving accurate or useful information.

Gate Keys

Not every portal requires a gate key to operate, but many do. To use such a portal, a traveler needs to have the gate key when he or she steps through. Many gate keys allow their portal to remain open for a short time, which lets multiple travelers pass through with the use of a single gate key.

Gate keys tend to be objects or phrases that are neither too common nor too rare. They aren't so common as to cause accidental use of a given portal, nor are they so rare that a portal can never be used. (Although both such portals can exist somewhere in Sigil, and these often lead to the wildest adventures.) Gate keys, once established, never change.

A gate key usually has a connection to its portal's destination, providing a clue to where a portal opens up to when the path isn't widely known. Numerous proprietors throughout Sigil claim to keep logs marking portals, their destinations, and the gate keys required to operate them (if any), and for a price they are usually willing to provide such information to those who ask. Check out Tivvum's Antiquities in the Market Ward when you're in need of a gate key.

Portals in Action

When any individual crosses the threshold of a portal while carrying the proper gate key (if a gate key is required to make the portal function), the archway that frames the portal flashes with arcane energy, and a ghostly image of a distant location can briefly be glimpsed through the open portal. The portal remains open for only a few seconds (long enough for a group of PCs to step through). Anyone who steps through vanishes from Sigil and instantly appears at the destination. Anything that's partially through a portal when it closes is teleported to the portal's destination.

Anyone in Sigil can use a portal to leave the city, but the converse is not necessarily true. The City of Doors seems to have the ability to keep out gods, demon princes, primordials, and similarly powerful beings. When such an entity attempts to use a portal to Sigil, nothing happens. If such an entity tries to rush through an active portal that a lesser being opened, the entity is forcibly expelled from the portal and pushed back to wherever it tried to enter from.

6

THE LADY OF PAIN

What keeps the City of Doors safe and functioning? What maintains order and refuses to allow Sigil to tumble into chaos and anarchy? The answer is simple, yet surprisingly complex: the Lady of Pain.

The Lady of Pain isn't a woman and isn't human. Although theories abound, the truth of the matter is that no one knows who or what the Lady of Pain actually is. She exists. She has an enduring connection to Sigil. And she stands as the law and the power in the City of Doors.

Some believe she is a god, but no pantheon claims her as a member. Some think she must be a demon prince or a devil lord, but others find that idea unacceptable. One or two ancient texts identify her as the embodiment of Sigil, or even as a proto-entity from the time before time. Most visitors to and inhabitants of Sigil don't really care one way or another. The simple truth is that the Lady of Pain exists, and that's all that matters.

The Lady remains distant from most of the day-to-day activities that take place in Sigil. You won't find a castle, a palace, or a temple with her name on it. Indeed, if anyone worships her they usually end up missing (presumed to be banished to the Mazes, see below) or turn up with their skin flayed from their bones. It is widely known that she accepts no prayers or sacrifices, and she reportedly punishes or destroys those that make such offerings.

The Lady of Pain never speaks. She never participates in council meetings or guild discussions or judicial inquiries. When she appears, she is seen drifting down the cobbled streets, her gown barely brushing the dusty surface as she passes by. Those familiar with the ways of Sigil know enough to move on during the Lady's sporadic forays through the streets. Anyone who has the bad sense to try to interfere with her passage receives painful gashes from her penetrating gaze.

Such appearances, rare and memorable though they might be, eventually end when the Lady passes through a wall or simply fades into nothingness, vanishing from sight without word or warning.

What is the Lady of Pain? She is the impassive protector of Sigil, inspiring awe and fear with her very presence. No one deals with the Lady. She doesn't give missions or serve as a patron. She makes no proclamations and issues no edicts. She is just the wonder and mystery and danger of Sigil made manifest. But she does have laws—or, at least, certain truths about Sigil are credited to her will.

The presence of the Lady keeps all inhabitants and visitors in line, making Sigil more or less safe for conducting business of all sorts. She keeps gods and other powerful entities out of the city. She prevents teleportation rituals and other magic from penetrating the borders of the City of Doors. She oversees the dabus that maintain the city. And she creates the Mazes that serve as the most prominent deterrent to conquest and chaos in Sigil—and which give the city its other name, the Cage.

THE MAZES

When a significant threat to Sigil appears, it doesn't last long. Powermongers, rabble-rousers, and malcontents who flaunt their ambitions and disdains quickly find themselves banished to the Mazes. These pocket dimensions swirl into existence to torment a single threat, whether that threat is an individual or a small group of conspirators.

Each maze appears as a small part of Sigil, such as an alleyway, courtyard, or cul-de-sac. This copy becomes a twisting labyrinth that has no beginning, no end, and no obvious exit points. A targeted individual might step through an archway, turn down an alley, or pass through a door in his or her own house and suddenly be spun into a newly created maze.

In a maze, a trapped individual doesn't starve or die of thirst: Food and drink appear at regular intervals. Each maze contains one hidden portal that can be used for escape. The prisoner just needs to find the door, and then determine what key is required to open it. For most, this possibility of escape is just a cruel hope that taunts them but never materializes. Every once in a great while, however, a prisoner finds a way to get out.

Of course, many disappearances that are blamed on the Mazes have no connection to these pocket dimensions at all, but such is the nature of life in the Cage. Those taken by one of the Mazes might eventually stumble out of their prison, chastened and changed, but most are never seen again.

THE DABUS

A unique race of intelligent beings, the dabus, lives in Sigil. They are never encountered anywhere else, neither in the natural world nor out among the planes. Dabus appear as pale-skinned humanoids with long and narrow bodies and features. They emanate a serene air, with their calm expressions, elegant horns, and shocks of white hair. Like the Lady of Pain, dabus float above the ground as they move about the city. Unlike the Lady, dabus are always around, visible and active as they perform their daily tasks and functions.

Dabus swarm like ants atop a crumb of food, appearing when something in Sigil needs to be repaired. They maintain the infrastructure of the city, making sure that the sewers never clog, the razor-vine never spreads completely out of control, and the cobblestones that line the streets are never cracked or broken. Most people in Sigil consider them to be nothing more than inscrutable workers, but the evidence suggests that they are something more.

As with the Lady of Pain, dozen of theories about the origin and purpose of the dabus exist. Are they living manifestations of the city? Servants of the Lady of Pain? The first inhabitants of the hollow ring that became Sigil? Does the City of Doors belong to the dabus, or do the dabus belong to the city? Each of these questions has multiple answers that are held as true and absolute. Here's what is actually known about the dabus.

For as long as there has been a Sigil, the dabus have been present.

Dabus never speak, and they rarely acknowledge or interact with other beings. Although their behavior reflects that displayed by the Lady of Pain, the dabus are not quite as distant and aloof as she tends to be.

When a dabus needs to communicate with someone, it does so with gestures and sign language, and occasionally in the form of a rebus.

Dabus are not combative by nature. Usually, they quietly float about the city, performing the tasks that fall to them without hesitation or complaint. They will fight if they must, however, and when they engage in combat, they show a remarkable courage and grace that rattles their opponents.

Though the dabus float above the ground when they move, they don't actually fly. They glide along, never touching the ground but also never soaring far above it either.

It is believed that the dabus live beneath Sigil, or that the city creates them when they are needed, or that the Lady sets them to their tasks with her own silent gaze.

Whatever the truth, dabus scour the city, making repairs, cleaning, landscaping, and otherwise keeping Sigil's ancient infrastructure from falling apart. Their work is never so perfect that the city is in danger of looking brand new, but they do keep the place presentable. Sometimes they even undertake extensive rebuilding projects, tearing down small sections of the city and reconstructing them—usually to the complaints of the displaced inhabitants.

Silent, serene, and dedicated, these mysterious servants also have a dark side. Dabus can appear in great numbers to quell riots, disperse crowds, or deal with the greatest threats to the stability of the city and the well-being of the Lady of Pain. They never react to normal crimes or minor disturbances, however, leaving such peacekeeping duties to anyone who wants to take them up.

SILENT WORKERS

Dabus work crews usually consist of three to five of the strange, silent beings. They silently float about the city to handle tasks, whether whitewashing a wall, painting a building, sweeping a street, pruning razorvine, or attacking a threat.

The examples below are typical dabus that usually float above the streets of Sigil. Other, more powerful versions can appear when the need is great or the danger seems potentially devastating to the city or the Lady of Pain.

Dabus Custodian	Level 15 Artillery
Medium immortal humanoid	XP 1,200

Initiative +11   **Senses** Perception +16; darkvision
HP 118; **Bloodied** 59
AC 27; **Fortitude** 27, **Reflex** 25, **Will** 25
Speed 8 (hover)

⊕ **Hammer** (standard; at-will) ✦ **Weapon**
+22 vs. AC; 1d10 + 5 damage.

⊙ **Psychic Ray** (standard; at-will) ✦ **Psychic**
Ranged 10; +20 vs. Will; 2d8 + 6 psychic damage, and the target is dazed (save ends).

✸ **Psychic Burst** (standard; recharge ⚄ ⚅) ✦ **Psychic**
Area burst 1 within 20; +18 vs. Will; 3d10 + 6 psychic damage, and the target is stunned (save ends).

Alignment Unaligned   **Languages** – (understands all)
Skills Streetwise +15

Str 16 (+10)	**Dex** 18 (+11)	**Wis** 18 (+11)
Con 22 (+13)	**Int** 16 (+10)	**Cha** 16 (+10)

Dabus Enforcer	Level 18 Controller
Medium immortal humanoid	XP 2,000

Initiative +14   **Senses** Perception +18; darkvision
HP 172; **Bloodied** 86
AC 32; **Fortitude** 30, **Reflex** 30, **Will** 29
Speed 8 (hover)

⊕ **Longsword** (standard; at-will) ✦ **Weapon**
+23 vs. AC; 1d10 + 7 damage.

⊙ **Psychic Rend** (standard; at-will) ✦ **Psychic**
Ranged 10; +22 vs. Will; 2d8 + 7 psychic damage, and the target slides 3 squares. The target is also stunned (save ends).

✸ **Mind Cage** (standard; recharge ⚄ ⚅) ✦ **Psychic**
Area burst 1 within 20; +22 vs. Will; 4d10 + 7 psychic damage, and the target takes ongoing 10 psychic damage and is immobilized (save ends both).

Alignment Unaligned   **Languages** – (understands all)
Skills Arcana +18, Nature +18

Str 16 (+12)	**Dex** 20 (+14)	**Wis** 17 (+13)
Con 20 (+14)	**Int** 18 (+13)	**Cha** 18 (+13)

RULES AND GOVERNANCE

In Sigil, anything can happen. That's part of the city's charm, and a state of affairs that lends an element of danger to everyday events. Walking down a Sigil street can involve avoiding the stare of the Lady of Pain, being hustled by a planar trader, running into a demon that's passing through, and meeting a being from a corner of a plane you'd never heard of before.

Conducting yourself in Sigil requires that you remember a few simple rules. When it comes to day-to-day affairs, always maintain your guard. It isn't like Sigil has a vigilant city watch around to deter every would-be assailant who might come hunting for you. When it comes to the big picture, the things that concern the usually peaceful fierceness of the Lady of Pain, keep your head down and your eyes averted. She tolerates (some might say ignores) petty squabbles and minor crimes, including fights, muggings, robberies, and even the occasional murder. But if you try to alter or interfere with the portals, or if you slaughter the dabus, or if you attempt to destroy the city, start a rebellion, or challenge the

Lady herself, then you must deal with the consequences of attracting both the attention and the wrath of the Lady of Pain.

THE BRINK OF ANARCHY

From a certain point of view, the Lady of Pain rules Sigil. Her presence keeps the place running smoothly and makes the streets more or less safe so that the business of the city can occur. On the other hand, she doesn't behave like a ruler at all. She issues no proclamations. She collects no taxes. She really doesn't seem all that interested in the welfare of her subjects beyond the fact that keeping the people of Sigil relatively content means that her city remains full and vibrant.

Law and order tend to be a personal affair. For the most part, you keep yourself safe by carrying a weapon or a spell and appearing to know what to do with it. Certain parts of Sigil can feel a lot like a wild frontier town where people are responsible for protecting themselves and taking the law into their own hands. Organized groups do operate throughout the city. They just have to operate at a level that doesn't make it appear as though they're threatening the sanctity or power of the Lady of Pain.

In the past, Sigil served as a headquarters for numerous factions. These philosophical fraternities helped keep Sigil vital by each running a different part of the city. In the aftermath of a terrible war between the factions, the Lady of Pain made a rare and stunning appearance before the surviving leaders. With a dabus in tow to communicate for her, the Lady proclaimed: *The city tolerates your faction no longer. Abandon it or die.* They complied, and Sigil no longer hosts any organized factions.

SIGIL'S CITIZENS

The residents of Sigil are as diverse a lot as you could ever expect to find. Any kind of sentient creature in the world—and from any place outside the world—can be found roaming the streets or residing here. The city is a place where racial animosity takes a back seat to more pragmatic concerns. No one who lives or visits here is likely to be attacked based simply on his or her basic nature, since almost everyone is here for the same reason: to benefit from what the city has to offer as the hub of the multiverse. The atmosphere in Sigil is similar to that of an armed truce; although isolated violence does break out from time to time, the residents of Sigil appreciate the need not to cause widespread havoc in the city, and they police themselves to keep things on an even keel.

SIGIL ADVISORY COUNCIL

Prominent and well-to-do citizens have banded together since the disappearance of the factions to fill the void left behind. The members meet regularly and wrap themselves in the pomp and prestige of the office they have created, sincerely working to maintain the peace in the City of Doors. Well spoken and charismatic, the group established a process of nomination and election to fill their ranks with worthy representatives. There are nine seats on the council.

The Advisors have little real authority. It is commonly said that if the Lady ever did appear before the council members to ask for advice, they would all flee in terror and never return.

Still, the Advisors step forward to speak on the city's behalf. So far, the Lady of Pain hasn't banished any of them to the Mazes or sliced any of them to bloody ribbons, so perhaps they have a bit more authority than certain citizens believe. Who can tell for sure? What is known about the Advisors is that they sometimes use their wealth to hire adventurers to deal with problems, and they even engage in humanitarian and charitable activities in the more upscale sections of the city. They sometimes cooperate with the Mutual Trade Association to push forth edicts and get things done.

Rhys, former leader of the Transcendent Order faction, serves on the council and is perhaps its most well-known member. She is a tiefling with style and attitude, and is considered a true asset to Sigil by those who know her.

SONS OF MERCY

The Sons of Mercy oversee Sigil's Prison, caring for the inmates until each has paid his or her debt and can be set free. The group also coordinates watch patrols throughout the city, but it has no real legal authority—the Sons of Mercy are little more than a group of concerned citizens voluntarily working to make Sigil's streets safe. Sworn to protect the innocent, uphold justice, and prove that crime doesn't pay, the Sons of Mercy are led by Arwyl Swan's Son, who trained among the Mercykillers faction when that organization still held sway in Sigil.

Without real authority or power beyond the walls of the Prison, the Sons of Mercy have limited success as a police force. Certainly, no one who runs into a Sons of Mercy patrol while operating on the wrong side of the law readily recognizes that patrol's right to administer justice. In most cases, the only way for the patrol to exercise any authority is through force of arms. If a patrol can get the upper hand, or demonstrate more power and ability than the opposition, then it usually succeeds. If not, the members of the patrol flee or take a beating for their trouble.

MUTUAL TRADE ASSOCIATION

Another self-started and self-regulated group to step to the forefront of Sigil politics is the Mutual Trade Association. A loose collection of guild masters and prominent independent merchants, the Traders have come together to protect their business interests as they relate to the City of Doors.

For a time, it appeared that the vacuum created by the fall of the factions was going to set the rich and well-connected against each other as different merchant lords vied for power and influence. Realizing that such a fierce competition could unduly attract the attention of the Lady of Pain, three of the top captains of commerce put aside their mutual animosity to form the Traders.

Although all three associates claim to have an equal say in how the Traders conduct business, the truth of the matter is that Shemeshka, a raavasta who controls a vast commercial empire and information-gathering network, has emerged as the de facto leader of the group. The other associates are Zadara and Estavan. Zadara, a reclusive storm giant entrepreneur, supplies funds to creative and daring individuals in return for hefty returns on her investments as well as the promise of future favors. Estavan, meanwhile, is an extremely powerful oni mage who serves as the face of the vast Planar Trade Consortium. In addition, numerous less influential members have joined the Traders for the benefits the organization provides.

The Traders do not interfere with the day-to-day affairs of the individual businesses that make up the association. In most cases, they don't even share business-related information. They do, however, look for solutions to problems that plague all the members, including crime waves, disrupted supply lines, taxes and tariffs, embattled trade routes, worker unrest, and other threats to profit and industry. Often, the Traders will enact solutions to problems affecting Sigil long before either the Sons of Mercy or the Sigil Advisory Council can get their acts together. As long as doing so helps business, then it's in the interest of the Traders to get things done.

Other Power Players

Other groups trying to enforce some kind of order on the chaos of Sigil tend to be more low-key and usually less civic-minded than the organizations discussed above. Armed merchant auxiliaries, for example, protect trade routes and warehouses, target gangs of robbers, and recover stolen goods. Neighborhood gangs have formed to combat increasing crime and violence, though these groups can be as violent and unpredictable as the ills they have been created to rectify. Finally, wealthy patrons of all stripes have taken to hiring bodyguards or putting militia units and adventurers on retainer so that they can call upon them at a moment's notice to deal with trouble that gets out of hand.

Sigil's Businesses and Services

Almost anything can be found in Sigil. Thanks to the multitude of portals and the enterprising businesses that seek to open the vastness of the planes to trade, there's a chance that something you want or need is on display in the next stall or shop window. Of course, locating exactly what you're searching for could take a while—Sigil's a big place with a lot of people, and nothing is ever straightforward or easy in the Cage.

Locals who are willing to show newcomers around or lead a body to a specific location are known as touts. A good tout also knows people and can make introductions if the price is right. Touts range from wily street urchins to rough-and-tumble cutters who look as capable of robbing you as providing safe passage, and the prices they charge for their services vary wildly as well. In general, you can hire a tout for about 100 gp per day, though some offer their services for less and others put a higher premium on the use of their skills. Touts can routinely be hired in markets, in taverns, near known portals, and around other places where newcomers congregate.

Another common purveyor of service is the courier. A courier makes money by delivering items or messages in a timely fashion, so most of the people engaged in this service are trustworthy and reliable. Couriers can carry just about anything that a normal individual can lug around; a letter, a small satchel, a small box or crate, and so forth. Some employ magic items, such as *bags of holding*, but these well-equipped couriers charge more for their services. For secret messages or other sensitive material, a few couriers provide a special service—they perform a ritual upon a small trinket (usually an unadorned ring or a carved wooden or stone tile with the courier's icon or crest upon it) that repeats the message stored within it when the named recipient activates it. For the most important packages, a courier undergoes a special ritual that magically binds the courier to the deliverable item. If the courier loses the package or fails to deliver it by the appointed hour, he or she begins to wither and die. Such ensorcelled couriers work hard to hang onto the items placed in their care and work even harder to recover any items that are lost or stolen along the way. Prices range from 50 gp for a mundane delivery service to as much as 10,000 gp for magically binding a package to a courier. Additional costs can be applied to deliveries to destinations outside Sigil.

Taverns abound in the City of Doors. One common saying is that there are as many taverns as portals in Sigil, and sometimes it seems like this remark isn't that far off. There are taverns that cater to particular tastes and clientele, fancy taverns, dives, holes in the wall, and places where even adventurers should feel afraid. Alehouses, wine cellars, pubs, and even places that serve rarer, more exotic fare can be found in different parts of the city. In general, a tavern provides a good place to get a lay of the land, to hear the news of the street, and to uncover any rumors of jobs, excitement, or patrons in need.

Inns tend to offer more services than the typical tavern, but there are exceptions to every rule. At an inn, you can usually secure lodging while you're in Sigil, and inns tend to provide fewer options for imbibing and more options to get a meal than the average tavern. As with taverns, you can find inns that cater to all tastes and needs, including those related to a customer's particular species. Oversized rooms for giants? Conveniences for the smaller races? Special dietary requirements? Thanks to the wide range of visitors that regularly pass through Sigil, all these options and more are provided for somewhere in the city.

Markets spring up throughout the city. Some, such as the Great Bazaar, are permanent affairs, while others appear and disappear with regularity. You can buy and sell all sorts of items at a variety of locations, from transitory stalls and tents, to brick-and-mortar shops, to folding tables set up in dark alleys or in the backs of dimly lit taverns. Markets are classified as either "day" or "night" markets. At day markets, you're more likely to find food, supplies, and other necessities of daily life. Some of the items for sale are the usual fare; common meats, vegetables, and fruits, for instance. Those who have a taste for the exotic can also find unusual food and drink from across the planes. Housewares, crafts, jewelry, clothing, and other basic necessities—from the common and mundane to the rare and unusual—also fill the stalls and display tables of the day markets.

The night markets are a different story. When darkness fills Sigil's sky, those who sell entertainment and pleasure appear to replace the daytime wares that cater to more mundane needs. The night markets, at once deadly and fascinating, cater to those seeking distraction, excitement, and a hint of danger. At the night markets, one's misfortune can become another's entertainment, especially when the shadows deepen. Musicians and bards, prophets and bawds, spell-sellers and purveyors of previously owned materials emerge from the spreading darkness to replace goods appropriate to the light of day with goods and services dedicated more to wants than to needs. Some find the night markets to be wild and unpredictable, but for others that's just what draws them out to shop as the darker parts of the city come alive. You need to know which market will best serve your needs for a particular desire; then you need to find the merchant you feel most comfortable dealing with—no matter what time of day you decide to shop.

THE WARDS OF SIGIL

When you first arrive in Sigil, it's easy to become confused and disoriented. To the uninitiated, Sigil's streets appear to be a chaotic scramble laid out haphazardly, in every direction, with no apparent plan or purpose. On the surface, this is true. But Sigil's citizens know that there are different parts to the city, and they know that those parts make sense. The city is divided into wards, and each ward's name speaks to what you can expect to find in that section of the city.

Where one ward starts and another ends isn't handled by official maps and property lines. You can usually tell where you are by the crowding of the buildings (or lack thereof), by the general upkeep and ambience of a neighborhood, and by the types of businesses found there. The poorer the ward, the more tightly packed and run-down the living conditions become.

Generally, everyone agrees that Sigil has six distinct wards, and these are spread out in a clockwise direction around the hollow ring. The six wards are The Lady's Ward, the Market Ward, the Guildhall Ward, the Clerk's Ward, the Lower Ward, and the Hive.

THE LADY'S WARD

The most influential and powerful within Sigil society live and work in The Lady's Ward, the richest of Sigil's sections. Within the unmarked boundaries of The Lady's Ward, a visitor will find the City Barracks, the Court, the Prison, and the Armory, as well as more than half of the city's temples. This ward tends to be the cleanest, quietest, and most upscale of all the areas in the City of Doors.

THE CHANT

Sigil's a major hub for planar trade, but it's not the biggest one in existence; the City of Brass in the Elemental Chaos owns the title as the mercantile center of the universe. Sigil does feature a staggering amount of trade in physical items, but that pales in comparison to the city's preeminent role as the information capital at the center of all things. News, rumors, gossip, and facts—collectively called "the chant" by Cagers—find their way here to be bought and sold.

Sigil's chant-brokers provide information to those who seek it, whether the seeker is an adventurer from the world looking for a map of a dominion in the Astral Sea, a githyanki searching for clues to a forgotten location in the Shadowfell, or an eladrin lord from the Feywild hoping to find something lost in the Elemental Chaos. Sigil is the place to find and buy things that can't be held: secrets, gateways, passwords, the true names of dead gods, how to wake a sleeping primordial, the answers to lost riddles. Nearly everything known or imagined can be found here—for a price.

No matter how powerful or all-seeing a chant-broker seems, though, one fact remains true: No one has all the information, and anyone who claims otherwise is lying.

This ward overflows with monuments, fountains, and statuary of all descriptions. It is at once majestic and cold, full of life but ultimately lifeless thanks to the restrained (some would say absent) energy level imposed upon the visible streets by the residents of the neighborhood. Behind the gilded gates and white-washed facades of the well-kept buildings, all manner of revelries and plots unwind in secret. And that's the truth of The Lady's Ward: The orderly streets hide a secret turbulence that roils and seethes just out of sight.

The rich and powerful aren't all charitable and honorable, either. Behind the image of respectability might hide the secret face of a crime lord, or a tyrant, or a dark wizard. Not that all the residents of The Lady's Ward are evil, but they certainly aren't all good and holy, either.

Street crime in the ward is kept to a minimum, thanks to both the proximity of the Prison and the private militias employed by the great families and wealthiest individuals living in the neighborhood. Of course, these private armies sometimes battle each other in addition to keeping the ward safe, but that's just life in The Lady's Ward.

Sons of Mercy Basher	Level 13 Soldier
Medium natural humanoid, human	XP 800

Initiative +11   **Senses** Perception +13
HP 130; **Bloodied** 65
AC 29; **Fortitude** 26, **Reflex** 24, **Will** 24
Speed 5

⊕ **Lightning Halberd** (standard; at-will) ✦ **Lightning, Weapon**
   Reach 2; +20 vs. AC; 2d10 + 4 lightning damage, and the target is marked until the end of the basher's next turn.

↯ **Powerful Strike** (standard; recharge ⚅ ⚆) ✦ **Lightning, Weapon**
   Requires a halberd; reach 2; +21 vs. AC; 3d10 + 6 lightning damage, and the target is knocked prone.

↗ **Crossbow** (standard; at-will) ✦ **Cold, Weapon**
   Ranged 15/30; +20 vs. AC; 1d8 + 8 cold damage, and the target is slowed (save ends).

Alignment Unaligned   **Languages** Common, Draconic
Skills Athletics +16, Streetwise +14
Str 20 (+11)   **Dex** 17 (+9)   **Wis** 14 (+8)
Con 18 (+10)   **Int** 12 (+7)   **Cha** 16 (+9)

Equipment chainmail, halberd, crossbow with 20 frost bolts

SONS OF MERCY PATROL

The typical Sons of Mercy patrol consists of three bashers and two wizards who make constant sweeps of the ward they are assigned to watch over and protect. More members can be called upon in situations that warrant additional firepower, but the Sons of Mercy don't have the unlimited resources necessary to really take control of the city's law-enforcement needs.

The examples on this page are typical Sons of Mercy members that usually patrol the streets of Sigil. The group does have access to higher-level members, though such individuals aren't normally sent out on routine patrols. They are leaders and special operatives within the group, saved for especially important missions.

Sons of Mercy Wizard	Level 14 Artillery
Medium natural humanoid, human	XP 1,000

Initiative +13   **Senses** Perception +15
HP 108; **Bloodied** 54
AC 26; **Fortitude** 25, **Reflex** 27, **Will** 26
Speed 6

⊕ **Quarterstaff** (standard; at-will) ✦ **Cold, Fire, Weapon**
   +21 vs. AC; 1d10 + 6 cold and fire damage.

◎ **Magic Missile** (standard; at-will) ✦ **Force**
   Ranged 20; +19 vs. Reflex; 2d4 + 4 force damage.

↗ **Icy Rays** (standard; recharge ⚃ ⚄ ⚅) ✦ **Cold**
   Ranged 10; two ray attacks on different targets; +19 vs. Reflex; 1d10 + 4 cold damage, and the target is immobilized until the end of the wizard's next turn.

↗ **Lightning Serpent** (standard; recharge ⚄ ⚅) ✦ **Lightning, Poison**
   Ranged 10; +19 vs. Reflex; 2d12 + 4 lightning damage, and the target takes ongoing 5 poison damage and is slowed (save ends both).

❊ **Thunderlance** (standard; encounter) ✦ **Thunder**
   Close blast 5; +19 vs. Reflex; 4d6 + 4 thunder damage, and the target is pushed 4 squares.

Alignment Unaligned   **Languages** Common, Elven
Skills Arcana +16, Diplomacy +17
Str 10 (+7)   **Dex** 22 (+13)   **Wis** 17 (+10)
Con 18 (+11)   **Int** 18 (+11)   **Cha** 20 (+12)

Equipment robes, quarterstaff, wand

Fey magic holds sway in the Gardens, a patch of greenery adjoining the noble district's most prestigious manors. An outer ring of lush and well-tended botanical wonders surrounds an inner circle of wild vegetation. Doors to the Feywild abound here. The inner circle alters its nature on a quarterly cycle, giving the Cage one of its few signs of seasonal change. In a succession of three-month intervals, it manifests as a deciduous forest (spring), a tropical jungle (summer), a thorn forest (autumn), and a coniferous forest (winter.) An ancient eladrin clan, the Bloodroot, protects the Gardens from interlopers. Members of its self-styled royal court change personalities as the vegetation of the inner circle shifts.

The sole sector of The Lady's Ward where the unwashed are permitted to gather is the Temple District. Here, great temples to the gods, funded by competing families, attract swarming crowds of worshipers. The gods cannot appear here, but that doesn't stop worshipers from competing in honor of their patron deities. Followers show their wealth and piety (in that order) by financing ever more impressive improvements.

Temples to dead and forgotten gods remain extravagantly staffed and attended. Certain families prefer to dedicate themselves to obscure deities, since an extinct god never steals your thunder or makes demands upon you.

Worship can be a thirsty business, and a band of expensive taverns rings the Temple District to cater to this need. Best known of them is the Silver Tankard, a celestial mead house constructed in imitation of a similar establishment in paradisiacal Hestavar.

Its fabled terrace is reserved for great heroes of law and virtue. The Silver Tankard is famed as the only known tavern run by a literal angel, the charismatic Aratha.

THE MARKET WARD

Buyers and sellers flock to the Market Ward, famed throughout the planes for its Grand Bazaar. Among its countless stalls, customers can purchase any item imaginable—and some not. The Market Ward is one of the smallest of Sigil's neighborhoods (roughly matched in size by the Guildhall Ward). The most cosmopolitan of Sigil's wards, this is where you go to buy the common, useful, and everyday items you need for life inside the city—and for stocking up before departing for parts unknown.

The streets of the Market Ward buzz with activity at all times of the day and night. The sellers and the goods change as day becomes night, but the markets are always busy and full of customers, merchants, and curious browsers. The busiest and most amazing of these marketplaces is the Grand Bazaar.

By day, the Grand Bazaar fills an enormous square with stalls, tents, folding tables, and portable shop booths, and the smells of flowers, fruit, meat, and other exotic and familiar scents hang like a cloud over the area. The crowded aisles are surrounded by hawkers calling potential customers to taste, smell, touch, and otherwise examine and eventually buy the wares piled high in every stall.

Not everything that's for sale is either tangible or ready to pick up and cart off. Some things that can be purchased are stored outside Sigil, such as an astral skiff, a demonic war engine, or a safe house in the Elemental Chaos. Other items, such as special weapons or armor, are crafted to order and take time to produce. Make sure you can trust the seller, or that you have a way to guarantee that what you just purchased will be available for pickup at the appointed time or when you step through a portal to somewhere else in the planes.

Similar types of merchandise tend to be clustered in aisles, forming rough groupings of categories of items so that customers can compare while shopping. Foodstuffs, adventuring supplies, household goods, clothing, furnishings, magic items, alchemical goods, scrolls and books, armor, and weaponry can each be found in a separate section of the Grand Bazaar.

Be wary of pickpockets and cutpurses that freely roam the marketplaces, since not everyone who's looking to part you from your money is necessarily a merchant. Con artists, hustlers, thieves, and scoundrels of all descriptions also make a living in the Market Ward.

Gambling halls can be found within the confines of the Market Ward, and many inns and taverns feature at least a table or two devoted to games of chance. At these places, a visitor can be parted from his money, whether that visitor is shopping or not.

A laneway annex to the Grand Bazaar called the Seeker's Plaza swarms with guides and touts ready for hire. They range from splendidly garbed sages to street-bred ragamuffins. More established types are

Above is a representation of how Sigil would look if it could be viewed from outside the city. The map on the facing page is a two-dimensional depiction of the various wards and districts of the city and how the two halves of the hollow ring connect.

ADVENTURERS' INNS

The Market Ward is a favorite destination for adventurers, and many tend to stay here while they're in Sigil, patronizing the various inns catering to the trade. Inns popular with planar explorers cluster together on the edge of the Grand Bazaar, including such notable places as these.

✦ The Golden Spout is celebrated for the softness of its bunks and the purity of its ale. The halfling proprietor, Vala Pearlseeker, once served as a cleric of Melora. For reasons she refuses to discuss, she now renounces the worship of all gods and instead caters to the needs of travelers.

✦ The daringly named Hand of Vecna, known for the wildness of its clientele, can be found across from the stalls

of weapons in the marketplace. Dragonborn innkeeper Zharam Yro permits entry to anyone, no matter how infamous, but he always requires payment in advance.

✦ The fortresslike Battlement charges premium prices for its well-secured rooms and access to its impregnable vault, a pocket dimension unto itself. Owner-operator Udar Kraa, a taciturn orc, personally heads its impressively equipped private guard.

✦ The Red Tabor (named after a handheld drum) suits gold-pinching guests willing to skimp on amenities, including cleanliness. The innkeeper, a touchy eladrin named Ambriel, throws out anyone who complains about the accommodations.

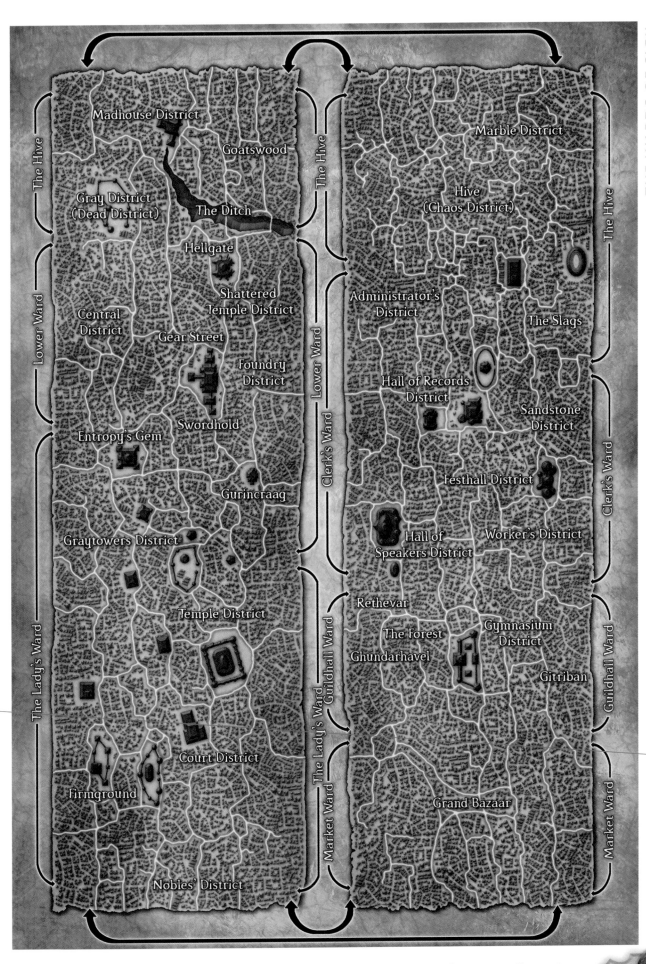

The Hive

The Hive

Madhouse District

Marble District

Goatswood

Gray District
(Dead District)

The Ditch

Hive
(Chaos District)

Hellgate

Administrator's
District

The Slags

Shattered
Temple District

Central
District

Gear Street

Hall of Records
District

Foundry
District

Sandstone
District

Swordhold

Festhall District

Entropy's Gem

Gurincraag

Worker's District

Graytowers District

Hall of
Speakers District

Rethevar

Temple District

The Forest

Gymnasium
District

Ghundarhavel

Gitriban

Court District

Firmground

Grand Bazaar

Nobles' District

The Hive · Lower Ward · The Lady's Ward

Clerk's Ward · Guildhall Ward · Market Ward

The Hive · Administrator's · Clerk's Ward · Guildhall Ward · Market Ward

6

paid by inns and vendors to steer business in their direction. Smudge-faced youngsters desperate for a patron often prove more loyal in the long run than any of the crowd in the Plaza.

Copperman Way, a wide avenue made possible when its owners bought and demolished an entire impoverished neighborhood, provides a small oasis for the recently wealthy. Its residents include the merchant lords, the self-made rich who have prospered in a single generation. Most made their fortunes primarily in Sigil, though a few adventurers who acquired treasure troves in the planar vastness can be found among their number.

The spokesperson for this rising merchant class is the dragonborn Drizu Kuri, a sweet-talking vendor of magic items. Once an explorer herself, she keeps tabs on every new adventuring crew that comes to the city, quickly making acquaintance with the most promising of them. Drizu maintains a network of informants and scholars who research possible treasure hauls. She funds adventuring parties in return for a share of the proceeds, often providing potential quests as a way of encouraging business.

THE GUILDHALL WARD

There aren't a lot of obvious differences between the Guildhall Ward and the Market Ward. If anything sets the Guildhall Ward apart, it's that it has more residential buildings than the Market Ward, and more crafters and artisans maintain workshops here and use the Market Ward as a place to sell their wares.

Since the decline of the factions, the guilds are once again rising to prominence in the City of Doors. The guilds monitor prices and wages throughout Sigil. Members meet to discuss business trends, exchange information, and promote employment. They offer training programs and apprenticeships, pool their resources to maintain work space and warehouses, and sometimes buy raw materials in bulk to share across the membership, depending on the businesses served by a particular guild.

Guild headquarters situated in this ward include the Order of Master Clerks and Scribes (which deals with copyists, record-keepers, and accountants), the Escort Guild (professional touts), the Council of Innkeepers, the Arcane Brotherhood (wizards and arcane scholars), and the Builders' Fellowship (carpenters and stonecutters). An Adventurers' Guild, established by Brin Konnet and his party of infamous cutters, is trying to find a foothold in Sigil, but so far few other adventurers and freebooters have agreed to join and pay the fees associated with membership in the organization.

THE CLERK'S WARD

By day, the scratching of pens on parchment fills the air throughout the Clerk's Ward. At night, when the sages and scribes retreat to their personal dens, studies, and libraries, the Civic Festhall comes alive with boisterous music and crowds looking for a good time.

Bureaucrats, scribes, sages, and scholars rule the Clerk's Ward by day, performing the behind-the-scenes work that keeps the city running. Here, keeping complete and accurate records is the passion and the purpose, and this activity allows the other wards to operate more or less smoothly. Laws, ownership deeds, proof of citizenry, payments and debts, arrests, and taxation—records of all these transactions and more are kept and maintained in the Clerk's Ward.

In general, the Clerk's Ward is the most tame and peaceful section of Sigil. Some might even refer to the place as dull. But it's the order and the dullness that makes the area so good for what it does. After all, nobody wants distractions that could lead to costly mistakes when it comes to the records of the City of Doors.

The Hall of Records dominates the ward, and it serves as the center of Sigil's financial world. Once controlled by the faction known as the Fated, the Hall of Records is now the domain of the Order of Master Clerks and Scribes. In the aftermath of the Faction War, taxes fell by the wayside. This situation worked out well for a while, but then the masses began to make noise about the fact that nothing was getting done throughout the city. Without any funds, many of the processes of government ground to a halt. So, the Order called for a series of new taxes, with postings that described exactly what the funds would be spent to accomplish, and taxation was returned to Sigil. Most think that the new taxes, reasonably inexpensive and with full disclosure on spending, are much better than the taxes in the days of the Fated. Still, there's always someone grumbling that taxes are too high.

The work of the Hall of Records includes registering merchants' bills of credit, setting official exchange rates for planar currency, registering property deeds and discovery claims, revising tax rolls, and recording defaults on debts. Records of the Court are also filed here, and proclamations by various higher-ups of the city are copied and posted for all to read.

Fine inns abound near the Hall of Records, since everyone knows that money attracts more money. You can also hire bodyguards, mercenaries, adventurers, wizards, and even thieves at any tavern.

The Civic Festhall, another prominent feature of the Clerk's Ward, serves as a place of pleasure, entertainment, and distractions from the usual problems of the day. Every night, the Festhall puts on some kind of show or performance, whether a concert, an opera, or a play. The Festhall also features a museum, an art gallery, a tavern, and a wine shop. Programs at the Festhall are designed to show its patrons a good and safe time, sometimes with a little culture thrown in.

The streets around the Festhall attract all kinds of artistic businesses, featuring curiosities from across the planes. These unusual artistic expressions some-times turn into fads that spread like wildfire through the city. Most burn out as quickly as they sprang up, but every once in a while a new flavor takes hold and works its way into Sigil's cultural consciousness.

The Lower Ward

Artisans and other skilled laborers dwell in the sulfurous haze of the Lower Ward, where the fires of the Elemental Chaos rise through lava-filled pools and chasms to power smithies and forges. The Great Foundry sits at the center of the ward, with warehouses, mills, forges, and small workshops sur-rounding it in ever-widening circles. The ward is named for the disproportionate number of portals to the Plane Below that can be accessed here.

People living and working in the Lower Ward tend to be stubborn, hard-working, and a bit secretive. It's a rough-and-tumble place, and those who frequent the area know that they have to be able to take care of themselves, since there's little in the way of law or protection on these hot, steamy streets.

Scalding steam and stinking smoke rise from the Great Foundry to form a layer of haze that hangs eter-nally over Sigil's rooftops. The workshops of smiths, glassblowers, and other artisans are clustered here. Vents from the Elemental Chaos lend them magical heat and other forms of energy. Tools, hinges, pots,

nails, and other goods made of iron pour forth from the workers in the Great Foundry on a regular basis. Since the fall of the factions, a group of bladelings (see *Manual of the Planes*, page 116) have taken up the responsibility of running the Great Foundry. Much of the city is just happy to have new goods to buy and sell, but some wonder about what deeper agenda the strange humanoids have put into play.

Elementals, demons, and other creatures of the Plane Below roam the streets of the Lower Ward. Some come to Sigil to conduct legitimate business (though most would balk at what the demons call legitimate), while others use the portals to handle darker, more dangerous deeds in the City of Doors. It isn't unusual to see archons working the forges and foundries, or to encounter barlguras or mariliths in the seedier taverns, or to discover a free-roaming elemental searching a dark alley or the ruins of an old workshop or warehouse.

The Shattered Temple, another prominent struc-ture in the ward, stands as a reminder of things that have gone away. Once the site of an imposing iron temple, today all that remains is a zone of destruc-tion. Not only is the god it was once dedicated to dead and forgotten, but the faction that held this place as its headquarters fled the city in the aftermath of the Faction War.

NICOLE ASHLEY CARDIFF

Parts of the Shattered Temple have been repaired so that it can be used, but only a small portion of the structure has been made whole. The rest remains a tumbled ruin. Many consider the place to be bad luck and the nexus of ill omens within the city. Most steer clear of the place and take the long way around to avoid it whenever they can.

With the demise of the factions, the ruin has become home to ghosts, specters, and other creatures from the Shadowfell. A number of doors to this plane are scattered about the ruins of the Shattered Temple, and every once in a while a brave (or foolish?) band of adventurers heads into the ruins in search of a portal. Among the things haunting the Temple is a clan of vampires known as the Stokril. The vampires are careful not to draw too much attention to themselves, but at least a few of the many who go missing in the Lower Ward can be chalked up to the nighttime activities of the Stokril clan.

The cavern complex called the Bones of Night extends beneath the streets of the Lower Ward. Located near the foul-smelling Ditch (the closest thing to a river running through the ward), the Bones of Night serves as a font of knowledge for those willing to appeal to dark powers and things that no longer walk among the living. Here, wizards, warlocks, scholars, sages, and those of darker trades come to learn from the dead.

The cavern complex is accessed through a gaping hole in a fire-gutted building. A ladder made of bone descends into the darkness below. As you step upon the ladder, the sound of what must be hundreds of chittering rats surrounds you, but it fades away as you descend into the Salon of Skulls. The grave dressings of hundreds of wealthy dead citizens decorate the entrance salon. Plush chairs, richly appointed tables, and thick tapestries fill the room, and burial shrouds hang as curtains to create private areas within. The walls of the salon are lined with shelves. Skulls of all shapes and sizes fill the shelves, including human, elf, eladrin, dwarf, tiefling, dragonborn, and more. A hole in the floor of the salon leads to the Catacombs, where even more skulls (as well as additional recently interred dead) are stored.

Lothar, the Master of Bones, consults his "library of skulls" for a fee when supplicants arrive to seek knowledge. Using the experiences and information provided by the dead, Lothar makes a fine living while also learning something of the seekers by the questions they ask. A stone golem and a pack of wererats serve Lothar and protect the Bones of Night.

THE HIVE

A labyrinth of hovels, shanties, and tents fills the Hive. This ward provides a home to the city's destitute, its criminals, and its ambitious up-and-comers. So named because its residents are packed together like hornets in a nest, the Hive comprises existence's most notorious slum. Decrepit tenements jut like broken teeth along its narrow, snaking streets. It's one of the worst places to live or visit, and life here can be deadly and extremely short. A bit of honest work can be found, but more common are the jobs best suited to the desperate and the insane. Not everyone here is bad or evil; the ward is also occupied by those who are down on their luck, who have been treated badly by life through no fault of their own, or who accidentally wandered into Sigil and can't find either a way out or a way to make a decent living. For these, the Hive is the only option.

Although legitimate businesses don't take up a lot of space in the Hive, things still get bought and sold around the ward. Thieves and robbers use fences to help them sell their stolen wares, and you can find a pawnbroker or a moneylender on almost every corner. Slave markets operate in secret in the Hive, popping up in different locations so that any authorities who care can't easily find them and shut them down. Entertainment is available in the Hive, from taverns serving cheap drinks to gladiator pits where the desperate are pitted against each other and against exotic monsters for the amusement of the crowd.

In sharp contrast to the ward's general squalor and noise, the area surrounding Sigil's vast Mortuary is pristine and silent. The faction once known as the Dustmen has formed the Mortuary Guild, and "dustman" has become a generic term for anyone who disposes of the dead. Dustman coaches gather the dead throughout the city, then cart the bodies to the Mortuary for processing. Within the Mortuary, doors to every plane are concentrated in perhaps the greatest numbers found anywhere in the city. The dustmen and their undead assistants send the city's corpses to other worlds for disposal. The doors within the Mortuary are not generally used for traveling around the planes. As often as not, these portals lead to great crematoriums, burial pits, necropolises, and other places dangerous to living creatures.

The dustmen seem to have a connection to the Shadowfell, and many revere the Raven Queen for her role in the final disposition of the dead.

Clans of goblins and orcs seem to be locked in a perpetual skirmish on the Hive's side of the Ditch. The clan leaders, Pruto of the orcs and Sojah of the goblins, wage a barely contained war for control of the area around the Ditch. Pruto uses his ferocious sons and daughters to lead strike teams against the goblins, while Sojah schemes and covertly hires mercenaries to steadily eliminate Pruto's brood.

At the very edge of the Hive, the Gatehouse overlooks the wretched ward. This arched tower with sprawling wings continues to serve as the place where the mad and the lost are administered by the people who once assembled under the faction of the

Bleak Cabal. When the factions were disbanded, the Bleakers shrugged, threw off the trappings of their organization, and simply went about the business of caring for their disturbed and insane charges. There are always long lines waiting to get into the Gatehouse. Many of Sigil's destitute have looked into the planes and found madness staring back at them, and these individuals find their way to the Gatehouse for care. Some come of their own accord, seeking help in their moments of lucidity. Others must be dragged, kicking and screaming, to the doors of the place.

The Gatehouse rings with the screams of the mad and the cries of the insane. Whether the bizarre nature of a strange corner of a distant plane has unhinged an inmate's mind, or an arcane scholar read the wrong scroll and is now haunted by apocalyptic visions of a distant realm that draws ever closer, the Gatehouse caregivers take each unfortunate's symptoms in stride and provide what help they can.

The Gatehouse Night Market appears every evening as the light of day gives way to the encroaching darkness of twilight and later. For those accustomed to shopping in the Market Ward, the Night Market is a plunge into the cold water of another world. It's dangerous, exciting, and exotic in ways that the average citizen can only dream about–and usually only wants to.

What can you find at the Night Market? All kinds of goods and services that don't appear in the stalls or on the shelves of the markets set up by day. From poisons and dangerous elixirs, to burglars and assassins for hire, if it's illicit, immoral, or profane, chances are you can find it in the Night Market.

In the Night Market, stolen goods are bought and sold. If you need someone to forge a document or perform a dangerous ritual, introductions can be made for the right price. Do you need illegal ritual components? Cursed magic items? Banned goods? Wander the Night Market, and you can probably find someone willing to sell what you want. Whether that individual actually has access to the item or service you paid for is an entirely different matter.

A blackened expanse of ruined metal buildings, many of them half-melted, is known as the Slags. This portion of the Hive houses the city's most repellent and antisocial entities. Inhabited by aberrations and their depraved mortal allies, it is treated as anathema by all but the bravest adventurers. The poorest of the poor dwell on the streets in this vicinity, their sleep bedeviled by the shrieks and rending noises accompanying the near-constant combat between its mutually hostile denizens.

It is said that the Slags are the result of a random portal that deposited warring demons into the streets of the Hive. The portal has long since closed, and most of the demons have departed for other realms, but evidence of the destructive battle remains, as well as lingering dangers that keep the Slags in ruins. Windblown balls of razorvine slice their way through the streets, adding to the dangers presented by wild worgs, dire animals, and areas of planar instability. Earthquakes rumble through the area on a regular basis, opening or closing cracks in the ground, rearranging rubble, and knocking down the few ruins still standing. The demon warriors also left behind caches of weapons and supplies, but these are trapped and extremely dangerous to anyone seeking to acquire their contents. Worse, the traps reestablish themselves through demonic magic, which makes it impossible to follow a foolish adventurer and simply take the prize after he or she has been reduced to a fine red mist.

THE KADYX

The worst threat rumored to roam the broken streets of the Slags is called the kadyx. No one has ever seen the kadyx in plain view and lived to describe it. When it is glimpsed by a fleeing observer, the observer reports seeing a glistening black scale or the flash of a scythelike claw. Legends claim that the kadyx came through the portal with the demon armies, and that it is a deadly carnivore of magical origin. It demonstrates a high degree of intelligence and even a twisted sense of humor, mostly seen in the way it leaves behind the remains of its victims. The bodies of warrior types are discovered with their armor intact, but the body inside reduced to nothing more than a fleshless pile of bones, and other victims are displayed in gruesome yet ironic ways.

The Kadyx, Demon War Drake	Level 21 Solo Skirmisher
Large elemental magical beast (demon, reptile)	XP 16,000

Initiative +21   **Senses** Perception +22; low-light vision
HP 784; **Bloodied** 392; see also *bloodied rage*
AC 35; **Fortitude** 35, **Reflex** 36, **Will** 34
Immune fear (while bloodied only)
Saving Throws +5
Speed 8
Action Points 2

⊕ **Bite** (standard; at-will)
    Reach 2; +26 vs. AC; 3d6 +8 damage; see also *bloodied rage*.
↯ **Claw Swipe** (standard; at-will) ✦ **Fire, Lightning**
    Close blast 2; +24 vs. AC; 2d6 + 7 fire and lightning damage.
↯ **Tail Sweep** (standard; at-will) ✦ **Fire, Lightning**
    Close burst 2; +24 vs. Reflex; 2d6 + 7 fire and lightning damage, and the target is pushed 1 square.
↯ **Dance of War** (standard; at-will) ✦ **Fire, Lightning**
    The war drake makes a claw swipe and a tail sweep attack, shifting 2 squares before each attack.
↯ **Demonic Glare** (minor 1/round; at-will) ✦ **Fear**
    Close blast 5; +24 vs. Will; the target is dazed and takes ongoing 10 damage (save ends both).
Bloodied Rage (while bloodied)
    The war drake gains a +4 bonus to attack rolls and makes an extra bite attack each round.

Alignment Chaotic evil   **Languages** Abyssal, Common
Str 26 (+18)   **Dex** 28 (+19)   **Wis** 24 (+17)
Con 20 (+15)   **Int** 18 (+14)   **Cha** 15 (+12)

FACES OF SIGIL

Among Sigil's diverse population, a number of individuals stand out as prominent or notable members of the constantly changing society of the Cage. Here are a few of them.

Adamok Ebon: Bladeling hunter, guide, and sometime-assassin for hire, known to be occasionally employed by Shemeshka the Marauder.

A'kin: Owner of the Friendly Fiend, an exceptional magical trinket shop. The polite and cultured raavasta (see *Manual of the Planes*, page 136) seemingly knows the secrets of everyone's business, and appears willing and eager to assist with his customers' any need. A'kin is as friendly as his shop's name, chatting easily with his customers and often gifting them with free trinkets . . . and answering all questions except those about himself.

Alluvius Ruskin: To most, the sweet old tiefling shop owner of Tivvum's Antiquities, a prominent gate-key shop in the Market Ward. But Lu—aside from being a skillful and dangerous wizard—has her own plans for the Cage: She wants to consume enough magic from the city to overthrow the Lady of Pain.

Arwyl Swan's Son: Human paladin from Cormyr on Toril and the leader of the Sons of Mercy. Arwyl finds the situation much improved from the days when the Mercykillers imposed their harsh brand of justice in the Cage. Mindful of those times, he tries to keep the Sons out of political entanglements and focused on seeing justice done.

Autochon the Bellringer: The armor-encased Master of Couriers. Very few messages passed between folks in the City of Doors don't travel by way of his messengers. His couriers are by far the finest in the city, many of them "silent couriers" enchanted to reveal their messages only to the proper recipient. Whispered rumors claim that no one has dared to attack Autochon's messengers since he made a profitable (yet horrifying) contract for their protection with the Temple of the Abyss in The Lady's Ward.

Balthazar Thames: An independent investigator and self-proclaimed "solver of mysteries, finder of lost objects, and friend for hire." Thames's services aren't cheap, but the deva is reliable and loyal to his clients.

Black Marian: Human fortuneteller at the Singing Fountain in The Lady's Ward. Marian can hear the future of any cutter who drinks from the fountain. When she's not telling fortunes, Marian sings for the crowds and sometimes passes along hidden messages within her metaphor-laden lyrics. Autochon the Bellringer considers Marian's message-songs a direct threat to his control over the city's couriers.

Caravan: One of Estavan's best human agents, Caravan has recently become disenchanted with his employer due to his exposure to Estavan's shady dealings. He remains loyal to the oni mage, though surreptitious offers of work from would-be employers have been tempting him to change jobs. Caravan's great strength, experience, and competence mark him as one of the Cage's most sought-after hirelings.

Estavan: Merchant lord of the Planar Trade Consortium, an extensive trade-and-transport company. As the Consortium's most visible agent, Estavan has status and influence in the City of Doors that far surpasses that accorded to a simple trader. Goods travel with the Consortium's caravans from one end of the planes to another and often pass through Sigil on the way. Estavan keeps constantly busy tracking those shipments, arranging new trades, hiring bashers to guard the transports, and checking up on Consortium affairs in the town of Tradegate—yet he still finds time to arrange the order of Sigil's business with Shemeshka the Marauder and Zadara, formerly his two biggest competitors and now his partners in a stranglehold over financial matters in the Cage. Estavan's (and the Consortium's) clients include such diverse cutters as A'kin, Alluvius Ruskin, and Kesto Brighteyes. Given Estavan's growing influence, more and more folks are asking: Who, exactly, owns the Planar Trade Consortium, and who truly controls all of its vast resources?

Fell, the Rogue Dabus: The source of much tension in the City of Doors. Unlike other dabus, Fell touches the ground when he walks and is quite friendly to those he meets. Whispered chant says that Fell betrayed the Lady of Pain. No one knows why the Lady suffers him to walk the streets of the Cage, and though many would love to punish Fell for his crime, they figure that his punishment—when it comes—will be by the Lady's hand.

Kesto Brighteyes: The gnome illusionist who runs the Parted Veil bookshop in the Lower Ward. The Parted Veil remains one of the best places in all of Sigil to research any topic—if Kesto doesn't have a book on something that interests a browser, he'll know someone who does.

Kylie: This young tiefling used to work for Autochon the Bellringer until she quit in the middle of a message delivery. Autochon would have sworn revenge except that his own master, Shemeshka the Marauder, ordered him to leave the girl alone. Kylie now runs her own growing gang of touts and couriers. Kylie knows a great number of the important folks in the city and has good contacts with many of them.

Lissandra the Gate-Seeker: An émigré from the world fascinated by the workings of Sigil's portals. Lissandra keeps a log of known portals and keys and constantly updates her information by questioning anyone using the portals. She's currently looking to hire adventurers to "obtain" Ramander the Wise's log-book so that information about all the portals in the city can be disseminated to the common people, where it belongs.

Lothar the Old: The Master of Bones maintains a vast skull "library" from which he has pulled enough information to rival any chant-broker. For a considerable fee, Master Lothar consults the bones for knowledge on virtually any subject. If necessary, his wererat servants search out and obtain particular skulls that hold specific secrets. Cagers say that only Master Lothar truly knows where all the bones in Sigil are buried, and they groan at the pun—but remember the truth.

Ramander the Wise: The "Master of Portals." Whenever this human mage's team of searchers locates a new portal, Ramander tries to buy the land it sits on and charges travelers a hefty fee for the use of the portal. If he cannot buy the land, he extorts the owner into paying him an even larger fee simply to retain the portal site. If thwarted, he resorts to darker tactics. Ramander skates on the thin edge of the Lady's laws against tampering with the city's portals. The city's residents mostly leave him to his business because Ramander works for Shemeshka the Marauder, and no one wants to threaten one of her favorite operatives. But even Shemeshka cannot protect the mage from the Lady's wrath, and everyone waits impatiently for the Master of Portals to find his own private portal—one that leads to an inescapable Maze.

Rhys: The lovely tiefling face of the Sigil Advisory Council. A natural advisor and balancing factor for the council, Rhys relies on her instincts for snap judgments that—to Sigil's benefit—turn out to be accurate more often than not.

Rule-of-Three: A wise man, a trickster, and a shrewd rogue. Appearing as a githzerai sage, Rule-of-Three can often be found at the Styx Oarsman tavern in the Lower Ward, dispensing advice in triplicate riddles that often contradict each other. His peculiar rules of commerce require him to ask for payment in sets of three: for example, three coins of different metals, or three pouches, each containing a separate valuable spice. In response, he gives three answers to every question. This practice relates to an abstruse philosophy claiming that everything in existence can be grouped into triads.

Some say this wrinkled, rail-thin sage is really the son of a demon prince. He laughs off such suggestions even as he reveals disturbingly reliable information about the Abyss.

Rule-of-Three collects intelligence on political events in Sigil and draws on extensive contacts in other planes as well. He occasionally acts as a mediator and broker for warring parties. As with anyone who knows more than he's telling, others project a grand agenda onto him. Surely a disheveled tavern rat couldn't really be planning to reignite the Blood War, or to unite demons and devils for an apocalyptic final battle against the gods . . . right?

Shemeshka the Marauder: The self-proclaimed "King of the Cross-Trade." Few dare to argue with the title; the raavasta's range of knowledge and secrets is matched only by her vicious temper. Shemeshka attained her position as Sigil's most prominent and powerful chant-broker through her vast network of spies. The raavasta's agents are everywhere, and their presence ensures that the power players of the city rely on Shemeshka for news on their enemies—and fear her for what she may be revealing about them. The fiend holds the strings of powerful movers such as Autochon the Bellringer and Ramander the Wise, having ensured their debt (and others') to her through convoluted plans that always end with her granting a "favor"—one that binds them to her eternally. Shemeshka has her hands in a great deal of the city's business, whether openly or through representatives. All of these factors—spies, secrets, control, and financial might—make Shemeshka the Marauder one of the most feared, hated, and powerful creatures in the City of Doors.

Tattershade, King of the Rats: This shadow fiend rules an underground wererat "kingdom" near the Ditch. The wererats mostly act as thieves in the Hive and in squalid parts of the Lower Ward, though folks in these areas have lately reported an increase in the frequency of actual attacks. The wererat twins Trick and Track act as Tattershade's lieutenants.

The Us: A pack of cranium rats whose combined intelligence reaches godlike proportions. The Us directs its mind-controlled servants to take actions the pack thinks will help it grow and gain power.

Vocar the Disobedient: A worn, wrinkled human named Vocar leads a fugitive existence in the Hive, hiding from the servants of Vecna. His empty eye socket and missing hand testify to his past as an exarch of the maimed god. Occasionally lucid but often babblingly mad, Vocar trades the awful truths he learned while serving the god of secrets for momentary shelter from his wrath. Those bargaining for his revelations are left to sort out which are reliable and which are figments of his shattered mind.

Most residents of Sigil believe that Vocar is simply mad. He wanders the Hive with a red cloth covering his missing eye while whispering a constant stream of strange utterances. People avoid him, and only the desperate or the equally insane have anything to do with him.

Zadara: Probably the wealthiest person in Sigil. Though few know the extent of her operations, Zadara has a hand in a good many enterprises. The storm giant has a talent for recognizing those whose plans have the potential to increase her fortune, and she provides them with enough gold to put their schemes into motion. She backs and funds the various works of Lissandra the Gate-Seeker, among others. Her main rivals for financial control over the Cage include her new "partners," Shemeshka the Marauder and Estavan of the Planar Trade Consortium. Rarely seen on the streets of Sigil, Zadara employs powerful door guards—two marut blademasters named Kubriel and Gog— to keep unwanted visitors out of her mansion.

6

Encounter Level 13 (4,800 XP)

SETUP

1 half-elf brigand captain (C)
1 human gladiator (G)
1 abyssal eviscerator (A)
5 dwarf thugs (D)

Use this encounter whenever the adventurers are exploring the streets of Sigil or trying to find a specific location somewhere in the Cage. This encounter works best during the twilight or night hours, when the streets are darker and more dangerous.

A gang of brigands waits to ambush anyone who enters this quiet, empty square.

As the adventurers approach the stairs down into this small square from the northern street, the first thing they notice is the pulsating glow of the strange vortex across from the fountain. None of the brigands are immediately visible.

Set this encounter in the Market Ward, the Clerk's Ward, the Lower Ward, or the Hive.

As the adventurers approach the square, read:
Stairs ahead of you lead down to an open square surrounded by dark buildings and darker alleyways. You can hear the low gurgle of water in the fountain at the center of the square, but the thing that most captures your attention is the strange, pulsating glow of swirling energy radiating in the darkness ahead.

Half-Elf Brigand Captain (C)	Level 13 Skirmisher
Medium natural humanoid	XP 800

Initiative +13   **Senses** Perception +12; low-light vision
HP 126; **Bloodied** 63
AC 27; **Fortitude** 25, **Reflex** 26, **Will** 24
Speed 6

⊕ **Longsword** (standard; at-will) ✦ **Weapon**
   +18 vs. AC; 1d8 + 8 damage, and the half-elf brigand captain shifts 1 square.

⊙ **Dagger** (standard; at-will) ✦ **Weapon**
   Ranged 5/10; +18 vs. AC; 1d4 + 6 damage.

↯/⤳ **Slash and Dash** (standard; recharge ⚄ ⚅ ⚀⚀)
   The half-elf brigand captain makes a longsword attack, shifts 2 squares, and makes a dagger attack.

↯ **Triggering Slash** (standard; recharge ⚄ ⚀⚀) ✦ **Weapon**
   +18 vs. AC; 2d8 + 8 damage, and one ally shifts 1 square and makes a melee basic attack as a free action.

Alignment Unaligned   **Languages** Common, Elven
Skills Athletics +15, Diplomacy +14, Insight +12, Stealth +16
| **Str** 18 (+10) | **Dex** 20 (+11) | **Wis** 12 (+7) |
| **Con** 14 (+8) | **Int** 10 (+6) | **Cha** 16 (+9) |
Equipment leather armor, longsword, 6 daggers

Perception Check

DC 18 *Somewhere to the west, a pack animal snorts.*
DC 25 *You notice a small figure crouching atop a nearby roof, watching intently as you approach the square.*

TACTICS

The brigands work well together and have learned how to incorporate the vortex into their tactics. The vortex is a random arcane event that appears in the same space on a couple of nights during every month. It appears according to no schedule, so the brigands check for its appearance on a regular basis and then use it to their advantage when it materializes.

The captain, the gladiator, and the demon stick to the shadows, hiding until the adventurers move into the square. The dwarf thugs maintain their position until they have clear shots; then they open fire and try to draw the adventurers deeper into the square.

The dwarf thugs stick to the roofs for as long as possible, firing down upon the adventurers with their crossbows. They attempt to concentrate fire on a single target whenever the opportunity presents itself, but they will spread their bolts around to keep the adventurers off balance.

The gladiator and the abyssal eviscerator rush from the dark alleyways once they can clearly spot a target in the square. Both attempt to force their opponents toward the vortex to take advantage of the aid it can provide them (see "Features of the Area").

The brigand captain moves through the shadows, looking to flank an opponent and strike with surprise before slipping away. He tries to work with the gladiator if possible, because he doesn't really trust the demon.

The brigands fight until only two remain, and then they attempt to escape, either through the dark alleys or into the sewer grate in the northwest alley.

Abyssal Eviscerator (A)	Level 14 Brute
Medium elemental humanoid (demon)	XP 1,000

Initiative +10   **Senses** Perception +9
HP 173; **Bloodied** 86
AC 26; **Fortitude** 28, **Reflex** 25, **Will** 24
Resist 15 variable (2/encounter)
Speed 6

⊕ **Claw** (standard; at-will)
   +17 vs. AC; 2d10 + 6 damage.

↯ **Grab** (standard; at-will)
   +15 vs. Reflex; 2d6 + 6 damage, and the target is grabbed.

↯ **Eviscerating Talons** (minor 1/round, 3/round while bloodied; at-will)
   Targets a creature grabbed by the abyssal eviscerator; no attack roll; 6 damage.

Alignment Chaotic evil   **Languages** Abyssal
Skills Athletics +18
| **Str** 23 (+13) | **Dex** 17 (+10) | **Wis** 15 (+9) |
| **Con** 23 (+13) | **Int** 7 (+5) | **Cha** 11 (+7) |

5 Dwarf Thugs (D)
Level 13 Minion

Medium natural humanoid — XP 200 each

Initiative +10   **Senses** Perception +10; low-light vision

HP 1; a missed attack never damages a minion.

AC 25; **Fortitude** 25, **Reflex** 23, **Will** 23

Saving Throws +5 against poison effects

Speed 5

⊕ **Warhammer** (standard; at-will) ✦ **Weapon**
+20 vs. AC; 9 damage.

⌁ **Crossbow** (standard; at-will) ✦ **Weapon**
Ranged 15/30; +20 vs. AC; 9 damage.

Aimed Shot
A dwarf thug gains a +2 bonus to attack rolls and deals an extra 3 damage with ranged attacks against creatures that don't have cover.

Combined Fire
Dwarf thugs can make a combined ranged attack against a single target. For each dwarf thug participating in a combined attack, increase the attack roll by 1 and the damage by 1.

Alignment Unaligned   **Languages** Common, Dwarven

Skills Athletics +17, Endurance +14, Stealth +15

Str 22 (+12)	**Dex** 18 (+10)	**Wis** 18 (+10)
Con 16 (+9)	**Int** 11 (+6)	**Cha** 10 (+6)

Equipment chainmail, warhammer, crossbow with 20 bolts

Human Gladiator (G)
Level 14 Elite Soldier

Medium natural humanoid — XP 2,000

Initiative +12   **Senses** Perception +9

Fighting Focus aura 1; each enemy that starts its turn within the aura is marked until the start of its next turn.

HP 276; **Bloodied** 138

AC 30; **Fortitude** 26, **Reflex** 26, **Will** 24

Saving Throws +2

Speed 6

Action Points 1

⊕ **Gladius** (standard; at-will) ✦ **Weapon**
+21 vs. AC; 2d8 + 6 damage.

✦ **Knock to the Dirt** (minor; encounter)
+19 vs. Fortitude; the target is knocked prone.

✦ **Well-Placed Kick** (minor; recharge ⚃ ⚅)
+19 vs. Reflex; the target is dazed and slowed (save ends both).

✦ **Sand in the Eyes** (minor; encounter)
+19 vs. Fortitude; the target is blinded (save ends).

⟵ **Gladius Display** (standard; at-will) ✦ **Weapon**
Close burst 1; targets enemies; +19 vs. Reflex; 2d8 + 6 damage.

Alignment Unaligned   **Languages** Common

Skills Acrobatics +15, Athletics +18

Str 22 (+13)	**Dex** 16 (+10)	**Wis** 14 (+9)
Con 18 (+11)	**Int** 12 (+8)	**Cha** 17 (+10)

Equipment light shield, scale armor, gladius (short sword)

DEVELOPMENT

If the brigands are defeated but any of them manage to escape, then they will gather allies and attempt to get revenge against the adventurers. This retaliatory attack might not happen for days or weeks, but the brigands will watch the adventurers from afar, get a sense of their patterns and habits, and then strike again when the characters least expect it. These brigands are part of a larger band of thieves and cutthroats operating in Sigil, and they don't take well to losing a battle.

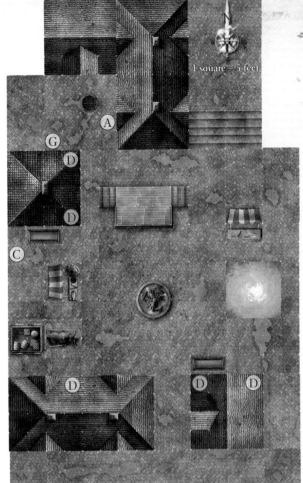

1 square = 5 feet

FEATURES OF THE AREA

Illumination: Dim light from the vortex in the square. Darkness in the alleys around the square.

Bench: Two benches in the square are difficult terrain.

Building: The buildings surrounding the square are locked tight and are 20 feet high. Anyone falling off a building roof takes 2d10 damage. A character can climb to the roof of a building with a DC 23 Athletics check.

Fountain: The fountain in the square gurgles with running water. The fountain is difficult terrain.

Oxcart: A cart laden with crates and barrels, hitched to the ox that pulls it, is parked next to a building. If the rope securing the ox is cut, the ox bolts at the first sign of trouble—pulling the cart along with it. It moves 6 squares each turn. Any creatures whose squares it moves through take 9 damage and are pushed 1 square out of the way.

Stalls: The stalls are empty. They are blocking terrain.

Vortex: The vortex is a swirling, pulsating cloud of arcane energy. Any creature that enters the vortex is attacked: +16 vs. Will; 1d6 + 6 damage, and the target is dazed (save ends). Whether the attack hits or misses, the target slides 1d6 + 1 squares west.

Encounter Level 15 (6,000 XP)

SETUP

3 cranium rat arcanist swarms (R)
2 wererat sewer guards (G)
2 elemental oozes (O)

Use this encounter whenever the adventurers are exploring the sewers of Sigil. They could be searching for a missing person or item, seeking a hidden lair or chamber beneath the streets, or looking for a portal to a specific location.

2 Wererat Sewer Guards (G)		Level 13 Skirmisher
Medium natural humanoid (shapechanger)		XP 800 each

Initiative +14   **Senses** Perception +14; low-light vision
HP 130; **Bloodied** 65
Regeneration 10 (if the wererat takes damage from a silvered weapon, its regeneration doesn't function on its next turn)
AC 27; **Fortitude** 25, **Reflex** 26, **Will** 24
Immune sewer fever (see below)
Speed 6, climb 4 (not in human form)
⊕ **Short Sword** (standard; at-will) ✦ **Poison, Weapon**
  +18 vs. AC; 1d10 + 6 damage, plus ongoing 10 poison damage (save ends).
⊕ **Bite** (standard; at-will) ✦ **Disease**
  +18 vs. AC; 1d6 + 4 damage, and the target takes ongoing 5 damage (save ends) and contracts sewer fever (see below).
⊗ **Crossbow** (standard; at-will) ✦ **Poison, Weapon**
  Ranged 15/30; +18 vs. AC; 1d8 + 6 poison damage, plus ongoing 5 poison damage (save ends).
✦ **Dance of Poison** (standard; encounter; recharges when first bloodied)
  The wererat makes two short sword attacks against one target, shifts up to 3 squares, and makes two short sword attacks against a different target.
Change Shape (minor; at-will) ✦ **Polymorph**
  A wererat can alter its physical form to appear as a dire rat or a unique human (see "Change Shape," *Monster Manual 2*, page 216). It loses its bite attack in human form.
Combat Advantage
  A wererat deals 2d6 extra damage on melee attacks against any target that grants it combat advantage.
Alignment Evil   **Languages** Common
Skills Bluff +15, Stealth +17, Streetwise +15, Thievery +17
Str 20 (+11)   **Dex** 22 (+12)   **Wis** 16 (+9)
Con 18 (+10)   **Int** 15 (+8)   **Cha** 18 (+10)
Equipment cloak, short sword

The section of the sewer the PCs travel to is controlled by a pack of cranium rats. When the adventurers arrive, only three swarms are currently

in residence. The rest of the pack is out and about on various errands and other business. That doesn't mean that the rats are defenseless. In addition to their own abilities, two wererat sewer guards serve as protection for the nest, and the cranium rats have also used their psychic powers to coax a pair of elemental oozes to roam the nearby waterways as further discouragement for intruders.

Set this encounter in sewers beneath the Market Ward, the Clerk's Ward, or The Lady's Ward.

The adventurers begin this encounter in the storage room, the southernmost room on the map.

As the adventurers enter the storeroom, read:
Stairs lead down into a dusty room full of crates and barrels. A large crack in the north wall opens into darkness. A foul smell emanates from the opening.

Perception Check
DC 18 *You notice a faint flicker of light deep within the darkness beyond the opening in the north wall.*
DC 25 *You hear the low gurgle of water somewhere in the darkness beyond the opening in the north wall.*

TACTICS

The wererat sewer guards work together to take down the most-powerful-looking opponent, setting up flanking situations to gain combat advantage. They have no problem hanging back and firing their crossbows, or falling back to use ranged attacks when they start taking a lot of damage. They use *dance of poison* at the first opportunity, and again after they become bloodied. They don't exactly work with the elemental oozes, but they do try to lure opponents toward the creatures so that the oozes get into the battle.

The elemental oozes attack any creature that is unfriendly to the cranium rats. Whenever an enemy gets within 10 squares of an ooze, the ooze notices it with its tremorsense and moves to attack on its turn. An ooze can flow freely into and out of the sewer water as part of a move action. Remember to use an ooze's *elemental backlash* when it takes damage, and its *elemental burst* when it is bloodied or killed. As long as at least one cranium rat swarm remains within 10 squares of an ooze, the ooze will keep fighting until it is destroyed. Without the influence of the swarm, an ooze attempts to flee the battle once it is bloodied.

Sewer Fever	Level 13 Disease	Endurance improve DC 23, maintain DC 18, worsen DC 17 or lower

The target is cured.	◄	Initial Effect: The target loses a healing surge.	◄►	The target takes a -2 penalty to AC, Fortitude, and Reflex.	►	Final State: The target takes a -2 penalty to AC, Fortitude, and Reflex. The target loses all healing surges and cannot regain hit points.

The cranium rat arcanist swarms have a group mind. Each swarm makes all of the other swarms within 10 squares of it smarter and more powerful. They leave the heavy lifting of battle to the wererats and oozes, preferring to hang back and use their ranged powers from a distance. When only one swarm remains, it attempts to escape deeper into the sewer.

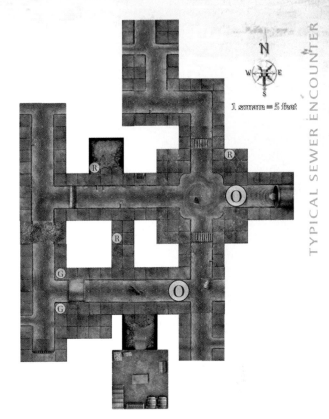

1 square = 5 feet

2 Elemental Oozes (O)		Level 12 Brute
Large elemental beast (blind, ooze)		XP 700 each

Initiative +9 **Senses** Perception +9; blindsight 10, tremorsense 10
HP 150; **Bloodied** 75
AC 24; **Fortitude** 26, **Reflex** 22, **Will** 22
Immune gaze; **Resist** 10 acid, cold, fire, lightning
Speed 4; see also *flowing form*

⊕ **Slam** (standard; at-will) ✦ **Cold, Fire, Lightning**
Reach 2; +15 vs. AC; 3d6 + 5 damage, and ongoing 10 cold, fire, and lightning damage (save ends).

Flowing Form (move; at-will)
The elemental ooze shifts 4 squares.

Elemental Backlash (immediate reaction, when the elemental ooze takes damage; at-will) ✦ **Cold, Fire, Lightning**
The elemental ooze releases elemental energy that deals 5 cold, fire, and lightning damage to all enemies adjacent to it.

↞ **Elemental Burst** (when first bloodied, and again when reduced to 0 hit points) ✦ **Cold, Fire, Lightning**
The elemental ooze releases a burst of elemental energy; close burst 2; +15 vs. Reflex; 3d10 + 6 cold, fire, and lightning damage, and the target is pushed 2 squares.

Alignment Unaligned	**Languages** —	
Str 24 (+13)	**Dex** 16 (+9)	**Wis** 16 (+9)
Con 20 (+11)	**Int** 4 (+3)	**Cha** 4 (+3)

3 Cranium Rat Arcanist Swarms (R)		Level 14 Controller
Medium natural beast (swarm)		XP 1,000 each

Initiative +16 **Senses** Perception +22; low-light vision
Mind Whispers aura 1; each enemy that begins its turn in the aura takes 5 psychic damage and a -2 penalty to attack rolls until the end of its next turn.
HP 141; **Bloodied** 70
AC 28; **Fortitude** 27; **Reflex** 25; **Will** 26
Resist half damage from melee and ranged attacks; **Vulnerable** 10 against close and area attacks
Speed 6, climb 3

⊕ **Swarm of Teeth** (standard; at-will)
+19 vs. AC; 1d8 + 5 damage, and ongoing 5 damage (save ends).

⊙ **Psychic Bolt** (standard; at-will) ✦ **Psychic**
Ranged 20; +18 vs. Will; 1d10 + 6 psychic damage, and the target is dazed (save ends).

✴ **Psychic Barrage** (standard; recharge ⚄ ⚅) ✦ **Psychic**
Area burst 1 within 10; +16 vs. Will; 2d10 + 6 psychic damage, and the target is stunned (save ends).

Group Mind
For each cranium rat swarm within 10 squares of any other one, increase attack and damage rolls by 1, and increase the Intelligence score of each swarm by 2.

Alignment Evil	**Languages** telepathy 10	
Str 18 (+11)	**Dex** 16 (+10)	**Wis** 17 (+10)
Con 21 (+12)	**Int** 10 (+7)	**Cha** 18 (+11)

DEVELOPMENT

If the adventurers defeat the cranium rats, they must eventually deal with the ramifications. The rest of the pack seeks revenge against them, and the cranium rats are experts at manipulating others by mental suggestions. The adventurers don't really want these creatures as long-term enemies, and they should look for ways to appease them and make amends.

FEATURES OF THE AREA

Illumination: Dim light from the sputtering torches hung sparingly throughout the area.

Bridges: Rickety planks cross the sewer channels in various places.

Lair: The alcove where one of the cranium rat swarms begins the encounter is the lair of the cranium rat pack. It contains two level 15 treasure parcels (see *Dungeon Master's Guide*, page 128).

Ladder: A ladder leads up to the streets above.

Rubble: Piles of rubble and trash are difficult terrain.

Sewer Water: The sludgy water flowing through the channels is 5 feet deep and is difficult terrain. It cost 2 squares of movement to move from the water onto the sewer platforms. Any creature that enters the water or starts its turn there takes 5 acid damage.

To some, the planes are inaccessible and unknown. These people are locked to a particular reality, unable to walk from world to world for reasons that usually involve ignorance or fear. There are those, however, who understand the ways of planes and portals, and for those select few (relatively speaking) the planes provide a wide and varied vista for trade, exploration, research, and adventure.

Whether they know the secrets of planar travel or just have a strong sword and some spells to sell, adventurers can make gold and find transport at any of the gate-towns scattered across existence. Bodyguards, couriers, and caravan guards hired to protect one of the constant trade caravans moving between Sigil and the planes are always in high demand.

A gate-town is any settlement, in the natural world or on the planes, built around a known portal to someplace else. Such portals are not the usual permanent teleportation circles that you can find in most civilized towns and cities, but actual gateways that open onto another plane of existence. The area around a gate-town takes on aspects of the plane on the other end of its portal, giving visitors an idea of what they can expect when they cross over to the other side. The planar energy that leaks through the portal causes this; the effect it has on the area depends on where the portal leads.

The other aspect of a gate-town's portal is convenience and reliability. It is always accessible (though it might have a cycle of times when it is open and times when it is closed), and you don't usually need a gate key to cause it to function. Gate-town portals to Sigil abide by all the known restrictions, however, including the fact that gods and other extremely powerful beings cannot use them.

These conduits between realities are always guarded and maintained by their communities, since they represent varying degrees of wealth and power to those that control them.

TRADEGATE

The bustling town of Tradegate, situated at the crossroads in the shadow of the Rumbling Hills, provides the natural world with a known and accessible gate to Sigil. Merchants from across the land come to sell local goods and buy exotic goods from across the planes that move through Sigil to the market in Tradegate. Sigil's Planar Trade Consortium runs Tradegate, using it as one of its key distribution centers along the caravan routes it maintains. Master Trader Duncam keeps a tight rein on access to the gate, however. You can't just come to Tradegate, stroll up to the ornate stone gate that stands like an arch in the middle of the town square, and step through it into Sigil. A special gate key is required to operate this portal, and Duncam reveals the key only to those he deems worthy of entering the City of Doors—and who can afford the 1,000 gp fee.

SLUMBER

The sleepy town of Slumber, resting in a quiet corner of the Shadowfell, features a misshapen stone gate to the Plane of Dreams. The land around Slumber fluctuates between giving off visions of contented dreams and terrible nightmares as the gate's cycle unfolds. It opens twice each month, and the land reflects which part of Dream the gate leads to when it activates. For three days in the middle of the month, the gate opens upon Dream's more fanciful and comforting regions, and the land around Slumber grows lighter and more vibrant in response. For three days at the end of the month, when the gate opens into the regions of nightmare, Slumber and the surrounding countryside take on a darker, more dangerous tone. Monsters roam the shadows, mostly out of sight. The mood of the town takes on a lunatic bent, and the usually sedate population allows its darker instincts to rise to the surface.

Excelsior

Among the shining ports of the Astral Sea, few are brighter than the gate-town of Excelsior. The streets here are paved with gold-flecked brick, and floating castles of paladin lords protect the port from pirates and other dangers. The glowing gate, like a pool of golden light radiating deep within the town's guarded perimeter, leads to the holy mountains of Celestia.

Bedlam

There's a crazy little burg in the Feywild known as Bedlam. Here, the streets seem a bit off kilter, and no building stands straight and tall. All the lines are askew, with no right angles anywhere, and the sounds of either uncontrollable crying or insane laughter echo in the shadowed alleys and behind covered windows throughout the town. The problem here is that the place is built around a gate to Pandemonium, the forgotten domain of madness and exile. Luckily for the people living in or visiting Bedlam, the gate only opens once every month, when the dark moon rises unseen above the land. The gate is said to open upon Madhouse, the citadel of the Bleak Cabal. While this might or might not be true, it is known that some former members of Sigil's disbanded faction have taken up residence in Bedlam to help keep in check those affected by Pandemonium's influence.

Plague-Mort

The ramshackle town of Plague-Mort occupies an unusually dark corner of the Shadowfell, where its gate that resembles a black pool of oil waits to transport travelers to the Abyss. Thanks to the influence of the Abyss that leaks through the gate, Plague-Mort follows the law of "might makes right." The strongest rule in Plague-Mort, and the current ruler goes by the name of Blackhelm. His enforcers, the Plague Hounds, are always looking for new recruits—and forced conscription is the normal method of hire for the Plague Hounds.

Moonstair

The town of Moonstair, built amid the ruins of the ancient troll kingdom of Vardar, serves as a trade outpost to the southwest of Nentir Vale. The town's most renowned feature is the Moon Door, a gate to the Feywild that opens whenever the moon is full and the sky is clear. The Moon Door sits atop an island of jagged stone that juts from the river beyond the westernmost point of the town. A wide ring of moss and flowering plants marks the spot where the gate appears when it opens. To reach the Moon Door, travelers traverse a series of smaller, rocky islets—the "moon stair" for which the town is named. The gate serves as a regular pathway between this part of the natural world and the eladrin castle-city of Celduilon in the Feywild.

Farren

Strange energy seems to flow through the town of Farren, nestled among the Mountains of Chaos in the natural world. Not a normal gate-town, Farren appears to have a one-way connection from someplace distant and outside the bounds of the multiverse. This connection flows from that strange and mysterious place to Farren—never the other way. The gate here, if that's what it can truly be called, appears as a cloud of slimy darkness trapped within a box canyon just beyond the limits of the town. The place feels wrong, and the inhabitants range from secretive and distant to noticeably insane. Mystics and prophets come to Farren to have visions or learn secrets, but the visions usually lead to madness, and the secrets provide nothing but death and destruction to those that hear them. Two or three times every year, the mountains rumble and the cloud comes alive with dancing energy. Abominations and aberrations of all kinds have appeared at these times, leading some to speculate that the gate—if gate it truly is—connects to the Far Realm.

Gloomport

The gate-town of Gloomport, located on the shore of the Glistening Sea in the natural world, provides one of the most stable and safest paths into the Shadowfell. Gloomport itself is a cold and dismal place, where a biting rain whips in from the sea on most days, and a dark, storm-filled cloud hangs over it even when the wind is calm and the rain isn't falling. To reach the Shadowfell, travelers board a ship and sail to the west—into the darker, stormier part of the sea. Eventually, the ship crosses over and the city of Gloomwrought appears on the horizon. Rising from the barren shore, the City of Midnight is a common destination for merchants and travelers of the planes.

Gleaming

The town of Gleaming, east of Nentir Vale, has a secret. The goods that brings merchants and travelers from far and wide come through a hidden gate that connects the town with the Astral Sea. The mayor of Gleaming, Berenda Farwalker, a halfling of great wisdom and charisma, guards the secret of the gate—as have her father, grandmother, and great-grandfather before her. The place radiates with the presence of the Astral Sea, and divine power flows through the region around the town. The gate leads to a neutral trading port in the Astral Sea, and through the gate the leaders of both sides conduct a brisk and secret exchange of goods from their respective worlds. For the right price, and if the need is great enough, Berenda will allow travelers to access the gate. She must know their business in the Astral Sea, however, and she must trust them implicitly before she grants them use of the gate.

A CONSPIRACY OF DOORS

A Conspiracy of Doors is a DUNGEONS & DRAGONS adventure for five player characters of 11th level. It can serve as an introduction to Sigil, the City of Doors, as well as a group of adventurers' first taste of action at the paragon tier.

INTRODUCTION

The Festival of Doors, one of the most beloved and profitable holidays celebrated in Sigil, fast approaches. Estavan, the Planar Trade Consortium's representative in Sigil, is worried about some recent events. Individually, none of these events seems to be a cause for concern. However, Estavan has spotted a pattern that has put him on edge. He believes that a secret attack has been launched against the Consortium, an attack associated with the upcoming holiday. Now Estavan needs to find adventurers to uncover the truth behind these attacks and reveal the conspiracy for all to see.

BACKGROUND

Once a deeply spiritual event, the Festival of Doors has become little more than an excuse to have a raucous celebration. No one puts more into the Festival of Doors than Sigil's elite upper class, and no one profits more from the needs of expensive celebrations than the merchants. The Planar Trade Consortium, in particular, has a monopoly on providing the most sought-after goods for the festival feasts, including the rare cavefire wine that has become essential to the celebration.

In the weeks leading up to the Festival of Doors, a number of seemingly unrelated setbacks have troubled the Consortium. Agents have disappeared. Trade caravans have been attacked. Cargo has been hijacked. Warehouses have been robbed and even set afire. Estavan, merchant lord of the Consortium, usually chalks up such happenings as part of the cost of doing business. However, as the Festival of Doors approaches, he has been disturbed by a gnawing intuition that he can't silence: The Consortium is under attack.

The three most recent disasters to befall the Consortium have resulted in a break in certain key supply lines that provide needed foodstuffs to Sigil. The City of Doors doesn't produce any of its own food; all the food necessary to feed the city must come from someplace else. And the only way the food makes the trip is in caravans such as those used by the Consortium, caravans that travel from distant planes through portals and gate-towns to eventually reach Sigil. Without a constant influx of supplies, Sigil would quickly run out of food and drink. Once this occurs, riots and looting would break out, the Lady of Pain would take notice, and the most apparent perpetrators of the trouble would be exiled to the Mazes—or worse.

Such a fate could be in Estavan's future unless he takes action now. The oni mage knows that punishment directed at him and the Consortium won't actually solve the coming crisis. The riots will continue, food and drink will grow more scarce, and people will begin either dying or fleeing the city in droves.

Estavan has come to the conclusion that these attacks are coordinated and part of a larger plan to disrupt and eventually destroy the City of Doors. If that plan is allowed to reach fruition, Estavan believes that all of existence will be in danger. The oni mage follows the school of thought that places Sigil as the linchpin of all existence. Without the linchpin, the theory goes, the planes themselves will spread farther apart. If the chaos that follows is slow and steady, the multiverse will slowly fade away. If it's more violent, the planes will fly apart in an immediate explosion of worlds-shattering destruction. Or so Estavan believes.

ADVENTURE SYNOPSIS

The adventure begins in a town or city in the natural world, wherever the adventurers kick back to relax between missions. An agent of the Planar Trade Consortium seeks them out and invites them to meet with her "high-up," the oni mage Estavan. In a secret meeting, far from the prying eyes of his unknown enemies, Estavan strikes a deal with the adventurers to reopen the supply lines and discover who is behind the attacks on the Consortium.

In the opening scene, Estavan reveals the truth about the multiverse to the adventures, confirming rumors they might have heard about Sigil or perhaps being the first to introduce them to the larger existence beyond the natural world. He wants them to acquire a gate key from a trusted source, an ancient wizard and reagent seller who goes by the name of Fesdin Crale. The gate key is supposed to take the adventurers to Sigil so that they can begin their investigation. However, Fesdin—who is actually a shape-changing lamia named Arthani—provides a gate key that instead transports the Consortium agents into a trap.

After defeating the threat, the adventurers track the lamia to the gate-town of Tradegate. They arrive in time to try to prevent Arthani from destroying the town's gate.

The next clue leads the adventurers to the Night Market in the City of Doors. Questioning the locals leads to an attack by the lamia's associates, which sends the characters to the source of the missing cavefire wine. The final encounter, in a warehouse in Sigil, pits the adventurers against the demon-summoner who is behind the current conspiracy.

Starting the Adventure

At the first break between missions in your ongoing campaign, when the adventurers are back in a town or city to buy supplies and recuperate, they are approached by a female tiefling. Read:

A young female tiefling dressed in traveling leathers and still covered in the dust of the road strides confidently toward you, a friendly smile playing across her lips. "Are you the cutters that put Kalaran in the dead book?" (Rephrase this question to reflect whatever key event has just happened in your campaign.)

Her manner of speaking should make it evident to the characters that this tiefling isn't a local. If they acknowledge that they are the people she's looking for, she plops down in the nearest chair and introduces herself.

"I'm Nera, and I represent the Planar Trade Consortium. My high-up, the exquisite Estavan, wants to offer you a job. The dark of it is, he can't just stroll into this fine establishment, since the locals aren't as tolerant as those of us from the City of Doors. He's waiting for you in the upstairs room at the end of the hall. Don't worry. For an oni mage, Estavan's pretty civilized. And he always offers the best jink. You know, coin? Gold? Platinum? Jink! Tell him Nera sent you."

She drops a small sack containing 10 pp (1,000 gp). "There's more where that came from, if Estavan thinks you can handle the job," Nera says as she rises and offers her farewell.

Meeting Estavan

If the adventurers take the payment and follow Nera's directions, they find a suite on the upper floor of the best inn in town. They can knock or simply walk in, and when they do, they get their first view of Estavan. Read:

The spacious room features a small table and enough chairs for all of you. Seated behind the table, sipping from a fragile cup, is a large ogrelike creature with powdered, pale blue skin, dressed in an immaculate red kimono. "Welcome, friends," he says in a booming voice. "I am Estavan, and I assure you that I mean you no harm. In fact, I wish to hire you for a very important job. Would any of you care for some Arborean spice tea?"

For an oni mage, Estavan is exceedingly polite and friendly. He dresses well, and great care seems to have gone into every aspect of his appearance. A flashy necklace hangs in his open collar for all to see, his nails are filed neatly, and his horns are polished to a shine. Despite this outward appearance of civility and manners, Estavan can be as manipulative

and merciless as he is ostentatious. For the purposes of this meeting, Estavan stays patient and interested in the adventurers for as long as it takes to win them over. His patience isn't unlimited, however, and he will defend himself if the adventurers attack.

Hopefully, it won't come to that, and Estavan does everything he can to make the adventurers feel comfortable with the arrangement. Read:

"The chant—excuse me—the situation is that the organization that I represent buys and sells goods throughout the planes of existence. You do realize that there is more to existence than just this tiny ball of dirt and water, don't you? The Planar Trade Consortium has interests in it all."

As the conversation unfolds, Estavan provides the following information:

Sigil: Sigil, the City of Doors, stands at the center of the multiverse, and all planes and worlds connect to it through its many portals.

Planar Trade Consortium: This conglomerate of trading concerns operates trading posts, markets, and caravans throughout the known planes of existence. Two of its most important centers of operation are the town of Tradegate in the natural world and Sigil. Recently, the Consortium has been the target of raids and other attacks that Estavan believes are the precursor to a more significant—and dangerous—event. Agents have disappeared, caravans have been hijacked, and supply lines have been cut off. These are harbingers, the oni mage believes, of a much larger plan to isolate Sigil. "If such a thing were to happen," Estavan insists, "the multiverse will shudder and perhaps begin to unravel."

Festival of Doors: The upcoming holiday known as the Festival of Doors, celebrated every year in Sigil, seems to be the focus of these attacks. Goods associated with the celebration are among those affected by the supply disruptions. Ice apples from the Elemental Chaos, glitterbeasts from the Feywild, and cavefire wine from the Shadowfell, among other traditional festival fare, have stopped flowing into the City of Doors. "The key to discovering who is behind this is to track the wine to its source," Estavan declares.

What do you want us to do? Investigate the attacks, follow the supply lines back to their sources, discover who is behind these attacks, and put a stop to it before the Festival of Doors starts in three days.

Why us? Estavan's usual agents are known to be operatives of the Consortium, and thus the oni mage believes that they are all being watched. "I need someone without a clear connection to my organization," he explains, "but someone who is also capable of getting this job done."

What's in it for us? "You have received an opening stipend. Complete the task, and you will also get this." Estavan places an astral diamond (worth 10,000 gp) on the table.

ENCOUNTER D1: DOORWAY TO DANGER

Encounter Level 11 (3,200 XP)

SETUP

1 battle wight commander (C)
2 battle wights (B)
1 wight life-eater (W)
1 ghost spider (S)

After Estavan gets the adventurers to agree to aid the Planar Trade Consortium, he sends them to find a trusted associate named Fesdin Crale. Read:

"Crale is a wizard and sage, a seller of things arcane and mysterious," Estavan explains. "Tell him that I have sent you, and he should be willing to sell you a gate key and the location of a portal to Sigil. That's where you should start your investigation, in the City of Doors. Good luck, my agents. Know that the fate of the multiverse might well rest in your hands."

If the PCs ask, Estavan says he doesn't have a gate key to give them and would prefer they seek out the appropriate local resources to get what they need. He directs the adventurers to an out-of-the-way shop called Crale's Arcane Wonders, in a run-down part of town. Here, the adventurers meet up with the wizard and sage known as Fesdin Crale. Read:

The dark little shop is crammed full of jars and bottles, scrolls and books, and all manner of strange and exotic items. Most of it appears to be junk, but when it comes to arcane matters, who can say for sure? The proprietor you see before you is an older human male who identifies himself as Fesdin Crale. "Why do you come to this place?" he asks, examining each of you in turn with his steely gaze.

Crale warms up to the adventurers after they mention that Estavan has sent them. He listens to their request, then nods and begins to rummage around the crowded shop. After a few moments, the wizard produces a small, rectangular plank made of smooth stone, about the size of a domino. Carved into one side of the plank is the stylized image of an arched doorway. He also produces a map showing the location of a narrow alley on the other side of town.

"A gate key to Sigil, as well as the location of the portal this gate key activates," Crale says. "I can let you have both for the mere cost of 100 gold."

If the adventurers pay, Crale thanks them and asks them to give his regards to Estavan. If they try to haggle, one of the adventurers can make a Diplomacy check to reduce the price. A result of 21 or higher gets Crale to accept 75 gp instead, "as a favor to my old friend Estavan."

THROUGH THE PORTAL

When the adventurers step through the portal while carrying the gate key, they are transported to a new location. However, it isn't their expected destination.

As the adventurers step into the portal, read:
You find yourself in a dark, close space. The smell of dirt, stone, and stale air surround you, and silence fills the dark.

The gate key has sent the adventurers to a secret crypt somewhere in a distant corner of the natural world. The key can return the adventurers, but it won't function again until an hour passes. (A PC can determine this information with a DC 16 Arcana check.)

Fesdin Crale (actually the lamia Arthani) has sent the adventurers into this trap.

As soon as the adventurers can see, read:
You find yourselves in a sealed crypt. Pillars hold up the massive stone ceiling, and thick webs fill parts of the chamber. Four coffins stand against the wall on the far side of the room.

TACTICS

The wights work together to destroy the living beings that have entered their tomb. The battle wights move to engage the adventurers in the center of the chamber, while the wight life-eater waits until they have moved past its hiding place so that it can spring out from behind them. It delays, if necessary, so that it can act later in the round.

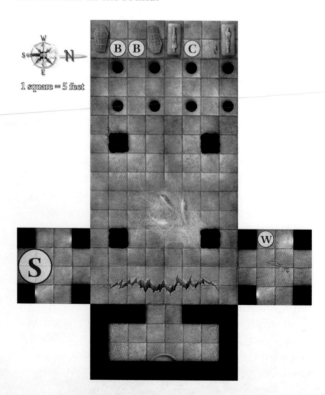

1 square = 5 feet

Ghost Spider (S) — Level 11 Elite Lurker

Ghost Spider (S)	Level 11 Elite Lurker
Large shadow beast (spider)	XP 1,200

Initiative +9   **Senses** Perception +7; tremorsense 10
HP 129; **Bloodied** 64
AC 25; **Fortitude** 25, **Reflex** 24, **Will** 22
Resist insubstantial
Saving Throws +2
Speed 6, climb 6 (spider climb), phasing
Action Points 1

⊕ **Ghost Claw** (standard; at-will) ✦ Necrotic
+14 vs. Reflex; 1d8 + 5 damage, and the target takes ongoing 5 necrotic damage and is weakened (save ends both).

⨂ **Phasing Attack** (standard; at-will)
The ghost spider makes two ghost claw attacks. The ghost spider can shift 6 squares between the attacks.

⨂ **Phasing Web** (move; recharge ⚅ ⚄ ⚃)
The ghost spider shifts 6 squares, phasing through enemies. It attacks each enemy it phases through; +14 vs. Fortitude; target is immobilized (save ends).

Alignment Unaligned   **Languages** —
Skills Athletics +15, Stealth +14

Str 20 (+10)	**Dex** 18 (+9)	**Wis** 15 (+7)
Con 20 (+10)	**Int** 1 (+0)	**Cha** 10 (+5)

Wight Life-Eater (W) — Level 10 Skirmisher

Wight Life-Eater (W)	Level 10 Skirmisher
Medium natural humanoid (undead)	XP 500

Initiative +9   **Senses** Perception +3; darkvision
HP 104; **Bloodied** 52
AC 24; **Fortitude** 22, **Reflex** 21, **Will** 21
Immune disease, poison; **Resist** 10 necrotic; **Vulnerable** 5 radiant
Speed 7

⊕ **Claw** (standard; at-will) ✦ Necrotic
+15 vs. AC; 2d6 + 5 necrotic damage, the target loses a healing surge, and the wight shifts 3 squares.

Alignment Evil   **Languages** Common
Skills Stealth +13

Str 18 (+9)	**Dex** 16 (+8)	**Wis** 6 (+3)
Con 16 (+8)	**Int** 10 (+5)	**Cha** 17 (+8)

Battle Wight Commander (C) — Level 12 Soldier (Leader)

Battle Wight Commander (C)	Level 12 Soldier (Leader)
Medium natural humanoid (undead)	XP 700

Initiative +12   **Senses** Perception +12; darkvision
HP 106; **Bloodied** 53
AC 28; **Fortitude** 26, **Reflex** 23, **Will** 26
Immune disease, poison; **Resist** 10 necrotic; **Vulnerable** 5 radiant
Speed 5

⊕ **Souldraining Longsword** (standard; at-will) ✦ Necrotic, Weapon
+18 vs. AC; 1d8 + 7 necrotic damage, and the target loses a healing surge and is immobilized and weakened (save ends both).

↗ **Soul Harvest** (standard; recharge ⚅ ⚄ ⚃) ✦ Healing, Necrotic
Ranged 5; affects an immobilized target only; +15 vs. Fortitude; 2d8 + 7 necrotic damage, and the battle wight commander and all undead allies within 2 squares of it regain 10 hit points.

Alignment Evil   **Languages** Common
Skills Intimidate +18

Str 24 (+13)	**Dex** 19 (+10)	**Wis** 14 (+7)
Con 22 (+12)	**Int** 15 (+7)	**Cha** 24 (+13)

Equipment plate armor, heavy shield, longsword

2 Battle Wights (B) — Level 9 Soldier

2 Battle Wights (B)	Level 9 Soldier
Medium natural humanoid (undead)	XP 400 each

Initiative +7   **Senses** Perception +3; darkvision
HP 98; **Bloodied** 49
AC 25; **Fortitude** 22, **Reflex** 18, **Will** 22
Immune disease, poison; **Resist** 10 necrotic; **Vulnerable** 5 radiant
Speed 5

⊕ **Souldraining Longsword** (standard; at-will) ✦ Necrotic, Weapon
+15 vs. AC; 1d8 + 5 necrotic damage, and the target loses a healing surge and is immobilized (save ends).

↗ **Soul Reaping** (standard; recharge ⚅ ⚃) ✦ Healing, Necrotic
Ranged 5; affects an immobilized target only; +12 vs. Fortitude; 2d8 + 5 necrotic damage, and the battle wight regains 10 hit points.

Alignment Evil   **Languages** Common
Skills Intimidate +14

Str 20 (+9)	**Dex** 13 (+5)	**Wis** 9 (+3)
Con 18 (+8)	**Int** 12 (+5)	**Cha** 20 (+9)

Equipment plate armor, heavy shield, longsword

The ghost spider phases into and out of the tomb to hunt, using part of the area as a lair. When living creatures enter the tomb, it attacks and inadvertently helps the wights. Although the wights seek to end humanoid life, they have no interest in the fluids and flesh that the ghost spider feasts upon.

If the ghost spider loses more than three-quarters of its hit points, it seeks to phase out of the tomb and escape.

The wights fight until they are destroyed.

DEVELOPMENT

The body in the northern side chamber is the real Fesdin Crale. He has obviously been drained of life by the wights. A character who makes a DC 16 Perception check finds a copper coin in his pocket. One side shows the icon of the Planar Trade Consortium (a long caravan moving through a portal); the other is engraved with the words "Crale's Arcane Wonders."

A pouch on Crale's belt holds a small journal in which the sage has kept a record of customers and transactions as well as other notes. The most recent entries seem to be tracking a series of disturbances related to portals that lead to Sigil. The final entry reads as follows:

"A creature called Arthani seems to be the common factor, though she never appears in the same shape twice. Estavan must be warned that Tradegate is the next target!"

FEATURES OF THE AREA

Illumination: Darkness.

Body: The dead body of the real Fesdin Crale. See "Development" for details.

Cracked Ground: Any creature that enters a square of cracked ground stops moving and falls prone.

Fountain: The fountain is actually a portal. A gate key is required to operate the portal.

Webs: Any creature that enters a square of webs stops moving and is immobilized (save ends).

Coffins: The coffins are used by the wights. The battle wight commander's coffin contains a level 12 magic item.

Encounter Level 13 (4,300 XP)

SETUP

1 lamia devourer (L)
2 mezzodemons (M)
6 cyclops guards (C)

If the adventurers take the coin they found on the dead merchant back to the shop, they find that the pretender who sent them into the trap has vacated the premises. In the back room, a door opens onto a small, empty space. Anyone carrying the coin who opens the door activates the portal to Tradegate.

If the characters don't have the wizard's coin or don't open the door in the back room, some other method of getting to Tradegate might be required. Estavan has already left the town, but Nera is still hanging out at the tavern, enjoying a short break from her regular duties for the Consortium. She can inform the adventurers about the portal to Tradegate in Crale's shop and give them a key to use it. If the PCs ask about a way to get to Sigil, she says, "There's a portal to Sigil in Tradegate, of course."

ARRIVING IN TRADEGATE

When the adventurers move through the portal into Tradegate, they discover that something isn't quite right in the usually bustling town. Read:

You step through the broken window of a deserted building into a quiet alley. The alley opens onto a wide street that leads south toward the town square. You notice that not only is the alley unusually quiet, but the entire town seems to be deserted. The only activity you immediately notice is in the town square, where glowing lights and the crackle of strange energy indicate that something is happening near the arched gate in the center of the square.

Perception Check
DC 18 *You spot large humanoids moving around the arched gate, each silhouetted against the glowing lights.*
DC 23 *People throughout the town have slumped over where they were standing or in the middle of some activity, and now they lay here and there, apparently fast asleep.*

Lamia Devourer (L)	Level 13 Elite Controller
Medium fey magical beast (shapechanger)	XP 1,600

Initiative +8   **Senses** Perception +13
Swarm's Embrace aura 1; an enemy that starts its turn in the aura takes 10 damage.
HP 260; **Bloodied** 130
AC 27; **Fortitude** 25, **Reflex** 24, **Will** 26
Resist half damage from melee and ranged attacks; **Vulnerable** 10 against close and area attacks.
Saving Throws +2
Speed 6, climb 6
Action Points 1
⊕ **Cursed Touch** (standard; at-will)
   +17 vs. Fortitude; 1d10 + 6 damage, and the target is dazed (save ends).
⟵ **Devouring Swarm** (standard; at-will)
   Close blast 5; targets enemies only; +15 vs. Fortitude; 3d6 + 4 damage.
⟵ **Swarm Burst** (standard; recharge ⚄ ⚅)
   Close burst 5; targets enemies only; +15 vs. Will; the target is pushed 3 squares and immobilized (save ends).
Change Shape (minor; at-will) ✦ **Polymorph**
   A lamia can alter its physical form to appear as an attractive Medium humanoid of any race or gender (see "Change Shape," *Monster Manual 2*, page 216).
Squeezing Swarm
   By altering its shape, a lamia can squeeze through small openings as if it were a Tiny creature (see "Squeeze," *Player's Handbook*, page 292).
Alignment Evil   **Languages** Common, Elven
Skills Arcana +14, Bluff +16, Insight +13
| **Str** 13 (+7) | **Dex** 14 (+8) | **Wis** 14 (+8) |
| **Con** 18 (+10) | **Int** 17 (+9) | **Cha** 21 (+11) |

6 Cyclops Guards (C)	Level 14 Minion
Large fey humanoid	XP 250 each

Initiative +10   **Senses** Perception +15; truesight 6
HP 1; a missed attack never damages a minion.
AC 27; **Fortitude** 26, **Reflex** 23, **Will** 23
Speed 6
⊕ **Battleaxe** (standard; at-will) ✦ **Weapon**
   Reach 2; +17 vs. AC; 7 damage.
✝ **Evil Eye** (immediate reaction, when a melee attack misses the cyclops guard; at-will)
   The cyclops guard makes a melee basic attack against the attacker.
Alignment Unaligned   **Languages** Elven
| **Str** 22 (+13) | **Dex** 16 (+10) | **Wis** 17 (+10) |
| **Con** 20 (+12) | **Int** 11 (+7) | **Cha** 11 (+7) |
Equipment hide armor, heavy shield, battleaxe

2 Mezzodemons (M)	Level 11 Soldier
Medium elemental humanoid (demon)	XP 600 each

Initiative +9   **Senses** Perception +13; darkvision
HP 113; **Bloodied** 56
AC 27; **Fortitude** 25, **Reflex** 22, **Will** 23
Resist 20 poison, 10 variable (2/encounter)
Speed 6
⊕ **Trident** (standard; at-will) ✦ **Weapon**
   Reach 2; +18 vs. AC; 1d8 + 5 damage.
✝ **Skewering Tines** (standard; at-will) ✦ **Weapon**
   Requires trident; reach 2; +18 vs. AC; 1d8 + 5 damage, ongoing 5 damage, and the target is restrained (save ends both). While the target is restrained, the mezzodemon can't make trident attacks.
⟵ **Poison Breath** (standard; recharge ⚄ ⚅) ✦ **Poison**
   Close blast 3; targets enemies; +16 vs. Fortitude; 2d6 + 3 poison damage, and ongoing 5 poison damage (save ends).
Alignment Chaotic evil   **Languages** Abyssal
Skills Intimidate +11
| **Str** 20 (+10) | **Dex** 15 (+7) | **Wis** 16 (+8) |
| **Con** 17 (+8) | **Int** 10 (+5) | **Cha** 13 (+6) |
Equipment trident

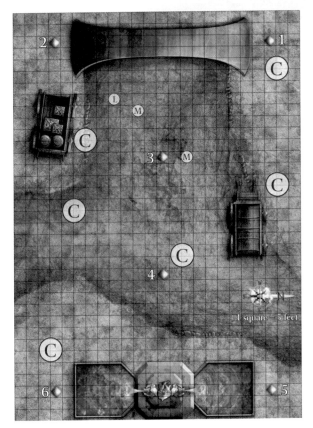

1 square = 5 feet

The lamia Arthani, who impersonated Fesdin Crale to send the adventurers into the crypt ambush, has performed a ritual to put the residents of Tradegate into a deep slumber. When the adventurers arrive, Arthani is in the process of completing a ritual to destroy the gate to Sigil.

When the adventurers approach the town square, read:
The arched gate is clearly the centerpiece of the town square. The icon of the Planar Trade Consortium is carved into the arch's keystone, and images of all kinds of doors decorate the rest of the ancient stone. Six glowing rods, each about 5 feet tall, jut from the ground in a pattern around the square. A one-eyed giant stands guard at each rod, and you also spot two insectlike demons wielding tridents hovering protectively near a female eladrin in a red gown. She's reading from a scroll as you approach.

TACTICS

The lamia devourer is on the verge of completing her ritual that will destroy the gate to Sigil. Unless she is in great danger, she uses a minor action each turn to make a DC 20 Arcana check and advance the ritual. She needs to achieve six successful checks before getting three failures. She uses *swarm burst* to clear enemies away from her, but prefers to use *devouring swarm* from a distance. See "The Ritual" for more details. If the ritual is disrupted and if six or more of the other monsters are defeated, Arthani flees through the gate to Sigil (she has a key).

The mezzodemons remain near Arthani to protect her. They try to use their *poison breath* attacks on restrained foes. They fight to the death.

The cyclops guards seek to engage the adventurers on the road, as they are reaching the square. If any of the PCs attempt to disturb the glowing rods, the guards move to attack them. They fight to the death.

THE RITUAL

Each round that Arthani achieves a success during the performance of the ritual, roll a d6. The result indicates which of the rods (numbered 1–6 on the map) draws energy from the gate. That rod emits energy in a close burst 2 that deals 5 damage to any of the lamia's enemies within the burst.

A character adjacent to one of the rods can remove it from the ground with a DC 18 Thievery check, a DC 23 Arcana check, or a DC 20 Strength check. A failed check deals 10 damage, pushes the character 2 squares, and knocks him prone.

If Arthani succeeds at the ritual, it doesn't destroy the gate as she had hoped, but it does lock it so that it no longer functions. Estavan will need to send powerful spellcasters at a later time to reverse the ritual and reestablish the portal to Sigil.

If all of the rods are removed, or if Arthani gets three failures, or if the adventurers otherwise defeat the lamia, the ritual fails.

DEVELOPMENT

If Arthani escapes through the gate, the adventurers must find Master Trader Duncam, wait for the slumber ritual to wear off in an hour, and then get a gate key from him so they can follow the lamia to Sigil. This gate key is a phrase, "the center of all things."

If Arthani is defeated, she collapses into a pile of dead and dying beetles. In the belt pouch that remains, the adventurers find three 1,000 gp gems and a flier for The House of Song, a festhall in the infamous Gatehouse Night Market in the Hive. One of the mezzodemons carries the same flier, though his has the name "Tarvas" scrawled upon it.

FEATURES OF THE AREA

Illumination: Bright light.

Arch: This stone arch occupies a prominent place in the town square. With the proper gate key, it opens a portal to Sigil.

Glowing Rods: These 5-foot-tall metal rods are inscribed with runes. They jut from the ground and glow with arcane brilliance. See "The Ritual" for additional details.

Wagons: The wagons are piled high with crates and barrels bound for Sigil, including such goods as ice apples, eladrin chocolate, and dwarven black ale.

ENCOUNTER D3: THE NIGHT MARKET

Encounter Level 13 (4,100 XP)

SETUP

Tarvas Demoncaller (T)
2 arctide runespiral demons (A)
2 bloodcry barlguras (B)
2 ogre bludgeoneers (O)

The adventurers follow Arthani or the clues the lamia left behind to Sigil. They arrive during the day, so they have time to do a little research or investigation before the Night Market opens.

EXPLORING SIGIL

The first thing the adventurers notice upon stepping through the portal is that Sigil is much more cosmopolitan and diverse than any other town or city they might have visited before. Not only do they see that all the usual races are represented, they also run into demons, devils, monstrous races, and creatures they have never encountered before. None of them act overtly hostile, but most carry themselves with confidence and bravado.

The second thing that the adventurers notice is that the horizon, where it can be seen through the crowds and the close-stacked buildings, curves up instead of down. A soft but persistent rain falls from above, but every so often the mist lifts enough to reveal a glimpse of the city hanging upside down above them.

As the adventurers explore the city, at some point call for a Perception check.

Perception Check

DC 23 *You notice a figure, bundled in a hooded cloak to stave off the rain, following you at a discreet distance.*

This agent of Tarvas Demoncaller (see "The Night Market," below, disappears into the crowd if the adventurers try to approach him.

RESEARCH

Visiting various locations around the city and asking the right questions accomplishes two things: It provides the adventurers with information, and it gets them noticed by all the wrong people. Here are some things the adventurers can learn around the city:

Arcana DC 25: Arthani had been visiting Sigil for the last few weeks, purchasing rituals and ancient spellbooks of all descriptions.

Diplomacy DC 15: The Festival of Doors celebration is coming up, but most citizens appear to be apprehensive about the holiday for some reason that no one is willing to talk about.

Insight DC 18: The city seems to be in a state of heightened tension, though you can't figure out what is causing this condition through observation.

Streetwise DC 18: Food, drink, and other essentials have been becoming increasingly more expensive and harder to come by. Small riots have broken out at a few market locations, and rumors abound that the citizens are becoming more restless and reckless in light of these unusual shortages.

Streetwise DC 23: The best source for acquiring cavefire wine is a trader named Tos, who sets up a stand in the Night Market when she's in Sigil.

THE NIGHT MARKET

When the adventurers head for the Gatehouse Night Market, whether to locate The House of Song or to look for the trader named Tos, they run into Tarvas Demoncaller and a few of his associates. If Arthani the lamia escaped after Encounter D2, she will also be on hand for this battle. Adjust the XP accordingly.

Tarvas Demoncaller is a wizard committed to spreading chaos and destruction. As a means to this end, he leads an effort to impede the flow of necessary supplies to Sigil's population. He won't fight in this encounter, however, so his statistics are provided in a later encounter.

2 Arctide Runespiral Demons (A)	Level 12 Artillery
Large elemental magical beast (demon)	XP 700 each

Initiative +12   **Senses** Perception +10
HP 97; **Bloodied** 48; see also *bloodied shock*
AC 24; **Fortitude** 23, **Reflex** 25, **Will** 23
Resist 15 variable (2/encounter)
Speed 7

⊕ **Bite** (standard; at-will)
+17 vs. AC; 1d6 + 5 damage.

↯ **Arcane Arc** (immediate interrupt, when an enemy moves adjacent to the arctide runespiral demon; at-will) ✦ **Lightning**
+17 vs. Reflex; 1d8 + 5 lightning damage.

↗ **Focused Strike** (standard; at-will) ✦ **Lightning**
Ranged 10; +19 vs. Reflex; 2d8 + 5 lightning damage.

⟸ **Bloodied Shock** (free, when first bloodied; encounter) ✦ **Lightning**
Close burst 1; +15 vs. Reflex; 1d8 + 5 lightning damage, and the target is dazed (save ends).

✳ **Charged Lightning Burst** (standard; at-will) ✦ **Lightning**
Area burst 2 within 10; +15 vs. Reflex; 1d8 + 5 lightning damage. The attack deals 1 extra lightning damage for each creature in the burst. Each ally damaged by the attack gains a +1 bonus to any recharge rolls at the start of its next turn.

Alignment Chaotic evil   **Languages** Abyssal
Str 15 (+8)   **Dex** 23 (+12)   **Wis** 19 (+10)
Con 19 (+10)   **Int** 7 (+4)   **Cha** 12 (+7)

2 Bloodcry Barlguras (B) Level 14 Brute
Large elemental beast (demon) XP 1,000 each

Initiative +11	**Senses** Perception +16; low-light vision

HP 174; **Bloodied** 87; see also *bloodcry*
AC 26; **Fortitude** 27, **Reflex** 24, **Will** 24
Resist 10 variable (1/encounter; see *Monster Manual* page 282)
Speed 8, climb 8

⊕ **Slam** (standard; at-will)
    Reach 2; +17 vs. AC; 2d8 + 6 damage, or 3d8 + 6 damage if the
    barlgura is bloodied, and the target is pushed 1 square.

✝ **Double Attack** (standard; at-will)
    The barlgura makes two slam attacks.

⬅ **Bloodcry** (free, when first bloodied; encounter)
    Close burst 3; targets enemies only; +15 vs. Will; 4d10 + 6
    damage, and the barlgura and all allies within 5 squares of it gain
    a +2 bonus to attack rolls until the end of the barlgura's next turn.

Alignment Chaotic evil   **Languages** Abyssal
Skills Athletics +18

Str 22 (+13)	**Dex** 18 (+11)	**Wis** 19 (+11)
Con 24 (+14)	**Int** 6 (+5)	**Cha** 12 (+8)

2 Ogre Bludgeoneers (O) Level 16 Minion
Large natural humanoid XP 350 each

Initiative +9	**Senses** Perception +9

HP 1; a missed attack never damages a minion.
AC 28; **Fortitude** 30, **Reflex** 24, **Will** 24
Speed 8

⊕ **Greatclub** (standard; at-will) ✦ **Weapon**
    Reach 2; +19 vs. AC; 9 damage.

Alignment Chaotic evil   **Languages** Giant

Str 23 (+14)	**Dex** 13 (+9)	**Wis** 13 (+9)
Con 25 (+15)	**Int** 4 (+5)	**Cha** 6 (+6)

Equipment hide armor, greatclub

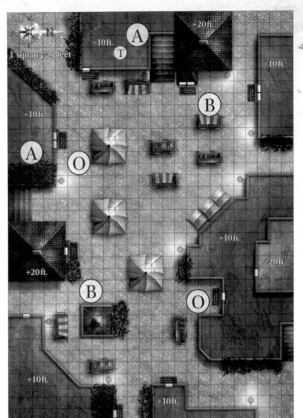

TACTICS

Thanks to his agents spread out around the city,
Tarvas has been keeping a watch on the adventurers, and he is alerted when they approach the Night
Market from the street to the northeast. He directs
his demons and hired thugs to attack the PCs, sticking around long enough to be noticed by them and to
trade a jibe or two before disappearing into the night.

If the lamia escaped in the previous encounter,
she starts out beside Tarvas and takes command of
the situation after the wizard departs. This time, she
battles to the death.

The barlguras wade in to make double attacks
each round, each demon concentrating on a single
foe. They move to stay close enough to as many enemies and allies as possible to take full advantage of
bloodcry when they become bloodied the first time.

The ogres are hired thugs that attempt to set up
flanks with the demons.

DEVELOPMENT

Tarvas doesn't stick around for this battle. He has
places to be and things to do in order to cause the
chaos he hopes to engender by the time the Festival
of Doors begins. He hopes that his underlings can
stop the adventurers.

After the battle ends, the adventurers can ask
around and locate the trader named Tos. With a bit of
coaxing, and maybe a bit of gold to loosen her tongue
(say, 500 gp), she'll reveal that the source of the cavefire
wine she sells to the Consortium is a cave in a remote
part of the Shadowfell. The adventurers must convince
Tos that they plan to reopen the trade corridors before
she tells them how to get to the cave, providing them
with the location of an appropriate portal and a key.

The House of Song festhall is located in the building that Tarvas stood atop at the beginning of the
battle. Inside, the adventurers discover that a back
room in the festhall has been converted into a sum-
moner's laboratory, complete with magic circles
and other paraphernalia. In his haste, Tarvas leaves
behind a level 13 magic item and notes concerning
a demon summoning ritual. A DC 25 Arcana check
reveals that it was used to send demons to Tos's cave.

FEATURES OF THE AREA

Illumination: Dim light.

Buildings: The flat-topped roofs are 10 feet above
the street, while the gabled roofs are 20 feet high. A
DC 15 Athletics check is needed to climb the walls.

Razorvine: These sharp patches deal 20 damage
to any creature that enters a square occupied by the
plant or starts its turn in one.

Tables and Tents: These portable shops pop up
when night falls. When the battle begins, the merchants scatter. Tables are difficult terrain, while tents
are blocking terrain.

Encounter Level 11 (3,200 XP)

SETUP

1 pod demon (D)
4 podspawn (P)
Falling rocks hazard

When the adventurers approach Tos's cave in the Shadowfell, they are greeted by a male who bears a striking resemblance to the independent merchant. It's her brother, Thom, who handles the production of cavefire wine. He appears to be greatly agitated when the adventurers arrive. He asks who they are and why they are here. If the adventurers tell Thom that Tos sent them, he immediately relaxes and relates some important information. Read:

"Tos told you that these caves are the source of our cavefire wine? Well, that source isn't doing so good right about now," he informs you. "The cavefire mushrooms we crush and ferment to make the wine appear to be dying, and I think I know what's killing them. There's a terrible monster in the caves, and I'm not able to chase it away. Perhaps you can take care of this for us."

QUESTIONING THOM

Here are some questions the adventurers might ask, and Thom's responses to them.

What's a cavefire mushroom? *"It's a rare fungus that grows within this network of caves. We've learned how to turn these mushrooms into cavefire wine. The taste is warm and soothing, and it has become a central element of Sigil's Festival of Doors."*

Why would someone want to keep you from selling the wine? *"Cavefire wine's purpose ranges from spiritual to celebratory, but it has become intertwined with the celebration of the Festival of Doors. Without it, many people in Sigil will believe that the festival has been ruined and that bad luck and ill fortune will follow them throughout the coming year."*

What kind of monster is in the cave? *"It's a large mass of disgusting goo that creates smaller versions of itself. It told me to get out of the cave when it arrived, and I haven't gone back in since."*

ENTERING THE CAVE

After the adventurers enter the cave, it takes them a few minutes to follow the winding passages toward the chamber where the cavefire mushrooms grow. The path to the main chamber is marked with arrows, so it's easy to find. The PCs approach the main chamber (depicted on the map) from the west.

When the adventurers enter the chamber, read:
The shadowy cave ahead is warm and moist. A central column divides the chamber. Water drips down the column to form a pool at its base. Deeper in the chamber, thick patches of mushrooms glow with a discernible light, though the intensity seems to drop noticeably as you approach.

Perception Check

DC 16 *A body floats, face down, in the pool of water.*
DC 21 *A telltale amount of dust and pebbles sprinkles down from cracks in the cave's ceiling.*
DC 23 *You notice faint sketches scrawled on the walls of the cave's central column of rock. The sketches seem to form some kind of symbols, but you have a hard time staring at them for too long.*

Falling Rocks	Level 13 Lurker
Hazard	XP 800

The caves rumble and shake, and suddenly rocks rain down from the ceiling above.

Hazard: A shower of rocks comes down in certain parts of the cave, as shown on the map.

Perception
- DC 18: A telltale amount of dust and pebbles sprinkles down from cracks in the cave's ceiling.
- DC 23: You notice faint sketches scrawled on the walls of the cave's central column of rock. The sketches seem to form some kind of symbols, but you have a hard time staring at them for too long.

Additional Skill: Dungeoneering
- DC 18: You recognize the unstable nature of the cracked and pitted ceiling, and you feel a slight shaking in the ground beneath your feet.

Initiative +2

Attack
Standard Action   **Area** special
Target: Each creature in area
Attack: +14 vs. Reflex
Hit: 1d10 + 6 damage, and the target is dazed (save ends).
Special: Each round, on the hazard's initiative count, roll a d6 to determine which zone or zones the rocks fall in during that round. The rocks attack each creature in each affected zone.

Countermeasures
- If a character spots the symbols on the central column, he or she can attempt a skill challenge to identify them and break the enchantment that has instigated this hazard.

  Each turn, if a character is adjacent to a symbol scrawled on the wall, that character can make a DC 18 Thievery check, a DC 18 Arcana check, or a DC 23 Religion check to disrupt the magic imbued within the symbol. A failure on any check causes the hazard to immediately attack, as described above.

  If the characters achieve 4 successes before they get 3 failures, the cave stops rumbling and the hazard no longer functions.

  If the characters fail the skill challenge, the hazard remains and the damage increases to 2d10 + 6. After an hour, the characters can attempt to disrupt the magical hazard again.

Pod Demon (D) **Level 15 Elite Artillery**
Large elemental humanoid (demon) XP 2,400

Initiative +12 **Senses** Perception +10; darkvision
HP 176; **Bloodied** 88
AC 27; **Fortitude** 25, **Reflex** 27, **Will** 29
Resist 15 variable (2/encounter)
Saving Throws +2
Speed 8
Action Points 1

Slam (standard; at-will) ✦ **Poison**
+20 vs. AC; 1d6 + 5 damage, and ongoing 5 poison damage (save ends).

Detonate Minion (minor 1/round; recharge ⚄ ⚅) ✦ **Poison**
Ranged 10; targets one podspawn; the podspawn explodes, dropping to 0 hit points and dealing 1d8 + 3 poison damage to each creature adjacent to the podspawn.

Spew Podspawn (standard; at-will) ✦ **Acid**
Close blast 3; +18 vs. Reflex; 2d6 + 5 acid damage.

Generate Podspawn (standard; recharges when first bloodied) ✦ **Poison**
Close burst 2; +18 vs. Reflex; 3d6 + 5 poison damage. *Effect:* If the pod demon has fewer than four podspawn, it spawns podspawn into unoccupied squares within the burst, bringing its total number of minions to four.

Fling Podspawn (standard; at-will) ✦ **Acid**
Area burst 1 within 10; +18 vs. Reflex; 2d6 + 5 acid damage.

Combat Advantage
A pod demon's attack deals 2d6 extra damage to any target granting combat advantage to it.

Spawn
If a pod demon has fewer than four podspawn at the start of its turn, it spawns one podspawn within 2 squares of it.

Transfer Essence (move; at-will) ✦ **Teleportation**
The pod demon swaps positions with a podspawn within 10 squares of it.

Alignment Evil **Languages** Abyssal, Common
Str 17 (+10) **Dex** 20 (+12) **Wis** 16 (+10)
Con 21 (+12) **Int** 12 (+8) **Cha** 24 (+14)

4 Podspawn (P) **Level 15 Minion Skirmisher**
Small elemental humanoid (demon) XP 300 or 0 if encountered with pod demon

Initiative +14 **Senses** Perception +6; darkvision
HP 1; a missed attack never damages a minion.
AC 29; **Fortitude** 28, **Reflex** 28, **Will** 25
Resist The podspawn shares any resistances that its pod demon progenitor has.
Speed 8

Corroding Slime (standard; at-will) ✦ **Acid**
+20 vs. AC; 12 acid damage.

Dangerous Proximity
Any enemy adjacent to a podspawn grants combat advantage to it.

Alignment Evil **Languages** Abyssal, Common
Str 13 (+8) **Dex** 20 (+12) **Wis** 8 (+6)
Con 21 (+12) **Int** 5 (+4) **Cha** 15 (+9)

Tactics

The hazard drops rocks each round on its turn. The adventurers can eliminate this hazard by succeeding on a skill challenge. Note that the falling rocks attack all creatures in the affected zone, including the pod demon and its spawn.

As soon as the pod demon realizes that intruders have entered the chamber, it orders its minions to

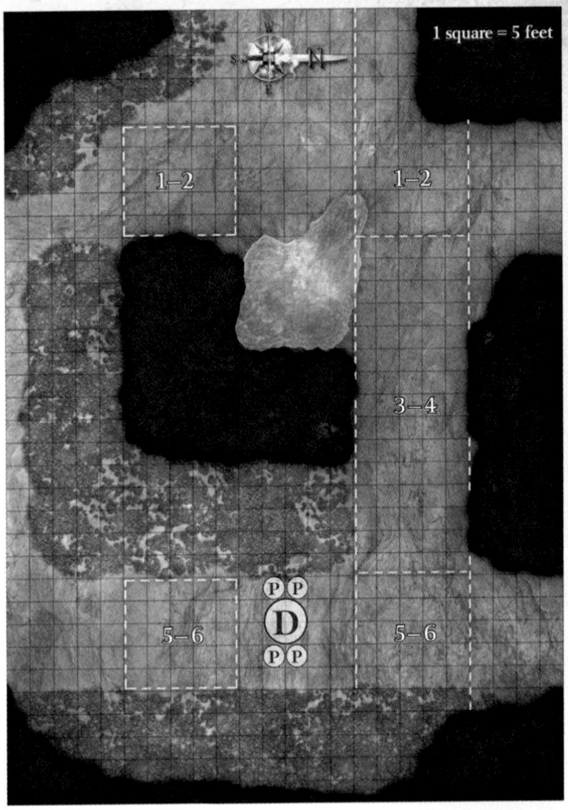

engage them and set up flanking situations for it to take advantage of. Then it moves in, takes advantage of combat advantage by employing its slam attack, and then spends a minor action to use *detonate minion*. It retreats after that to use its ranged attacks. Every round at the start of its turn, it spawns one podspawn within 2 squares of its position. When it has two or fewer minions remaining, it uses *generate podspawn* to create more. The pod demon is a demented and twisted creature that fights to the death.

Development

The presence of the demon causes the cavefire mushrooms to grow sick and die. As soon as the PCs defeat the demon, the mushrooms begin to improve.

The body belongs to the cultist who accompanied the demon and set up the falling rocks hazard. After he completed his ritual, the pod demon killed him.

A DC 16 Perception check allows the adventurers to discover 500 gp and a note that shows the location of a Planar Trade Consortium warehouse in Sigil's Market Ward.

Features of the Area

Illumination: Dim light. The gloom of the Shadowfell mutes light sources used in this area, reducing the radius illuminated by 50 percent. For example, a torch illuminates 2 squares instead of 5. Magical light sources are unaffected.

Mushroom Patch: These patches of faintly glowing mushrooms are difficult terrain.

Pool: The pool of water is 3 feet deep.

Encounter Level 15 (6,300 XP)

SETUP

Tarvas Demoncaller (T)
1 needle demon (N)
2 vrock swordwings (V)
2 immolith deathragers (D)

The adventurers return to Sigil on the day of the Festival of Doors. The celebration is set to kick off at nightfall, in just a few hours, but a grand soiree seems to be the furthest thing from the minds of the citizens. Read:

The streets of Sigil appear to be on the verge of chaos and violence. Angry protestors fill the Market Ward, exchanging nasty words with merchants and each other as tempers grow exceedingly thin. More dabus than usual float in plain view, and even these mysterious creatures seem to be nervous and on edge. "Where's our cavefire wine?" one protestor calls out. Another shouts, "I heard that all shipments have stopped. How will we survive without food and water?" A rock occasionally sails out of the crowd to narrowly miss a merchant's head.

IN SIGIL

Here are some things the adventurers might want to do upon returning to the City of Doors.

Seek Out Estavan: The adventurers can find Estavan in his office in the Clerk's Ward. He appears more agitated than when last they met, and he leaps up and starts asking questions as soon as they enter the office. He wants to know what they've found out, because he feels more and more certain that something bad is about to happen. If they didn't find the clue about the warehouse, Estavan tells them that he has been out of contact with the manager of the place and he is overdue for a report from that location. He asks them to go check it out for him while he explores a few last leads. If they did find the clue and mention it, Estavan asks them to go ahead and see what's going on there. "Hurry," he implores them. " I believe that Sigil and the multiverse have no time remaining for us to waste."

Look for Tarvas Demoncaller: The adventurers might decide to go back to The House of Song and seek out Tarvas. A DC 23 Streetwise check points the adventurers toward a warehouse in the Market Ward. "Strange things have been happening all over the

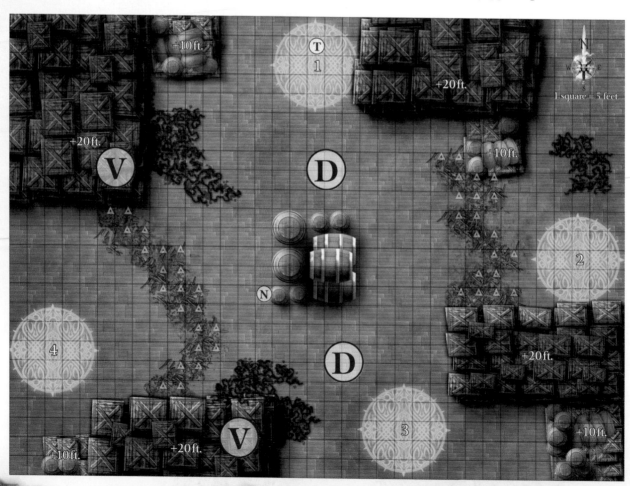

city," one local tells them, "but the weirdness appears to be centered on that building."

Tarvas Demoncaller (T) — Level 15 Controller (Leader)
Medium natural humanoid, human   XP 1,200

Initiative +9   **Senses** Perception +12; darkvision

Demonic Command aura sight; demons in the aura gain a +1 bonus to attack rolls and a +2 bonus to damage rolls.

HP 140; **Bloodied** 70; see also *demon link*

AC 29; **Fortitude** 24, **Reflex** 27, **Will** 28

Speed 6

⊕ **Quarterstaff** (standard; at-will) ✦ **Weapon**
     +20 vs. AC; 1d8 + 6 damage.

✝ **Touch of the Demon** (standard, usable only while bloodied; at-will)
     +20 vs. AC; 2d8 + 6 damage.

↗ **Elemental Bolt** (standard; at-will) ✦ **Fire, Lightning**
     Ranged 5; +18 vs. Reflex; 1d8 +6 fire and lightning damage.

❊ **Explosive Summoning** (standard; at-will)
     Area burst 1 within 10; Tarvas summons a small demon that appears in a square adjacent to him and then moves up to 10 squares and explodes; +17 vs. Reflex; 1d10 + 6 damage, and the target is slowed (save ends).

❊ **Demonic Wrath** (standard; recharge ⚄⚅)
     Area burst 1 within 20; +17 vs. Reflex; 4d8 + 5 damage, and the target takes ongoing 5 damage (save ends).

Demon Link (minor; at-will) ✦ **Healing**
     Tarvas can transfer up to 22 damage he has taken to a demon within 5 squares of him. He cannot transfer more hit points than the demon has remaining.

Alignment Chaotic evil   **Languages** Abyssal, Common
Skills Arcana +16, Insight +17, Intimidate +17, Stealth +14

Str 12 (+8)	**Dex** 15 (+9)	**Wis** 21 (+12)
Con 12 (+8)	**Int** 18 (+11)	**Cha** 20 (+12)

Equipment robes, quarterstaff

2 Vrock Swordwings (V) — Level 14 Skirmisher
Large elemental humanoid (demon)   XP 1,000 each

Initiative +13   **Senses** Perception +14; darkvision

HP 140; **Bloodied** 70; see also *spores of madness*

AC 28; **Fortitude** 26, **Reflex** 24, **Will** 24

Resist 10 variable (2/encounter)

Speed 6, fly 8; see also *flyby attack*

⊕ **Falchion** (standard; at-will) ✦ **Weapon**
     Reach 2; +19 vs. AC; 2d8 + 7 damage.

✝ **Flyby Attack** (standard; at-will)
     The vrock flies up to 8 squares and makes one falchion attack at any point during that movement. The vrock doesn't provoke opportunity attacks when moving away from the target of the attack.

↞ **Frightful Screech** (standard; recharge ⚄⚅)
     Close burst 3; deafened creatures are immune; +18 vs. Will; the target is pushed 3 squares and immobilized until the end of the vrock's next turn.

↞ **Spores of Madness** (free, when first bloodied; encounter) ✦ **Poison**
     Close burst 2; demons are immune; +17 vs. Will; 1d10 + 5 poison damage, and the target is dazed (save ends).

Alignment Chaotic evil   **Languages** Abyssal
Skills Bluff +16, Insight +14

Str 23 (+13)	**Dex** 19 (+11)	**Wis** 15 (+9)
Con 20 (+12)	**Int** 12 (+8)	**Cha** 19 (+11)

THE WAREHOUSE

This large building is one of many used by the Planar Trade Consortium to store goods before they are loaded on caravans or distributed to the markets in Sigil. This particular location has been commandeered by Tarvas Demoncaller, chosen because he seeks revenge against the Planar Trade Consortium for some real or imagined slight. He hopes that by disrupting trade into Sigil, he can cast doubt upon the Consortium's ability to provide for the city. Cutting off the flow of goods, he hopes, will lead to a level of panic and rioting that would be enough to send the Lady of Pain on a rampage and result in the banishment or even the destruction of the Consortium.

2 Immolith Deathragers (D) — Level 15 Brute
Large elemental magical beast (demon, fire, undead)   XP 1,200 each

Initiative +11   **Senses** Perception +9

Flaming Aura (Fire) aura 1; any creature that enters or starts its turn in the aura takes 10 fire damage.

HP 185; **Bloodied** 92

AC 27; **Fortitude** 30, **Reflex** 27, **Will** 28

Immune disease, fire, poison; **Resist** 15 variable (2/encounter); **Vulnerable** 10 radiant

Speed 6

⊕ **Claw** (standard; at-will) ✦ **Fire**
     Reach 4; +18 vs. AC; 3d6 + 6 fire damage, and ongoing 10 fire damage (save ends).

↞ **Deathrage** (free; when first bloodied and again when reduced to 0 hit points) ✦ **Fire**
     Close burst 4; +17 vs. AC; 3d10 + 6 fire damage.

Alignment Chaotic evil   **Languages** Abyssal

Str 25 (+14)	**Dex** 18 (+11)	**Wis** 15 (+9)
Con 25 (+14)	**Int** 9 (+6)	**Cha** 20 (+12)

Needle Demon (N) — Level 12 Controller
Medium elemental humanoid (demon)   XP 700

Initiative +10   **Senses** Perception +9; darkvision

HP 123; **Bloodied** 61

AC 26; **Fortitude** 23, **Reflex** 23, **Will** 25

Resist 15 variable (2/encounter)

Speed 6

⊕ **Claw** (standard; at-will)
     +17 vs. AC; 2d6 + 5 damage.

✝ **Claws of Betrayal** (standard; requires combat advantage against each target; at-will)
     The needle demon makes two claw attacks. If both attacks hit the same target, the target takes ongoing 10 damage (save ends).

✝ **Tail Whip** (immediate reaction, when an enemy moves into a square adjacent to the needle demon; at-will)
     +17 vs. AC; 1d6 + 2 damage.

↞ **Rage of the Betrayed** (standard; recharge ⚄⚅) ✦ **Charm**
     Close blast 5; targets enemies; +16 vs. Will; the target is dominated (save ends).

Alignment Chaotic evil   **Languages** Abyssal
Skills Bluff +17, Insight +14, Intimidate +17

Str 16 (+9)	**Dex** 19 (+10)	**Wis** 17 (+9)
Con 19 (+10)	**Int** 14 (+8)	**Cha** 22 (+12)

This encounter concludes on the next page.

This encounter is continued from the previous page.

Exploring the outside of the warehouse yields few clues. The place's only windows are located high on the walls, near the 30-foot roof line. Flashes of light appear at irregular intervals, briefly illuminating the dirt-caked windows. A massive cargo door at the front of the building is locked from the inside. A normal door, situated in the alley on the eastern side of the building, is also locked. It can be opened with a DC 25 Thievery check. The encounter assumes that the adventurers enter the warehouse through this door.

When the adventurers enter the warehouse, read:

Towering containers fill large portions of the massive interior. Much of the place sits in darkness, though a pool of dim light that occasionally flashes into brightness occupies a section near the center of the building. As you draw closer, you can see that the contents of some of the containers have been spilled across open sections of floor. A glowing circle inscribed on the floor seems to be the source of the dim light, and you hear a voice chanting in a strange language somewhere among the crates and barrels ahead of you.

TACTICS

Tarvas Demoncaller is in the midst of a ritual designed to alter and corrupt the goods that come through portals to Sigil. He chants in Abyssal, calling on the power of demons to aid him in his effort to foment chaos.

Tarvas makes sure to stay within line of sight of his demon servants to allow them to take advantage of his *demonic command* aura. Each round, he uses a minor action to advance his ritual. Doing this causes him to teleport from one magic circle to another. See "The Ritual" for details. His preferred standard action is to use *demonic wrath* whenever it is available; otherwise, he falls back on *explosive summoning* or *elemental bolt*, as appropriate.

The needle demon waits for the immoliths to wade into battle before joining them. It seeks to use *rage of the betrayed* to dominate a foe. If that isn't ready, it seeks combat advantage and uses of *claws of betrayal*.

The immoliths move forward to take up space, slow the intruders down, and pound on them as often as possible.

The vrock swordwings fly from high point to high point, making *flyby attacks* along the way. If any enemies get close to its perch, a vrock unleashes its *frightful screech*.

Tarvas and his servants fight to the death.

THE RITUAL

Each round at the beginning of his turn, Tarvas uses a minor action to continue his ritual. Roll a d20. The result determines which magic circle he teleports to:

1–5 = circle 1; 6–10 = circle 2; 11–15 = circle 3; 16–20 = circle 4. If the result indicates the circle he already occupies, roll again.

When Tarvas teleports, the circle he leaves flashes with abyssal energy. This effect deals 5 damage to any creature that isn't a demon that is standing in or adjacent to the circle. He also attempts a DC 25 Arcana check. If he achieves 10 successes before getting 3 failures, he completes the ritual (see "Ending the Adventure"). If he gets 3 failures, the ritual doesn't work and he flies into a terrible rage. When this happens, he stops hopping from circle to circle and turns his full attention to destroying the meddlesome adventurers.

FEATURES OF THE AREA

Illumination: Dim light around the magic circles inscribed on the floor. Darkness throughout the rest of the building.

Containers: Large containers, crates, and barrels are stacked high throughout the warehouse's massive interior. Some of these stacks are 10 feet high, others 20 feet high. A DC 20 Athletics check is required to climb the stacked containers.

Magic Circles: These glowing runes, inscribed on the floor of the warehouse, are part of the ritual that Tarvas is conducting to temporarily shut down Sigil's portals. See "The Ritual" for details on how Tarvas uses them in this encounter.

Razorvine: These sharp patches deal 20 damage to any creature that enters a square occupied by the plant or starts its turn in one.

Scattered Goods: Items spilled from broken containers form difficult terrain across the floor.

ENDING THE ADVENTURE

If the adventurers defeat Tarvas and the ritual fails, Sigil slowly goes back to normal. The Festival of Doors comes off without any further complications, except that some of the usual celebratory accompaniments are in short supply. Estavan thanks the adventurers, gives them the astral diamond he promised, and hurries to get his caravans moving again.

If Tarvas completes the ritual, Sigil goes through 24 hours of upheaval as incoming food and beverages are discovered to be rancid and spoiled, and trade goods of every kind are warped and corroded. Riots spread quickly throughout the streets. The Lady of Pain makes a multitude of appearances, and citizens disappear as she works to restore order. Estavan (and Tarvas, if he survived) disappears during this time, and the adventurers receive no additional reward for their efforts. The fate of the Planar Trade Consortium and Estavan are left to the needs of your campaign.

INDEX

NEW MONSTERS

Every new monster in this book appears on the following list, which is sorted alphabetically by level and monster role. Monster leaders are indicated with an (L).

Monster	Level and Role	Page
Crazed Human Rabble	2 Minion	121
Orryn Glittercave	4 Defender	33
Hobgoblin Legionnaire of Avernus	5 Soldier (L)	113
Young Blue Dragon Goblin Ally	6 Solo Artillery	111
Adamantine Horse of Xarn	7 Brute	149
Satisfied Adamantine Horse of Xarn	8 Brute	149
Zombie Hulk of Orcus	8 Brute	117
Pleased Adamantine Horse of Xarn	10 Brute	149
Snaketongue Wyvern	10 Skirmisher	119
Wight Life-Eater	10 Skirmisher	213
Dragonborn Gladiator of Tiamat	10 Soldier	123
Ghost Spider	11 Elite Lurker	213
Loathsome Chanter	11 Minion	76
Chosen Mezzodemon	11 Soldier	115
Elemental Ooze	12 Brute	207
Ettin Spirit-Talker of Demogorgon	12 Elite Controller (L)	107

Monster	Level and Role	Page
Lamia Devourer	13 Elite Controller	214
Dwarf Thug	13 Minion	205
Half-Elf Brigand Captain	13 Skirmisher	204
Wererat Sewer Guard	13 Skirmisher	206
Sons of Mercy Basher	13 Soldier	195
Sons of Mercy Wizard	14 Artillery	195
Abyssal Eviscerator	14 Brute	204
Bloodcry Barlgura	14 Brute	217
Cranium Rat Arcanist Swarm	14 Controller	207
Vrock Swordwing	14 Skirmisher	221
Human Gladiator	14 Elite Soldier	205
Dabus Custodian	15 Artillery	191
Immolith Deathrager	15 Brute	221
Tarvas Demoncaller	15 Controller (L)	221
Fey Bodak Skulk	16 Lurker	109
Dabus Enforcer	18 Controller	191
The Kadyx, Demon War Drake	21 Solo Skirmisher	201

IMPROVE YOUR GAME WITH A BOOKMARK.

Add D&D Insider™ to your Favorites and bring more to your characters and campaigns with a constantly growing source of new content, tools, articles, applications, and more.

Whether you're a player, a DM—or both—D&DI will help you spend less time prepping for your game and more time playing it.

SUBSCRIBE NOW AT DNDINSIDER.COM

D&D
INSIDER
NEVER SPLIT THE PARTY